# Energy Budgets
# at Risk™

T0327696

Founded in 1807, John Wiley & Sons is the oldest independent publishing company in the United States. With offices in North America, Europe, Australia and Asia, Wiley is globally committed to developing and marketing print and electronic products and services for our customers' professional and personal knowledge and understanding.

The Wiley Finance series contains books written specifically for finance and investment professionals as well as sophisticated individual investors and their financial advisors. Book topics range from portfolio management to e-commerce, risk management, financial engineering, valuation and financial instrument analysis, as well as much more.

For a list of available titles, please visit our Web site at www.Wiley Finance.com.

# Energy Budgets at Risk (EBaR)®

*A Risk Management Approach to Energy Purchase and Efficiency Choices*

JERRY JACKSON

John Wiley & Sons, Inc.

Copyright © 2008 by Jerry Jackson. All rights reserved

Published by John Wiley & Sons, Inc., Hoboken, New Jersey.

Published simultaneously in Canada.

No part of this publication may be reproduced, stored in a retrieval system, or transmitted in any form or by any means, electronic, mechanical, photocopying, recording, scanning, or otherwise, except as permitted under Section 107 or 108 of the 1976 United States Copyright Act, without either the prior written permission of the Publisher, or authorization through payment of the appropriate per-copy fee to the Copyright Clearance Center, Inc., 222 Rosewood Drive, Danvers, MA 01923, (978) 750-8400, fax (978) 646-4470, or on the web at www.copyright.com. Requests to the Publisher for permission should be addressed to the Permissions Department, John Wiley & Sons, Inc., 111 River Street, Hoboken, NJ 07030, (201) 748-6011, fax (201) 748-6008, or online at http://www.wiley.com/go/permissions.

Limit of Liability/Disclaimer of Warranty: While the publisher and author have used their best efforts in preparing this book, they make no representations or warranties with respect to the accuracy or completeness of the contents of this book and specifically disclaim any implied warranties of merchantability or fitness for a particular purpose. No warranty may be created or extended by sales representatives or written sales materials. The advice and strategies contained herein may not be suitable for your situation. You should consult with a professional where appropriate. Neither the publisher nor author shall be liable for any loss of profit or any other commercial damages, including but not limited to special, incidental, consequential, or other damages.

For general information on our other products and services or for technical support, please contact our Customer Care Department within the United States at (800) 762-2974, outside the United States at (317) 572-3993 or fax (317) 572-4002.

Wiley publishes in a variety of print and electronic formats and by print-on-demand. Some material included with standard print versions of this book may not be included in e-books or in print-on-demand. If this book refers to media such as a CD or DVD that is not included in the version you purchased, you may download this material at http://booksupport.wiley.com. For more information about Wiley products, visit www.wiley.com.

*Library of Congress Cataloging-in-Publication Data:*

Jackson, Jerry, 1945–
    Energy Budgets At Risk (EBAR) : a risk management approach to energy purchase and efficiency choices / Jerry Jackson.
        p. cm. – (Wiley finance series)
    Includes bibliographical references and index.
    ISBN 978-0-470-19767-7 (cloth)
    1. Power resources–Costs–Management.  2. Energy consumption–Costs.  I. Title.
    HD9502.A2J34  2008
    658.2'6–dc22
                                                                    2007042812

10  9  8  7  6  5  4  3  2  1

# Contents

# Preface

**R**ecent energy price increases and volatility have created severe energy budgeting and planning difficulties for many commercial, institutional, industrial, and government organizations. Uncertainty over energy prices, equipment performance, weather, and other factors make it exceedingly difficult to assess costs and benefits of energy-efficiency investments. In areas with competitive energy markets, those decisions are even more complex. A recent U.S. Business Roundtable CEO Economic Outlook Survey identified energy costs as one of the two top cost pressures faced by their businesses—right behind health care.

Energy Budgets at Risk (EBaR),* described in this book, is a new quantitative approach to evaluating energy-efficiency investments by using modern risk management tools. EBaR can also incorporate energy purchase decisions for organizations in competitive energy markets, providing an integrated investment-purchase analysis. Organizations can now apply investment analysis to energy-related decisions in a manner that is consistent with their financial investment analysis.

The most remarkable outcome of EBaR analysis is that its application increases cash flow. Annualized net savings can be 30 percent or more of current energy costs.

## VALUE AT RISK (VaR) APPROACH TO FACILITY ENERGY RISK MANAGEMENT

In late 2005, I began planning a series of continuing education workshops at Texas A&M University to provide energy customers with a financial framework specifically developed to evaluate energy-efficiency investments under current market conditions, which for some customers in Texas included a near doubling of energy prices since 2002. Having worked with energy customers for 30 years, I knew that most energy-efficiency investments are

---

*Energy Budgets at Risk (EBaR)®, Energy Budgets at Risk™, and EBaR™ are trademarks belonging to Jerry Jackson.

evaluated, at least in the screening phase, with a short payback criterion that excludes many of the most profitable investments. For example, a recent study of more than 9,000 small and medium U.S. manufacturing firms who participated in free energy audits, provided in part by Texas A&M University, found an average payback of 15 months was required to prompt efficiency investments. This is consistent with my own observations from working with individual organizations.

Payback analysis is primarily used to limit investment risk. Short paybacks require all savings to occur in the near future—the least risky portion of the planning horizon. However, a heavy price accompanies this traditional payback analysis. As much as 30 percent of current energy bills can be cost-effectively eliminated if energy-efficiency investments are evaluated with more appropriate investment tools. Organizations are desperately in need of a new approach to evaluate energy-efficiency investments in today's costly and uncertain energy markets.

Based on my study and experience with organizations making energy-efficiency investments, I felt that any new financial investment framework designed to replace or supplement traditional analysis would have to include the two most prominent features of payback analysis: a simple decision rule and the ability to limit risk. A review of current financial investment tools revealed that while energy-efficiency investment analysis has been stuck on payback, a remarkable transformation has occurred in financial industry investment and risk management analysis. Various at-risk measures show the probability that an investment portfolio will sustain a specific loss, which provides a simple decision rule to manage returns and risks. The impacts of adding new investments to a portfolio can be evaluated in terms of expected returns and risk associated with the portfolio.

Recasting energy efficiency as a portfolio and investment analysis problem permits an application of the same simple at-risk decision rules to energy-related investments and energy risk management. Budget risk associated with current energy-using equipment is quantified and financial characteristics of efficiency investments and their impacts are determined with quantitative analysis.

The result, Energy Budgets at Risk (EBaR), is a new energy management framework that reduces energy costs and measures energy investment risk by extending and applying Value at Risk (VaR), a widely-used risk management tool developed in the financial industry and applied by virtually all investment fund and portfolio managers on Wall Street. EBaR quantitatively determines energy budget risk and provides energy risk management investment strategies that reduce cost and, at the same time, meet budget flexibility and risk tolerance requirements of individual organizations.

Furthermore, investments based on EBaR analysis result in increased cash flows by providing energy budget savings greater than investment costs.

EBaR investments provide the same financial bottom line impact as an increase in revenues. In a process customized to meet the risk tolerance of individual organizations, EBaR applies quantitative risk management analysis that has been developed and vetted in the financial community to guide facility owners and managers in making efficiency investment and purchase choices in today's challenging energy markets.

## AN EBaR FACILITY ENERGY RISK MANAGEMENT STANDARD

JP Morgan's RiskMetrics service was instrumental in establishing VaR as a standard financial risk management tool in the 1990s. No similar resource has been available to show energy and financial managers how to develop and apply risk management techniques to minimize energy costs, subject to organizational risk tolerance. *Energy Budgets at Risk* provides such a guide.

The fact that managing energy budget risk increases cash flow is no more surprising than the fact that managing financial investment risk with a diversified portfolio can be expected to provide greater returns than investing only in low-risk government securities. However, prior to publication of *Energy Budgets at Risk*, few resources were available to guide formal risk management associated with investment in energy-efficient technologies and energy purchases. This is not to suggest that many enterprising energy managers have not developed their own risk management strategies; however, no commonly accepted quantitative methodology existed to guide energy managers and others in the assessment of facility energy-related risks—at least no methodologies that were comparable to risk management methodologies applied in financial applications.

The objective of this book is to provide such a methodology and roadmap that energy managers, corporate executives and government officials can use to understand and implement best practice strategies for facility energy risk management.

## APPLYING EBaR AT YOUR FACILITY

*Energy Budgets at Risk* provides background information required to understand energy cost, price, efficiency, and related issues that are important in developing a balanced approach to facility energy risk management. EBaR concepts and applications are introduced and described in sufficient detail to support applications at individual facilities.

This section describes features of *Energy Budgets at Risk* that facilitate an evaluation and application of EBaR at your facility.

## What Exactly is EBaR Analysis?

EBaR analysis develops and applies a series of equations describing your facility's energy use and operating characteristics. These equations are combined with weather data and energy price forecasts with a widely used software process called Monte Carlo analysis. Graphical and tabular outputs provide representations of risks and returns for any energy efficiency investment. EBaR analysis also incorporates energy purchase options for facilities in competitive energy markets.

## How Much Can I Save?

A brief detour to the Appendix provides information to assess potential energy and financial benefits of an EBaR analysis. This appendix provides excerpts from MAISY® facility energy use data (http://www.maisy.com) on more than one million business, institutional, and government buildings. Data are detailed by business type and operating hours. Using these data, readers can calculate several energy use statistics for their facility and compare them to data on similar facilities to see how much energy use can be reduced. Applying your electric prices and natural gas prices provides a general indication of the financial rewards associated with an EBaR strategy.

While these calculations are only general estimates, they provide a reasonable basis for determining the value of an EBaR application at your facility.[1]

## Detailed Case Study Examples

All concepts and applications are illustrated with a detailed case study application to an Austin, Texas office building. Monthly facility energy use data, Austin weather data, and other facility data are used to illustrate concepts, data development, equation parameter estimation, and application in EBaR analysis. Readers can substitute data for their facilities and use each of the steps in Chapters 8–10 as a template for their own EBaR analysis.

## What Software Is Required?

Excel software was used to develop all required data relationships and characterizations in this book. Each of the data development steps is described in detail in Chapter 8 along with documentation of required Excel menu options.

Monte Carlo software applies the relationships and data developed with Excel software to generate distributions of efficiency investment risks and returns. Monte Carlo software is used in all financial risk management applications and is available in a variety of commercial software packages. The Monte Carlo process is described in Chapter 7. Many of these software packages are Excel add-ins, permitting Excel to serve as the software platform for the data development, Monte Carlo analysis, and output tables and graphs.

All of the tables and graphs used in Chapters 9 through 12 to present the case study results were developed using Excel.

Energy risk management software customized to support all aspects of EBaR analysis is also available at energybudgetsatrisk.com.

## IS AN EBaR STRATEGY RIGHT FOR YOUR ORGANIZATION?

EBaR is a compelling application. Common sense says that managing risks is a more profitable strategy than avoiding risks. Incorporating risk in traditional investment analysis by using short paybacks or high internal rate of return thresholds avoids rather than manages risk. The evidence is overwhelming that nearly every business, institution, and government agency can reduce energy bills with cost-effective energy-efficiency investments.

### Is It Worth the Effort?

Every new initiative incurs a cost. Is developing an EBaR analysis and strategy likely to be a good investment of time and resources for your organization?

**Energy Savings**   As indicated in the previous section, the Appendix, which provides information on energy use characteristics of over one million facilities, can be used to benchmark your current energy use to other facilities in your business and operating hours category. Your energy use compared to the more efficient facilities represented in the tables provides a good indication of potential efficiency savings.

**Efficiency Investments as a New Revenue Source**   Energy savings developed from information in the Appendix are multiplied by the average price of electricity and natural gas to estimate potential savings in energy costs. When the cost of the investment is amortized over the lifetime of the equipment, these investments nearly always increase cash flow. That is, the value of energy savings more than offsets the cost of financing.

Efficiency investments can be viewed as generating a new revenue or income stream. Lease and lease purchase financing offered by energy service companies, manufacturers and financial organizations described in Chapter 3 support this income-enhancing strategy.

## Is My Facility Big Enough?

Because EBaR is a scalable application, the answer to this question is an unequivocal yes. Anyone considering reading this book is concerned enough about energy costs to invest at least a minimal effort to manage those costs. EBaR scalability means that small organizations can apply the process to evaluate the simplest and most promising efficiency investments first and then extend the analysis over time.

## Organization Type

Organizations differ in their management and decision-making structure, budget flexibility, and risk tolerance. Commercial, institutional, industrial, and government agencies face different constraints and options in considering energy budget risks, efficiency investments, and energy purchase decisions.

The EBaR framework applies equally to all organization types. Budget flexibility and risk tolerance are parameters of the analysis specified by users. EBaR strategic choices reflect budget and risk characteristics of individual users.

## From Do-It-Yourself to Turnkey Projects

EBaR analysis provides value regardless of the extent to which efficiency projects are self-performed by an organization.

Organizations who conduct their own analysis, make their own equipment purchases, and self-perform or contract for installation should certainly have a detailed understanding of EBaR concepts and applications.

Organizations at the other end of the spectrum, who contract out analysis, engineering, financing, and other efficiency tasks, should have an equally thorough understanding of EBaR. For instance, performance contracts require energy service companies to conduct all tasks associated with energy-efficiency investments—from analysis to monitoring savings of the installed equipment. Performance contracts also guarantee energy savings and commit energy service companies to make reimbursements for savings that fall short of the guaranteed amount. While this approach would seem to offer a risk-free option to achieve improved energy efficiency, performance contracts can suffer from either underinvestment or overinvestment in efficient technologies. In addition, efficiency improvements achieved under performance contracts may do little to reduce energy budget volatility—an important consideration for government agencies and institutions whose only option to addressing higher energy costs is to reduce services.

Energy managers or contract officers with responsibility for performance contractor selection and contract negotiation should conduct their own energy risk management analysis or require vendors to present the results of EBaR analysis to evaluate competing bids and to insure that contractors meet the needs of the organization.

## GOING GREEN, CARBON FOOTPRINTS, AND EBaR

The list of companies, municipalities, institutions, and other organizations publicly committing to carbon reductions and other green policies is growing by the day. The primary opportunity to meet these environmental goals is through energy efficiency investments that reduce energy use.

Many organizations reluctant to undertake carbon-reducing initiatives assume these actions will increase operating costs, resulting in reduced earnings or, for government and nonprofit organizations, a reduced level of services. *Energy Budgets at Risk* shows that carbon and other greenhouse gas emissions can be reduced with energy cost savings more than offsetting the cost of energy-efficiency investments. Thus, achieving carbon-reducing goals with EBaR analysis can add to the financial bottom line.

New carbon-trading mechanisms established both by government and private interests and the growing use of "efficiency certificates" in individual states pass incentives to reduce energy use through to individual facility owners. For instance, efficiency certificates permit individual facility owners to sell efficiency improvement credits to utilities who are required to meet requirements of "efficiency portfolio standards." These market mechanisms provide additional financial incentives to invest in energy efficiency.

The EBaR analytical framework is ideally suited to integrate carbon-reduction and other green objectives in a capital budgeting approach that comprehensively considers benefits, costs, and risks associated with energy efficiency investments.

## WHO SHOULD READ THIS BOOK?

*Energy Budgets at Risk* is written for a nontechnical audience. The material is directly relevant to actual decisions faced by facility energy managers, financial managers and executives in business, institutions, and government. Concepts and applications are introduced and described in sufficient detail to support applications at individual facilities.

*Energy Budgets at Risk* provides background information required to understand the various energy cost, price, efficiency, and related issues that are important in developing a balanced approach to facility energy risk management. Analytical concepts are limited, and sufficient background material is included to explain and illustrate all applications.

This book is designed to serve five separate but related audiences with whom I have interacted over the last 30 years. The first group is composed of building owners, facility managers, and others on the front line who are responsible for electric, natural gas, and fuel oil budgets in commercial, industrial, government, and institutional buildings and facilities. This audience will learn how to develop, apply and present a comprehensive, consistent financial risk management framework to evaluate energy budget risk, alternative energy-efficiency investments, and, in competitive markets, how to integrate efficiency investment decisions with purchase decisions.

The second audience is composed of CEOs, CFOs, CROs (chief risk officers), administrators, and managers whose organizations have already begun adopting quantitative management approaches in other areas such as Six Sigma quality measurement. For these decision makers, *Energy Budgets at Risk* provides another tool in the expanding portfolio of management analytics. For organizations just beginning to consider quantitative options for measuring and managing risk, *Energy Budgets at Risk* provides a perfect starting point. An energy budget and efficiency investment application provides an intuitive introduction to modern risk management concepts and tools, and, additionally provides immediate cash flow benefits.

The third audience, energy service companies (ESCOs), MEPs (mechanical, electrical and plumbing firms), consulting engineers, architects, and other design professionals who provide energy-efficiency services, typically struggles to present efficiency options to their clients. More efficient choices nearly always cost more initially but with proper financing will increase cash flows. However, many owners feel uncomfortable with anything other than the traditional least-cost option. An EBaR analysis intuitively demonstrates that making a trade-off between initial cost and future energy budgets will better meet owner objectives.

The fourth audience is government policy makers and electric utilities program planners. Simply providing consumers with energy-efficiency technology information and encouraging them to use traditional investment evaluations like net present value analysis have relatively little impact on efficiency-investment decisions. *Energy Budgets at Risk* tackles this problem by providing policy makers and program planners with a new investment analysis tool that can be bundled with energy-efficient technology information to increase the impact of current information programs. Promoting EBaR and other new information initiatives that better fit existing decision-making requirements is a promising approach to encourage greater energy efficiency.

The final audience includes advanced undergraduate and graduate university students. *Energy Budgets at Risk* provides the financial framework to evaluate energy efficiency and green building choices required in architectural design, construction, facilities management, and mechanical engineering disciplines. Also, students in business, finance, and industrial engineering will find *Energy Budgets at Risk* instructive as an introduction to quantitative risk management applications to evaluate market risks and capital budgeting investment decisions.

## ORGANIZATION OF THE BOOK

This book has been organized to assist readers in understanding and applying information on energy markets, risk management, EBaR concepts and analysis, and individual facility applications.

Chapter 1 provides an overview of the EBaR process and background information on energy markets and future energy prices. The role of EBar in promoting green objectives at individual facilities and through government policies is also described.

A summary of mainstream efficiency technologies is provided as background in Chapter 2. An engineering background is not required to review information on available efficiency options or to follow the case study analysis discussed in later chapters.

Chapters 3 and 4 provide detail on facility energy costs, and traditional capital budgeting practices applied to energy-efficiency investments.

Chapters 5 and 6 present a brief history of the development of financial industry risk management and a discussion of its application to energy-efficiency decision making.

Chapters 7 and 8 describe EBaR analysis components whose application to energy budget risk, investment analysis and risk and competitive market analyses are illustrated in Chapters 9 through 11.

Readers who want to go right to the financial bottom line can take a quick look at Chapter 12, EBaR Reports, to see results of the Austin office case study and how EBaR decision variables can be presented for management consideration.

Finally, the Appendix provides information that answers the question of whether developing an EBaR analysis is worth the effort for a given organization. Information on energy-use characteristics of more than one million business, institutional, and government buildings in the United States provides a basis for readers to develop a general estimate of the potential financial savings available with an EBaR analysis.

## energybudgetsatrisk.com

Energybudgetsatrisk.com is a companion web site for this book. Web contents include energy risk management software customized to support all aspects of EBaR analysis, additional discussion of EBaR-related issues and a section devoted to frequently asked questions about EBaR application. Questions concerning EBaR related topics may be addressed to the author via e-mail through the web site.

Information on EBaR workshops and training is also posted on energybudgetsatrisk.com.

Jerry Jackson

# Energy Markets and Budgets at Risk

High, erratic energy prices have created financial crises for many businesses, institutions, and government agencies over the last several years.

This chapter provides background information on energy markets and price trends, and introduces basic Energy Budgets at Risk (EBaR) concepts. The potential role of EBaR in meeting green objectives and supporting energy policy options is also discussed.

## RECENT PRICE INCREASES

As of mid-2007, average U.S. natural gas and oil prices for commercial sector (nonresidential and nonindustrial) establishments were 100 and 250 percent higher than 1999 levels (Figure 1.1). Electricity price increases in this period vary considerably by state; Figure 1.1 shows commercial sector electric prices relative to 1999 for the four most populous U.S. states of California, New York, Texas and Florida. Electric price increases over the 1999 to 2007 period range from 36 percent in California to 54 percent in Florida.

Prices in Figure 1.1 are actual prices that do not take inflation into account. Figure 1.2 shows prices adjusted for inflation. 2007 average real (inflation-adjusted) U.S. commercial sector natural gas and oil prices are 61 and 184 percent higher than 1999 levels. Real electricity price increases range from 11 (California) to 26 (Florida) percent of 1999 values. These inflation-adjusted series provide a general indication of energy price increases relative to all prices.[1]

Energy price increases and the volatility of recent years have transformed a small component of operating costs into a threat to operating reserves and profits for many organizations. Energy-intensive organizations

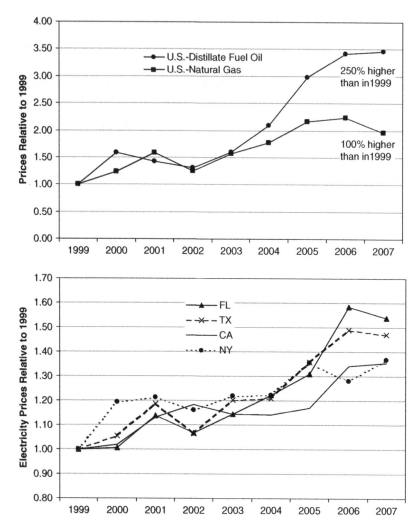

**FIGURE 1.1** Commercial sector energy prices relative to 1999
*Source:* Energy Information Administration, http://www.eia.doe.gov/, June 2007. Estimates for 2007 are based on the first three months of the year.

have been critically affected, and recent financial reports frequently identify energy costs as a primary cause of disappointing earnings. The U.S. Business Roundtable's fourth-quarter, 2006, CEO Economic Outlook Survey identified energy costs as one of the top two cost pressures faced by their businesses.[2]

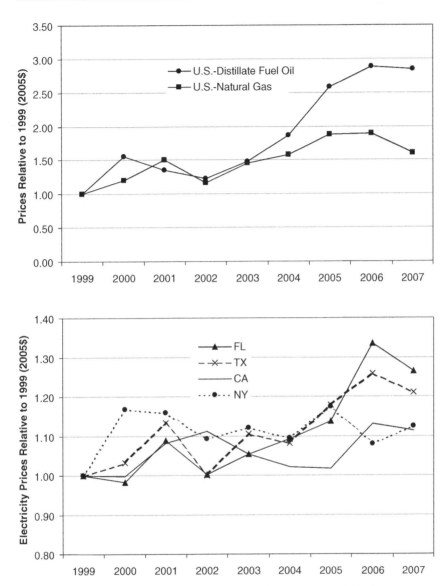

**FIGURE 1.2** Commercial sector energy prices relative to 1999 (2005$)
*Source:* Energy Information Administration, http://www.eia.doe.gov/, June 2007.
Estimates for 2007 are based on the first three months of the year. Price index data
from US Department of Commerce, available at http://www.gpoaccess.gov/eop/
2007/B3.xls.

## APPLYING RISK MANAGEMENT TO ENERGY BUDGETS

Evaluating risk associated with energy costs and taking steps to reduce cost and risk exposure in today's energy markets require a process different from traditional energy management approaches. Current high energy prices and volatility mean that using last year's energy costs as an estimate of next year's budget and evaluating energy-reducing investments with simple payback or internal rate of return hurdle rates (minimum acceptable rates) will expose organizations to an unnecessary level of risk and bypass profitable efficiency investments.

### ENERGY EFFICIENCY INVESTMENTS INCLUDE

- The purchase of new, more efficient energy-using equipment to replace existing equipment—for example, the purchase of new high-efficiency fluorescent lamps and ballasts.
- The modification of existing equipment or structural characteristics to operate more efficiently. Adjusting airflow in a ventilation system and installing solar-radiation deflecting roofing are examples of this activity.
- Redesign of existing energy-using systems such as delamping (disconnecting existing lighting fixtures) and replacement of standard fluorescent light fixtures with light and motion detectors. Modifying constant air volume ventilation systems to variable air volume designs is another redesign example.
- Installation of systems to change the operation of energy-using equipment. For example, energy management and control systems use computerized controls for everything from lighting to heating, ventilation, and air conditioning systems.

This book introduces a new framework to evaluate and quantify energy cost risks, energy efficiency investments, and energy purchase decisions based on risk management tools refined over the last decade in the financial industry. Energy Budgets at Risk (EBaR) analysis explicitly recognizes risk tolerance of individual organizations and risks associated with specific investment decisions.

EBaR is more than a tool to address recent energy price increases; it provides an entirely new framework to bring energy efficiency investment and purchase decisions up to date using best practice risk management tools. Even in relatively low-cost energy areas, organizations can expect to achieve annual net energy costs savings ranging from 20 to 30 percent of current energy bills (net savings are annual savings minus the annual cost of the investment amortized over its lifetime). EBaR can be viewed as an addition to the increasingly quantitative portfolio of management tools required in today's fast-paced competitive markets.

*Energy Budgets at Risk* shows organizations how to evaluate and manage energy risk in a way that best meets the organization's budget flexibility and risk tolerance.

## ENERGY BUDGETS AT RISK WORKSHOPS

This book and the EBaR process have grown out of my consulting practice and a series of energy risk management workshops I developed at Texas A&M University. Comments and questions from my consulting clients and from the broad spectrum of workshop attendees from commercial, institutional, and government agencies make it clear that the tenor of energy concerns has changed dramatically over the last several years. Organizations are eager to reduce energy costs, but lack the ability to make sound financial decisions with respect to energy-efficiency investments. Energy managers are generally aware of many of the options available to improve energy efficiency; however, they readily admit they do not know how to evaluate and prioritize the alternatives or, most importantly, how to make the financial case to their management. CFOs and public administrators almost universally view energy efficiency as a different kind of capital budgeting problem—one that is most conveniently handled with very short payback thresholds, which, unfortunately, exclude many attractive options.

Organizations operating in competitive electricity and natural gas markets face even greater challenges. Energy pricing options can vary in a dozen dimensions, such as contract time period and use of hourly spot market pricing. Because pricing contract terms impact efficiency investment returns and efficiency investments impact competitive price quotes, efficiency investment and purchasing decisions should be made simultaneously. However, efficiency and purchasing decisions are almost always considered separately, usually by different departments within a single organization.

The end result is that individual organizations are losing tens of thousands, hundreds of thousands and in some cases millions of dollars per year in unnecessary energy costs. Remarkably, these neglected opportunities more than pay for themselves, increasing cash flows to provide the equivalent of new revenue opportunities.

Problems presented by two of my workshop attendees are representative of the difficulties many organizations are experiencing. The first attendee is the hands-on owner of a Texas restaurant chain. His electricity bills had more than doubled over the last several years and were cutting deeply into his profits. He was concerned that prices would continue to rise and had recently invested in a dozen different energy-efficiency technologies to cover all the bases. Unfortunately, the return on his investment was small because several of his investments had little impact on his energy bills relative to their cost.

The second attendee is an energy manager at a retail grocery chain who manages more than $5 million per year in energy costs. He knew that he could save substantially with energy efficiency investments—his local equipment suppliers were marketing their efficiency products to him. He did not know how to compare the various investments, however, nor did he know how to evaluate which investments he should undertake with his limited capital budget. To make matters more difficult, his current competitive electricity market contract was about to expire, and competing suppliers were offering many different pricing options. Faced with a seemingly overwhelming number of choices, he had procrastinated for six months at the time of the workshop—the cost of indecision to his company, by my calculations, was running at about $100,000 per month. Of course these opportunity costs are not typically evaluated, so neither he nor his management were aware of the lost revenue opportunity.

*Energy Budgets at Risk* shows readers how to avoid these and other energy-related investment and purchase problems. The book is written for a nontechnical audience. Concepts and applications such as probability distributions and Monte Carlo analysis are introduced and described in sufficient detail to enable readers to understand and apply EBaR analysis at their organizations.

## AN ENERGY BUDGETS AT RISK (EBaR) OVERVIEW

In spite of financial challenges created by recent energy price increases, few organizations apply more than a rudimentary approach to evaluate energy price risk and energy efficiency investment options (Chapter 4 discusses this issue in more detail). Payback analysis is the predominant financial analysis tool used to qualify energy efficiency investments, though conservative internal rate of return hurdle rates or equivalent evaluations are sometimes applied. In competitive energy markets, energy purchase decisions and efficiency investments are almost universally considered separately rather than as part of a coordinated energy risk management process. Energy-related decision making is virtually the same for most organizations as it was in 1972 before energy prices began their modern volatile trajectory. Using short payback periods is a reasonably effective strategy to limit risk since it limits analysis to the near term, where there is the least uncertainty; however, it also ignores some of the most profitable energy efficiency investments.

CFOs and financial administrators in most of these organizations deal with other kinds of financial risk in a much different manner. Most organizations apply sophisticated financial risk management techniques, or hire firms to apply this analysis, in order to maximize returns on financial portfolios and pension funds. Advances in quantitative financial analysis, especially over the last decade, provide an impressive ability to quantify risks and rewards associated with various investment strategies and portfolios. Value at risk, earnings at risk and other at risk measures are now a standard part of the financial risk management vocabulary.

The following sections illustrate how modern risk management techniques are used in EBaR analysis to address energy budget and efficiency investment risks.

## Energy Budgeting Under Uncertainty

Although managing facility energy costs and managing financial investments appear to have little in common, they reflect remarkably similar challenges: how best to evaluate and make investment decisions in the face of uncertainty. Analyzing energy budget risk can even be cast as a portfolio problem. Each energy-using system in a facility can be considered an investment characterized in part by its operating costs. Past years' experiences can be used to characterize variability in energy prices and energy use resulting from weather variations, facility utilization and so on—thereby providing a distribution of likely facility energy budgets for the coming year. Figure 1.3 shows an expected budget of $100,000 along with a distribution of other budget outcomes that might occur based on past experience. The area under portions of the distribution, relative to the total area under the curve, shows the probability that an outcome will occur between the two points on the energy budget axis as shown for energy budgets of less than $60,000 and more than $120,000 in Figure 1.3.

## Applying at Risk Analysis to the Energy Budget Process

Readers familiar with the widely used Value at Risk (VaR) financial analysis will recognize the similarity between this energy budget analysis and VaR

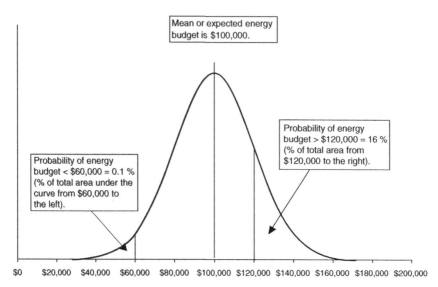

**FIGURE 1.3**   Distribution of Likely Energy Budget Outcomes

analysis. VaR analysis, with a history that traces back to 1922,[3] was popularized by JP Morgan in the early 1990s and is now widely used in financial analysis to assess risks associated with investments and financial portfolios. As indicated in Figure 1.4, VaR statistics show the maximum daily, weekly or monthly portfolio loss that can be expected to occur based on a specified confidence level. A variety of other "at risk" measures such as Earnings at Risk, Profits at Risk and Cash Flow at Risk have been developed. Technical analysis related to estimation of these VaR-related risk measures is now an active area of academic and applied research. U.S. and international financial regulatory agencies have adopted VaR analysis to evaluate financial institutions' risk exposure. As indicated in the lower panel of Figure 1.4, EBaR reflects an energy budget-counterpart to VaR analysis.

### Including New Energy-Efficiency Investments

EBaR analysis can be applied to evaluate new energy-efficient investments—such as replacing existing fluorescent ballasts and lamps with new high efficiency products. Future variations in electric price and uncertainty over the number of hours each fixture will operate result in a distribution of likely returns on this investment. Returns can be measured as annual energy cost savings and an internal rate of return, IRR. The internal rate of return

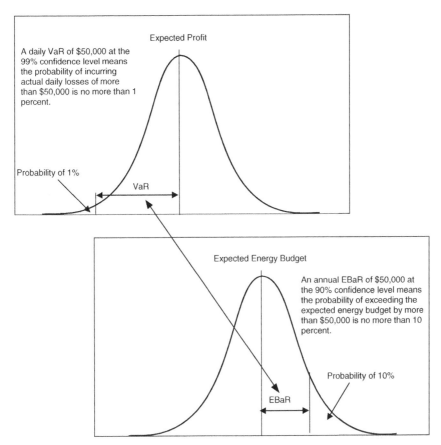

Expected Profit

A daily VaR of $50,000 at the 99% confidence level means the probability of incurring actual daily losses of more than $50,000 is no more than 1 percent.

Probability of 1%

VaR

Expected Energy Budget

An annual EBaR of $50,000 at the 90% confidence level means the probability of exceeding the expected energy budget by more than $50,000 is no more than 10 percent.

Probability of 10%

EBaR

**FIGURE 1.4** Correspondence of VaR and EBaR Analysis Concepts

reflects the effective yield on the efficiency investment (investment basics are covered in Chapter 4).

Figure 1.5 shows a hypothetical distribution of annual savings reflecting potential variations in electricity price and operating hours. In this example, the investment cost is $80,000; annual savings are $40,000; and the annual financing cost to pay for the investment over ten years at a 12 percent interest rate is approximately $14,000. Deducting annual financing costs from annual energy cost savings provides an annual cash flow increase of $26,000 per year. However, the payback for this investment is two years, which is more than many organizations accept in traditional efficiency screening analysis.

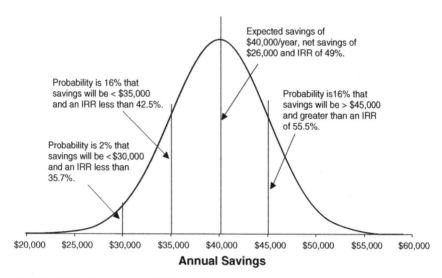

**FIGURE 1.5**  Hypothetical Lighting Investment Analysis

At the expected value, the internal rate of return is 49 percent. Traditional budgeting practices would recommend this investment if the $40,000 were a guaranteed return—that is, if there was no uncertainty. Of course, there is uncertainty regarding electricity price and operating hours so this investment is rejected based on its failure to meet the organization's payback threshold. The EBaR investment distribution shows, however, only a 2 percent probability that the savings will be less than $30,000 per year. Savings of $30,000 per year provide an internal rate of return of 35.7 percent and an increased cash flow of $16,000 per year. Information on the distribution of investment returns provides insights on investments like this that fail traditional payback or internal rate of return hurdle rates but provide attractive returns and can generate significant cash flows with little risk.

What happens to total energy budget risk with this investment? Subtracting the annual amortized cost of the investment from the annual energy savings and applying the same calculations as above provide a new distribution of expected energy budgets (Figure 1.6). Expected savings were $40,000; however, the amortized cost of financing the investment offsets some of the savings in the new budget to give a new net savings of $26,000 per year. The new distribution reflects a smaller expected energy budget and less variation in potential outcomes, that is, less energy budget risk. The figure shows that while the expected or average energy budget will drop by $26,000, the "worst case" outcome defined by the EBaR probability of

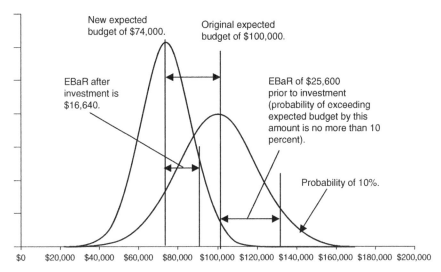

**FIGURE 1.6**    Total Energy Budgets at Risk after the Investment

10 percent declines by $34,960. Thus, the investment reduced the expected budget but it reduced even more the exposure to extreme budgets that can occur with high energy prices, weather, and other events.

## Management and Decision-Making Advantages

The EBaR representations above are only part of the process; however, the intuitive appeal of this approach is obvious—rather than trying to make investment decisions based on a traditional single estimate of expected energy savings, the entire range of investment outcomes and their probability of occurrence should be considered. This inclusive representation allows individual organizations to better understand the risks and rewards of alternative energy strategies, and this understanding accommodates their ability and desire to bear risks. As shown in Chapter 9, assessing uncertainty using this distribution-based analysis is accomplished with Monte Carlo analysis, an accepted and easy-to-apply-approach to treating uncertainty that has been applied in financial and many other application areas for decades.

One reason that VaR analysis is so widely used is its distillation of the many dimensions of information on return and risk into a single decision variable. EBaR decision variables provide the same advantage. For instance, if $EBaR_{irr,90}$, the smallest internal rate of return likely at the 90 percent confidence level, is greater than a given threshold, say, a return of 25 percent, the investment will be recommended for further consideration. An $EBaR_{irr,90}$ of 45 percent means that there is no more than a 10 percent probability that the internal rate of return will be less than 45. A more conservative EBaR statistic for the investment, say $EBaR_{irr,95} = 0.35$, permits only a 5 percent chance of achieving a return of less than 35 percent.

From a management perspective, knowing that an investment has an $EBaR_{irr,90} = 0.45$ and $EBaR_{irr,95} = 0.35$ provides much more information

## ENERGY BUDGETS AT RISK (EBaR) DECISION VARIABLES

EBaR provides three primary decision variables that measure budget and investment risk.

### Energy Budgets

$EBaR_{budget,x}$ is the budget form of the EBaR statistic showing the largest expected energy budget variance (difference between the expected budget and actual energy costs) at a given confidence level, x, typically, 90 or 95 percent. An $EBaR_{budget,,95} = \$50,000$ indicates that the likelihood of experiencing a budget variance of $50,000 or less is 95 percent.

### Efficiency Investment

$EBaR_{irr,x}$ is an investment form of the EBaR statistic showing the smallest expected investment internal rate of return (IRR) at a given confidence level, x, typically, 90 or 95 percent. An $EBaR_{irr,95} = 35$ percent indicates that the likelihood of achieving an internal rate of return of 35 percent or more is 95 percent. Chapter 4 discusses internal rate of return and other investment basics.

$EBaR_{netsav,x}$ is the smallest net savings (energy cost savings minus amortized cost of the equipment, including financing costs) at a given confidence level, x. An $EBaR_{netsav,x} = \$30,000$ indicates a 95 percent likelihood of achieving a net savings of $30,000 or more.

than traditional payback and IRR because it reflects the investment return conditioned on an organization's risk tolerance. Even in cases where decision makers are unwilling to accept almost any risk (perhaps using a confidence level of 97.5 percent), EBaR still provides advantages over traditional measures because it recognizes variations in uncertainty that occur across different efficiency technologies.

Thus, EBaR replaces the single-dimension decision variable, payback (or an IRR hurdle rate), with a single-dimension decision variable, $EBaR_{irr,x}$, where x is the confidence level. The difference is that payback and traditional IRR analysis is based on initial cost and a single estimate of expected savings, whereas EBaR analysis is based on initial cost and likely distributions of expected savings with an explicit consideration of risk. Short payback periods accommodate risk by only accepting almost sure bets, while EBaR analysis identifies desirable investments based on both investment returns and the associated risk. In other words, EBaR-based analysis manages risk, while payback analysis attempts to avoid risk by setting conservative investment criteria.

It is worth repeating that the EBaR decision variable, $EBaR_{irr,x}$, is a simple, intuitive and meaningful decision variable: a necessary requirement as capital budgeting requests are bumped up the chain of command for consideration. While intuitive graphs and tables like those in Chapters 9 and 10 can be used to visually convey an additional layer of information on the trade-off between risks and returns, the value of $EBaR_{irr,x}$ alone is sufficient to qualify investments for consideration by upper management. Making investment decisions based on values of EBaR decisions variables does not require understanding the application details of EBaR analysis.

There are, of course, differences in financial portfolio and energy-related investment analysis. Portfolio managers can sell a financial instrument if its performance is lagging and replace it with another. Energy efficiency investments reflect a physical investment, so a bad investment cannot generally be sold. However, these differences are subtle compared to the overall approach provided by modern financial risk management and can be incorporated in efficiency investments analysis.

## Bottom-Line Advantages

What impact can EBaR have on an organization's energy expenditures? Analysis of current energy investment behavior and existing energy efficiency technologies indicates that most organizations can achieve annual savings of 20 to 30 percent of energy costs beyond the annual costs associated with financing the investments. That is, cash flow can be expected to increase by as much as 30 percent of current energy budgets beginning the first day after the investment occurs.

A $100,000 efficiency investment in an office building that, based on the engineering calculations, pays for itself and provides additional savings of, say, $50,000 each year sounds too good to be true. After all, if this potential existed wouldn't the energy manager make the same savings calculations and make the investment without having to resort to more complicated analysis to be convinced that a "free" $50,000 per year is a good option? The answer typically is no. For instance, a recent comprehensive study of 9,000 small and medium manufacturers found an average payback of 15 months was required to prompt an energy-saving investment after a free detailed energy audit had been conducted and conveyed to facility managers and owners.[4] This criterion is equivalent to a return of about 70 percent. If a company borrows money at 10 percent it would realize a net return, after making annual interest and principal payments, of about 60 percent. Ignoring an investment of $100,000 to reap a profit of $50,000 per year does indeed seem paradoxical.

## THE ENERGY PARADOX AND EFFICIENCY GAP

By the late 1970s it became apparent that corporate, government, and institutional decision-makers were more reluctant to invest in energy efficiency technologies than in other investments. This enigma was identified as the "energy paradox" or "efficiency gap." It was assumed at that time that information programs and the maturing of new energy-efficient technologies would remove most of this investment barrier. However, the efficiency gap has persisted at approximately the same level for a quarter century. This result has continued to puzzle most energy economists. Explanations have been debated in dozens of articles in the interim without any compelling empirical evidence of the cause.

The example of manufacturers currently requiring a 15-month payback in the "Bottom Line Advantages" section is just one of many examples that illustrate the fact that this investment behavior is still the rule. Studies by the Department of Energy and many other organizations confirm this shortsighted investment strategy.

As indicated in Chapter 4, the energy paradox or efficiency gap is primarily a result of decision-maker use of payback requirements to screen energy efficiency investment risk. EBaR analysis overcomes the limitations of this traditional approach.

The primary explanation for this seeming anomaly has already been mentioned above. Decision makers apply short payback periods to protect against the risk of bad investment outcomes. A mean or expected payback of 15 months may be considered necessary to limit the probability of a bad investment outcome to an acceptable level of, say, 5 percent. To be effective, rules of thumb must reflect worst-case scenarios—in this case, perhaps a technology that costs more to install, incurs greater operating and maintenance expense, and performs less effectively than planned. However, likely distributions of individual efficiency technologies vary considerably so worst-case rules of thumb reject many good investments. Evidence from studies of investment behavior indicates that most current investment decisions are guided by this attempt to limit risk, resulting in a large potential for energy efficiency savings when EBaR analysis is applied.

In summary, EBaR provides organizations with a new framework to evaluate energy budget risks and rewards of energy-related decisions. This process transforms traditional energy efficiency and energy purchase decisions into a financial analysis framework compatible with best financial practices in today's business world. Applying this investment analysis framework can be expected to increase cash flows by 20 to 30 percent or more of current energy costs for most organizations.

## A LOOK BACK AT ENERGY PRICES

Most businesses, institutions, and government agencies are acutely aware of recent energy cost increases. Appropriate organizational responses to increased energy costs depend in part on expectations about future energy prices. While forecasting the exact level of energy prices at specific times is a dicey proposition, sufficient information exists on energy markets and market trends to develop reasonable expectations on future energy price trends based on past trends and factors that are expected to influence those trends in the future. This section summarizes historical price trends and relationships beginning in 1972, the year before the first oil embargo.

Energy sources are substitutable to varying extents in providing energy-related services. Oil, natural gas, and electricity can all be used to provide space heating, water heating, and manufacturing process uses; coal, natural gas and oil are substitutes in the generation of electricity. Since fuel choices generally require the purchase of long-lasting equipment designed for the energy source, substitution impacts take some time to play out. Markets for energy sources differ; for instance, oil prices are determined in a world market while natural gas prices reflect geographic supply constraints.

The end result is that the price of individual fuels is jointly determined by a complicated mix of demand and supply relationships that exist across economic sectors and geographic areas. Historical price series for oil, natural gas and electricity are presented in the sections that follow.

## Oil Price Trends

The best place to start understanding energy price trends is with oil because of the influence oil prices have on other fuels and energy sources. Two major oil price spikes have occurred in the last 35 years. Figure 1.7 shows the crude oil composite acquisition cost by refiners. The first oil embargo by Arab states in 1973, which more than doubled prices, was followed by another curtailment in 1979. By 1981, oil prices were five times their 1972 level. However, by 1986, prices had fallen to $23 per barrel (in 2005 dollars), just double that of 1972. Oil prices fluctuated within a range of +/– $9 per barrel for 18 years through 2003. Since 1999, real oil prices have tripled from $20 to $60 per barrel. (All of the charts in this section show "real" prices rather than "nominal" prices; that is, the historical prices have been adjusted for inflation.)

## Natural Gas Price Trends

The average U.S. price commercial customers paid for natural gas over the 1972 to 2007 period is shown in Figure 1.8.

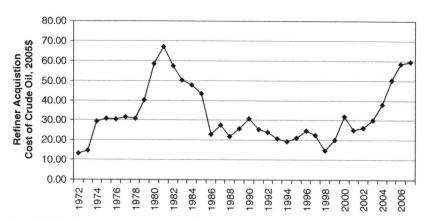

**FIGURE 1.7**   U.S. 1972–2007 Crude Oil Composite Acquisition Cost by Refiners (2005 dollars per barrel)
*Source:* Energy Information Administration, 5/29/2007. Data through 2006 are actual; 2007 is estimated based on monthly series through September.

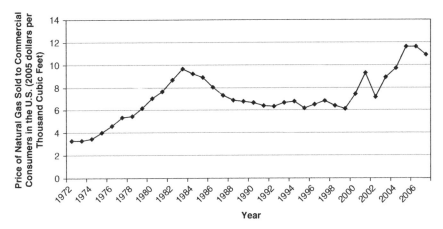

**FIGURE 1.8** U.S. Price of Natural Gas Sold to Commercial Consumers (2005 dollars per thousand cubic foot)
*Source:* Energy Information Administration, 11/11/2007. Data through 2006 are actual; 2007 is estimated based on monthly series through August.

The correlation between oil and gas prices is illustrated in Figure 1.9 where oil and gas series of Figures 1.7 and 1.8 are plotted as annual values divided by the series average. The relationship between oil and gas prices is a stable relationship with oil prices influencing natural gas prices, but natural gas prices having little influence on oil prices.[5] In other words, increases or decreases in world oil prices are reflected in increases or decreases in domestic natural gas prices. However, when gas prices increase because of excess demand, there is an imperceptible impact on world oil markets because of the small size of North American gas markets compared to the world oil market. The recent tendency of natural gas prices to exceed oil prices on a dollars per Btu basis (Btu or British thermal units are a measure of energy content) is reflected in the figure suggesting that demand for natural gas in the North American gas market is greater relative to its supply than the relationship of world oil demand to oil supply.

## Electricity Price Trends

Approximately 30 percent of electric utility operating costs (including depreciation) are determined by fuel costs; consequently, changes in generator fuels have a muted impact on electricity prices. From 1972 to 1974, the price of coal, which accounts for about 50 percent of generation capacity, rose dramatically and then steadily declined until 2003 (see Figure 1.10).

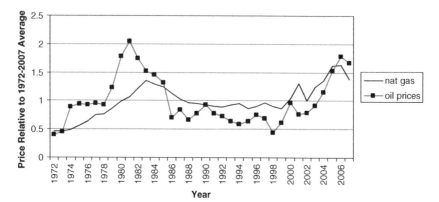

**FIGURE 1.9** Comparison of Oil and Commercial Natural Gas Price Series
*Source:* Energy Information Administration, 5/31/2007. Data through 2006 are
actual; 2007 is estimated based on monthly series through March.

With price increases in the last several years, the 2007 price of coal stands
at about its 1972 level in real terms. Nuclear power is currently used for
about 21 percent of utility customer generation; however, uranium costs
are a much smaller part of operating cost than with fossil fuel plants. 1972
uranium prices are unavailable; however, 2005 uranium prices are about 40
percent of their 1981 value.

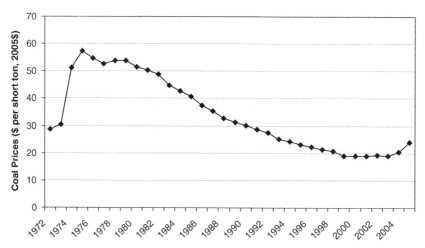

**FIGURE 1.10** 1972–2005 Coal Prices, 2005 Dollars per Short Ton
*Source:* Energy Information Administration, Annual Energy Review, 2006.

Other generating energy sources for utility customers include natural gas (17 percent), oil (2 percent), hydro (8 percent) and renewables (2 percent).

## ELECTRICITY GENERATION ENERGY SOURCES

The following table shows U.S. utility and independent power producer generation by energy source.

| Fuel type | % Generation |
|-----------|--------------|
| Coal | 50.4 |
| Nuclear | 20.1 |
| Natural Gas | 18.8 |
| Hydroelectric | 7.3 |
| Other Renewables | 1.7 |
| Oil | 1.5 |

*Source:* Net Generation by Energy Source by Type of Producer, data for electric utilities, electric power chp and independent power producers, 2006, http://www.eia.doe.gov/cneaf/electricity/epa/epat1p1.html

U.S. historical electric prices in Figure 1.11 reflect generating fuel price trends as well as technological advances in turbine design. Although natural gas fuels only about 20 percent of total electric generation, increases in natural gas prices since 2000 have put significant upward pressure on electricity rates in many parts of the United States. Natural gas generators account for about 75 percent of generators added in the last decade and most peaking units that provide electricity in peak summer or winter periods. As a fuel for electricity supplied at the margin, natural gas prices have considerable impact on the price of electricity. As indicated in Figure 1.1 shown at the beginning of this chapter, electric prices have increased substantially in many states reflecting increased natural gas prices. The moderating impact of states with a greater portion of generation provided by coal or nuclear generators has held national average price increases since 1999 to about 9 percent in real terms (Figure 1.11).

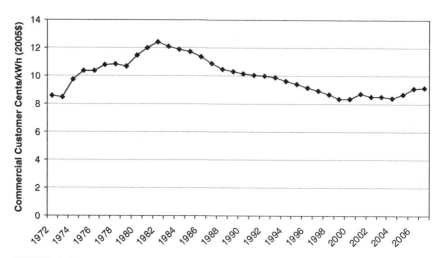

**FIGURE 1.11**   1972–2007 U.S. Commercial Electricity Prices (2005 cents per kWh)
*Source:* Energy Information Administration, Electric Power Monthly with data through July 2007, 11/11/2007.

## A LOOK FORWARD: ENERGY DEMAND AND SUPPLY FACTORS

Energy prices are determined by demand and supply. Excess supply results in lower prices, and excess demand results in higher prices. Regulated electric and natural gas utilities pass along market-determined prices to their customers with a different process from competitive energy providers; however, in the end, all energy customers pay prices determined primarily by market forces. A number of demand and supply factors are especially interesting in the context of forecasting future price trends because they reflect new trends or, as sometimes happens, because they are often mentioned in the popular press as important but in reality are likely to have little impact on energy prices in the foreseeable future. Some of these factors are discussed in the section below.

### Robust Economic Growth in Developing Countries

Globalization of the world economy, liberalized trade policies, and the introduction of competitive market reforms have contributed to unprecedented growth in less developed countries. Economic growth in Asian countries has been remarkable. Annual economic growth averaging more than 9 percent has been sustained since 1978 in China, a country of 1.3 billion people. By comparison, the United States has a population of 300 million and real economic growth averaging 3 percent over the same period. The Department of Energy's "Energy Information Agency" (EIA) forecasts China's 2006 oil consumption to increase by about half a million barrels per day, soaking up nearly 40 percent of the annual increase in world supplies. China, the third-largest net importer of oil, following the United States and Japan, will soon achieve second-place status.[6]

The EIA estimates an increase in energy use in non-OECD countries (mostly developing nations) *four times* that of OECD countries between 2004 and 2030.[7]

## Economic Growth in the United States and Other Developed Countries

Globalization has contributed to an unprecedented period of sustained economic growth for developed countries as well as less developed countries. Increased incomes result in larger houses, more appliances, greater demand for services and consumer goods—all of which increase the demand for energy. The steady growth of developed nations provides a background against which growth in developing countries has strained energy supply capabilities since 1999. Most forecasts reflect a healthy U.S. economic growth of about 3 percent through 2010 with only slightly lower growth through 2015.

## Innovation and New Technology Development

The discussion of efficient end-use (space heating, lighting, and so on) technologies in Chapter 2 illustrates the potential demand-reducing impact of efficiency improvements achieved through innovation and technology developments that improve on existing energy-using equipment. A number of technologies reduce energy use in more unconventional ways. One such technology is a combined heat and power system (CHP), which uses natural gas to generate electricity at the facility site and captures waste heat from the generation process for space heating, water heating, air conditioning, or process uses. This technology reduces the overall demand for energy because it captures and uses heat from the generation process. CHP units can achieve 90 percent efficiency. That is, only 10 percent of the energy input used in the system is lost to the environment compared to central power plants where about 68 percent of the energy input is lost (average U.S. electric system efficiency is about 32 percent). Cool storage systems are another attractive technology that use electricity in off-peak hours to generate chilled water or ice that can be used to cool buildings during peak summer hours. While total energy use is no less, the ability to use lower-cost off-peak electricity to generate cold water or ice reduces both customer and utility system costs.

Innovation in the form of increased equipment efficiency and new technology developments reflects the single greatest potential impact on future demand for energy. However, new technologies take time to develop and reach the commercialization stage; consequently, for the near future (the next decade), the benefit of technology innovation and development will primarily take the form of the application of more efficient technologies currently on the market.

## Oil and Natural Gas Exploration and Production

The market supply reaction to high oil and natural gas prices is as expected. Oil and natural gas rotary rigs are used to drill for, explore, and develop oil and gas wells. The number of North American rotary rigs in operation has increased from 625 in 1999 to 1,649 in 2006 and 1801 in November 2007.[8] Increased exploration and production in non-OPEC countries including former Soviet Union republics, Africa, and even Brazil will also help meet growing demand. Considerable time is required to find and bring new oil sources to the market so any significant relief from current market responses is likely to be at least five or more years in the future.

Declines in production in mature oil fields offset some of the new production. For instance, Mexico's huge Cantarell oil field, one of the largest in the world, reported a year-over-year decline of 13 percent in June 2006. A July, 2007 International Energy Agency report estimates a decline of about 4 percent per year in all existing fields.

Will increased production reduce prices to 1990 levels? If new oil production required only drilling more wells in existing oil fields, the marginal cost of adding new production would be about the same as wells producing in the 1990s, and the price of oil could be expected to fall back close to the 1990s levels. However, new production is successively harder to find and to reach, and consequently costs more. The production costs of new sources determine the market price of oil. While technology advances in exploration and production help limit cost increases, increased cost of producing oil from deep-water wells and other more difficult-to-reach oil deposits can be expected to set a floor for oil prices that is significantly higher than oil prices in the 1990s.

## OPEC Reaction

The Organization of the Petroleum Exporting Countries (OPEC), which includes Algeria, Angola, Indonesia, Iran, Iraq, Kuwait, Libya, Nigeria, Qatar,

Saudi Arabia, the United Arab Emirates, and Venezuela, supplies about 40 percent of the world's oil. In market conditions with tight supplies, OPEC member increases or reductions in production can significantly impact oil prices. As recently as March, 2006, OPEC members publicly identified a world oil price target in the $50 to $60/barrel range as "appropriate."

Weakness of the dollar and observations that the sustained higher price levels seem to have relatively little impact on economic activity appear to have prompted OPEC to replace the earlier range with an OPEC target of $60 to $65/barrel beginning in mid-2007.[9] Continued weakening of the dollar through the end of 2007 will likely keep the target in a higher range of $70 to $75/barrel.

Higher oil prices could potentially slow world economies enough to offset higher prices with a greater reduction in oil consumption and encourage development of conventional and unconventional supply development in non-OPEC countries. While there is some consolation in expecting that OPEC will move to limit prices that stay much above $75/barrel for extended periods of time, the downside is that a price below $75/barrel is likely to cause a restriction in OPEC oil production, boosting the price back above the $75 mark.

It is important to note that OPEC targets exclude speculation and risk premiums. As discussed in the $100/barrel oil section below, the current view that these factors add about $25 to the current price means that OPEC has little incentive to increase output in today's $90–100/barrel market.

## New Oil Extraction Technologies

A variety of technologies is expected to play a role in the future supply of liquid fuels including oil sands, ultraheavy oils, gas-to-liquids, and coal-to-liquids technologies. While these technologies will contribute significantly to liquid fuels supply at some point, they are economical only when competing with high oil prices, with most technologies requiring oil to be in the $50-plus/barrel range. Consequently, these technologies cannot be expected to reduce oil prices below that breakeven point—a far cry from $20/barrel in 1999 (inflation-adjusted to 2005 dollars, referred to in following text as 2005$).

## Renewable Technologies

With the exception of biomass, wind, and passive solar technologies, renewable energy is still an expensive proposition. Although ethanol is expected to contribute increasingly to liquid fuels with the help of government subsidies, renewable sources of electric generation in the baseline or reference

EIA forecast accounts for no more than about 6 percent of new electric generation energy sources from 2006 to 2030. Coal is forecast to provide 54 percent, natural gas 36 percent, and nuclear 4 percent of new generation fuel sources. Cost-effective fuel cells, photovoltaic, and other renewable technologies are still too far in the horizon to influence energy prices in the foreseeable future.

The ability to buy green electricity from most utilities and power providers and publicity over renewable energy portfolio standards, suggest that renewables are making great headway in replacing conventional energy sources. For instance, there is substantial news coverage of state-mandated renewable portfolio standards requiring power producers to include certain percentages of renewable energy sources in their portfolio of electric production technologies. The reality is that relatively little generation capacity is provided with sources other than existing hydro and biomass. New renewable energy sources consist mostly of wind generation (Table 1.1). Biomass includes generators that use methane from organic waste sites to fuel electric generation turbines; however, the number of waste sites limits new biomass contributions. The number of new hydro sites is also limited. Wind generation is economically competitive in many areas; however, electricity is intermittently available, especially on the hottest summer days when it is

**TABLE 1.1**   U.S. Energy Consumption by Energy Source, 2001–2004 (Quadrillion Btu)

| Energy Source | 2001 | 2002 | 2003 | 2004 | 2005 |
|---|---|---|---|---|---|
| Total | 96.563 | 98.101 | 98.450 | 100.586 | 100.942 |
| Fossil Fuels | 83.138 | 83.994 | 84.386 | 86.191 | 86.451 |
|    Coal | 21.914 | 21.904 | 22.321 | 22.466 | 22.785 |
|    Coal Coke Net Imports | 0.029 | 0.061 | 0.051 | 0.138 | 0.044 |
|    Natural Gas | 22.861 | 23.628 | 22.967 | 22.993 | 22.886 |
|    Petroleum | 38.333 | 38.401 | 39.047 | 40.594 | 40.735 |
| Electricity Net Imports | 0.075 | 0.072 | 0.022 | 0.039 | 0.084 |
| Nuclear Electric Power | 8.033 | 8.143 | 7.959 | 8.222 | 8.160 |
| Renewable Energy | 5.465 | 6.067 | 6.321 | 6.433 | 6.588 |
|    Conventional Hydroelectric | 2.242 | 2.689 | 2.825 | 2.690 | 2.703 |
|    Geothermal Energy | 0.311 | 0.328 | 0.331 | 0.341 | 0.343 |
|    Biomass | 2.777 | 2.880 | 2.988 | 3.196 | 3.298 |
|    Solar Energy | 0.065 | 0.064 | 0.064 | 0.064 | 0.066 |
|    Wind Energy | 0.070 | 0.105 | 0.115 | 0.142 | 0.178 |

*Source:* Energy Information Administration, August 2005, http://www.eia.doe.gov/ cneaf/solar.renewables/page/trends/table1.html.

most needed. For instance, the Electric Reliability Council of Texas counts only 2.6 percent of rated generation towards meeting capacity requirements. While wind is an important resource in reducing emissions by replacing coal and natural gas driven power plants, increased wind-generated electricity will have little impact on electricity prices.

Research and development of renewable technologies is intense and can be expected to provide promising results in the future; however, renewable energy supply contributions are unlikely to be great enough to reduce energy prices in the current planning horizon.

## Other Factors

Many other demand and supply factors enter into the market determination of energy prices, including consumer price response, building and appliance efficiency standards, automobile efficiency standards, and so on. The most comprehensive and accessible description of these factors is provided in the Energy Information Administration's Monthly and Annual Energy Outlooks (http://www.eia.doe.gov/oiaf/forecasting.html).

## Interpreting $100/Barrel Oil

As of November 2007, oil prices are approaching $100/barrel, nearly equal to the $101.70 (in today's dollars) reached in 1980. The current price reflects a near doubling of the lowest oil price in 2007. How does one interpret this latest spike in oil prices and what does it mean for the longer-term energy price outlook?

Slower than expected production responses to higher oil prices, increasing restrictions placed on foreign participation in oil production by some oil-producing nations, smaller than expected impacts of higher oil prices on world economies, and continuing global economic growth are frequently mentioned as factors suggesting that growing world oil demand will continue to apply pressure on supply. Oil prices also reflect a decline in the dollar and a risk premium associated with current geopolitical uncertainties. It is generally believed that the risk premium reflected in the current price is approximately $25/barrel.

It is important to remember that NYMEX (New York Mercantile Exchange) oil prices quoted in the news are based on commodity futures contracts for the coming month. Commodity prices are volatile and can include, as the current situation demonstrates, a substantial risk and speculative component. Dissecting current futures market prices to determine how much of the $100/barrel price is likely to remain as markets gain additional supply and demand information over time and how much reflects unfounded speculation is difficult. Continued uncertainty concerning supply and demand balances along with geopolitical risks could keep oil prices in the $90–$100/barrel or higher for some time. On the other hand, early signs that the market is not as tight as anticipated and that higher oil prices are significantly reducing world economic growth could quickly deflate oil prices.

A consensus view at this time is that oil prices may go higher but will fall back to the $70 to $75 per barrel range in the reasonably near future with continuing modest declines over time as oil production increases. This consensus forecast is presented in the next section.

## ENERGY PRICE FORECASTS

Viewing historical price series and considering important demand and supply factors provide an interesting context for evaluating whether future price forecasts seem reasonable. However it is difficult to determine whether prices are likely to:

- Decline as they did following the price spike in the early 1980s.
- Continue increasing because of continuing shifts in demand and supply balances associated with new factors such as economic growth in less developed countries.
- Follow some other path.

A modeling process is required to identify the most likely path for future energy prices. The following sections describe a comprehensive modeling approach developed and applied by the U.S. Department of Energy.

### Putting Demand and Supply Together

Determining how the interplay of demand and supply factors will impact energy prices beyond the near future requires the use of forecasting models. The most widely referenced energy forecasting model is the Energy Information Administration's (EIA) National Energy Modeling System (NEMS).[10] NEMS is used to develop projections for EIA forecasts. In addition to providing energy demand, supply, and price forecasts, NEMS is used to evaluate policy issues requested by Congress and executive branch agencies.

Other organizations, including economic and energy consulting firms, and other government bodies have also developed and used forecasting models to estimate future energy demand, supply, and prices. Modeling methodologies differ among these organizations, which reflect their focus and resources. A consensus forecast based on EIA and published information from other forecast sources in mid-2007 reflects a scenario with a moderation of current high prices. However, demand is expected to grow at a rate that will continue to apply pressure on fossil fuel supply, keeping prices significantly higher than the 1990s.

Since the NEMS model forecast is consistent with the consensus forecast, its results are presented in Figure 1.12. A comparison with other forecast results is also included in Table 1.2 on page 30. Before presenting the EIA NEMS forecast, it is useful to consider the modeling process to develop an appreciation for the way in which forecasting models can reflect detailed demand and supply factors.

## The Modeling Process

NEMS uses a market-based approach that forecasts energy demand for individual sectors for each of the nine U.S. census divisions. NEMS forecasts

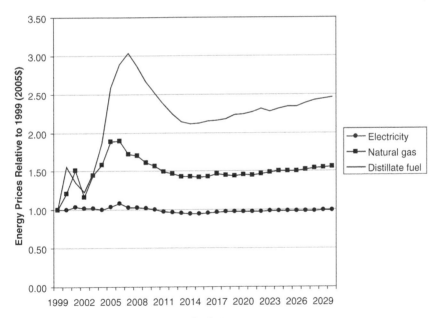

**FIGURE 1.12**   Annual Energy Outlook 2007
*Source:* Annual Energy Outlook 2007, with Projections to 2030, February 2007, Energy Information Administration, U.S. Department of Energy, Washington, DC 20585, www.eia.doe.gov/oiaf/aeo/ Historical prices are from Energy Information Administration, June 2007.

energy demand, supply, and prices through 2030. Energy supply modules represent regional markets including the North American Electric Reliability Council regions and subregions for electricity; and the Petroleum Administration for Defense Districts (PADDs) for refineries. NEMS includes macroeconomic and international modules to reflect economic growth and impacts of world energy markets. NEMS balances energy supply and demand for each energy source and energy demand sector. The simulation system determines prices paid by energy consumers and received by suppliers with feedbacks to economic activity and fuel supply modules. NEMS also reflects the impacts and costs of legislation and environmental regulations.

A detailed description of NEMS is beyond the scope of this discussion; however, a summary of one of the demand elements will provide readers with a better understanding of the modeling process. The NEMS residential and commercial demand modules apply a modeling technique called end-use modeling to forecasting energy use. This modeling approach was developed, in part by the author, at Oak Ridge National Laboratory in 1976 and forms the basis for nearly all energy policy models in use today including models used by state agencies in California and Indiana.[11]

End-use models explicitly represent energy use consumed by individual energy-using equipment, sum the energy use to the building type level and then to the sector (residential, commercial). This approach is sometimes called a bottom-up approach for obvious reasons. The modeling approach is intuitive; for instance, in the residential sector, each household occupies a dwelling unit, requiring space heating, air conditioning and equipment including water heaters, refrigerators, dish and clothes washers, and so on. Energy use of each end-use equipment is determined from engineering and/or statistical analysis. From one year to the next, the number of households increases, new dwelling unit construction takes place, and some dwelling units are demolished. New dwelling units require new end-use equipment. End-use equipment that wears out is replaced with new equipment. Some households purchase new end-use equipment. Households make equipment efficiency choices based on energy prices and the cost of equipment. Appliance and building efficiency standards restrict the efficiency choices that households can make. Household behavioral responses to energy price increases, like turning thermostats down, are represented as well as fuel switching in response to changes in relative fuel prices.

Industrial and transportation demand modules reflect somewhat different methodologies; however, each module reflects, to the extent possible, specific energy technology classes, fuel choices, energy price responses, economic, technology, and other factors. Additional modules include macroeconomic, international, electricity market, renewable fuels, oil and gas supply, natural gas transmission and distribution, petroleum market, and coal market.

Relationships in each of the modules are represented with mathematical equations whose parameters are typically estimated econometrically or represent engineering-based analysis. These relationships and parameter estimation are described in more detail in the previously referenced NEMS documentation.

Models applied by other organizations are less detailed than the NEMS model because they are not used to evaluate costs and benefits of alternative federal and state policy prescriptions. However, all models represent the same basic supply and demand relationships. Results from NEMS and several alternative models are presented in the next section.

## The Consensus: High Prices for the Foreseeable Future

The baseline or reference EIA NEMS energy price forecasts are shown in Figure 1.12 for commercial sector distillate oil, natural gas, and electricity, measured as a ratio of 1999 prices in 2005 dollars.[12] The commercial sector excludes industrial (manufacturing), residential, transportation, and utility activities. Industrial sector prices are typically less than commercial for the largest industrial customers; however, most industrial customers face energy prices close to those represented by the commercial prices presented in this chapter. Inflation effects have been removed from historical and future prices. For reference, 2015 prices are $49.87 per barrel for oil, $8.73 per thousand cubic feet for natural gas and 8.0 cents per kWh for electricity (all in 2005 dollars).

As indicated in Figure 1.12, future commercial sector fuel oil prices are expected to moderate by about 2015 and remain two to two-and-a-half times their 1999 value through the forecast period. Natural gas is expected to moderate to about one-and-one half times its 1999 value. While the U.S. average commercial sector electricity price more or less maintains its 1999 value, regional variations reflected in Figure 1.1 shown at the beginning of this chapter will continue as a result of elevated natural gas prices.

The baseline forecast shown in Figure 1.12 represents a significant departure from history with the prediction that fossil fuel energy prices will maintain a higher price plateau than experienced in the past. Though many factors are involved, one can summarize this outcome as reflecting a demand/supply relationship that requires the continued use of higher-cost supply options to meet demands of a growing world economy.

## Comparison Forecasts

The Energy Information Administration provides a comparison of its forecasts with those of other organizations in its 2007 Annual Energy Outlook documentation (AEO2007). Table 1.2 summarizes this comparison with forecast information for 2015.

While AEO2007 forecasts of world oil prices are on the high side by an average of 9 percent of alternative forecasts, commercial natural gas and electricity prices are on the low side by an average of 12 percent for each. EIA provides a variety of easily accessible data and analyses on its forecast Web page at http://www.eia.doe.gov/oiaf/forecasting.html, where interested readers can learn more on a variety of topics related to energy demand, supply, and price forecasting.

It is important to remember that these price forecasts do not attempt to account for unexpected events such as hurricane damage to offshore wells, wars, or unforeseen economic downturns. Any of these or similar factors could cause prices to spike or to drop; however, the resulting excess demand or excess supply would likely be worked off within a relatively short time period.

In summary, all publicly available forecasts indicate that increases in supply can be expected to reduce current high energy prices through the middle of the next decade; however, demand pressures and higher fossil fuel

**TABLE 1.2** Comparison of 2007 Annual Energy Outlook and Alternative Forecasts, 2015 Prices (2005$)

| | AEO2007 | GII | IEA | EVA | EEA | DB | SEER |
|---|---|---|---|---|---|---|---|
| World oil prices | 49.87 | 46.54 | 47.8 | 42.35 | 49.8 | 40.11 | 45.27 |
| Commercial customer natural gas prices | 8.73 | 10.5 | n/a | n/a | 9.98 | n/a | 8.83 |
| Commercial customer electric prices | 8.0 | 9.2 | n/a | 8.7 | n/a | n/a | n/a |

*Source:* Annual Energy Outlook 2007, with Projections to 2030, February 2007, Energy Information Administration, U.S. Department of Energy, Washington, DC 20585.

Table abbreviations:
GII    Global Insights, Inc.
EVA    Energy Ventures Analysis, Inc.
IEA    International Energy Agency
DB    Deutsche Bank, AG
EEA    Energy and Environmental Analysis, Inc.
SEER    Strategic Energy and Economic Research, Inc.

production costs will usher in a new era of higher natural gas and oil prices. U.S. electricity prices are not expected to increase on average; however, areas that rely heavily on natural gas generation will experience price increases as new gas-fired capacity additions are added to the generating mix.

## An Increasingly Likely Contrary Forecast

Forecasters tend to follow the pack, thereby avoiding being singled out if future events do not confirm the forecaster's predictions. Increased cost of oil production will almost certainly provide a new higher floor to oil prices compared to the past. While an economic slowdown or some other event may temporarily create an excess supply of oil with falling oil prices, forecasting a higher oil price plateau is a safe bet.

However, the prospects of healthy world economic growth, declines in existing production, and increasing difficulty associated with new production could conceivably lead to even tighter oil markets in the future. This outcome is predicted by the July 2007 International Energy Agency—Medium-Term Oil Market Report. Supply difficulties are forecasted to begin in 2009 with a "crunch" by 2012.[13]

Those who share the IEA's more pessimistic view of world oil markets see the current $100/barrel oil prices as further proof that supply and demand conditions are tighter than generally recognized and that the impacts of greater non-OECD country growth have been underestimated while the ability of oil producers to respond to increased oil prices has been overestimated.

Prices much lower than those predicted in the consensus forecast described in the previous section seem unlikely; however, the IAE's analysis suggests a reasonable likelihood that energy prices will be greater than those represented by the consensus forecast. While $100/barrel oil prices initially appear to be unsustainable because of their expected drag on economic growth, a more limited impact on global economic growth than expected could keep oil prices considerably higher than the consensus forecast.

The important information in the contrary forecast is not the $/barrel estimate; rather it is that there is a reasonable probability that oil prices, and by extension other energy prices, will be higher than presented in the consensus forecast.

## Recession Impacts

Economic recessions reduce demand pressure and can create significant declines in energy commodity prices (natural gas, oil, and other fossil fuels). Consequently, an unexpected decline in economic activity will most likely create a temporary deviation from predicted energy price paths. However, on recovery, the same factors will come back into play, and energy prices can be expected to return to their forecast values.

While a temporary recession-caused reduction in energy prices may reduce facility energy costs, economic factors increase the importance of cash flow advantages of efficiency investments identified through EBaR analysis. Efficiency investments that qualify in recessionary periods will provide greater returns when energy prices recover, providing an effective hedge against the coming price increase.

## GOING GREEN—THE CRITICAL ROLE OF EFFICIENCY INVESTMENTS

An increasing number of corporations and government organizations are undertaking sustainability initiatives including green building design and operations intended to reduce greenhouse gas emissions. Virtually all of these initiatives involve reductions in energy use. For instance, reduced building energy use is a major component in achieving the U.S. Green Building Councils LEED (Leadership in Energy and Environment Design, http://www.usgbc.org/) certification. Organizations are also investing in energy efficiency to qualify their buildings with an Energy Star rating from the U.S. Environmental Protection Agency (http://energystar.gov/).

An interesting innovation that facilitates this desire to achieve green goals is the Chicago Climate Exchange (CCX, http://www.chicagoclimatex.com). CCX is the first legally binding greenhouse gas emissions allowance trading system. CCX members make a commitment to meet reductions in annual greenhouse gas emissions with reductions beyond the target level claimed as surplus allowances that can be sold or saved for future use. Members whose emissions exceed their targets must purchase contracts to offset excess emissions. Indirectly generated greenhouse gas emissions from purchased energy are also included in the greenhouse gas emissions accounting.

Current CCX members read like a sample of who's who in business, education, and government, including Rolls-Royce, Ford Motor Company, Dow Corning, DuPont, Steelcase Inc., Eastman Kodak Company, American Electric Power, DTE Energy, Motorola, Sony Electronics, the cities of Chicago, Oakland, Melbourne, Australia and Portland, the State of New Mexico, IBM, Intel Corporation, Michigan State University, and many more.

The CCX framework is important because it offers a market-based system in which organizations that can most efficiently reduce energy use are encouraged to achieve energy reductions. On the other hand, those who are less able to contribute physical reductions in emissions pay others to achieve their reduction goals.

Other new carbon-trading mechanisms are being established both by government and private interests and the growing use of "efficiency certificates" in individual states pass incentives to reduce energy use through to individual facility owners. For instance, efficiency certificates permit individual facility owners to sell efficiency improvement credits to utilities who are required to meet requirements of "efficiency portfolio standards." These market mechanisms provide a prominent role for efficiency investments in meeting organization and social goals to reduce carbon and other greenhouse gas emissions.

Carbon taxes are increasingly discussed as a policy tool to encourage emissions reductions. Tax impacts are likely to affect individual commercial, institutional, and manufacturing facilities based on their energy use, providing additional incentives to invest in energy-efficient equipment.

Energy efficiency is sure to be at the center of future green initiatives. Organizations who develop the EBaR framework now to address efficiency investments will be well positioned to mitigate cost impacts that develop in the future.

## EBaR AS A POLICY OPTION

It became apparent in the late 1970s that building owners and managers were not responding to higher energy prices and energy saving investments as policy makers expected. Returns on efficiency investments were five or six times the cost of borrowing. Why wouldn't rational business investors take advantage of that gap and make money on those investments? The so-called energy paradox or efficiency gap has been studied extensively, and many incentive and information programs have been advocated and initiated by federal and state governments specifically to address this problem with little verification that these programs have the desired impact. In fact, a recent study by Resources for The Future, concluded that one of these programs, a university-managed free energy audit program targeted to small and medium-sized manufacturers, appeared to have little or no impact on energy efficiency investments.[14]

The evidence is overwhelming that individual organizations continue to make energy efficiency investments that reflect paybacks of, on average, about one-and-one-half years with comparable internal rates of return of about 50 percent. The Department of Energy and other organizations have evaluated equipment technologies currently in use and, compared to technologies considered cost effective, have identified unachieved potential efficiency savings of 20 to 50 percent. An International Energy Agency study estimates a comparable efficiency gap of 30 percent in OECD (developed) countries.

The many recent strategies promoted by municipal, state, and federal agencies, advocacy groups, and private organizations to address environmental and energy problems include efficiency improvements high on the list, but these strategies are short on details as to how such efficiency improvements are to be achieved. Most plans recommend expansion of utility efficiency incentive programs; however, current utility and other incentive programs are relatively inefficient because they do not address the crux of the efficiency gap—that is, the use of short paybacks and high internal rate of return traditionally used to limit risk.

Providing EBaR educational programs to help decision makers better understand and address energy price risk can significantly extend the impact of efficiency incentives and other efficiency-oriented programs.

## SUMMARY

Current high and erratic energy prices have created financial difficulties for many businesses, institutions, and government agencies. In the best-forecast scenario, natural gas and oil prices are likely to be 50 to 100 percent higher than their 1999 levels, after adjusting for inflation. Electricity prices vary significantly by utility; however, high natural gas prices are likely to keep electric prices 20 percent or more above their 1999 levels in many areas.

In spite of these challenges organizations do not yet consider energy efficiency investments with financial risk management tools. Most organizations apply payback or internal rate of return (IRR) analysis using conservative thresholds to qualify efficiency investments for further evaluation. These rules of thumb are designed to limit risk associated with efficiency investments; however, like all rules of thumb, they are designed to prevent worst-case scenarios. Consequently, many profitable efficiency investments are excluded from consideration.

By applying financial risk management analysis to the energy efficiency investment decisions in a process called Energy Budgets at Risk (EBaR), payback and IRR rules are replaced by decision variables that reflect both the return on the efficiency investment and its risk. For instance, an $EBaR_{irr,mean}$ of 65 percent and an $EBaR_{irr,95}$, of 45 percent means that the expected internal rate of return on the investment is 65 percent and there is no more than a 5 percent probability that the internal rate of return will be less than 45 percent.

From a management perspective, knowing the expected return and probabilities associated with other outcomes provides much more information than traditional payback and IRR hurdle rate because it permits investment decisions conditioned on an organization's risk tolerance.

Organizations in competitive electricity and natural gas markets can include energy purchase decisions as part of the EBaR process to simultaneously consider the feedback between efficiency and purchase decisions, reducing both energy costs and the price paid for energy.

EBaR allows organizations to manage energy cost risks rather than attempting to avoid risks. Most organizations can reduce annual energy costs from 20 to 30 percent even after paying the annual amortized cost of the investment. That is, organizations who implement EBaR practices can increase cash flows by an amount equal to 20 to 30 percent of their current energy costs.

## CHAPTER 2

# Facility Efficiency Options

This chapter begins with a brief review of facility energy management options. The second section describes basic energy efficiency opportunities that are available to reduce buildings energy use. The chapter closes with a brief discussion on calculating efficiency investment costs and savings and a note to nonenergy engineers.

## FACILITY ENERGY MANAGEMENT

Prior to the tumultuous 1970s, responsibility for energy management along with many other duties typically rested with the building engineer, facility manager, or, in the case of smaller buildings, the building owner. Among the various tasks—including space management, waste management, security, maintenance and so on—energy management was a small role. The unprecedented increases in energy prices after 1972 propelled energy management to the forefront of facility management concerns. On closer inspection, building and energy systems designs in nearly all facilities used much more energy than required to provide energy-related services.

For example, one popular heating, ventilation, and air conditioning (HVAC) system design used a dual-duct distribution system that distributed hot and cold air in side-by-side ducts and mixed the hot and cold air to achieve the desired temperature in each space. In addition, lighting intensity was several times more than what was required in most spaces. Early remedies to reduce energy use included resetting thermostats and delamping—that is, disconnecting one out of every three or four fluorescent fixtures. Most of these early measures were stopgaps, designed to reduce the impact of increased energy bills.

In the late 1970s, the science of facility energy management began developing with a more narrow facility manager focus on energy issues. The energy services industry began developing at about the same time to provide services required to respond more appropriately to increased energy prices.

Energy use reductions achieved by energy managers depend in large part on the characteristics of energy-efficient technologies. Approaches to facility energy management and a description of energy efficiency technologies are included in the remainder of this chapter.

## The Energy Manager and the Energy Services Industry

Facility energy management came into its own as a recognized specialty in the late 1970s and early 1980s. The Association of Energy Engineers (AEE, http://www.aeecenter.com) was formed in 1977 to support facility energy management, and it continues to provide publications, training, and certification in facility energy management. According to the 2007 AEE survey of its more than 9,000 members, 86 percent of its energy managers hold college degrees, and 77 percent hold at least one certification offered by the AEE.[1] The role of energy manager has become much more challenging over time as dozens of new technologies have been introduced. Knowledge of HVAC, lighting, motors, refrigeration, and other energy technologies as well as an ability to analyze facility energy use data are required to manage facility energy use in today's energy markets.

An independent energy service industry also took shape at the same time that energy management was developing as a specialty. Energy service companies, or ESCOs, specialize in assessment, design, and installation of energy efficiency projects as well as maintenance and tune-ups of existing energy systems. A 2007 report from Lawrence Berkeley National Laboratory (LBNL) estimated ESCO revenues at about $3.6 billion in 2006.[2] Except for the period between 2000 and 2004, when the looming expectation of retail competition slowed growth, the ESCO industry has grown at about 20 percent per year since 1990. In 2006, LBNL estimated more than 80 percent of ESCO revenue was derived from institutional customer facilities, including federal, state, and local, government and education; with about 9 percent from commercial sector applications and 6 percent from industrial facilities.

In addition to traditional ESCO companies, many equipment manufacturers, mechanical and electrical firms, and engineering and consulting firms provide energy services included under the ESCO services umbrella.

The development of energy management as a professional specialty and the emergence of an energy service industry mean that today's building owners and managers have a variety of options for managing facility energy use. These options include maintaining an in-house staff to continuously evaluate energy performance, maintain systems, develop capital budgeting proposals (that is, proposals for investment in energy efficiency) and oversee projects completed by in-house staff and/or contractors. At the other end of the spectrum, energy management functions can be completely outsourced to a single ESCO company or managed by a consulting engineer.

## Energy Manager as Investment Advisor

Regardless of how facility energy management is accomplished, today's energy market challenges can better be met if facility energy manager authority and responsibility is extended beyond the traditional role of monitoring energy use and maintaining energy systems with sporadic submittals of energy efficiency investment projects for approval. Traditionally, requests for energy efficiency investments move up the chain of approval only if they meet conservative payback or internal rate of return thresholds. Proposals are typically considered with a single estimated energy budget savings or a high and a low savings estimate.

Most energy managers possess valuable information on facility energy use characteristics, energy-using equipment in the facility, and information on energy efficiency options. These resources can be used more effectively if facility energy managers are also viewed as investment advisors who identify and analyze returns that are available with energy efficiency investments. Knowledge of facilities and energy systems makes energy managers and their staff important participants in assessing uncertainty surrounding efficiency investments. This assessment is required in any risk management approach to energy budgeting.

Along with increased authority for the energy manager comes increased responsibility and accountability so energy managers must also be provided a framework to evaluate and communicate opportunities for efficiency investment and analysis to management.

A review of the significant energy efficiency investment opportunities that exist in most facilities provides an appreciation for the value that can be provided by energy managers acting as efficiency investment advisors.

## EFFICIENCY OPTIONS

A variety of sources provide comprehensive descriptions of energy-efficient technologies. Since the objective of this section is to provide a sense of available efficiency options and their potential returns, a brief summary of some of the most important technologies and technology classes is provided. The Energy Star Building Manual (http://www.energystar.gov/ia/business/BUM.pdf) provides an excellent and generally, nontechnical description of efficiency options and is recommended as a general reference for those who are unfamiliar with current energy system efficiency options.

Energy efficiency technologies are described approximately in order of importance and priority for the typical commercial, institutional, and government building. These technologies also apply to the building-related energy use in industrial facilities. Evaluation and installation priority recognize the importance of considering and implementing some efficiency options before others. For instance, interior lighting changes will reduce waste heat loads on air conditioning. As such, heating, ventilation, and air conditioning tune-ups should ideally be implemented after lighting changes have been completed.

In an effort to establish the approximate order of importance of energy-efficient technologies it is useful to consider how energy is used in facilities. The combination of the amount of energy used and efficiency improvement options for each end use determines total potential energy savings. Figure 2.1 shows the average end-use electricity use for all U.S. commercial, institutional. and government buildings in 2007. Space heating, which is not included in the figure, varies widely by geographic location and can range from about 5 to 25 percent of total building energy use.

As the Figure 2.1 shows, lighting is the predominant end use followed by air conditioning, miscellaneous uses, and ventilation (the distribution of heat and air conditioning). Refrigeration is next in importance, but is

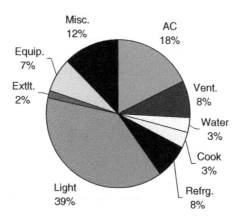

**FIGURE 2.1** Average 2007 Commercial, Institutional and Government End-Use Percentages
*Source:* Market Analysis and Information System (MAISY®) data.
http://www.maisy.com.

primarily found in food stores, restaurants, and refrigerated warehouses. Electric equipment and appliances are followed in importance by water heating, cooking, and exterior lighting. These end-use percentages vary by business type and by individual facilities within business types; however, the end-use distribution provides a reasonably good picture of end-use targets for efficiency investments.

A discussion of the following efficiency applications is provided in following sections:

- Lighting.
- Other internal and external loads.
- Commissioning and recommissioning.
- Heating, ventilation and air conditioning.
- Combined heat and power.
- Cool storage and other demand response technologies.

## Lighting

Lighting is the all-star of energy efficiency options and technologies. Figure 2.2 shows what has happened to energy use requirements of the

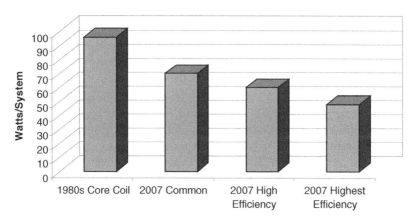

**FIGURE 2.2** Comparison of Common Fluorescent Lighting System Electricity Use
*Source:* H. Sach, S. Nadel, J. Thorne Amann, M. Tuazon, E. Mendelshon, L. Rainer, G. Todesco, D. Shipley, and M. Adelaar, "Emerging Energy-Saving Technologies and Practices for the Buildings Sector as of 2004," Report Number A042, October 2004, American Council for an Energy-Efficient Economy, http://acee.org.

## ELECTRICITY AND LIGHTING TERMINOLOGY

Several definitions are important in understanding the way electricity use is measured and discussed.

A **watt** is a unit of power—that is, a measure of energy conversion per unit of time. In the case of a light bulb, electric energy is converted to light (electromagnetic radiation) and heat (thermal energy). A 100 watt light bulb converts twice as much energy per second as a 50 watt light bulb. More specifically, a 100 watt light bulb converts 100 Joules—a measure of energy—every second into heat and light.

A **watt hour** is the amount of energy used in one hour by an appliance that requires one watt of power to operate.

A **kilowatt (KW)** is 1,000 watts and **kilowatt hour (kWh)** is 1,000 watthours. A kWh is the energy used by an appliance that requires one watt of power operating for 1000 hours, the energy used by an appliance that requires 1000 watts of power for one hour or any multiple of watts and hours that equals 1,000.

Electric bills for commercial, institutional, government, and manufacturing establishments are typically computed using the maximum KW in the month (referred to by utilities as the **KW demand**) and the **monthly energy** or kWh used in a month (often referred to by utilities as the energy use).

The 12 part in the **T12** and the 8 part of the **T8 fluorescent lamps** refer to the diameter of the lamp but are commonly used to differentiate higher efficiencies of T8 lamps compared to T12 lamps.

A **ballast** regulates power flow through fluorescent and high intensity discharge lamps (*HID*). Lamp system energy use is comprised of energy requirements for the ballast and all of the lamps controlled by the ballast.

**Btu** is also a measure of energy. 3,412 Btus are equivalent to 1 kilowatt hour (kWh). In one hour a 1,000 watt (1 KW) resistance space heater converts 1 kW of electric energy into 3,412 Btu's of thermal energy or heat.

most common fluorescent lighting system—that is, the four-foot two-lamp fluorescent lighting system. Throughout the 1980s, the standard lighting system was a core-coil ballast, which used about 16 watts of electricity, and two lamps, which each used 40 watts for a total connected load of 96 watts. Based on these figures, a facility that operated for 4000 hours per year would use 384 kWh (96 watts × 4000 hours = 384 kilowatt-hours (kWh) of energy use) for each system. At the current average commercial price of 9.6 cents per kWh, the cost of operating a single four-foot lamp system would be $36.86 per year with the 1980s technology.

A common two-lamp system in use today is a high-efficiency magnetic ballast and high-efficiency T12 lamp set that uses a total of about 70 watts (depending on lamp and ballast specifics) for a total of 280 kWh per year with a savings of $9.98 per system. DOE ballast standards effectively prohibit the use of magnetic ballasts with most T12 lamps beginning in 2005 for new and renovation applications and 2010 for replacement systems. Ballasts last ten years or more, however, so many of these systems will be in place for some time.

A typical high-efficiency system in use today uses high-efficiency T8 lamps and electronic ballast for a total of approximately 60 watts per system.

The highest efficiency fluorescent system, introduced in 2002, is the so-called super T8 system costing about $5 more than the typical system with energy use of 48 watts, which is exactly one-half of the 1980s 4-foot 2-lamp fluorescent lighting system. In addition, the super T8 systems provide 15 to 20 percent greater light (lumen) output than regular T8 systems and have lifetimes of 30,000 hours compared to the standard 20,000 hours.

While the history of fluorescent lamp systems reflects improvements in technology associated with ballasts and lamps, several other lighting applications provide significant increases in efficiency by substituting a new technology in an existing use. Compact fluorescent lamps provide about 3 to 4 times the light output per watt input and last 10 times (10,000 hours) as long as incandescent lamps. Light emitting diode (LED) exit signs are a perfect replacement for incandescent or compact fluorescent signs. LED exit signs use about 5 watts compared to about 40 watts for an incandescent lamp and 10 watts for a compact fluorescent lamp. LED signs also have lifetimes of 10 or more years; whereas incandescent lamps have lifetimes of three months and compact fluorescent lamps have lifetimes of several years.

High intensity discharge (HID) lamps (halogen parabolic aluminized reflector, or PAR, metal halide and high pressure sodium lamps) can replace less efficient incandescent and mercury vapor lamps with savings as much as 75 percent, depending on the lamp and the application.

In addition to efficiency increases illustrated with the examples above, the following options exist to reduce lighting energy use:

- Reduced lighting levels: Buildings have been and continue to be overlit. A design of 2.5 watts per square foot was not uncommon for an office building in the 1970s; however, today's lighting systems are often designed to less than 1.0 watt per square foot. Delamping, or removing/ disconnecting lamps in older buildings, can be an effective approach to reducing overhead lighting, especially when combined with task lighting.
- Reflectors, which are mirrored surfaces inside the fixture that reflect light to work surfaces, and high lumen output lamps also reduce the number of light fixtures required to provide an appropriate illumination level.
- Occupancy sensors automatically turn off lights when spaces are unoccupied.
- Continuous dimming electronic ballasts use photocells in areas that receive natural daylight to reduce light output and power consumption depending on the amount of natural lighting received.
- Energy management systems (EMS) and or timers provide control over operating hours and can significantly impact lighting electricity use.
- Day lighting that employs optimized design for new buildings can significantly reduce lighting energy use.

Reduced lighting electricity use also reduces air conditioning and ventilation uses by reducing heat generated by lighting systems. While heating season energy use increases somewhat without this waste heat, the offsetting impact is small.

Taken together, lighting system changes including new high-efficiency systems and operational changes can reduce electricity use in most buildings by 20 to 30 percent and pay for itself in two to three years. No other end use provides such large potential savings to such a wide segment of the building sector.

## Other Internal and External Loads

*Loads* are a generic term used to describe electric power requirements. Internal loads reflect power requirements generated inside a building whereas external loads reflect those generated from outside sources. Lighting is an internal load while a hot day (with the transfer of heat from outside to inside) provides external loads for an air conditioning system.

Lighting is by far the greatest single internal load in most facilities (refrigeration in food sales facilities and manufacturing processes being obvious exceptions). Reductions in other loads can also be significant. For instance, switching to an Energy Star PC and monitor can save 100 watts. Savings in an area with 30 computers would reduce annual electricity bills by $1,152 if the computers are active for 4,000 hours per year at the national average commercial electricity price of 9.6 cents per kWh. In addition, 10,236 fewer Btus per hour are put into the air to be removed by the air conditioning system. If the space is in an interior area that requires air conditioning year round, an additional annual savings of approximately $500 is realized. The savings would actually be even greater than the total of $1,652 for the space since this internal load contributes directly to the peak electricity use that, because of electric billing practices, carries an electricity cost that is more than the cost of electricity use for other hours (electric billing practices are covered in Chapter 3).

Properly sized, high-efficiency, and variable-speed motors represent an attractive energy saving option. A variety of other equipment contributes to internal loads. Kitchen uses, refrigerated vending machines, domestic hot water, and virtually any appliance or equipment that uses energy within a facility create waste heat. A variety of new control technologies exists to reduce energy use in plug loads and other uses (plug loads refer to electricity use associated with equipment that is plugged into wall outlets).

Changes in the building shell can significantly reduce external loads. While adding insulation to exterior walls in an office building would generally not be cost effective, adding window film to reduce solar heat gain, window shading, roof insulation, and installation of light-colored roofing are viable options with attractive economics in many geographic areas.

## Commissioning and Recommissioning

Commissioning occurs in a new building when the capabilities of building HVAC, controls and electrical systems are verified to be consistent with system design. Recommissioning or a building tune-up is the reevaluation of building systems and the modification required to meet both initial design specifications and current operational needs. This inclusion of current operational needs in recommissioning is important since initial system designs that do not match internal building requirements can significantly affect HVAC performance. For instance, many building HVAC systems are designed and installed to serve the greatest likely loads prior to building occupancy with the result that many systems are poorly tuned for current uses.

The Texas A&M University Energy Systems Laboratory reports average energy cost savings of about 20 percent in their application of recommissioning over 300 buildings. Simple paybacks averaged less than two years.[3] Recommissioning projects typically include a site visit, data collection and analysis to identify potential measures and associated costs. More detailed analysis is applied to each source of system inefficiency and system changes are completed. Energy use and environment improvements are evaluated and compared to initial estimates. Facility staff training is typically provided to help maintain systems in their recommissioned state.

## Heating, Ventilation, and Air Conditioning

Changes in the efficiency of heating, ventilation, and air conditioning systems are nearly as dramatic as those achieved in lighting over the last thirty years. Chiller systems efficiency has doubled; dual-duct, terminal reheat, and multizone ventilation systems that provide a constant air volume are being replaced with variable air volume systems that can respond to the varying needs of individual spaces. Building energy management and control systems significantly reduce energy use and improve comfort levels.

Economizers can be an effective approach to reduce air conditioning loads in certain geographic areas. Economizers use outside air to cool interior spaces when the outside temperature or the temperature and relative humidity conditions are appropriate.

Ventilation systems move hot and cold air through a building to deliver heating and air conditioning. When used in combination with variable-speed drives (motors), variable air volume retrofits can cut ventilation requirements by as much as half.

Appropriately sized, variable-speed drives can also reduce costs of transporting hot and chilled water through building spaces.

Boiler retrofitting with new efficient burners, reset controls that reduce steam pressure, and heat exchangers that capture waste heat in flue gas economizers for use in preheating boiler water are effective efficiency options. Boiler replacement with a more appropriately sized higher-efficiency boiler can also provide large efficiency gains. Advanced controls, which include energy management and control systems (EMCS) and direct digital controls (DDC), can optimize operation of HVAC and lighting systems in a sophisticated process that continuously monitors and adjusts delivery of services in both occupied and unoccupied hours.

## Combined Heat and Power

Combined heat and power technologies are used to generate electricity at a facility and to apply the waste heat, which is provided as a by-product of generation, to space heating, domestic water heating, air conditioning, process, and other uses. Central fossil-fuel fired utility power generating plants reflect, on average, an efficiency of about 32 percent. That is, 32 percent of energy content in the fossil fuel is converted to electricity with the rest of the energy released to the atmosphere in the form of heat. Combined heat and power (CHP), or cogeneration can achieve efficiencies of as much as 85 to 90 percent by using the waste heat for end-use services, as illustrated in Figure 2.3.

CHP applications can reduce facility energy costs and reduce total emissions. In addition to reducing purchased electricity, CHP sites reduce their purchases of natural gas and other fossil fuels because they have a new source of thermal (heat) energy. CHP has been used for decades by universities, hospitals, and many manufacturing industries to capture part of the thermal energy produced in the generation process.

There has been greater interest in CHP since the late 1990s when electric reliability problems arose in California and some areas on the U.S. East Coast. Recent increases in the price of natural gas, which is used to fuel CHP systems, have reduced the economic advantage of CHP in many areas; however, CHP is still an attractive option in many applications. Most on-site generators are driven with natural-gas-fueled reciprocating engines although a newer technology, microturbines, is increasingly being selected for CHP systems, in part because of their minimal emissions characteristics and their ability to provide higher quality power. While fuel cells will also eventually drive CHP systems, this technology is too expensive to allow it to compete commercially now with reciprocating engine and microturbine systems.

An interesting development in the CHP industry is the effort to achieve a plug-and-play system design that minimizes the engineering, design, and implementation efforts required to integrate CHP systems with building energy systems. This strategy is reflected in the United Technology (parent company of Carrier Corporation)–Capstone microturbine integrated system that comes as a package to provide combined heating, cooling, and electric power with 3, 4, 5 or 6 60 kW microturbines and an absorption chiller/heater

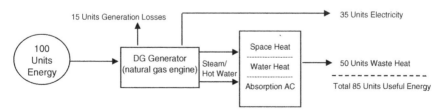

**FIGURE 2.3**  Combined Heat and Power Schematic

from Carrier. Efficiencies of these systems reach 90 percent, and the packaging avoids custom design and integration of the microturbines with the heating and air conditioning systems.

The economics of a CHP system is determined by first calculating the savings derived by avoiding purchases of electricity and natural gas (displaced by use of thermal energy from the CHP system instead of, for instance, thermal energy generated by burning natural gas in a boiler). The cost of natural gas purchases to fuel the engine or microturbine is then calculated along with operating and maintenance expenses and subtracted from the avoided energy costs. This net savings must be great enough over the life of the CHP system to pay for the system including its financing costs. These calculations can be somewhat complicated with respect to avoided electricity costs because CHP systems reduce both electricity used during each month (the billed energy or kWh charge) and the peak electricity use charge (the billing demand or peak kW). In addition, many utilities use a "ratchet" clause in their tariffs that apply a minimum demand charge that is often as high as 80 percent of the annual maximum kW use. Thus, reduction of the kW demand in a peak month can reduce bills for the following 11 months.

CHP systems also provide a source of emergency power, that, used in place of an emergency generator, can significantly reduce the comparative cost of the system. CHP is considered an attractive option for many companies—11 percent of respondents to the Association of Energy Engineers 2007 survey identified CHP as the highest priority for application at their facility in the near future.[4]

## Cool Storage and Other Demand Response Technologies

Cool storage uses less expensive off-peak electricity to generate chilled water or ice that can supplement or replace air conditioning needs during times of peak electric system use. Demand response technologies allow electric utility customers to curtail or shift loads from peak hours to off-peak hours. While these technologies may not reduce total energy use and in some cases may actually increase overall energy use, they are included in this section because they reduce the demand for on-peak generating capacity (that is, power plants) and electric distribution systems, which are becoming increasingly more costly. That is, they reduce the demand on overall electric generation resources.

Demand response has become a primary instrument for utilities to relieve peak summer generating demands and especially congestion on transmission and distribution lines. Many utilities and independent system operators (ISOs) responsible for managing the electric grid within specific geographic regions offer special incentives to customers who can curtail electricity use during periods when the generation and grid system is stressed. While traditional commercial, institutional, and government facilities have difficulty shifting loads to off-peak hours, many organizations are finding it financially beneficial to employ their emergency generation to reduce loads in these periods. Because some of the emergency generators are quite large, the financial benefit can be substantial. While traditional diesel-fired generators are typically restricted to the number of hours they can operate each year (often 200 hours), natural gas generators with the appropriate emissions controls can avoid this limitation.

## Analysis Priority

Interaction of internal and external loads, and energy systems within buildings makes the analysis priority important in evaluating costs and benefits of the various efficiency options. For instance, benefits of lighting controls would be much greater based on current lighting technologies compared to analysis after a lighting upgrade is completed.

Efficiency technologies are ideally evaluated sequentially with the most fundamental options first. Lighting efficiency options should generally be considered first because of impacts on HVAC energy requirements; at the same time, lighting energy use is not impacted by most other efficiency options. Simultaneous or iterative evaluations along with several rounds of whole building systems evaluation may be required to identify an optimal efficiency investment strategy.

## CALCULATING COST AND SAVINGS

The question that undoubtedly occurs after reading the preceding efficiency options section is how much do the various options cost and how much do they reduce energy bills? If a facility has not considered lighting and HVAC efficiency upgrades or conducted a recommissioning effort, it is likely that net cost reductions can reach and even exceed 30 percent of current energy costs after costs of the equipment have been amortized over equipment lifetimes.

A variety of factors determine both cost and savings estimates associated with each efficiency investment including:

1. Current system efficiencies.
2. Unique characteristics of energy systems and facilities.

3. Energy price structures including electricity demand charges, ratchet clauses, incentives. and end-use energy cost (discussed in Chapter 3).
4. Future energy prices.
5. Future weather.
6. Actual performance of efficiency investments.
7. Operating and maintenance costs associated with efficiency investments.

Items 1 and 2 in the list above are characteristics of each facility and can be evaluated by inspection and/or monitoring. This information is usually developed by the facility energy manager, an equipment supplier, an ESCO, or by a consulting firm or consulting engineer. Energy prices are more complicated than the average prices presented in the previous chapter and referenced in this chapter. As shown in the following chapter, the price of energy associated with each end use is different, and each efficiency option reflects its own avoided costs (the cost of the energy saved) because of the way energy prices are structured.

A brief detour to the Appendix provides information to estimate potential financial benefits of an EBaR analysis. This appendix provides information on energy use characteristics based on analysis of more than one million business, institutional, and government buildings drawn from the widely used MAISY energy use databases (http://www.maisy.com). Data are detailed by business type and operating hours. Using these data, readers can calculate several energy use statistics for their facility and compare them to data on similar facilities to see how much energy use can be reduced. Transferring information from the appropriate table and the reader's energy use statistics to the tables in the Appendix along with average utility electric prices and natural gas prices provides a general indication of the energy cost savings associated with an EBaR strategy.

Items 4 through 7 reflect cost inputs that are uncertain. However, ranges of these inputs can be applied to determine a range of costs where the cost range reflects any desired level of certainty. Addressing these later items is the role of the EBaR analysis framework. Chapter 10 provides answers to the questions of how much efficiency options cost and how much they save.

## SUMMARY: A WORD TO NONENERGY ENGINEERS

If you are not an engineer or are unfamiliar with the efficiency technologies mentioned above, you may wonder whether the EBaR process is too technical to apply at your facility. If you are a financial or operating executive or manager with responsibility for energy budgets and investments, you may be questioning the value of learning about the EBaR process without having a more detailed understanding of the technical aspects of efficiency investments.

However, no particular technical insights are required to follow the examples used in this book or to understand the risk management approach applied in EBaR. A limited number of common, easy-to-understand technologies are explained and used in the examples. Once familiar with these applications you will have gained a thorough understanding of the EBaR process and a better understanding of how technology detail fits into the application of EBaR analysis.

If your position does not require directly dealing with equipment manufacturers, ESCOs and other parties providing the efficiency technologies and analysis, you will not need technical information beyond what is provided in this book. If you are a facility or energy manager without technical knowledge of many of the efficiency systems, you will find an understanding of some basic characteristics of energy systems useful. As mentioned above, the Energy Star Building Manual (http://www.energystar.gov/ia/business/BUM.pdf) provides an excellent and generally nontechnical description of energy efficiency technologies.

Finally, readers should remember that detail on the EBaR analysis process is provided in following chapters to guide those who want to develop their own EBaR analysis system. As an alternative, software that automatically performs each of the analytical steps in a comprehensive package is available at energybudgetsatrisk.com.

## CHAPTER 3

# The Nature of Energy
# Costs and Prices

Energy-efficient technologies, as described in the previous chapter, help determine how much energy use can be reduced. Energy savings multiplied by the energy price determines energy costs savings. However, energy prices vary monthly for fuel oil and natural gas, and electricity prices can vary hourly making cost calculations more difficult. This chapter describes these energy price details, why they exist, and how utilities reflect seasonal and temporal cost characteristic in their rates.

While electric market deregulation has stalled in the United States, active competitive markets have been established in several states. Issues related to competitive market pricing and insights on buying power in competitive markets are also included in this chapter.

Several other topics related to energy cost are discussed here, including identifying costs associated with individual end uses (lighting, space heating, air conditioning and so on), incentives and subsidies available for energy-efficiency investments and financing options that can be used to pay for efficiency investments.

## ENERGY PRICE OVERVIEW

Energy prices are determined differently for each energy source. Fuel oil is sold like gasoline with a dollar per gallon quote that varies with oil market prices. Geographic variations in the cost of fuel oil depend largely on geographic variations in transportation costs.

Natural gas bills are based on total natural gas used in the billing month where the price of gas is determined both by gas distribution costs and the market price of natural gas. Pipeline and distribution systems differ across the country, creating natural gas price differentials across geographic sub-markets. In deregulated natural gas markets, these prices can change more quickly than in some regulated markets, depending on the competitive pricing option elected by the gas customer; however, the price is basically determined by the North American market for natural gas along with regional market conditions.

Both regulated electric utilities and competitive electric providers pass along the cost of providing electricity service to their customers with electric rates that are often quite complicated. Details on how these costs are determined differ between regulated and deregulated markets. From a customer perspective, the primary advantage of being in a deregulated market is an increased number of pricing options and the potential to reduce electricity costs relative to what they would have been in a regulated market. On the other hand, about half of all customers in regulated markets pay less in electric rates than they cost the utility to provide service, so some customers will see costs of their electric service increase in a deregulated market relative to what those costs would have been under regulation.

It is likely that deregulation successes in Texas and New York will eventually restart the national movement to deregulation that faltered after the California market meltdown in 2000 and 2001. However, this renewal is not likely to begin any time soon. The delay in the deregulation movement is partly a result of increased electric prices, caused by an increase in natural gas prices that occurred at the same time that deregulation became effective in many states. The coincidence of increased electric prices and deregulation has caused considerable public criticism of the deregulation process in many deregulated states. While some improvements are called for in most deregulated markets, the ability of consumers to shop for power and a competitive mechanism that more closely matches electricity prices with the cost of serving individual customers provides significant consumer benefits. From an individual facility perspective, the important issue is to work within the existing market system to reduce energy costs and manage risk.

Since the price paid for electricity is determined by the cost of providing electric service, understanding electric industry cost structures is important to understanding how electricity rates are structured and options that exist for customers to reduce electricity costs.

## ELECTRIC COSTS AND RATES

This section summarizes the cost structure of utilities and the process by which costs are translated into rate structures for commercial, institutional, government, and manufacturing customers.

Facilities in regulated and deregulated markets pay for the same services: generation, transmission, and distribution of electricity. In deregulated markets rates have been unbundled so facilities that buy power from competitive providers pay a charge associated with generation of electricity provided by the retail electricity provider along with transmission and distribution (T&D) charges that go to the local T&D company (the "wires" part of the old regulated utility). This discussion proceeds by describing the basic regulated electric utility framework with notes on differences that apply to facilities in deregulated areas. Other differences to be considered in deregulated markets are addressed in a following section.

The term *retail electricity provider* (REP) is used to designate a deregulated provider of electricity. This designation is consistent with usage in Texas, the most active deregulated market. Other designations are used in other states; for instance, New York designates competitive electricity providers and companies that provide energy-efficiency services as "energy service companies" or ESCOs. We prefer to use the terms energy service companies and ESCOs in its more traditional application to refer to companies whose primary focus is providing energy-efficiency services and to refer to competitive electricity providers as retail electricity providers.

While electric utility rate details and structures vary considerably across the United States, basic utility cost-of-service analysis and rate design are similar. Utility cost categories include:

- Customer service costs include billing, customer service, and other fixed costs associated with each customer.
- Transmission costs are associated with high voltage transmissions of electricity.
- Distribution costs are associated with lower voltage distribution to customers and
- Electric generation costs.

Utilities attempt to pass along the cost in each of these categories to customers using rates that are equitable based on the demand each customer makes on different cost components of the utility system. Utilities also attempt to use rates that are easy for their customers to understand and do not change unnecessarily over time.

In deregulated areas, cost-of-service components are separated or unbundled so that utility customers who buy power from a retail electricity provider pay the customer service, transmission, and distribution charges set by the local T&D company and a charge for electricity negotiated with their retail electricity provider. Determining appropriate customer cost allocation for the T&D and generation components is a complicated process. A description of the electric generation process illustrates the complexity under which utility generation systems are planned and operate.

## Electric Utility Generation

Utility generation is accomplished with a portfolio of generation resources that vary in their relationship of capital costs to operating costs. Achieving lower operating cost typically requires greater initial or capital costs. As indicated in Figure 3.1, baseload units are designed to run all day every day, except when down for maintenance. The least-cost option to provide electricity under these operating conditions is a large coal-fired or nuclear power plant. These plants are more expensive to build but less expensive to run compared to other generating options. They also require longer periods to start up.

At the other end of the spectrum are peaking units that may only be needed a relatively small number of hours during the year. The cost of providing peak power is minimized for these less-frequently used plants by selecting generating options whose initial capital cost is the least, even though their fuel costs are considerably higher than baseload units. Peaking units are nearly always fueled with natural gas and can be brought on line quickly from a cold start to meet increased demand. Intermediate units fill the gap between baseload and peaking units providing power for longer time periods than peak hours but less than continuous operation. Intermediate units typically are less expensive to operate than peaking units and are fueled by natural gas or coal. In addition to using their own generating facilities, utilities buy and, in some cases, sell power to other utilities. Given the importance of fuel costs in the generating process, many regulated utilities use complex hedging strategies to protect their customers against adverse fuel price movements.

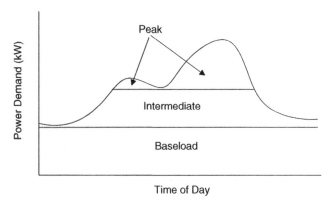

**FIGURE 3.1** Baseload, Intermediate and Peaking Generating Capacity

## Cost of Service

Costs associated with dispatching baseload, intermediate, and peak generating units as required to meet utility customer's electricity demand results in a cost of service that varies hourly and seasonally. The cost of producing power during peak periods can be more than triple the cost of power production during off-peak hours.

Determining how each utility customer's facility hourly electricity use matches up with the utility's use of baseload, intermediate, and peaking units provides a basis for calculating how much each customer should pay for the electricity services it receives. For regulated utilities, these calculations are not computed for each customer; instead a limited number of customer rate classes are selected for a utility cost-of-service study. These classes typically include residential, small general service (small commercial, institutional, government, manufacturing), general service (medium and large customers in the above categories), and large general service (typically larger manufacturing customers who take electricity at the primary voltage). Hourly load profiles for the individual classes are then developed from load research surveys that provide a sampling of 15-minute kW use for customers in each class.

Customer class hourly load information permits utilities to calculate each class's contributions to the total cost of providing electric service. Two general types of cost are considered:

- Operating costs are based on fuel, maintenance, and other operating costs.
- Capital costs reflect costs associated with transmission and distribution systems and generating plants. Since the utility must provide maximum power needs of customers, allocation of capital costs to the customer class is based on maximum kW use by the customer class in different time intervals.

The resulting operating and capital cost calculations for each rate class provide an estimate of operating costs as $/kWh (total electricity use) and a capital cost as $/kW (maximum electricity use). This distinction is maintained in customer bills as energy charges ($/kWh) and demand charges ($/kW) except for residential and small nonresidential customers whose rates include only an energy charge.

The customer's demand charge is often subject to a ratchet clause that specifies a demand charge based on the greater of (1) current month's peak kW or demand or (2) a percentage of the highest peak demand of the previous 11 months. Eighty percent is often used with the result that the demand component of the bill is determined by the greatest 15-minutes of electricity use in the month or 80 percent of the maximum over the previous 11 months (so-called demand meters typically record peak kW based on 15-minute intervals). The cost-of-service concept in this case is that the customer is requiring the utility to provide capacity to supply the customer's maximum kW need regardless of the customer's demand fluctuations from month to month.

Cost-of-service analysis is much more detailed and complicated than presented above, and significant resources are used both to conduct the cost-of-service studies and to debate the appropriateness and accuracy of the analysis in public service commission rate hearings. However, the general characterizations presented here explain the basic nature of utility rate design. The impacts of these rate designs on individual customer bills are discussed below. Impacts on efficiency investment analysis are an important factor considered in later chapters.

### Electric Rates, kWh, kW and Electricity Bills

For most facilities the total electric bill equals the sum of an energy charge (total kWh use in the month times a $/kWh energy rate) and a demand charge (peak kW use in the month times a $/kW rate) plus a customer charge.

For example, Table 3.1 shows a bill calculation for a facility that used 200,000 kWh in a month with a peak demand of 800 kW. The energy charge is $14,000 (200,000 times an energy charge of $0.07/kwh) and the demand charge is $8,000 (800 times $10.00/kW) for a total bill of $22,000. The average kWh price ($/kWh) is calculated by dividing $22,000 by 200,000 kWh to get $0.11/kWh.

Facility hourly energy use characteristics determine both the monthly total kWh and monthly peak kW. The more peaked a facility's hourly electric profile, the larger the demand charge and the greater the average kWh price. This impact can be substantial. Consider the simple commercial customer rate for facilities in the Austin Energy E06 rate class shown in Table 3.2. The energy charge for all kWh used in the month is $0.0514/kWh and the

**TABLE 3.1**   Example Bill Calculation

| Category | Rate | Use | Charge |
|---|---|---|---|
| Energy (kWh) | $0.07/kWh | 200,000 kWh | $14,000 |
| Demand (kW) | $10.00/kW | 800 | $8,000 |
| Total (per kWh) | $0.11/kWh | | $22,000 |

**TABLE 3.2**   Austin Energy E06 Rates

| Charge | Rate: Winter Months | Rate: Summer Months |
|---|---|---|
| Energy (kWh) | $0.0514/kWh | $0.0514/kWh |
| Demand (kW) | $12.65/kW | $14.03/kW |

*Source:* Austin Energy, City of Austin Electric Rate Schedule, June 1, 2007. http://www.austinenergy.com/About%20Us/Rates/rateSummary.pdf

demand charge is $12.65/kW in the winter (November through April) and $14.03/kW in the summer (May through October).

To consider the separate impacts of energy and demand charges, bills for three hypothetical 250,000 square foot office buildings in Austin are evaluated in Table 3.3. Each customer uses 300,000 kWh in the month but peak kW use varies from a low of 641 kW to a high of 1,190 kW. The peaked nature of load profiles is described by the load factor where:

Load factor = (month kWh/hours in month)/peak kW.

The number in parentheses is the average hourly kW use calculated by dividing the total of all kWh by the number of hours in the month. Thus, the load factor is the average demand divided by the peak demand. A load factor of 0.5 means the peak demand was twice the monthly average kW. Load factors for the customers in Table 3.3 are 0.65 (641 peak kW), 0.5 (833 peak kW) and 0.35 (1,190 kW). This range is reasonably characteristic of the spread in office building load factors in central Texas.

The monthly summer bill for the three customers ranges from $24,413 to $32,116, a difference of 32 percent. The highest demand charge is nearly double that of the lowest. Each customer was subject to the same energy and demand rates, used the same amount of total electricity in the month but the average kWh price varies from 8.1 cents/kWh to 10.7 cents/kWh.

Recognizing the separate roles of energy and demand costs is important in considering efficiency investments, because individual investments can have very different impacts on billed kWh and billed peak kW. For instance,

**TABLE 3.3**   Comparison of Bills with Different Load Factors

| kWh/Month | Peak kW | kWh Charge | kW Charge | Total Charge | $/kWh |
|---|---|---|---|---|---|
| 300,000 | 641 | $15,420 | $8,993 | $24,413 | $0.081 |
| 300,000 | 833 | $15,420 | $11,687 | $27,107 | $0.090 |
| 300,000 | 1,190 | $15,420 | $16,696 | $32,116 | $0.107 |

high efficiency exterior building lights do not impact peak kW charges while high efficiency interior lights impact peak kW directly through reduced lighting electricity use and indirectly through reduced air conditioning use that typically occurs during peak hours.

Most commercial, government, institutional, and manufacturing customers are demand-metered and billed both energy and demand charges. Energy and demand charges vary substantially by utility, even within the same state. The demand component of energy bills typically falls in the range of 20 to 60 percent of the monthly bill.

Smaller customers with billing demands less than 10 or 20 kW, are usually billed only on their kWh use (a demand of 20 kW is approximately consistent with a 7,500 square foot office building).

## Time of Use (TOU) Pricing

Larger customers are often metered with "interval" meters (also called interval data recorders or IDRs) that record energy use and demand at 15-minute intervals throughout the month. Peak demands of 500 or 1000 kW thresholds are often the thresholds for requiring interval metering. Thresholds can be much lower; for instance, California requires all customers with demand less than 200 kW to have interval meters. Interval meters are used with time-of-use (TOU) rates that typically charge different rates during weekdays for off-peak and peak hours. Some rate schedules include shoulder periods between the off-peak and peak period. These rates also vary by season.

The time-of-use rates for Pacific Gas and Electric Company's E-19 rate schedule is shown in Table 3.4. Peak periods are noon to 6:00 P.M. from May 1 through October 31. Partial-peak summer periods are 8:30 A.M. to noon and 6:00 P.M. to 9:30 P.M. and 8:30 A.M. to noon in the winter. All other hours are off peak. Demand charges are calculated separately for

**TABLE 3.4**   PGE Time-of-Use-Rates

| Rate | Demand Rates ($/kW) | Energy Rates ($/kWh) |
|------|---------------------|----------------------|
| Peak Summer | $15.02 | $0.144 |
| Part-Peak Summer | $3.57 | $0.106 |
| Maximum Demand Summer | $6.74 | |
| Off-Peak Summer | | $0.076 |
| Part-Peak Winter | $1.85 | $0.097 |
| Off-Peak Winter | | $0.079 |
| Maximum Demand Winter | $6.74 | |

peak and part-peak periods. The maximum demand charge is the maximum demand regardless of time period. Energy charges are calculated using total kWh used in each time period and the $/kWh charge in Table 3.4.

Customer variations in energy and peak demand characteristics illustrated in Table 3.3 occur in the real world as indicated by the chart showing average normalized August load shapes for a sample of PG&E office facilities billed under the E-19 rate schedule (Figure 3.2). Load shapes are normalized by dividing each hour's kW load by the sum for the day. Variation in load shapes results in significantly different average energy prices with facilities having the most peaked shapes paying more on kWh basis.

Figure 3.3 shows average annual electricity price ($/kWh) graphed against the ratio of August average day peak kW to daily average kW (a value of 2.0 means the peak kW is two times the daily average kW; higher values mean more peaked load shapes) for a sample of office buildings in the PG&E service area. Clearly, the extent to which a facility's electricity use is concentrated in more expensive peak hours carries a considerable penalty with the least peaked facility paying about 12.4 cents/kWh and the most peaked paying 18.1 cents/kWh.

Not surprisingly, the primary economic benefit of many energy-efficiency investments is provided by reducing peak-period energy use and, in some cases, shifting energy to off-peak hours. However, economic

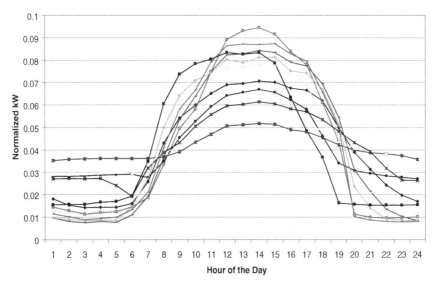

**FIGURE 3.2** PG&E Office Building Load Shapes

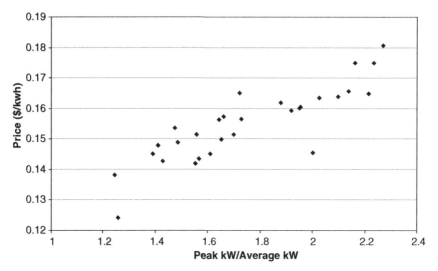

**FIGURE 3.3**   PG&E Office Building Price and Peak Kw Relationship

evaluation of these technologies becomes more difficult since information is required on hourly impacts of efficiency investments throughout the day.

One reason that buildings are generally energy inefficient is that, historically, electric rates have not provided price incentives for customers to reduce electricity use in the most expensive times of the day except through a single demand charge. TOU rates improve price signals provided to electric utility customers and provide an opportunity for proactive utility customers to significantly reduce energy costs.

## DEREGULATED ELECTRIC MARKETS

Facilities operating in a deregulated market can replace the generation portion of electric service provided by their local T&D company with generation supplied by a competitive provider. It would seem that such a change could be made in a reasonably transparent way with relatively little disruption to operation of electricity markets. Unfortunately, the road to deregulation has been a bumpy one; however, it is not without its success stories. These successes, notably in Texas and New York, will likely reignite the movement towards deregulation at some point in the future. The history of this process is briefly recounted below, along with several topics relevant for facilities that currently operate in competitive electric markets.

Deregulation of wholesale electricity markets (power sales by generators to utilities) began in earnest in mid-1990s as a result of passage of the Energy Policy Act of 1992 and resulting Federal Energy Regulatory (FERC) orders that opened interstate transmission access to nonutilities and required utilities to provide electronic information on available transmission capacity. Wholesale market deregulation was a success in generating competition among generating companies, though an overbuilt market eventually resulted in wholesale electric price collapse and a number of bankruptcies.

The deregulation of retail markets where competitors are allowed to sell electricity over the distribution utility's wires has had mixed results.

## The Theory of Retail Electric Competition

The competitive model provides goods and services at minimum cost to consumers. Competitive market price signals are the most efficient way of communicating from consumers to producers and visa versa. Less developed countries have made phenomenal economic strides in recent years, largely by moving from various forms of central planning to more competitive markets. The electric industry was the last in a long line of industry deregulation that started in the 1970s, industries that included trucking, telecommunications, airlines and more.

One of the appeals of deregulation, besides promising lower electricity prices and greater consumer choice, was the prospect of ridding states of the regulatory process for utilities. Under a regulated system, utilities make decisions with respect to adding new generating capacity and, unless those decisions can be proved imprudent, the utility's customers pay for the investment costs. The fact that utilities earn a rate of return on their investments in the electric system means that utilities have an incentive to invest more in capital than they would otherwise.

States are responsible for regulating utilities; consequently each state developed its own approach to deregulation. All state plans, however, were designed to maintain regulation of physical transmission and distribution (T&D) systems. The opening of wholesale power markets in the mid-1990s meant that a retail electricity provider could set up shop in upstate New York, buy power from a generator in Pennsylvania, and sell it to a New York City customer after adding in the transmission and distribution charges required to move the power and distribute it in New York City. Ideally this approach would transfer risks associated with ill-advised generation investments from utility ratepayers to generation companies who would compete with each other and drive the price of electric generation to its minimum competitive level.

A retail customer could then shop for the best commodity portion (the non-T&D component) of his electricity service and enter into a contract with the most desirable terms. Besides providing choices with respect to competitive retail providers and prices, the competitive model provides a variety of contract terms that can be structured to meet the customer's risk preferences.

Another advantage of competitive markets is achieved by moving away from electricity prices that are determined by rate classes. In regulated markets about half of electric customers cost more to serve than they provide in revenue and half cost less. For instance, a customer whose peak demand occurs at night with low energy use during the day may be billed as if the peak demand occurred during the day (billing demand is often the maximum demand during the month regardless of when it occurs). This customer is paying much more than the cost of service. Since the total revenue of all customers in a rate class matches the total cost of serving the rate class, those who cost less, like the night peaking customer, are subsidizing customers who are charged less than they cost to serve. With only four or five rate classes, the regulated system can be very inefficient in charging individual customers a price that reflects their true cost of service.

In competitive markets, retail electric providers seek out the lower cost-of-service customers, offer a savings over their regulated provider and still make a profit. On the other hand, retail providers will accept customers who are more expensive to serve only if they pay more than they were paying to the regulated utility. The end result is that individual customers will receive electricity bills that more accurately reflect the cost of providing service. More accurate pricing will encourage more efficient use of electric services.

The arguments for competitive markets are compelling and were enthusiastically accepted by many state legislators in the late 1990s. Large commercial and manufacturing customers who have enough market power, resources, and expertise to take advantage of the benefits of retail competition were active in promoting retail competition. A number of energy companies who were positioning themselves to take advantage of business opportunities were also lobbying for active retail markets.

As indicated in the next section, however, deregulation did not work as planned in many states.

## Retail Markets in Practice

The advent of competitive retail markets was eagerly awaited by some and not so eagerly by others; however, in the late 1990s it appeared that deregulated electricity markets were right around the corner for nearly all states.

Legislatures moved to deregulate their states under the promise that deregulated markets would lower electricity prices and make their states more competitive for future economic development.

State legislatures began implementing competitive retail electricity markets (competition by electricity providers to residential, commercial, public, and industrial utility customers) with California first in 1998. Unfortunately, the first state plan to deregulate was also the most poorly designed. Previously regulated utilities were required by the state to divest generation resources, purchase generated power on the market, and provide the power to customers under the proviso that rates would not increase—however, the price companies had to pay for power skyrocketed because of increases in natural gas prices in 2000 and 2001, requiring utilities to sell power for less than they were buying it. A number of other factors contributed to the California debacle; however, the end result included utility bankruptcy and a halt to the competitive market. Enron was a high-profile player in exaggerating shortages and increasing prices; however, the California initiative collapsed under the weight of its own lack of foresight.

Another problem experienced by a number of states related to the way electricity rates were unbundled. Costs of transmission and distribution had to be backed out of the delivered price determined by utility's cost-of-service data. Without an appropriate disaggregation of costs, new entrants into the market in many cases did not have enough "headroom" to purchase and distribute electricity competitively, given the existing transmission and distribution charges that had to be included in the delivered price. Virginia is a good example of a state that provided so little headroom that effective competition never developed with the state returning to a cost-of-service regulatory oversight at the end of 2008.

While the California deregulation plan foundered because of flawed design, a handful of additional states, most notably New York and Texas, have succeeded in developing reasonably robust competitive markets. While residential and smaller nonresidential customers have lower participation rates, the market for medium and larger electricity users is active in both states. It is likely that success in Texas and New York will at some point reignite the movement towards electric deregulation in most other states. Approximately two dozen states were in the process of deregulating electric markets until the meltdown of the California market in 2001. Some of these states revised or postponed deregulation plans; most of the rest have relatively tepid competition.[1]

Retail natural gas customers also face active competitive markets in a handful of states. State programs vary widely and are described by the Energy Information Administration at http://www.eia.doe.gov/oil_gas/natural_gas/restructure/restructure.html.

A number of benefits are provided to customers in deregulated states that are not available in regulated markets. At the same time, competitive markets have reduced utility focus on energy efficiency in several ways that hamper energy risk management. Suggestions for taking advantage of the unique features of competitive markets and avoiding some of their pitfalls appear in the next section.

### Insights on Buying Competitive Power

Integrating competitive energy purchases and efficiency investments is an important part of energy risk management discussed in detail in Chapter 11. However, this current chapter is an appropriate place to include comments on dealing with competitive electric providers based on my experience in working with utility customers in deregulated markets:

**REPs Primarily Want to Sell Electricity**  This statement is not meant to be pejorative and not meant to offend those retail electricity providers (REPs) who are committed to helping customers consider efficiency investments. However, the core business of most REPs is selling electricity—a much less costly process with more immediate returns than selling efficient technology applications. Selling electricity and selling efficiency services are two different processes requiring different skill sets and usually requiring co-ordinating decisions in two different areas of the customer's management structure—typically a difficult sales proposition. Many REPs advertise efficiency services, sometimes in partnership with energy service companies; however, in dealing with REPs it is wise to take the lead in insuring that efficiency impacts on electricity price bids and the impact of pricing products on efficiency investments are appropriately considered as described in Chapter 11.

**Electric Purchases that Ignore Efficiency Can Be Costly**  REPs evaluate facility electricity use patterns and conduct analysis of hourly load histories to evaluate weather sensitivity and to determine the cost of providing power in off-peak and peak periods. An REP price bid often is quoted only in $/kWh even though hourly loads and peak demand have been used to compute energy costs and distribution costs that include demand charges. Price bids may also include kWh and kW ranges in which a facility must operate or face penalty charges. That is, a contract with an REP may contain clauses that impact the return on efficient technology investments.

Some of the financial benefits of efficiency investments will be lost if price bids are based on preinvestment load shapes.

**Locking in Prices Carries a Risk**   Many times I have heard the comment "I want to lock in prices so I can go ahead and make decisions about efficiency investments." While locking in prices with long-term contracts removes uncertainty concerning electricity prices, it also carries the risk that market energy prices may fall below the contract price. The difference between the contract price and the lower market price represents the cost of hedging that was achieved with fixed rates. Long-term commitments with penalties for both overuse or underuse can also limit future options for efficiency investments over the period of the contract. A competitive market energy risk management approach considers the costs and benefits of pricing options *and* efficiency options together.

**Include Renegotiation Clauses**   Some organizations (primarily government) require fixed price contracts. However, a renegotiation clause that allows you to renegotiate electricity prices if the wholesale price of power drops below a specified level can remove some of the risk of going with a fixed price.

**Shop Your Energy; Price Bids Can Vary Significantly**   The first time I compared price bids for a Texas energy contract, I was surprised at the variation in prices offered by REPs. The difference between annual high and low bids was 12 percent and more than $2 million. Many organizations are reluctant to select a new REP; however, unless the REP goes out of business the only downside that can occur is with billing and administrative services. Line maintenance and other physical services will continue to be provided by the distribution utility that serves your facility's area.

**Check Your Bills**   It is hard to believe, but enough errors are made in REP billing statements to make checking your bills necessary. Check meter readings to make sure they are consistent with the billing statement, and make sure that the proper rate is applied to each component of facility electricity use.

**Work with REP Representatives to Learn About Energy Market Conditions** REP representatives are usually happy to discuss pricing options, their view of energy markets, and specifics relevant to the options they present. If the REP representative appears primarily to be a sales person without any industry knowledge, ask for another representative or contact another REP.

**Consider Alternative Pricing Options**   This is where a relationship with a knowledgeable REP representative is important. A variety of pricing options is now offered to take advantage of falling prices, but include enough hedging protection to meet your risk tolerance. REP representatives will usually be happy to discuss these options.

**Consider Contract Options** Medium and large customers can negotiate contract terms to include almost any energy-related issue of interest. For instance, optional contract extensions can be specified to protect against having to go into the market when prices appear unusually high. Organizations with multiple meters can ask for price quotes for individual meters or groups of meters based on load factors (the extent to which loads are peaked) from several suppliers and split their energy purchases. Prices can be locked in for future periods, even if the current contract has not yet terminated.

**Retail Market Pricing Options** The most significant advantage to being in a competitive electricity market is the opportunity to get competing bids on alternative pricing products structured to meet organizational risk considerations.

While a long-term fixed price contract may be desirable, benefits from reduced energy prices cannot be captured if they occur. Consequently the potential costs and benefits of all available pricing products should be considered. Incorporating the various pricing options in an EBaR process is described in more detail in Chapter 11; however, it is useful in this discussion of energy costs and prices to provide a brief overview of some of the pricing options available in today's competitive markets.

REPs are in a continuous process of buying contracts for energy to fulfill their obligations to sell energy to their customers. An REP could avoid most risk by buying contracts that lock in prices for future delivery of electricity and selling service contracts to their customers based on those fixed prices. If contracts are perfectly matched to its sales obligations, the REP has hedged all of its risk.

While hedging can reduce risk of loss; it limits gains that can be made from beneficial movements in market prices. For instance, consider the June purchase of a forward contract for $0.09/kWh in August to cover contracted energy commodity sales to customers at $0.09/kWh in August. If the spot price in six months goes above $0.09/kWh, we have saved money compared to buying electricity on the spot market for delivery to our customers; however, if the price drops below $0.09/kWh we have incurred a cost represented by the difference between $0.09/kWh and the current spot market.

REPs use information on likely future market price movements along with a variety of financial risk management instruments that are associated with commodity (electricity) purchases in an attempt to maximize their profits—subject to an acceptable level of risk. Other financial instruments like options, which give the buyer the right, but not the obligation, to buy energy at specific prices in the future, can be used to manage energy price risk with a variety of strategies.

When markets first opened to competition, pricing options were relatively limited and consisted primarily of a choice in the term of the contract, ranging from monthly to three years or more of fixed electricity prices. Competition and price volatility soon prompted REPs to extend their offerings, permitting customers to participate in some of the same kind of hedging practiced by REPs. A sampling of pricing products is included below:

- Fixed rates for periods ranging from one month to three or more years.
- Block rates tied to a specific block of kWh purchases for specific time periods on specific days.
- Spot pricing based on market clearing prices (MCPE in Texas).
- "Heat rate" contracts that tie electric prices to the future price of natural gas.
- Caps, collars, and floors that limit up, down, or both up and down price movements.
- Purchase contracts for some or all required electricity for one or more future months.

For products structured to simply pass-through market prices and other costs (for instance, distribution costs), there is little or no risk exposure to the REP so the contract includes what comes down to a service charge. For other products that expose the REP to risk, facility energy-use patterns become important and are part of the REP's pricing calculations.

Electric customers can avoid hedging and purchase all their electricity on the spot market (known as "going naked" in commodity market terminology). At the other extreme, fixed-price contracts for maximum terms provide a fully hedged position; that is, all risk is eliminated with respect to knowledge of future prices. Most customers will find a position between these two extremes to be most attractive. Quantitative evaluation of costs and benefits associated with the various pricing options is discussed in Chapter 11.

## END-USE COSTS

Costs per kWh can vary significantly by end use because of demand charges and time-of-use billing. End uses such as exterior lighting that primarily operate during less expensive off-peak hours are less costly and therefore provide smaller savings for each kWh reduction. On the other hand, end

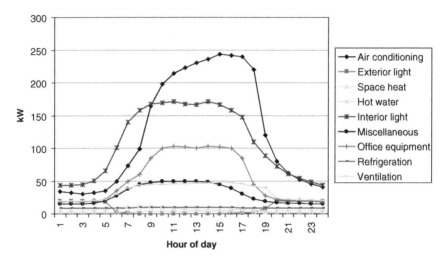

**FIGURE 3.4** End-Use Load Shapes

uses like air conditioning use more electricity at expensive times of the day and become more important efficiency investment targets.

Figure 3.4 shows August hourly load profiles for typical office building end uses in the PG&E service area for a day in August for a building that uses about 2.0 million kWh per year. Each end use provides a different kWh (electricity use for the day) and peak kW (maximum electricity use in the day) contribution to total facility energy use and hourly load profile; consequently, a different electricity price is associated with each end use.

Table 3.5 shows contributions of each of the end uses to energy and demand charges along with a daily $/kWh price using the PG&E E-19 rates shown in Table 3.4. $/kWh prices range from 6.8 cents/kWh for exterior lighting to 19.5 cents/kWh for air conditioning. In other words, reducing air conditioning by 1 kWh saves almost 3 times as much money as reducing exterior lighting by the same amount. Figure 3.5 shows daily $/kWh price for each end use in graphical form.

The substantial variation in energy prices and avoided costs illustrates that:

- Some end uses are more valuable than others in reducing energy bills.
- Energy pricing must be an integral component of facility energy risk management.

**TABLE 3.5**  Energy and Demand Charges by End Use ($)

| End Use | Peak charges kWh | Peak charges kW | Part-peak charges kWh | Part-peak charges kW | Maximum Demand kW | Maximum Demand Total Charges | Maximum Demand $/kWh |
|---|---|---|---|---|---|---|---|
| Air conditioning | 235.48 | 122.02 | 146.31 | 26.47 | 54.75 | 585.03 | 0.195 |
| Exterior light | 0.71 | 1.05 | 5.49 | 2.41 | 4.54 | 14.20 | 0.068 |
| Space heat | 5.96 | 3.34 | 7.24 | 1.50 | 2.84 | 20.88 | 0.130 |
| Hot water | 3.72 | 2.07 | 3.14 | 0.49 | 0.93 | 10.35 | 0.145 |
| Interior light | 156.91 | 85.95 | 123.70 | 20.34 | 38.57 | 425.47 | 0.163 |
| Miscellaneous | 40.97 | 24.64 | 33.45 | 5.86 | 11.06 | 115.97 | 0.161 |
| Office equipment | 91.60 | 51.57 | 59.89 | 12.26 | 23.14 | 238.45 | 0.184 |
| Refrigeration | 9.46 | 4.88 | 8.71 | 1.16 | 2.19 | 26.39 | 0.124 |
| Ventilation | 46.22 | 23.84 | 37.38 | 5.46 | 10.70 | 123.59 | 0.151 |
|  |  |  |  |  | Total | 1,560.34 | 0.166 |

## INCENTIVES TO REDUCE ENERGY USE

Electric utilities, at the behest of state utility regulatory agencies, developed active incentive programs in the 1980s through the mid-1990s in an attempt to integrate conservation or as is more currently known, demand-side management (DSM) or efficiency programs. Costs and benefits of programs

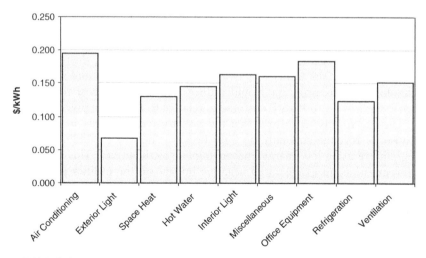

**FIGURE 3.5**  $/kWh by End

were evaluated from utility, customer, and societal perspectives. Based on this analysis, individual DSM programs were developed and offered to utility customers. Programs ranged from free energy audits and compact fluorescent light bulb give-aways to incentives to switch from electric space heating to natural gas space heating.

## New Interest in Efficiency

With the prospect of deregulated electricity markets looming in the mid-1990s, conservation and energy-efficiency programs were dropped by most utilities. The turmoil created by deregulation in California, the impacts of the Enron meltdown, and the glut of new generating capacity permitted the focus on utility-sponsored energy-efficiency programs to slowly fade.

Within the last several years, however, economic growth, constraints of existing transmission and distribution systems, and generating capacity shortfalls have begun to move efficiency programs back to the forefront in planning by utilities and regulators. In addition, concerns over emissions, especially $CO_2$, have added emphasis to the potential benefits from utility investments in their customers' buildings and equipment efficiency. In deregulated markets, dealing with efficiency issues falls to distribution utilities that maintain the transmission and distribution of power to customers within their former service areas.

The concept of integrated resource planning (IRP) that is still, at least formally, required by utilities in many states requires utilities to evaluate all available options to provide service to their customers. Consider an energy-efficiency technology that reduces the peaked nature of the load shapes shown in Figure 3.2. If a PG&E-funded program to install the technologies is less costly than generating or paying for the peak energy, then the least-cost option is for the utility to pay contractors to purchase and install the technologies. This program would reduce total resource cost to provide electric services to all PG&E customers, relative to the alternatives.

The rub to this scenario is that the investor-owned utility is worse off because its revenue suddenly declines because the office buildings in the program are using less energy and paying less to the utility. This reduction in revenues has an exaggerated negative impact on the utilities profits, so unless special arrangements are made to make the utility whole, utilities have a disincentive to promote efficiency programs.

This difficulty has been recognized for years, and a number of states have attempted to encourage efficiency programs by decoupling revenues and sales to estimate lost revenues and make an adjustment or adjust the utility's allowed rate of return.[2]

## Utility Incentives

Many regulated utilities offer incentives to reduce energy use at critical times and to invest in technologies that reduce demands on transmission, distribution, and generation resources. Incentive levels are typically based on a measure of the utility's avoided costs associated with the customer's use of specific technologies.

Southern California Edison (SCE) programs summarized below (http://www.sce.com/RebatesandSavings/LargeBusiness/) provide an example of incentives. In the case of SCE, these incentives are funded by a charge applied to each customer's bill within the SCE service territory. The California Public Utility Commissions oversees SCE's efficiency program plan, though the programs are administered by SCE.

Utility incentives fall into several categories and are illustrated with SCE program details. These categories are discussed below.

**End-Use Equipment**    End-use incentives improve facility efficiency by replacing existing equipment with more efficient equipment. Specific SCE rebates are shown in Table 3.6. The term "up to" indicates that rebates depend on the type of equipment; rebates are limited to 100 percent of the materials and labor installation costs.

**Performance Efficiency**    Performance incentives tie incentive payments to electricity use reduction achievements rather than specific technologies. SCE's performance program includes retrofit and new equipment installations. Incentives are based on the activity and annual kWh savings. Incentives can cover up to 50 percent of the cost of each measure.

- Fluorescent, metal halide, or other lighting installations; LED traffic or pedestrian signals; and lighting controls provide incentive payments of $0.05 per kWh.
- Chiller systems, cooling towers, packaged units greater than 12 tons, refrigeration systems, and some major system replacements provide incentive payments of $0.14 per kWh.
- Air compressors, EMS controls, injection molding machines, motors, server virtualization, variable frequency drives, process load, or other specialized equipment provide payments of $0.08 per kWh.

**Self-Generation**    SCE customers who use renewable or energy-efficiency self-generation can save up to $4,500/kW.

**TABLE 3.6**   SCE End-Use Equipment Incentives

| Lighting (per lamp, fixture, or device, unless noted) | Incentive |
| --- | --- |
| Screw-in compact fluorescent lamps | up to $5.00 |
| Hardwired fluorescent fixtures | up to $22.50 |
| High-efficiency exit signs | $27.00 |
| T-8 or T-5 lamps with electronic ballasts | up to $7.50 |
| HID fixtures (exterior) | up to $100 |
| Occupancy sensors | up to $44.00 |
| Photocells | $7.00 |
| Time clocks | $36.00 |
| LED channel signs (red) | up to $6 |
| High bay fixtures (interior T-8, T-5) | $100 |

| Refrigeration (lf—per linear foot; pd—per device) | Incentive |
| --- | --- |
| Night cover for display cases | $9.00 lf |
| New refrigeration display case with doors | up to $200 lf |
| Antisweat heat controls | $ 14.00 lf |
| Insulation of bare suction lines | $1.00 lf |
| Cooler or freezer door gaskets | $4.00 lf |
| Evaporative fan controller | $75 pd |
| Vending machine controller | $90 pd |
| ECM and PSC motors | $20 pd |
| Special doors with low/no antisweat heat | $50 pd |
| Square foot of trip curtains for walk-in boxes | $3.00 pd |
| Autoclosers for coolers or freezers | up to $50 pd |

| Food Service (per unit) | Incentive |
| --- | --- |
| Commercial connectionless steamers | up to $750 |
| Insulated holding cabinets | up to $300 |
| Commercial electric fryer | $200 |
| Commercial ice machines | up to $500 |
| Commercial electric griddle | $300 |
| Commercial electric combination oven | $1,000 |
| Commercial electric convection oven | $350 |
| Solid door reach-in refrigerators and freezers | up to $500 |
| Glass door reach-in refrigerators | up to $300 |

| Air Conditioners | Incentive |
| --- | --- |
| Variable frequency drives | $80.00 per horsepower |
| Reflective window film | $1.35 per square foot |
| Packaged terminal air conditioners less than 2 tons | $100.00 per unit |
| Advanced evaporative coolers | $123.00 per ton |

| Premium Efficiency motors | Incentive |
| --- | --- |
| Motors 1–2 HP | $35.00 |
| Motors 3–5 HP | $40.00 |
| Motors 5 HP | $50.00 |
| . . . | |
| Motors 200 HP | $1,260.00 |

**Demand Response**   Utility demand response (DR) programs pay customers to curtail their electricity use at certain times. Utility system operators who are responsible for scheduling generation resources in specific geographic areas also use DR resources to respond to capacity shortages during peak periods. Some SCE DR programs include:

- **The Capacity Bidding Program.** CBP participants receive guaranteed payments for agreeing to reduce loads when requested plus energy payments based on kWh reductions achieved. For a two to six hour day-of option, the average payment credit from May through October is $12.65/kW.
- **Time of Use-Base Interruptible Program.** The TOU-BIP is an interruptible rate for customers whose monthly demand is more than 200 kW and who are willing to curtail at least 15 percent of maximum demand. A minimum curtailment amount is 100 kW. Payments are made as a bill credit, regardless of whether an interruptible event occurs. Credits of as much as $16.45/kW are provided for peak period curtailment applied to the difference of the average monthly customer peak kW and a prespecified firm service level.
- **Demand Bidding Program.** The DBP is an Internet-based bidding program that offers customers with demand greater than 200 kW to bid for at least 30 kW reductions in electricity use on a day-of or day-ahead basis. Payments are 50 cents/kWh for a day-ahead and 60 cents/kWh for a day-of curtailment.

**Summary of Utility Incentives**   Utility incentives available from Southern California Edison (SCE) are presented above to provide examples of energy use incentives offered by utilities. While the efficiency incentives offered by SCE are both extensive and reflect a higher avoided cost (and therefore higher customer payments) than most areas, they provide a measure of the magnitude of savings available in service areas with serious programs.

Utilities' programs should be considered for each facility as part of an efficiency investment analysis. Facilities in competitive markets may also have significant incentives available from local transmission and distribution utilities.

## Other Incentives

Independent system operators (ISO), state agencies, and federal government agencies provide a variety of additional incentives. The incentives range from programs like those illustrated for SCE in the previous section to tax incentives provided by states and more recently by the federal government as part of the 2005 Energy Policy Act.

These incentives, together with utility incentives, can pay for a significant portion of many energy-efficiency investments and must be included in EBaR analysis.

## FINANCING ENERGY-EFFICIENCY INVESTMENTS

Three basic financing options are used for energy-efficiency investments including:

- Internal financing.
- Debt financing.
- Lease and lease-purchase agreements.

Each of these options is summarized below. Energy performance contracting, an increasingly popular option for undertaking efficiency investments, is also discussed in this section.

### Internal Financing

Internal financing pays for investments from current operating or capital accounts. Internal financing is the easiest financing method, requiring no contract negotiations and immediate access to funds. All savings and equipment depreciation are captured by the organization. The problem with internal funding from operating budgets is that total available funds for investments are typically not large. Efficiency investments funded from capital budgets can be larger; however, limited capital budgets may preclude many attractive efficiency investments.

In practice, internal financing with operating budgets is often used for projects with low costs and high returns (short paybacks), while capital budgets are used for larger projects. Competition for capital budgets typically limits the number of energy-efficiency investments funded this way, especially since energy-efficiency projects are often evaluated with more conservative payback or internal rate of return hurdle rates than other capital budgeting projects. Consequently, internal financing typically does not allow an organization to gain full advantage of the increase in cash flow offered by efficient technology investment options.

### Debt Financing

Debt financing acquires funds through loans, bonds, and other debt instruments. Debt is repaid over a period of time that may or may not reflect the lifetime of the efficiency investment. Debt financing in the form of bonds is a common way of financing efficiency projects for public facilities. Debt financing for private organizations is typically secured through a private lending institution.

## Lease and Lease-Purchase Agreements

The most attractive financing option for many applications is a lease or lease-purchase agreement financed by a vendor or other organization such as a bank or other credit organization. The financing agreement may continue over a period that is different from the lifetime of the efficiency investment. Equipment is typically provided to the facility owner with little or no initial payment and with payments that can extend for a decade or more. Leasing arrangements provide a flexible method of financing efficiency investments.

Leases can be structured to provide ownership to the facility or to assign ownership to the lessor; consequently, depreciation and tax considerations must be considered in a lease or lease-purchase agreement.

## Performance Contracting

Performance contracting is becoming an increasingly popular way of managing all aspects of energy-efficiency investments. Performance contractors are energy service companies who conduct all of the tasks associated with energy-efficiency investments from analysis to monitoring savings of the installed equipment. Performance contracting financing is usually provided by the performance contractor and can include debt or lease and lease-purchase agreements. Performance contracts guarantee energy savings and commit energy service companies to make reimbursements for savings that fall short of the guaranteed amount. While this approach provides convenience and transfers investment risk to the contractor, performance contracts can suffer from either underinvestment or overinvestment in efficient technologies, limiting the benefits to the facility owner.

Working closely with performance contractors to evaluate EBaR measures and limiting the extent of the savings guarantees can provide energy-efficiency investments that are more beneficial for both the facility owner and for the energy performance firm.

## SUMMARY

Energy cost savings are determined by reductions in energy use and the price paid for energy. This chapter describes determinants of electricity, natural gas, and fuel oil cost of service and pricing. The evolution of deregulation and competitive electric markets and electricity pricing products is described, and several comments are provided for energy customers who are new to purchasing electricity in deregulated markets.

Incentives to install energy-efficient equipment provided by utilities, states, and the federal government can significantly reduce project costs. Incentive payments offered by Southern California Edison are presented as an example of utility incentives.

Financing options are discussed. Long-term lease and lease-purchase agreements offered by equipment manufacturers, energy service companies and financial organizations provide a convenient form of financing that can significantly increase cash flow benefits of efficiency investments.

## CHAPTER 4

# Capital Budgeting: Theory and Practice

**C**apital budgeting is the process of determining which long-term projects should be undertaken. Energy-efficiency investments are typically considered part of the capital budgeting decision-making process. The capital budgeting analysis framework recommended in finance and managerial economics textbooks is the net present value method (NPV) that converts future costs and savings into current (that is, present) values to compare with the cost of the investment. Difficulties arise, however, when applying NPV analysis because of uncertainties associated with future values of variables used in the NPV calculations.

Decision makers have adapted to these NPV analysis difficulties by developing simpler decision-rules like payback analysis that are used along with or in place of NPV analysis. However, these simplified decision-rules can exclude many profitable efficiency investments, leading to underinvestment in energy efficiency technologies and excessive energy costs and budget volatility. Underinvestment in energy-efficiency options also means that opportunities to increase cash flow are being ignored.

Energy Budgets at Risk (EBaR) provides intuitive decision rules based on a risk management approach to capital budgeting analysis. To appreciate the advantages of the EBaR approach, it is useful to consider traditional NPV financial analysis, how traditional analysis attempts to address uncertainty and risk, and why payback is such a popular capital budgeting screening tool.

This chapter describes current practices in energy-efficiency capital budgeting.

## NET PRESENT VALUE AND IRR ANALYSIS

Net present value (NPV) analysis translates all costs and benefits associated with an investment to the present time to determine the desirability of making an investment. NPV concepts are described in this section.

### Time Value of Money

$100 today has a different value from $100 a year from now. $100 today can be invested in a high-yield savings account with a 5 percent interest rate, so its value in a year will be $105. If interest is compounded annually we also know that $100 today is equivalent to $110.25 ($105 at the end of the first year times 1.05 interest equals 110.25—with 25 cents the bonus from compounding) in two years.

Working backwards, any future amount, A, can be evaluated as a present value (or discounted to the present) with the following formula:

$$PV = A/(1.0 + i)^t \qquad (4.1)$$

Where $i$ is the interest rate and $t$ is the time period. The critical variable in this calculation is, of course, the interest rate, $i$. Different rates can be used when considering the time value of money for corporations, government agencies, or other organizations; however, this distinction is not important here. For now $i$ is considered to be a cost of capital, more specifically the cost of borrowing funds to pay for a capital investment.

The ability to discount future values and cash flows back to the present permits us to put any future amount or series of future amounts in present terms and compare their values to make financial decisions. Future values that have been discounted to the present are referred to as discounted values. The process of converting future values to present values is called discounting.

Discounting is an important element of financial analysis. Income streams with different time periods, mixed income streams, and income streams that begin one or two years in the future can all be discounted to their present value to provide a common basis for comparison.

### Net Present Value

Suppose an efficiency investment opportunity requires an initial investment of $I$ and provides annual energy budget savings of $S$. How do we know if the investment is attractive? The preferred approach taught in university finance and managerial economics courses is to proceed with the investment if the net present value (NPV) is greater than zero. NPV is defined as the sum of discounted savings minus the investment cost, that is:

$$\text{NPV} = \sum_{t=1}^{T} S/(1+i)^t - I \tag{4.2}$$

NPV is the present value of the savings *beyond* the cost of the investment. A negative net present value indicates that the investment will not pay for itself with savings while a positive NPV is the discounted or present value of the stream of savings beyond the cost of the initial investment. An NPV of $0 means the investment will return a discounted or present value exactly equal to the up-front investment cost, *I*. In this case the investor will be indifferent as to the investment.

If the NPV of an investment is greater than zero, finance theory designates it a good investment; however, if a limited amount of capital is available to invest and several different investment opportunities exist with different initial investment amounts, how can these investments be prioritized? For example, is an NPV of $1,000 on an initial investment of $4,500 with a lifetime of 5 years better than $5,000 on an investment of $9,500 with a lifetime of 10 years? The NPV of $5,000 obviously provides a greater return; however, how much of it is because of the larger initial investment or the longer lifetime?

## Internal Rate of Return (IRR)

Using another investment evaluation measure related to NPV solves this problem, but it requires considering investments from a slightly different perspective. Assume now the investment *I* is to be made in either the efficiency option or in an annuity that makes a uniform series of cash payments each year. An annuity is a series of fixed payments over a fixed period of time. Car payments and mortgage payments are the kind of annuity we will consider here—though in this case we will be receiving payments on our initial investment instead of making payments on an amount borrowed. Further assume that the lifetimes of the efficiency option and the annuity are the same and that the interest rate paid with the annuity option is known. To recap, the two investment options are:

1. Investment in an efficiency option that saves *S* yearly on an initial investment of *I*.
2. Investment in an annuity that will repay the initial investment plus interest over the term of the annuity.

Which investment should be chosen? To make the comparison, the effective interest rate represented by the investment in the efficiency option must be determined. In other words, if the efficiency investment is viewed as an annuity where payments are received in the form of energy budget savings over the term of the investment, an equivalent interest rate can be calculated and compared to the rate promised by the annuity.

The uniform-series capital-recovery factor equation can be used to determine the equivalent interest rate on the efficiency investment. The equation is

$$S = I^*[i/[1 - (1 + i)^{-T}]$$  (4.3)

Where $S$ is the savings, $I$ is the investment, $*$ is a multiplication operator, and the value of $i$ must be calculated using the equation. This is the same equation for calculating car and mortgage payments where an initial investment (the cost of the car) and an interest rate (i) are used to calculate the payment, $S$. In the efficiency application, however, an annual savings (S) and an initial investment (I) are used to determine the equivalent interest rate, $i$.

The calculated interest rate is called the internal rate of return (IRR). If the savings are large relative to the initial investment, the IRR is large. On the other hand, a poor investment will result in a low IRR.

The IRR now provides a useful measure to compare alternative efficiency investments. One can easily determine which investments are most profitable without having to adjust for size of the investments, savings, and investment lifetime (how long the equipment lasts): investments with higher IRRs are more profitable. Furthermore, the IRR can be compared to interest earned on other investments or to the cost of capital to determine if an investment is wise. An IRR of 10 percent is not a good investment if the cost of capital is 12 percent. On the other hand an IRR of 35 percent with a cost of capital of 12 percent reflects an annual profit of 23 percent on the original investment.

## IRR and NPV

The previous section defined the IRR as the equivalent rate of interest on an annuity that costs $I$ and pays $S$ each year for $T$ years. Greater annuity payments mean higher interest rates. That definition was presented first, because it is the most intuitive. However, an equivalent definition of IRR is the interest rate in Equation 4.2 required to make the NPV equal zero. That is, the IRR is the interest rate at which the investment would just break even. Thus, NPV and IRR analyses provide equivalent results when applied to determine the profitability of an investment, and NPV and IRR analyses are usually considered as interchangeable. The IRR measure is not without its deficiencies, however. For instance, a positive IRR can obscure the fact that returns on an investment can be negative for one or more periods, a fact that could enter into capital budgeting decisions. However, NPV and IRR investment analyses are considered acceptable approaches to consider capital budgeting decisions.

## Traditional Finance Theory and Uncertainty

The evaluation of capital budgeting presented so far is eminently reasonable—that is, an unassailable accounting framework that requires only a few calculations to determine the effectiveness of an energy-efficiency investment. The fly in the ointment when the theory is applied to actual investments is dealing with uncertainty that surrounds many of the variables in the calculations.

Before continuing, it is useful to recognize the distinction that some writers make between risk and uncertainty. Beginning with Frank Knight, one of the first economists to address risk and uncertainty in 1921, uncertainty is often used to characterize an outcome where there is no information available, distinguishing it from the term *risk,* which is associated with a process where some information on outcomes exists. This terminology is inconsistent with common applications of these terms; the terms *risk* and *uncertainty* are applied in this book consistent with the following more common usage. Risk is defined as the probability or likelihood of a negative outcome; for example, there is a risk associated with a specific energy-efficiency investment. *Uncertainty* means that the outcome is uncertain but not necessarily unquantifiable. That is, the statement that the commute time from office to home is uncertain does not mean that the time is unknowable, only that there are a variety of potential outcomes.

The first step in introducing uncertainty into capital budgeting analysis is to develop a way to represent variables whose outcome is uncertain. Savings associated with a new air conditioning system depend on the weather, among other factors. An engineering heat load model (an engineering model of a building that represents heat gains and losses) can be used to relate air conditioning electricity use to variations in weather variables. The model can then be applied with historical weather data to develop an estimate of the probability distribution of air conditioning electricity use based on the distribution of actual weather over the last 30 years. This process provides a distribution of likely air conditioning electricity savings. Equation 4.2, however, requires a single estimate of $S$, so the expected value, or average, of the savings ($E[S]$) is used in place of the single point estimate of the savings value, $S$. The resulting NPV is then also an expected value, $E[NPV]$.

The use of expected values provides little advantage in real world situations since the single savings value, $S$ of Equation 4.2, probably already reflected an expected value and NPV was probably being interpreted as an expected value as well. The other change in the NPV equation related to uncertainty is the addition of a risk premium, $r$, to the interest rate in the denominator that is used to discount future savings values. A positive value of $r$ increases the discount rate and reduces the value of future savings (the denominator is larger). Since the actual value of $S$ that will be realized is uncertain, $r$ must have a value greater than zero; otherwise a risky investment (one with a distribution of $S$ values) would have equal or greater value than a certain investment. A riskier investment will have a higher risk premium reducing the value of future savings to a greater extent than a less risky investment.

Considering the savings component as the only uncertain input in the NPV calculation provides the new NPV formulation:

$$E[\text{NPV}] = \sum_{t=1}^{T} E[S]/(1 + i + r)^{i} - I \qquad (4.4)$$

$E[.]$ denotes the expected or average value likely to occur and $r$ is a risk premium used to reflect risk associated with the investment. An investment is viewed as desirable if expected NPV is positive. Given the risk-averse nature of decision makers (a topic discussed in the next chapter) the term $r$ is expected to play a significant role in reducing the value of future savings associated with uncertain investments.

Applying this equation to investments, identical in every way except that savings associated with the second investment are more uncertain, provides a greater NPV for the first investment (the term $r$ in the denominator of the second investment is larger making the savings term smaller).

How does a decision maker apply this equation to evaluate an energy-efficiency investment? The standard textbook answer is that a discount rate (in this case $i + r$) comparable to returns on investments of equal risk should be applied in the NPV calculation. The problem, of course, is that investments of equal risk are difficult, if not impossible, to determine.

Traditional finance approaches to recognize risk are acknowledged as less than satisfactory by nearly all practitioners and by many academicians. For instance, a recommended alternative to including a risk factor in the discount rate is to adjust savings, $S$, by a "certainty equivalent factor" that reflects a reduction in the value of the savings because of the associated risk. Of course, specifying the certainty equivalence factor and risk premiums to be applied in the NPV equation requires "a large amount of judgement."[1]

## REAL OPTIONS—WHEN PROCRASTINATION PAYS

NPV and IRR analyses do not provide information on the value of waiting to make an irreversible investment. Efficiency investments are irreversible because the cost of removing an efficiency technology is usually prohibitive. That is, preserving the option to invest in the future has some value—hence there is a real options value to postponing an investment. If the real options value is negative, waiting to make a decision incurs costs as was the case with the grocery chain energy manager who was procrastinating on a decision to make even the most basic efficiency investments.

An example illustrates the real options issue. Assume a microturbine system installation, A, is being considered to provide power to an essential computer room with plans to use the waste heat in an absorption air conditioning system for the same room. The NPV analysis identifies a savings of $100 per year for the five-year life of the equipment, and the equipment will cost $200. The manufacturer of a competing microturbine system, B, is developing a new design that will increase the system's energy cost savings by 100 percent relative to system A with a system cost of $250. The manufacturer will have the system developed and verified by an independent laboratory and ready to install in one year. The manufacturer's representative confides, however, that the engineers feel there is a 50 percent chance that the system efficiency will improve by 100 percent and a 50 percent chance that the new system will provide the same efficiency as system A.

A real option analysis helps determine whether it is better to invest now or wait for a year to see if system B would be a smart choice. For system A the NPV is:

$$NPV = 92.59 + 85.73 + 79.38 + 73.50 + 68.06 - 200 = \$199.27$$
$$\text{(Option 1)}$$

Where the $100 per year savings is discounted by 8 percent per year (first year is divided by 1.08, second year by $1.08^2$, and so on). $200 is the initial cost paid at the outset so it is not discounted. The NPV shows a discounted net profit of $199.27.

What if the decision is delayed for a year? If system B turns out to have the same efficiency as A, system A will be chosen as originally planned because system B costs $50 more. The first year's savings of $92.59 will be lost and, because the present value of a $200 investment one year out is $185.19, the investment cost, in present terms, is $14.81 less. The NPV for this delayed decision is:

$$NPV = 0 + 85.73 + 79.38 + 73.50 + 68.06 + 63.02 - 185.19 = \$184.50$$
$$\text{(Option 2: choosing system A)}$$

However, if the system operates as manufacturer B claims, the NPV in that scenario is:

$$NPV = 0 + 171.47 + 158.77 + 147.01 + 136.12 + 126.04 - 231.48 = \$507.93$$
(Option 2: choosing system B)

Depending on the outcome of the next year's testing, the net present value of Option 2 will either be less or more than the NPV of Option 1. Since each of the Option 2 outcomes has a 50 percent probability of occurrence, the expected value of waiting a year is determined by multiplying each NPV in Option 2 by 0.5 to get a \$346.22. There is value to waiting to see how system B develops; the real option value is the difference in the two NPVs, \$146.95.

In order for real options values to come into play in capital budgeting, the investment must be irreversible and waiting one or more periods must eliminate some of the uncertainty associated with the decision.

Option values have an impact on energy-efficiency investments primarily with respect to postponing decisions:

- Regarding new technologies.
- In light of possible tax or other benefits that might be lost with current investments.
- To preserve capital for more urgent unforeseen uses.

This last item can be important. Investing in an irreversible asset given limited capital access means there is a cost associated with not having capital to use for other purposes that may have a greater bearing on the long-term financial health of the organization.

## CAPITAL BUDGETING IN PRACTICE

Considering the difficulties in applying recommended NPV analysis in practical applications, it is not surprising that most organizations use other capital budgeting analysis approaches in conjunction with or in place of NPV analysis. Capital budgeting includes investments in many different long-term investments in addition to energy efficiency including plant expansion, equipment upgrades, new market entry, and so on. An organization's general approach to capital budgeting analysis sets the stage for more specific applications like energy efficiency. This section provides information on general analysis approaches used by most organizations.

## Capital Budgeting Analysis Tools

A review of studies of corporate capital budgeting practices provided only two surveys specifically focused on energy-efficiency investments; however, a detailed series of case studies on energy-efficiency investment decision making indicates that energy-efficiency investments are viewed similarly to other investments that reduce operating cost.[2]

While results vary somewhat by study, payback (PB) analysis (investment cost divided by annual savings) clearly plays a preeminent role as a capital budgeting investment tool, used by from 56 to 94 percent of firms. These studies also indicate that most firms use multiple investment criteria with internal rate of return (IRR), NPV, and PB the three most-used analysis tools. The most thorough evaluation of multiple investment criteria use found that only 4 percent of firms used single investment criteria (all of those were PB), 28 percent used two, 32 percent used three, and 36 percent used four investment criteria. Of the surveyed firms that use more than one criterion, only 5 percent omit PB from their investment analysis.[3]

Available evidence indicates that PB analysis plays an even more prominent role in its application to evaluating energy-efficiency investments than other capital budgeting applications and that required payback thresholds are extremely short.

## Payback Analysis as Risk Filter

Payback (PB) analysis is used to limit risk associated with capital investments. Frank Lefley, who has studied capital budgeting practices in detail, found 71.5 percent of manufacturers in a 1994 survey said they use PB to limit risk while only 17.4 percent adjusted the discount rate in NPV analysis.[4] Ross's earlier series of 12 energy-efficiency case studies found a near unanimous use of PB in assessing energy-efficiency investments.

Why do organizations use the simplistic PB analysis rather the NPV analysis taught in business schools? The answer is that there is significant value, from a management perspective, in using simple, easy-to-apply rules-of-thumb as a risk-screening tool as long as the costs of simplifying the process are not too great.

The following sections show how risk is avoided with PB analysis and illustrate why the unrecognized costs of using PB for energy-efficiency analysis is so great.

**Why Organizations Use Payback**    How do you define risk? While definitions vary, an appropriate characterization for energy-efficiency investment analysis is the following: the probability of a negative outcome. An efficiency investment is risky if the probability of a negative outcome is great and not very risky if the probability of a negative outcome is more remote. More specifically the risk associated with a capital investment can be defined as the probability that the investment will provide an internal rate of return less than some required threshold such as the cost of capital, or a higher threshold, say 20 percent. A conceptual representation might look like the probability distribution of investment outcomes shown in Figure 4.1. The expected IRR is the engineering-based estimate, and the distribution might roughly represent experience with past projects, a judgmental expectation on variations likely to occur, or perhaps something as intuitive as "savings could be + or − 50 percent of the engineering estimate." If an organization's risk tolerance is 10 percent, meaning it is willing to take no more than a 10 percent chance that the investment will have a negative outcome (IRR < 20 percent), this investment would be rejected because, although its expected IRR is 40 percent, there is a 25 percent probability that the investment will end up achieving an IRR of less than 20 percent.

Recall from the section above on IRR and NPV that the internal rate of return of an investment can be determined by setting NPV equal to zero in Equation 4.2 and solving the resulting Equation 4.5 for the $i$ variable which is IRR.

$$I = \sum_{t=1}^{T} S/(1+i)^t \qquad (4.5)$$

The internal rate of return (IRR) reflects the energy cost savings as a comparable annualized rate of return on the initial investment. For example, a 20 percent IRR means savings are equal to the return earned on an annuity

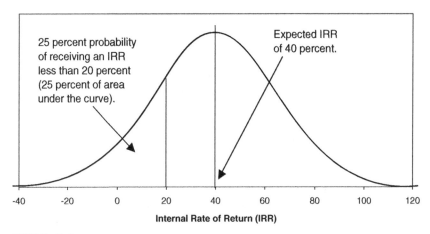

**FIGURE 4.1** Investment Outcomes

if the same amount of money were invested to be repaid at 20 percent compounded annually for the life of the efficiency investment.

Since PB (payback) is the investment amount divided by annual savings (PB = $I/S$), a unique relationship exists between PB and IRR for any investment time horizon, $T$. Consequently, for each IRR value on the horizontal axis of the probability distribution, there is a unique PB value.

What would the distribution look like for investments that just barely meet the risk tolerance of 10 percent and IRR threshold of 20 percent? Figure 4.2 shows this conceptual representation. The probability of achieving less than a 20 percent IRR (equivalent to a five-year payback) is just less than 10 percent (the area of the curve to the left of the 20 percent IRR). The expected value or engineering calculation in this case is an IRR of 70 percent (equivalent to a PB of about 15 months). In this situation, using a 15-month payback or a 70 percent IRR hurdle rate to evaluate energy-efficient investments actually reflects a desire to limit the risk of receiving a 20 percent or smaller IRR to less than 10 percent.

In this situation, simple payback results can be reliably used to screen efficiency investments based on risk analysis if:

1. All technologies have the same distribution of expected savings.
2. All technologies have the same lifetime (a unique relationship exists between payback and IRR only if the lifetime is fixed).

Assuming that these two conditions hold, an organization's use of a PB threshold to avoid risky projects is equivalent to rejecting projects based on the distribution of expected savings and the organization's risk tolerance. PB is also easy to understand and easy to compute, requiring only an estimate

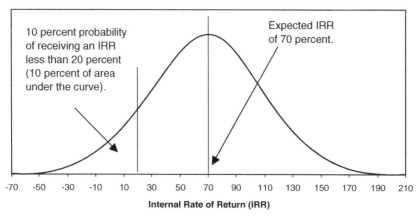

**FIGURE 4.2**  Acceptable Investment Savings Distribution

of initial costs and annual savings and it is an easy tool to use in prioritizing investments.

The problem with PB analysis is that the two assumptions required to make PB an accurate analytical tool are not fulfilled with most energy-efficiency investments.

**Why Payback Is a Bad Choice for Efficiency Investments**  Rules of thumb are never accepted as the most accurate analysis; consequently, they implicitly reflect a level of error that is acceptable to those who use them. While payback analysis (PB) may reflect reasonable screening criteria for some capital budgeting decisions, recent energy price increases and the availability of the large array of energy-efficient technologies result in an unacceptably high cost associated with its application as an energy-efficiency-screening tool.

As indicated in the previous section, PB is a perfect proxy for evaluating efficiency-investment risk only if technologies have the same lifetimes and display the same distribution of energy savings. Given the wide array of efficiency technologies, variations in energy prices by fuel type, equipment lifetimes, and other details in an efficiency-investment decision, PB is an exceedingly poor tool to use in addressing investment risk.

More specifically, PB-based risk analysis suffers from a number of deficiencies, whose importance has grown in recent years, including:

- PB does not consider savings beyond the PB threshold. For instance, PB analysis would not distinguish between a fluorescent lamp that has a life of 20,000 hours versus one with a life of 30,000 hours.
- PB provides no information on the nature of investment risk.
- PB risk analysis implicitly assumes all investments reflect the same distribution of outcomes.
- PB, like all rules of thumb, is designed for worst case scenarios.

The last two deficiencies are illustrated in Figure 4.3 where a new technology has been added to the general distribution represented in Figure 4.2 above. The new technology has an expected payback that is longer (1.65 versus 1.25 years or 15 months) and a lower expected IRR (60 percent rather than 70 percent); however, the smaller variation in outcomes provides a more peaked distribution with the result that there is less risk associated with the new investment than the threshold investment described earlier: there is only a 2.3 percent probability that the IRR will be lower than 20 percent. However, the new technology will be rejected as an investment because its expected values are an inaccurate translation to its risk profile.

High and volatile energy prices, an expansive array of energy-efficiency technologies, the value of excluded investments because of a worst-case

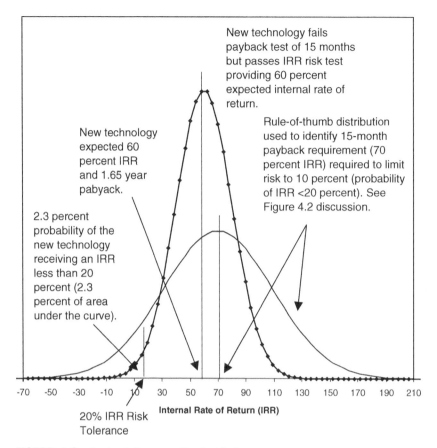

New technology fails payback test of 15 months but passes IRR risk test providing 60 percent expected internal rate of return.

New technology expected 60 percent IRR and 1.65 year pabyack.

Rule-of-thumb distribution used to identify 15-month payback requirement (70 percent IRR) required to limit risk to 10 percent (probability of IRR <20 percent). See Figure 4.2 discussion.

2.3 percent probability of the new technology receiving an IRR less than 20 percent (2.3 percent of area under the curve).

20% IRR Risk Tolerance

**Internal Rate of Return (IRR)**

**FIGURE 4.3** Payback Bypasses Profitable Investments

threshold design, and the inability of PB to directly assess or measure risk make PB an ineffective tool to manage investment risk and a significant source of operating cost losses.

## Other Traditional Risk Analysis Approaches

Other analysis frameworks are sometimes used to limit investment risk. Advantages and disadvantages of some of these alternatives are discussed below.

**IRR Hurdle Rates.** A traditional approach to dealing with risk is to compare the internal rate of return (IRR) based on an engineering estimate of savings and current energy prices, to a high hurdle rate (for example, a 50 percent rate). The investment is considered further if the IRR estimate is greater than the hurdle rate. While this approach improves on PB analysis in considering savings beyond the payback period, it suffers from most of the other problems associated with payback analysis detailed in the preceding section. That is, it provides little information on the nature of risk, implicitly assumes all investments reflect the same distribution of outcomes and is designed for worst case scenarios.

**NPV with Risk-Adjusted Discount Rates.** In practice this approach is rarely used as a primary risk evaluation tool. Determining the appropriate risk premium for efficiency investments is, at best, problematic.

**Scenario And Sensitivity Analysis.** While scenario and sensitivity analyses are often used in other financial analysis, their application to evaluate efficiency investment uncertainty using alternative operating and energy price assumptions is rare. The extensive presentation of decision variables and outcome distributions typically provided as analysis outcomes is incompatible with a general preference by decision makers for simple decision rules.

## SUMMARY

Today's energy markets are considerably more challenging than those that existed before the first oil embargo in 1973; however, efficiency investment analysis approaches have changed little in the intervening years. Factors that should be explicitly incorporated in energy-efficiency capital budgeting decisions include:

- Uncertainty associated with energy prices.
- A comprehensive consideration of energy-efficiency options.
- Uncertainty associated with energy-efficiency operating characteristics.
- Electric utility rate structures.
- Incentives from utilities, state, and federal sources including tax incentives.
- Opportunities to use financial hedges (for larger organizations).
- Efficiency choices integrated with competitive energy purchase decisions (for organizations in deregulated markets).

Traditional net present value analysis advocated in finance and managerial economics textbooks is incapable of adequately addressing most of these issues, which explains the prevalent use of payback and other rule-of-thumb approaches, such as high IRR hurdle rates to screen energy-efficiency investments for risk. Following chapters show how an application of EBaR provides a comprehensive framework to address each of these issues.

## CHAPTER 5

# Facility Energy Risk Management Foundations

**R**isk management (RM) is the process of evaluating risk, considering alternatives to address the risk, developing a strategy, and implementing appropriate procedures. Continuous evaluation and revision are required to keep risk management strategies current. Enterprise risk management (ERM) includes management of an organization's risk ranging from accidental loss to strategic risks associated with external threats to the organization. ERM is increasingly being viewed as an important part of management policies and chief risk officer positions, which are common in financial businesses, are beginning to appear in other industries. Energy risk management is a subset of general business risks that include demand for products or services, costs of inputs, and production, and related activities.[1]

Risk and risk management objectives must be quantified to develop a formal energy risk management framework such as EBaR. The development and application of probability distributions, described in Chapter 7, provide the quantitative building blocks used to assess energy budget and investment risk. Before beginning the application of these quantitative elements in EBaR analysis, it is useful to consider the historical development of financial risk management. Events that moved financial risk management to its current state have recent counterparts in the area of facility energy management. Understanding how financial risk management practices developed provides insight on the transformation that awaits the facility energy management field. This review of the development of the most widely used risk measure, value at risk (VaR), also provides important insights on risk measure characteristics required to provide both analytical rigor and management decision-making acceptance.

The remainder of this chapter discusses the applicability of risk management to capital budgeting and the development of financial risk management. The chapter ends with discussion of energy efficiency value at risk application issues.

## CAPITAL BUDGETING AND RISK MANAGEMENT

The discussion of capital budgeting analysis in Chapter 4 makes it clear that investment risk is typically not incorporated in a formal way in many capital budgeting analyses. Many capital budgeting decisions involve a variety of uncertainties that are difficult to quantify. For instance, expanding a production line might require considering domestic and international product demand, competitor pricing, competitor strategies and other factors. Formal comprehensive quantitative frameworks provide less value in these situations where judgment and qualitative factors are so difficult to quantify. There is limited value in attempting to quantify relationships that, by necessity, include a large component of judgment based on industry and other experience.

Capital budgeting decisions related to facility energy efficiency investments are considerably more focused than most investment decisions and therefore much more amenable to formal risk analysis. For instance, an energy-efficiency investment provides a more efficient use of energy and lower facility operating cost. The return on this investment does not depend on product demand or competitor strategies; as long as the facility operates, the investment will provide a return consistent with the quantitative relationships that comprise an energy risk management analysis.

Consequently, facility energy efficiency investment reflects an unusual opportunity, within the broad scope of capital budgeting applications, to apply quantitative financial risk management techniques. It was exactly this insight that prompted my efforts to develop the EBaR analysis framework.

## A BRIEF HISTORY OF FINANCIAL RISK ANALYSIS (VaR)

The development of financial analysis using tools based on probability distributions is a remarkable story; development of analysis techniques revolutionized an entire industry and helped spawn new financial products and services. This transformation began in the same year as the first energy embargo in 1973. This initial date is of interest because it reflects the first year that a transformation should have begun in financial analysis of energy-efficiency investments. The last section in this chapter includes a discussion of some of the issues that explain why energy-efficiency related financial innovation failed to materialize.

A brief overview of the history and development of one of the most important financial risk management class of tools, Value at Risk (VaR), puts probability distribution applications in a real-world context and at the same time projects the application of these principles to energy risk. VaR measures are defined here as a statistic that can be applied to measure the risk associated with a portfolio of financial investments. More specifically, the present-day definition of VaR is the worst loss expected from a portfolio over a specific time period, given a probability of occurrence or confidence level. A daily VaR of $1 million at a 99 percent confidence level means the probability is no more than 1 percent that the portfolio will sustain losses of $1 million within the next day. Figure 5.1 graphically illustrates this distribution of profits associated with holding a portfolio over for a day.

The application of a VaR approach in EBaR is apparent from the description of the three primary EBaR statistics described in earlier chapters. The $EBaR_{budget}$ statistic shows the largest expected energy budget variance (difference between the expected budget and actual) at a given confidence level, $EBaR_{IRR}$ shows the smallest expected internal rate of return at a given confidence level, while $EBaR_{netsave}$ shows the smallest expected net savings (savings after investment financing costs are deducted).

VaR representations have evolved over time, as the historical summary below indicates. Each step in the development of today's VaR representations has been an attempt to provide an improved quantitative, intuitive measure of investment risk.

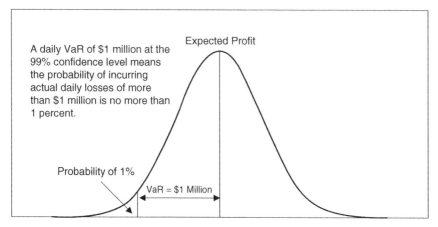

**FIGURE 5.1** Value at Risk

## Setting the Stage

The interest in and development of VaR grew out of the stock market crash in 1973–1974. The framework for this development; however, had been developed much earlier and is detailed below.

**Early Portfolio Theory**  Portfolio theory describes how investors can optimize their portfolios by diversifying investments and how assets should be priced to reflect risk. Several intuitive discussions of portfolio diversification appeared in the literature in the 1920s and 1930s; however, the first quantitative example did not appear until 1945 in a nontechnical paper.[2]

It wasn't until 1952 when Harry Markowitz, a young graduate student at the University of Chicago, published a paper entitled "Portfolio Selection" that a mathematical or quantitative solution was provided to guide development of an efficient portfolio that maximizes returns subject to some level of risk.[3] This process is achieved through diversification of investments within a portfolio. A portfolio with assets on the "efficiency frontier" can achieve no greater returns unless the portfolio owner accepts a greater level of risk. Markowitz used the statistical variance of return as a measure of risk in his quantitative analysis. Portfolio Selection provided a quantitative way of incorporating risk and return in a consistent mathematical representation that could be used to evaluate investment portfolios. Markowitz published a book in 1959 providing more details on how to apply his optimization process. Portfolio Selection (also the name of the book) provided the groundwork for most of the achievements in financial risk management. Markowitz received a Nobel prize for his work in 1990.

Application of the analysis was difficult without the benefit of a computer, so widespread recognition and use of Markowtiz's approach awaited both computing power and a market nudge in the early 1970s.

**Volatility and Derivatives**  The stock market crash that began in December 1972 and continued to September 1974 decimated the market. The Standard & Poor's 500 index fell 43 percent. Loss in equity values reached 50 percent. Prior to the 1973–1974 crash, risk was not a priority concern in portfolio market management strategy. Huge losses by some previously high-flying funds changed that focus.

A number of other events created substantial new risks that were not particularly worrisome in previous years. The Bretton Woods system was established near the end of World War II (1944) to regulate the international monetary system. The system required each country to maintain exchange rates within a 1 percent range. The Bretton Woods agreement collapsed in 1971, allowing exchange rates to float creating significant new foreign exchange volatility.

The first OPEC oil embargo shocked energy markets in 1973; natural gas markets were partially deregulated beginning in 1978. Both events ushered in the current period of energy price volatility.

Inflation and U.S. monetary policies beginning in the 1970s helped generate new volatility in interest rates, prices, and a variety of financial instruments.

This new environment of volatility increased the demand for financial instruments to manage risk. The market for derivatives provides a mechanism for organizations to transfer risk to those who are willing and able to accept the risk. Derivatives are financial instruments whose value is based on the value of another asset. Derivatives include futures contracts to buy or sell at some date in the future and options contracts that provide the right but not the obligation to buy or sell at a prespecified price during some time period. The Chicago Mercantile Exchange which has traded agricultural futures for more than one hundred years introduced financial futures contracts. Currency futures in 1972 were followed by Treasury bill, bond, currency, and many other futures.

The New York Mercantile Exchange established the first market for heating oil futures in 1978, followed by gasoline futures in 1981 and crude oil futures in 1983. Natural gas and electricity futures and related instruments such as weather derivatives have been introduced to help manage energy commodity price risk.

It wasn't until Fischer Black and Myron Scholes published a seminal paper on a procedure for pricing financial options in 1973 that options pricing reflected a mathematical process based in part on an application of the normal probability density function described in Chapter 7.

Peter Bernstein in his engaging narrative on risk[4] notes the coincidence of the Chicago Board Options Exchange (CBOE) opening a month prior to the Black and Scholes publication and the introduction of a hand-held calculator that could perform the calculations required with the Black-Sholes model. The CBOE was the first to provide options traders with standardized contracts and a market for trading and market regulation.

The new world of volatility in foreign exchange markets, interest rates, inflation, commodity prices, including energy, and the mathematical framework required to evaluate and price risk options set the stage for development of quantitative risk management techniques and tools. The computing power to support analysis (especially the introduction of the PC and smaller servers beginning in the early 1980s) and growth of the financial data industry that provides historical price data for use in the new quantitative tool applications provided inputs to the process. The increased demand for protection from volatility matched by an increasing supply of agents willing to assume risk has propelled the U.S. derivatives market to a total U.S. value of $145 trillion as of the first quarter 2007.[5]

## Modern VaR Statistics

In the 1970s and 1980s as the derivative markets grew and quantitative applications to portfolio and derivative analysis became more common, the importance of quantitative risk measures became more obvious. In 1975 the SEC used a rudimentary VaR analysis in updating its capital requirements for securities firms. The objective was to make sure firms held sufficient assets to meet obligations to their customers. In meeting capital requirements, percentage adjustments were made to various classes of securities to reflect a cushion against market losses if the assets had to be liquidated. In 1980, percentages were updated to cover losses that might be incurred in a 30-day liquidation period based on historical data analysis at a 95 percent confidence level. These statistics reflected a VaR application consistent with modern applications. Individual financial organizations refined and extended the SEC statistics developing proprietary VaR statistics.

In the early 1990s, JP Morgan developed a VaR system that used historical data and aggregated information across the entire firm to develop a variety of VaR measures. One of the measures computed a one-day VaR at a 95 percent confidence level based on a normal probability density function (see Chapter 7 for a discussion of normal probability density functions).

JP Morgan publicized its risk management applications through a service called RiskMetrics beginning in 1994 and is considered to have been the primary vehicle through which VaR was publicized in the early 1990s.

Banks, investment companies, hedge funds, and other financial organizations have developed their own proprietary VaR analysis. The refinement of technical components of VaR-related analysis is an active area of research by both academics and research department staff in financial organizations.

VaR measures have become institutionalized through U.S. and international regulation of banks and other financial institutions. VaR is the most widely recognized class of risk management tools.

VaR has its share of critics, often with respect to technical implementation issues. Some critics complain that VaR provides a single statistic that is subject to errors that are not apparent and that VaR provides misleading information by collapsing risk concerns to a single statistic. This argument that VaR oversimplifies risk management is actually a criticism of one of VaR's greatest strengths: the ability to synthesize a risk measure that is intuitive and can provide information in a way that decision makers can understand and use as a basis for action. There are certainly arguments to

## ENERGY EFFICIENCY AS A PORTFOLIO PROBLEM

EBaR recasts energy efficiency investment analysis as a portfolio problem, where the portfolio consists of energy-using technologies and financial risk management tools can be applied to evaluate portfolio optimization.

be made that many other dimensions of risk should be considered; however, one of the greatest challenges in applying information on risk is to present a metric that decision makers understand and feel comfortable applying. VaR and its related risk measures appear to have evolved as the best approach to including critical information in an intuitive decision variable.

VaR provides organizations with a way to evaluate and measure risk, specify acceptable levels of risk, balance financial decisions throughout organizations based on risk tolerance, and respond to market information on changes in risk exposure.

## APPLYING A VaR APPROACH TO FACILITY ENERGY RISK MANAGEMENT

The stock market crash of 1973–1974 and the oil embargo of 1973 were both defining moments in the development of financial and energy markets, respectively. Financial markets embarked on a frenetic path developing new tools and ways of dealing with risk while facility energy management continued with traditional practices and never effectively incorporated risk in addressing energy efficiency investments.

One must ask why energy risk management analysis did not develop along paths parallel to those in the financial industry and what is the potential for an energy risk management framework like EBaR in light of limited energy risk management activity of the past?

More specifically, this section discusses the following questions:

- What are the quantitative requirements for providing meaningful energy risk management decision-making information, and are these applications feasible?

- If a quantitative risk management application is feasible, what impediments have kept energy risk management from developing? Can these impediments be removed?
- What is the prognosis for development of facility energy risk management as a standard best practice?

## Quantitative Requirements/Feasibility

The quantitative application of an energy risk management process can be defined as an empirical process that characterizes and evaluates:

1. Energy budget risk represented as a distribution of energy cost outcomes.
2. The distribution of efficiency investment returns and risks associated with alternative investment strategies.
3. In competitive markets, risks and rewards of alternative energy purchase options.

The quantitative applications required to support these objectives are no more difficult, and in many ways easier, than their financial industry counterparts. Distributions of variables that affect energy costs and efficiency investment returns are applied in the same way as in financial analysis. There are no technical impediments to implementing a quantitative energy risk management analysis based on Value at Risk methodologies.

## Impediments

If there are no technical impediments to developing a facility energy risk management program along the lines of financial Value at Risk analysis, one must ask why energy risk management analysis has not developed along a parallel path. A follow-up question is: What is the potential for an energy risk management framework like EBaR in light of limited energy risk management activity of the past?

The following factors are important in explaining the lagging development of facility energy risk management and identifying issues that should be addressed in implementing an EBaR strategy.

**A VaR Application Is Not Obvious**   Value at Risk (VaR) is defined as a risk management tool for liquid assets like stocks, bonds, and derivatives. The response to a deteriorating risk position is to sell assets that have made the portfolio too risky. VaR analysis is not intuitively viewed as applicable to irreversible investments like lighting retrofits.

Energy efficiency investments are real, irreversible assets that are different from liquid assets because the investment cannot be sold if it is performing poorly. Risk analysis, in this case, must be modified to consider the "real option" value of postponing the investment decision for some time period, if there is likely to be more information in the future that narrows the uncertainty associated with the investment return.

Including the value of real options in a facility energy risk management application is a logical extension of the basic VaR analysis.

**Energy Is Viewed Like Other Operating Costs—Not as a New Revenue Source**   Energy costs are considered part of operating costs and are not usually considered investment opportunities that can generate income. Most operating costs can be reduced only with reduced services or negotiating lower-cost contracts. However, energy costs are different. Profitable investments increase revenue by reducing energy costs more than the amortized cost of the investment. Thus energy efficiency reflects an overlooked source of revenue. While this concept is generally accepted at a conceptual level, it is not typically viewed or pursued as a revenue opportunity.

**No Framework Has Been Available to Guide Efficiency Risk Management** JP Morgan's RiskMetrics was instrumental in establishing VaR as a risk management tool. No similar resource has been available to show energy and financial managers how to develop and apply risk management techniques to minimize energy costs, subject to organizational risk tolerance. The objective of *Energy Budgets at Risk* is to provide such a resource.

**Lack of Incentives**   Financial firms profit by virtue of savvy investment decisions, and decision makers are well compensated for making good investments. Individuals in most organizations have little incentive to pursue efficiency investments beyond the sure-thing criteria and as pointed out below, suffer from a variety of disincentives. Consequently, there has been little motivation from within organizations to adopt energy risk management strategies for efficiency investments.

**Hidden Costs of Inaction**   Energy costs are obvious; however, costs of inaction with respect to energy efficiency investments are not obvious. The opportunity costs of missed investment opportunities are hardly ever recognized.

**Benchmarking Difficulties**   Uncertainty over energy costs savings contributes to procrastination and inaction. Energy use and potential energy savings are difficult to benchmark. Every building has different uses, operating hours, internal loads, and other factors that make it difficult to assess how the energy management function is working within an organization.

The appendix in this book provides the first source of national energy use and energy savings benchmarks. These data are based on analysis of over one million businesses, institutions, and government agencies.

**Energy Management Has Not Been a Priority**   Until the high and volatile energy prices of recent years and recent concerns over environmental issues, energy management has not been a priority for most organizations. Attempting to reduce energy costs and manage energy risk is a relatively new experience for most organizations.

No framework has existed to guide organizations in considering energy analysis or risk management, so energy decisions continue to be made as they were three decades ago.

**Individual Risk Behavior and Agency Problems**   This inability to evaluate investment risk accurately then leads to greater risk aversion in individual decision making than most organizations desire. When decision makers' interests diverge from the organization's interest, an agency problem is said to exist. Both of these problems limit efficiency investment decision-making.

**Individual Risk-Averse Behavior**   The concept of the rational economic agent has so permeated business and management fields that only recently has there been general recognition of the fact that individuals react to risk in ways that can be very different than predicted by traditional business management practices.

Many of the revelations of research in finance behavior help explain why individual decision makers are reluctant to consider energy efficiency.[6] Individuals are risk averse, fear failure to a greater extent than they embrace success, are most comfortable following simple decision rules, respond to incentives in different ways depending on how the incentive is presented, value the status quo in unexpected ways, and so on. Uncertainty creates a desire to procrastinate, and hunches are often used to guide decision making.

While many of these tendencies are no surprise to experienced managers, these observations help explain the reluctance of energy and financial managers to invest in energy efficiency, given the uncertainty surrounding such investments. The lack of a risk assessment framework for energy efficiency capital budgeting discourages managers and staff from pursuing efficiency investments and promotes the natural tendency towards risk-averse behavior.

Incentives to promote risk-neutral decisions and guidelines to protect an energy manager from the vagaries of uncontrollable factors, such as weather deviations in the year following an HVAC investment, are both required to encourage behavior that reflects the best interests of the organization.

**Agency Problems**   Principals empower agents to act in their behalf. A corporation empowers its officers to act on its behalf to maximize profits; a building owner empowers the energy manager to make energy-efficiency investments to benefit the owner. As long as the agent's interests are aligned with the principal's, this relationship works well, providing expert decision making at the agent level. When agent interests and actions diverge from the principal's, an agency or principal-agent problem exists. For instance, managers are evaluated annually and, if performing well, may expect to receive promotions and new positions within several years; so there is an incentive to invest only in projects that can pay off in the short term.

The lack of employee incentives tied to profitable energy efficiency investments and lack of accountability for bypassed investment reinforce the natural tendency to avoid sticking your neck out. With current approaches to capital budgeting for energy efficiency, investments that are never made reflect an uncertain opportunity cost that is difficult to calculate and unlikely to be evaluated after the fact. Unless the avoided investment is obvious, avoiding an efficiency investment incurs little cost for the decision maker and avoids all risks associated with the investment.

Agency problems can be difficult to assess and rectify because the agent typically has more information on the problem—information that would be difficult for the manager to obtain and evaluate. This is especially true with modern energy-efficient technologies.

Effective energy risk management programs must specifically address individual risk-adverse behavior and agency problems.

### Overestimating Efforts Required to Reduce Uncertainty   Greater uncertainty leads to more risk-averse choices. When the cost of reducing uncertainty is smaller than benefits of making a decision with more information, an investment in reducing uncertainty is desirable.

A problem arises with these calculations when the decision maker knows little about the process required to resolve the uncertainty. Individuals are uncomfortable attempting to synthesize information on unfamiliar topics. The cost of gaining sufficient additional information to make better decisions is unknown until after the effort has been expended; however, the required level of effort is typically overestimated. The feeling of not knowing enough to know what to ask makes the information development process seem more complicated than it really is.

Using a contractor or consulting engineer to reduce decision-related uncertainty carries its own set of additional concerns. What is the cost? How reliable are the results, and so on. Faced with potential difficulties of learning more about the decision factors, decision makers usually fall short in gaining information desirable in making decisions.

The retail grocery energy manager described in Chapter 1 suffered from this reluctance to develop a more knowledgeable decision framework, which contributed to his reluctance to make a decision. An effective approach when one is facing the kind of information overload the energy manager was facing is to select one of the most important end uses (lighting or refrigeration in this case), develop information on technologies associated with the end use, and use EBaR to make efficiency investment decisions with this more limited problem definition. While there are some drawbacks associated with this focused analysis, it provides an approach that can more manageably reduce uncertainty and decision-making procrastination.

## PROGNOSIS

All of the impediments listed above can be addressed by:

- Evaluating potential benefits and costs of applying an EBaR strategy using information in this book, including the energy and cost saving benchmarking evaluations in the Appendix.
- Modifying relevant organizational factors to address the issues described in the previous section.
- Implementing an EBaR strategy.

Organizational changes related to agency and incentive issues that align organizational energy investment goals with goals of managers and staffs are especially important. Project-related financial incentives are an important strategy and can be designed in several ways including an energy efficiency commission based on energy savings. In addition to providing benefits for achieving efficiency improvements, responsibility for failing to take advantage of bypassed opportunities should also be included in a management strategy.

Useful management strategies are easier to envision if the concept of an energy manager as an investment advisor is considered. As an energy efficiency investment advisor, the energy manager is given increased authority and increased accountability. An efficiency investment manager should earn greater compensation for better investments and should stand ready to justify bypassed investments.

The history of VaR development described in earlier sections in this chapter reflects the interaction of a large number of forces that transformed an entire industry over 30 years. While many developments in the financial sector seem more dramatic than those relating to facility energy management, they are similar in many ways.

Similarities include:

- Volatility in energy prices, unprecedented price levels.
- New efficiency technologies (compare to new financial instruments in the form of new derivatives).
- Availability of price and other analysis-required data.
- Adequate computing power.
- Availability of EBaR, an analytical process that applies analysis vetted in the financial industry.
- Recent real options analysis developments.
- Significant cost penalties for organizations that ignore energy risk.
- Large returns available to market players who take advantage of these new resources.
- The widely-held view that there is an urgent need to better address energy-efficiency investments.

The motivations, incentives, and capabilities are now available to transform the traditional practice of facility energy-efficiency investment and energy purchase analysis into a modern risk management process.

How soon will facility energy risk management take hold? The fact that all of these components exist at one time, rather than representing a progression of developments over many years suggests that facility energy efficiency and energy purchase decision making could be rapidly transformed.

Increased focus on efficiency investment benefits associated with a strained electric utility delivery system and the desire to reduce greenhouse gas emissions, especially carbon footprint reductions and carbon trading, can be expected to accelerate the move to facility energy risk management.

## SUMMARY

Risk management (RM) is the process of evaluating risk, considering alternatives to address the risk, developing a strategy and implementing procedures. Most capital budgeting problems include factors that are difficult to quantify and are thus less amenable to quantitative risk management analysis. Energy-efficiency investments provide a unique opportunity to apply quantitative approaches developed in financial risk management. The historical development of the primary financial risk management analytical tool, Value at Risk (VaR) is presented in this chapter to illustrate similarities in developments in financial markets and today's energy markets.

Factors that have impeded development of quantitative risk management approaches in facility energy managements are discussed. Today's high and volatile energy prices, significant financial impacts on many organizations' financial health, and the availability of EBaR as a new tool to assist in managing energy risk lay the groundwork for rapid adoption of quantitative energy risk management solutions. Electric utility focus on increasing customer efficiency and increased interest in reducing carbon emissions is likely to play an important role in promoting the application of facility energy risk management.

## CHAPTER 6

# EBaR Concepts and Results

**O**ne reason that VaR applications are so widely used is their ability to concisely define and present the dimensions of risk most important to decision makers. A successful energy risk management analysis must translate energy risk analysis into similarly intuitive decision variables. This chapter presents EBaR reports that are designed to serve decision makers in evaluating energy budget risk and energy-efficiency investments.

The first section provides a conceptual review of EBaR analysis results from which the information in the report is drawn. The second section translates those concepts into items designed for management decision making.

## ENERGY BUDGETS AT RISK (EBaR) OVERVIEW

EBaR is a new quantitative approach to evaluate energy-efficiency investments, using modern risk management tools developed in the financial sector. For organizations in competitive energy markets, EBaR can also incorporate energy purchase decisions providing an integrated investment-purchase analysis. This competitive market extension to energy purchases is provided in Chapter 11 after basic EBaR applications are presented.

For most organizations, the EBaR process can be expected to reduce energy costs by 20 to 30 percent after paying for costs of the investments amortized over their lifetimes. That is, organizations can expect to increase cash flow by an amount equal to between 20 and 30 percent of current energy costs.

The recommendations of traditional capital budgeting analysis, as taught in university finance and managerial economics courses (net present value analysis), were shown in Chapter 4 to be unsatisfactory in practical situations where there is uncertainty over future energy prices, energy cost savings, and other factors. Traditional methods such as requiring low paybacks or high internal rates of return (IRR) were also shown to perform poorly as risk filters because they exclude many profitable investments.

EBaR replaces risk avoidance of traditional approaches with risk management that achieves savings consistent with each organization's risk tolerance.

Rather than using point estimates of variables that are important in investments analysis (for example, future electricity prices) each variable is represented by a probability distribution that shows the probability of each possible outcome. Monte Carlo analysis, a widely used analytical technique, is applied to calculate the probability distribution of energy budgets and energy-efficiency investment outcomes based on distributions of variables applied in these calculations.

EBaR provides information on two separate dimensions of energy risk. The first is energy budget risk; that is, risk associated with the current composition of energy-using technologies in a facility under current operating conditions. The second risk dimension reflects risk associated with specific energy-efficiency investments. This second application area utilizes information on the efficient technology costs, monthly and hourly energy use reductions, energy prices and rate structures, weather, operating characteristics, and other variables.

EBaR provides three primary decision variables:

$EBaR_{budget}$ describes current energy budget risk

$EBaR_{irr}$ and $EBaR_{netsav}$ assess the return on new energy-efficiency investments

## Energy Budgets: $EBaR_{budget,x}$

$EBaR_{budget,x}$ is the budget form of the EBaR statistic showing the largest expected energy budget variance (difference between the expected budget and actual costs) at a given confidence level, x, typically, 90 or 95 percent.

Every decision variable reflects some degree of uncertainty. Traditional measures typically ignore the uncertainty aspect, while risk management approaches attempt to quantify and provide decision makers with information on the level of uncertainty associated with a decision variable. As this and following chapters illustrate, this quantification provides considerably more information relevant to the decision process than single-point estimates of payback and internal rate of return.

## VARIANCE DEFINITIONS

The statistical term **variance** refers to the spread of a probability distribution as described in the following chapter.

The term **budget variance** refers to the variation of actual energy costs from budgeted costs.

*Variance* used in this book as a single term always refers to the statistical distribution spread; deviations of energy cost from budgeted cost is referred to only as *budget variance*.

EBaR$_{budget,x}$ is calculated using distributions of all important variables that impact energy costs including weather, energy prices, operating conditions, and other factors.

Figure 6.1 shows an expected budget of $100,000 along with a distribution of other budget outcomes that may occur. The area under portions of the distribution, relative to the total area under the curve, shows the

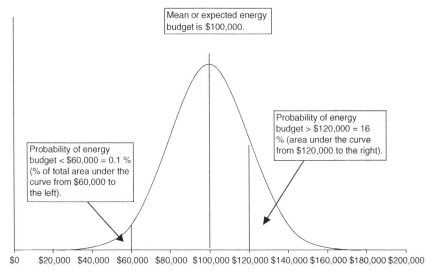

**FIGURE 6.1** Distribution of Likely Energy Budget Outcomes

probability that an outcome will occur between any two points on the energy budget axis as shown for energy budgets of less than $60,000 and more than $120,000 in Figure 6.1.

The development and application of EBaR budget analysis is described in detail in Chapters 8 and 9.

## Efficiency Investments: EBaR$_{irr,x}$ and EBaR$_{netsav,x}$

EBaR$_{irr,x}$ is an investment form of the EBaR statistic showing the smallest expected investment internal rate of return (IRR) at a given confidence level, x, typically, 90 or 95 percent. EBaR$_{netsav,x}$ is the smallest net savings (energy cost savings minus amortized cost of the equipment, including financing costs) at a given confidence level, x (usually the same confidence level as reported for EBaR$_{irr,x}$). The internal rate of return (IRR) and the net savings are the two most important variables considered in the investment decisions. Net savings reflect the "profit" associated with the project; an important answer to the question "is the project worthwhile?" The net savings statistic provides a way to evaluate project benefits with costs that are not explicitly included in EBaR$_{irr}$ including expenses associated with management evaluation, contracting and purchasing functions, and other overhead expenses, along with potential operational disruptions and other hidden project costs. Projects with high EBaR$_{irr}$ and low EBaR$_{netsav}$ may not provide enough savings to offset indirect costs that are not included explicitly in the investment cost.

EBaR$_{irr,x}$ and EBaR$_{netsav,x}$ are calculated using information on the variation of all important variables that impact the return on energy-efficiency investments including weather, energy prices, and operating conditions, along with potential variations in energy use and cost characteristics of efficiency technologies.

EBaR$_{irr,x}$ and EBaR$_{netsav,x}$ analysis is applied to evaluate new energy-efficient investments such as replacing existing fluorescent ballasts and lamps with new high-efficiency products. Future variations in electric price and uncertainty over the number of hours that each fixture will operate result in a distribution of likely returns on this investment. EBaR$_{irr,x}$ provides the internal rate of return achieved with the new technology. EBaR$_{netsav,x}$ provides net savings achieved with the new technology.

Figure 6.2 shows the hypothetical distribution of annual savings reflecting potential variations in electricity price and operating hours used as an example in Chapter 1. The investment cost is $80,000, expected annual savings are $40,000, and the annual finance cost to pay for the investment over ten years at 12 percent interest is about $14,000 with an expected annual net savings of $26,000. The payback for this investment is two years, a

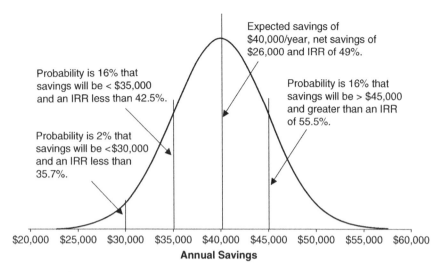

**FIGURE 6.2** Hypothetical Lighting Investment Analysis

value that might disqualify this investment in traditional efficiency screening analysis. At the expected value, the internal rate of return is 49 percent. The $EBaR_{irr,x}$ investment distribution shows there is only a 2 percent probability that the savings will be less than $30,000 per year with a corresponding internal rate of return on this outcome of 35.7 percent, well beyond the cost of capital. With 12 percent financing, the probability that cash flows (net savings) will be less than $16,000 per year is only 2 percent.

The lighting efficiency investment described in the previous paragraph is clearly attractive and presumably will be undertaken. The impact of the new investment on the total energy budget is determined with the EBaR budget analysis, $EBaR_{budget,x}$. Subtracting the annual amortized cost of the investment from the annual energy savings and applying the same calculations used to develop the energy budget distribution in Figure 6.1 provides a new distribution of expected energy budgets (Figure 6.3).

Expected energy cost savings are $40,000. Subtracting the amortized cost of financing the investment yields a net savings of $26,000 per year. The new distribution reflects a smaller expected energy budget and less variation in potential outcomes, that is, less energy budget risk. The figure shows that a worst-case budget variance outcome, defined in this example by the EBaR probability of 10 percent is reduced from 25,600 to $16,640.

The development and application of EBaR for efficiency investments, $EBaR_{irr,x}$, is described in detail in Chapter 10.

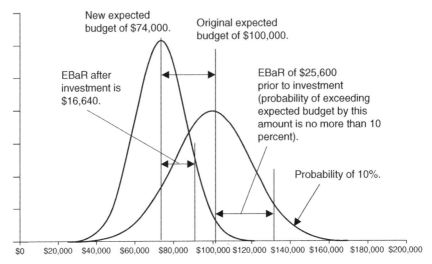

**FIGURE 6.3**   Total Energy Budgets at Risk After the Investment

## EBaR MANAGEMENT PRESENTATIONS

Most energy managers quickly recognize the value of an EBaR analysis, but they raise two concerns. The first is how to develop the data required to support the analysis, and the second is whether management will understand the analysis.

Data development is illustrated in the next several chapters. Presentation of results to management decision makers is the focus of this section.

EBaR is an effective energy risk management tool because it provides essential management information relevant to investment decisions: reliable analysis results provided as intuitive, meaningful decision variables.

The details of probability distribution developments and other analytical activities should not be included in a recommendation to management any more than the description of heat gain equations used in an engineering computer model. Of course, this information should be available to support decisions and for management to assess, if desired. The reality is the analytical process described in following chapters is much easier to follow than the supporting engineering analysis, which is nearly always accepted without management review. A suggested management presentation includes the following information.

**TABLE 6.1**   Expected Energy Budget and Expected Maximum Budget Variance

| EBaR Measure | Value | Description |
|---|---|---|
| $EBaR_{budget,mean}$ | $100,000 | The most likely energy budget for next year. |
| $EBaR_{budget,90}$ | $25,600 | The maximum expected budget variance at a 90 percent confidence level. The probability of a greater budget variance is less than 10 percent. |
| $EBaR_{budget,97.5}$ | $39,200 | The maximum expected budget variance at a 97.5 percent confidence level. The probability of a greater budget variance is less than 2.5 percent. |

## Energy Budget Risk

What information should the energy manager provide to management? The initial analysis of current budget risk shown in Figure 6.1 reveals an expected budget of $100,000 and an $EBaR_{budget,90}$ of $25,600 meaning that there is less than a 10 percent chance that the energy budget variance will be greater than $25,600. An outcome with a probability less than 2.5 percent can be included to show a worst-case scenario.

From a management perspective these EBaR values likely tell us all we need to know about budget risk. To recap, the EBaR values are presented in Table 6.1. A graphic representation is shown in Figure 6.4.

These three pieces of information already tell management more about the coming year's expected budget than would have been provided using last year's costs as a basis for budget planning.

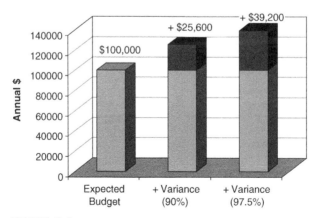

**FIGURE 6.4**   Energy Budget and Budget Variance

The EBaR$_{budget,mean}$ = \$100,000 statement is based on information on likely prices and other factors, like weather, that can be expected to differ next year as compared to last year. Budget variance estimates EBaR$_{budget,90}$ = \$25,600 and EBaR$_{budget,97.5}$ = \$39,200 also reflect improved information, because they use all information available to estimate likely budget variations rather than relying on budget variance from last year or the last several years where weather and other factors may have been unusual.

EBaR analysis recognizes weather uncertainty by providing an expected budget estimate based on both normal weather and a distribution of weather outcomes around the normal weather. Distributions reflecting likely outcomes are also developed for other factors that impact energy use and used in developing the EbaR$_{budget}$ values.

Follow-up questions might include: how likely is the budget variance to be greater than \$30,000? How likely is the budget to be less than \$75,000? What is the budget variance if we use a 95 percent confidence level? The energy manager or analyst who developed the EBaR analysis can easily respond to these additional questions.

## Efficiency Investment Risk

Energy managers are often asked to provide information on efficiency investments; however, the traditional presentations consisting of payback and/or IRR provide decision-makers with almost no information on investment risks and rewards. However, investment analysis results can be presented with intuitive EBaR decision variables similar to those used in the EBaR$_{budget}$ presentation. Referring back to the lighting efficiency investment referenced in the preceding section, analysis results are shown in Tables 6.2 and 6.3 and Figures 6.5 and 6.6.

**TABLE 6.2**   EBaR Expected Investment Results

| Mean or Expected Investment Results for Lighting Program | Value | Description |
|---|---|---|
| Investment cost | \$80,000 | |
| Expected annual savings | \$40,000 | |
| Payback | 2.0 years | |
| Annual finance cost | \$14,000 | Repayment of investment cost plus financing |
| EBaR$_{irr,mean}$ | 49.0% | Expected internal rate of return (IRR) |
| EBaR$_{netsav,mean}$ | \$26,000 | Expected net savings |

**TABLE 6.3**  EBaR Investment Risk Analysis

| Measure | Value | Description | Measure | Value | Description |
|---|---|---|---|---|---|
| EBaR$_{irr,90}$ | 31.4 | Minimum expected IRR at 90% confidence level | EBaR$_{netsav,90}$ | $19,600 | Minimum expected annual net savings at 90% confidence level |
| EBaR$_{irr,97.5}$ | 27.4 | Minimum expected IRR at 97.5% confidence level | EBaR$_{netsav,97.5}$ | $16,100 | Minimum expected annual net savings at 97.5% confidence level |
| Risk | 0.1% | Probability IRR < IRR$_{limit}$(20%) | | | |

The expected or most likely annual savings is $40,000. Note that the payback of 2.0 years is presented. This measure is included because it is a traditional investment measure and likely to be considered, at least implicitly by decision makers who have relied on payback in the past. Including payback also illustrates the limitations of this traditional measure relative to the information provided with risk analysis.

Table 6.2 shows the internal rate of return (IRR) of 49 percent. With a financing cost of $14,000/year, the annual net savings (EBaR$_{netsav,mean}$) is $26,000.

Table 6.3 shows investment risk. The EBaR$_{netsav,90}$ investment statistic indicates a 10 percent probability that the net savings (savings minus financing costs) will be less than $19,600 per year while EBaR$_{irr,90}$ indicates a

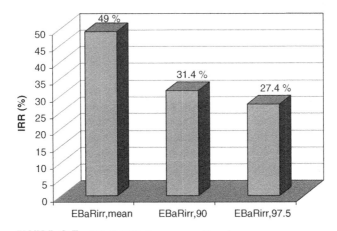

**FIGURE 6.5**  EBaR IRR Investment Results

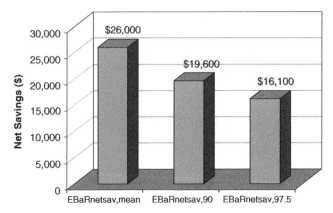

**FIGURE 6.6**   EBaR Net Savings Results

10 percent probability of an internal rate of return less than 31.4 percent. At a 97.5 percent confidence level there is less than a 2.5 percent chance that annual net savings and IRR will be less than $16,100 and 27.4 percent respectively.

EBaR analysis results, with just a few entries have provided a great deal more information concerning risk and rewards associated with this project than traditional payback or IRR analysis. A 90 percent confidence level excludes all but the most unlikely outcomes while a 97.5 percent confidence level excludes nearly all unlikely outcomes. This analysis nearly guarantees a minimum of $16,100 increase in annual cash flow.

The final row of the table indicates a probability of less than 0.1 percent that the investment will return less than the 20 percent required rate of return. This statistic reflects the EBaR definition of risk: the probability of an unacceptable investment return, that is, a return of less than $IRR_{limit}$.

## Investment Impacts on Budget Risk

The impact of energy-efficiency investments on the expected annual budget, $EBaR_{budget,mean}$ and budget variance, $EBaR_{budget,x}$, can easily be determined and should be included in the management presentation to show expected reductions in energy budgets and reduced budget risk (Table 6.4).

The budget impacts of the investment shown in Table 6.4 reflect a reduction in the expected energy budget of $40,000 or $26,000 if financing costs are deducted.

Results from Table 6.4 show both the reductions in the expected budget and the reduction in the budget variance, or budget risk. These results are shown graphically in Figure 6.7 as before and after expected budgets and expected budgets plus budget variance at both confidence levels.

**TABLE 6.4**   Efficiency Investment Impact on Energy Budget Risk

| Measure | Before | After | Difference | Description |
|---|---|---|---|---|
| $EBaR_{budget,mean}$ | $100,000 | $74,000 | −$26,000 | Largest expected budget variance |
| $EBaR_{budget,90}$ | $25,600 | $16,640 | −$8,960 | Maximum budget variance at a 90 percent confidence level (probability of a greater budget variance is less than 10 percent). |
| $EBaR_{budget,97.5}$ | $39,200 | $25,480 | −$13,780 | Maximum expected budget variance at a 97.5 percent confidence level (probability of a greater budget variance is less than 2.5 percent). |

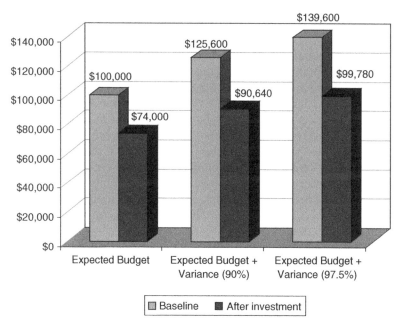

**FIGURE 6.7**   EBaR Energy-Efficiency Investment Results

**TABLE 6.5** EBaR Energy-Efficiency Investment: Opportunity Cost Analysis

| Confidence Level | Annual Savings | Total Discounted Savings | IRR | Description |
|---|---|---|---|---|
| Mean | $26,000 | $146,906 | 49.0 | Expected opportunity costs. |
| 90% | $19,600 | $110,744 | 31.4 | Probability is 90% that values will be greater than these. |
| 97.5% | $16,100 | $90,969 | 27.4 | Probability is 97.5% that values will be greater than these. |

## Opportunity Costs

Bypassing investments in energy efficiency incurs a cost of forgone savings that would have been achieved over the lifetime of the equipment or measure. Future savings must be discounted to determine a present value. A discount rate of 12 percent is used in Table 6.5. As with efficiency savings, these expected opportunity costs reflect a distribution.

An opportunity cost evaluation provides information not only on annual forgone savings but also forgone savings over the life of the measure and the forgone increase in the capitalized value of the business.

Tables 6.5 and 6.6 and Figures 6.8 and 6.9 show these costs.

Capitalization factors reflect the discounting process applied in rule-of-thumb valuations of facility assets. Capitalization factors are applied to annual income (revenue minus expenses) to determine the value of the asset. Capitalization factors (cap factors) reflect both a discounting of future cash flows and a limitation on the number of years used in the asset value calculation to come up with the asset value based on future cash flows. Cap factors vary by industry and location, and reflect a variety of factors with respect to the market for similar assets; however, cap factors are widely used to estimate asset value.

**TABLE 6.6** EBaR Energy-Efficiency Investment: Forgone Capital Value Increases

| Capitalization factor | Expected | 90% probability | 97.5% probability |
|---|---|---|---|
| 5 | $130,000 | $98,000 | $80,500 |
| 8 | $208,000 | $156,800 | $128,800 |
| 10 | $260,000 | $196,000 | $161,000 |

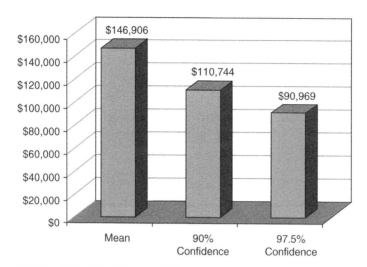

**FIGURE 6.8**  EBaR Energy-Efficiency Investment: Opportunity
Cost Analysis

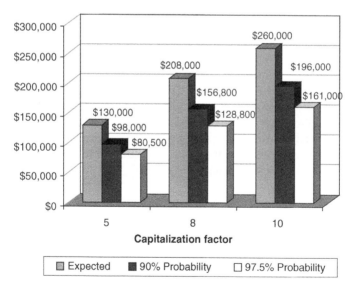

**FIGURE 6.9**  EBaR Energy-Efficiency Investment: Opportunity
Cost Analysis

Thus, investments in energy efficiency provide returns in two separate categories:

- Savings in annual operating costs
- Increases in the capital value of the facility

The presentation of opportunity costs is especially important in transforming energy-related budgeting into its more appropriate strategic investment analysis.

## SUMMARY

EBaR analysis captures all significant sources of uncertainty concerning energy budgets and efficiency investments. Budget risks and risks associated with efficiency investments are defined by distributions that reflect uncertainty in energy cost and investment-related factors. EBaR statistics provide expected budgets and investment returns as well as deviations from these expected values associated with uncertainty.

A successful energy risk management analysis must translate energy risk analysis into intuitive decision variables. This chapter presents EBaR reports designed to serve decision makers in evaluating energy budget risk and energy-efficiency investments.

Together, Tables 6.1 through 6.6 and corresponding figures provide an intuitive, concise statement of budget risk and the costs and benefits of an energy-efficiency investment. Mean IRR, net savings and budget variance reflect the expected values of these variables, while alternative values show worst-case outcomes at various confidence levels. Using a limited number of decision variables, this information presentation provides a much more comprehensive view of investment outcomes than traditional single-point estimates of payback and internal rate of return (IRR).

## CHAPTER 7

# Beginning Empirical EBaR
# Analysis: Risk and Probability
# Distributions

Traditional energy budgeting and investment analysis do not address risk directly. Historical budget variances (difference between energy cost and energy budget) provide some measure of the uncertainty associated with energy budgeting, while conservative investment paybacks or internal rates of return (IRR) are used to avoid investment risks.

EBaR addresses risk by explicitly representing uncertainty in energy budgeting and investment analysis. The first step in this process, formally defining risk and risk tolerance, is addressed in the first section of this chapter. The remainder of this chapter provides conceptual background on probability distributions. Probability distributions are central to the concept of risk and risk tolerance, and their development and application provide the primary quantitative vehicle used in risk management analysis and EBaR.

The application of probability distributions in EBaR is handled with Monte Carlo software described in a later section, so it is not necessary for readers to be able to manually apply the concepts described in this chapter. Rather, the objective is to provide the conceptual background necessary to understand the process and feel confident using software that performs the processes described here.

## ENERGY RISK

Definitions of risk depend on the application. An effective definition of risk and risk tolerance should be intuitive, easy to apply, and quantitatively meaningful.

---

## RISK DEFINITIONS

**Risk** The numerical probability of a negative financial outcome.

**Risk Tolerance** The maximum acceptable probability of a negative financial outcome.

---

### Definitions

With respect to energy management applications, a useful definition of risk and one that has been referenced in preceding chapters is the numerical probability of a negative financial outcome. More formally, an energy budget risk is the probability (or likelihood) that energy costs will exceed some dollar amount, and energy-efficiency investment risk is the risk that the return on the investment will fall short of a target return. Probability or likelihood is measured from zero to one with the value zero indicating that the event will never occur and one indicating that it will occur with certainty. Probabilities are also measured as percentages ranging from zero to 100 percent. A probability of 25 percent means that there is a one-in-four chance that the event will occur.

The risk definition then suggests the definition of risk tolerance: the maximum acceptable probability of a negative financial outcome. An efficiency investment is too risky if the probability of achieving *less than* the required internal rate of return on the investment is greater than the organization's risk tolerance of say, 5 percent. Similarly, the organization is at risk if the probability is more than 5 percent that next year's energy costs will exceed the energy budget by more than the energy budget contingency of, say $10,000.

These definitions of energy-related risks and risk tolerance are simple, consistent with normal use of the terms, and provide a convenient and meaningful way of measuring and evaluating risk. This risk definition is also closely related to the traditional definition of financial risk based on the statistical variance of returns associated with an investment.

Interpreting risk and risk management with probabilities requires a general understanding of probability distributions.

## PROBABILITY DISTRIBUTION FUNDAMENTALS

A quantitative characterization of potential outcomes of a process such as energy use in a building or an efficiency investment provides the basis for quantifying risk and risk tolerance. This section provides background on the development and interpretation of probability distributions that reflect these outcomes.

Risk management analysis requires that each variable that helps determine energy costs or investment return and is subject to any significant degree of uncertainty must be represented by a distribution of outcomes.

EBaR analysis applies two primary approaches to estimating these distributions including:

- Statistical analysis of historical data
- Nonstatistical specifications of distribution values

## Developing Distributions

Ideally, distributions reflecting the variation in outcomes of individual variables that impact energy costs would be based on historical observations of variable values. Several difficulties are encountered in attempting to develop distributions directly from historical data.

To illustrate these difficulties, consider an experiment where 100 coins are tossed in the air, and the number of heads is counted. If the experiment is repeated 50 times, the number of heads (the outcomes) forms a distribution. This distribution reflects the fact that when a coin is actually tossed 100 times in an experiment, the number of heads will not be exactly 50; it may be 48, 53 or some other number though we expect it to be reasonably close to 50. Figure 7.1 reflects the distribution of coin toss outcomes for 50 experiments.

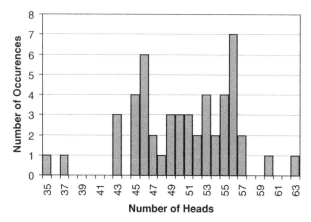

**FIGURE 7.1** Distribution of Coin Toss Outcomes for 50 Experiments

Figure 7.1 results were not actually determined by tossing a coin 5,000 times (100 tosses times 50 experiments); the coin tosses were simulated with a random number generator (RNG). An RNG is a mathematical process that generates a series of numbers lacking a pattern; that is, the values generated by an RNG are random. For instance, the RAND function in Excel provides a random number between 0 and 1.

Entering the RAND function (=RAND()) in each of 100 worksheet cells and defining a tails outcome as a value less than 0.5 and heads outcome as a value greater than 0.5 provide a simulation of 100 coin tosses. Repeating the RNG process 50 times generates the equivalent of 100 manual coin tosses repeated 50 times, providing data for a graph similar to that shown in 7.1. Using Excel to create 100 random numbers for 50 outcomes using this process is tedious; however, the process is trivial when performed with software; a software routine with an RNG process was used to generate the data in Figure 7.1.

Does an RNG-calculated process actually reflect the same result as tossing a coin? The answer is yes, assuming (1) the coin toss is a fair toss with exactly a 50 percent probability of heads and tails and (2) the RNG is a true random number generator. In reality coins may not give a completely equal chance of heads and tails, and computationally determined random numbers are not true random numbers (anything generated by a process has to, in some way, eventually reflect a pattern). However, any differences between actual coin tosses and coin tosses simulated with RNGs are indistinguishable for our purposes (and nearly all other purposes as well).

Having established RNGs as an appropriate way of simulating coin toss outcomes, consider characteristics of the distribution. In these 50 experiments some values we expected to see (58 and 44) did not show up, and the shape of the distribution is not quite as expected: for instance, the expected value of 50 occurs less often than five other outcomes.

These results are expained by the fact that only 50 coin toss experiments were used (that is the 50 observations represents a small sample). How will the distribution look when the number of experiments is increased from 50 to 200? The new distribution is shown in Figure 7.2. The Y-axis on the graph is the relative frequency of heads occurrence in the 200 experiments, rather than the number of heads occurrences. The relative frequency is the number of occurrences for each outcome divided by the total number of occurrences (200) and is the sample-data–based estimate of the probability of achieving that outcome.

Even with 200 coin toss experiments the distribution is sparse and shows an outcome of 57 heads as most likely, when we know that the most likely value should be 50.

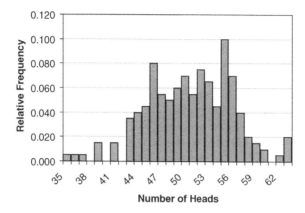

**FIGURE 7.2** Distribution of Coin Toss Outcomes for 200 Experiments

Increasing the number of experiments from 200 to 100,000 provides a final distribution shown in Figure 7.3. The number of heads outcomes that occurred in 100,000 tosses ranges from 29 to 71 and the relative frequency with which any one value of heads tosses occurred ranges from nearly zero up to 0.08 for the expected value of 50.

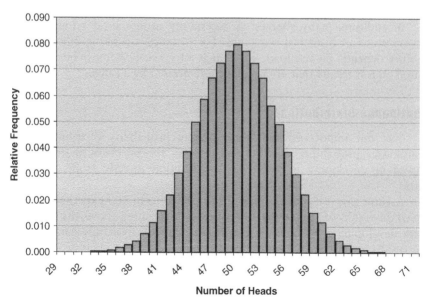

**FIGURE 7.3** Distribution of Coin Toss Outcomes for 100,000 Experiments

Comparing the change in shape from Figure 7.1 to 7.2 to 7.3 suggests that the shape is converging to the bell-shaped curve shown in Figure 7.3. It can be shown mathematically that the bell-shaped or normal distribution does in fact reflect the true distribution of coin toss outcomes.[1]

These figures are referred to as probability distributions because they show the distribution of outcomes and probabilities, or relative frequencies, for each of the possible outcomes. Once the probability distribution of a variable is known, it is easy to determine the probability of any event or combination of events related to the variable.

This example illustrates three important issues related to risk management applications including:

1. Observed outcomes can be used to estimate probabilities associated with each outcome.
2. Random number generators (RNG) can be used to simulate outcomes of various processes.
3. A large number of observations is required to develop reliable quantitative characterizations of probability distributions *directly* from observed data.

The last issue is problematic because most data series associated with uncertain variables related to energy cost have relatively few data points to define the true distribution.

In addition, many sources of uncertainty cannot be developed from observations of historical outcomes. For instance, operating efficiency of motors depends on the load, so a range of efficiencies must be specified based on test results that are usually characterized by a range.

## Continuous Distributions

A short but important step from discrete probability distributions to continuous probability distributions resolves the problems that are observed in developing a probability distribution directly from observed data.

Assume that we actually flipped the 100 coins in 200 experiments and saved the results of each of the 100 coin tosses. As noted above, the problem with developing a probability distribution directly from this data is that the results are sparse. We cannot calculate probabilities of getting 41 heads because, in 200 experiments, the result never occurred, though we know that the true probability is greater than zero because lower values occurred in this sample. In addition, we know from Figure 7.3 the shape of the distribution with a limited sample is not very accurate.

One way to handle this situation is to use information from the sample of 200 experiments along with a mathematical representation of the distribution to estimate the true distribution more accurately using only the 200 experimental results. As indicated above, the true distribution of the number-of-heads experiment can be accurately represented by the bell-shaped or normal distribution. Continuous distributions like the normal distribution are represented with equations that have few parameters—in the case of the normal distribution only the mean and the standard deviation are required to completely specify the distribution shown in Figure 7.3.

Knowing that the true distribution is a normal distribution with a mean of 50, an estimate of the standard deviation is all that is required to use the mathematical form of the distribution to determine the probability of any outcome. The standard deviation is a measure of the spread or dispersion of data around the mean value and can easily be calculated as 4.97 from the 200 sample points using the Excel STDEV function.

The formula for the normal distribution is:

$$\frac{1}{\sigma\sqrt{2\pi}}\exp\left(-\frac{(x-\mu)^2}{2\sigma^2}\right) \tag{7.1}$$

Specifying the two parameters represented by the Greek letter mu (the mean) and the Greek letter sigma (standard deviation) provides the normal probability distribution or as the mathematical representation is known, the normal probability density function (Figure 7.4). Since the area under

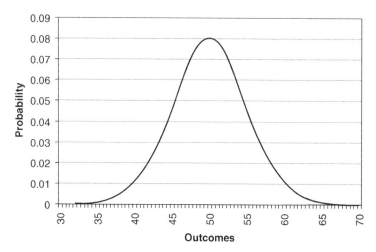

**FIGURE 7.4**  Normal Distribution Defined with Sample Standard Deviation

probability density functions equals 1.0, the probability of an event defined by two points on the X-axis is calculated as the area under the curve between the two points. For instance, the area under the curve from the value of 60 to the far right is 0.023, meaning that the probability of observing a heads outcome of 60 or more in 100 tosses is just 0.023 or 2.3 percent.

A visual comparison of the Figures 7.3 and 7.4 shows the probability density function estimated from the standard deviation (Figure 7.4) is nearly identical to that calculated from results of the 100,000 observed experimental results reflected in Figure 7.3.

Important characteristics of continuous probability distributions illustrated in this section include:

1. Given the specification of a mathematical distribution, only a few parameters need to be estimated to provide a comprehensive characterization of outcome probabilities.
2. Mathematical distributions parameters can be estimated from a sample of data.
3. The area under probability density functions between two outcomes defines the probability of occurrence of outcomes in that range.

Thus, data on energy prices, weather, and other observable variables can be used to calculate a standard deviation and estimate a probability density function. The standard deviation of monthly heating and cooling degree days published by the U.S. National Climatic Data Center are used in exactly this way to define weather distributions in the next chapter.

## Developing Continuous Distributions with Most-Likely or Extreme Value Probabilities

What happens when little or no observed data exists or when data that exist do not reflect important influences on future distributions of the variable? As indicated in the previous section, the distribution of outcomes can be represented with information on the mean and standard deviation using a normal distribution.

The mean of the distribution is generally not too difficult to estimate in most situations; it corresponds to a best guess expected value or to the engineering estimates provided by manufacturers or by in-house analysis.

However with little or no observed data, the standard deviation cannot be estimated, and a value for the standard deviation is difficult to estimate because the statistic does not have an intuitive interpretation. Fortunately, the standard deviation can be estimated indirectly. The mean and the probability of either (1) a likely range of values or (2) likely high and low values are sufficient to determine the standard deviation of a normal distribution.

This is an important characteristic of normal and other mathematically-defined distributions because identifying the probability of a likely range of values or the probability of extreme values can usually be determined with a reasonable degree of confidence by decision makers. While resulting probability distributions are based on a combination of limited observed data and subjective judgment or even subjective judgment alone, this process is an important step in developing more accurate assessments of energy-related risk. Often these distributions reflect information that can be developed reasonably accurately with limited observations or calculations. For instance, observations over several weeks can be used to define a range of evening operating hours of a lighting system used by janitorial services. Manufacturer ranges of efficiencies and lifetimes can be used to specify distribution ranges for those variables.

In some cases, these distributions will reflect expert opinion, or the analyst's judgment. For instance, estimates of a likely range of future energy prices could be based on the forecasts presented in Chapter 1. When information beyond that available in historical data exists and is relevant in defining an input variable distribution, it should always be incorporated. Typically, the only way to incorporate such information is to specify an expected value and a range of most likely or extreme values.

**Most Likely Values Approach**    The most likely values approach defines a normal distribution using the mean and a range of most likely outcomes. For instance, having experienced natural gas price volatility over the past several years, a building owner may feel there is a 90 percent probability that gas prices will in be in a range of $2.00 per 1,000 cubic feet higher or lower relative to the current price of $10.00.

The challenge is to go from this probability statement to a full probability distribution for natural gas prices. The previous section described the process of defining a normal distribution with the mean and the standard deviation. The same process is used here; however, one has to work backwards from the probability statement and the values of the most likely boundary values to determine the value for the standard deviation. Once the standard deviation is determined, the complete distribution can be defined as it was in the previous section.

The mathematical representation of the normal distribution can be applied to define probabilities associated with likely ranges of the variable of interest. In Figure 7.5 the area under the distribution curve between the two vertical lines in each of the three sets of boundary values reflects the probability of an outcome occurring between the high and low boundaries. The

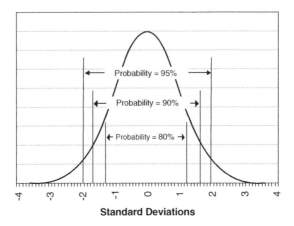

**Standard Deviations**

**FIGURE 7.5**   Normal Distribution Likely Values
Probabilities

values of the x-axis are defined in terms of standard deviations. The
relationship represented in the figure holds for all normal distributions.
That figure and Table 7.1 indicate that a range of 1.64 times the standard
deviation on either side of the mean value includes 90 percent of all
outcomes. Considering the original probability statement that there is a 90
percent probability that the price of natural gas will be +/− $2.00 from the
mean implies that $2.00 = 1.64 times the standard deviation. That is, the
standard deviation equals 1.22.

More generally, when a most-likely range is specified:

$$\text{Standard deviation} = \text{distance from mean}/\text{NSDp} \qquad (7.2)$$

Where NSDp reflects the appropriate number of standard deviations,
given the probability specification p.

Standard deviations from the mean for any probability range can be
developed from tables of standard normal distributions included in every
statistics textbook (and on the Web, of course). The number of standard deviations for the most frequently used probabilities are included in Table 7.1.

**TABLE 7.1**   Probabilities Associated with Standard Deviation Ranges in Normal
Distributions

| Number of standard deviations from the mean (NSDp) | Probability of outcomes in this range (%) |
|:---:|:---:|
| 1.28 | 80 |
| 1.64 | 90 |
| 1.96 | 95 |

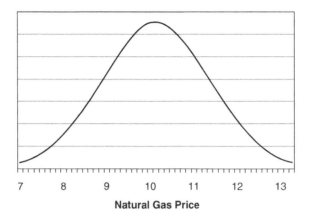

Natural Gas Price

**FIGURE 7.6** Distribution of Natural Gas Prices

With a mean of $10.00 and a standard deviation of $1.22, the natural gas price distribution is shown in Figure 7.6.

To use the most-likely values approach with a normal distribution, the following requirements must be met:

1. The mean must be specified.
2. A range of likely values centered on the mean must be specified with high and low values that are equal distance from the mean.
3. A probability associated with the range of likely values must be specified.
4. Equation 7.2 must be applied to determine the standard deviation.

**Other "Continuous" Distributions**　The procedure using a normal distribution requires symmetry around the mean. Some distributions in EBaR applications are not symmetrical. Triangular or piecewise distributions provide easy ways of representing these distributions.

Triangular distributions, not surprisingly, are triangular in shape and include a modal (most likely value) as well as likely high extreme and low extreme values. All (or nearly all) outcomes are assumed to fall between the high and low.

The triangular distribution shown in Figure 7.7 reflects a most likely price of $10.00 with extremes of $5.00 and $12.00 per 1,000 cubic feet.

Multiple expected value ranges are consistent with a piecewise distribution like that shown in Figure 7.8. The most likely price is $10 with an 80 percent probability of outcomes in the $7 to $11 range and extreme prices of $5 and $12.

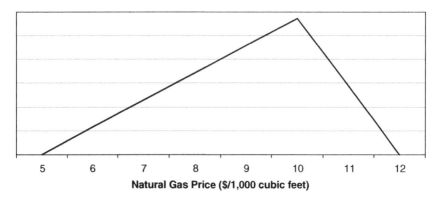

**Natural Gas Price ($/1,000 cubic feet)**

**FIGURE 7.7** Triangular Probability Distribution

While triangular and piecewise distributions are not continuous functions according to the mathematical definition of continuity (points where two straight lines meet are points of discontinuity), they are applied in the same way as continuous functions and, for our purposes are considered continuous.

Triangular and piecewise distributions are easy to develop and apply; however, normal distributions are used in the remaining examples in this book to keep attention focused on application issues related to energy risk management rather than digress on issues related to the mechanics of alternative distribution development.

**Extreme Values Approach** An approach that is the mathematical equivalent to the most likely values approach but differs in the nature of its

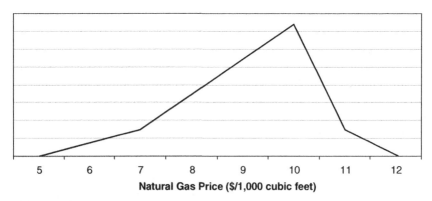

**Natural Gas Price ($/1,000 cubic feet)**

**FIGURE 7.8** Piecewise Probability Distribution

specification of uncertainty is the extreme values approach. The extreme values approach identifies the probability of "unlikely" extremes. Returning to the natural gas distribution problem, the probability statement that there is a 90 percent probability that gas prices will be plus or minus $2.00 relative to the current $10.00 price is equivalent to specifying a 5 percent probability that natural gas prices will exceed $12.00 or specifying a 5 percent chance that it will drop below $8.00.

As with the most likely values approach, triangular and piecewise probability distributions can be applied to reflect nonsymmetrical distributions; for example, a 5 percent probability that natural gas price will exceed $12.00 or specifying a 5 percent chance that it will drop below $4.00.

Since specifying most likely values and extreme values is mathematically equivalent, distribution probabilities that are stated as extreme values can be converted to their most likely values specification and applied as described above.

## Probability Distribution Recap

Probability distributions provide a way of quantitatively representing the probability of an event or a series of events. Discrete distributions can be estimated by observing outcomes and computing the relative frequency or probability of each outcome. Continuous probability distributions can also be estimated by using their mathematical formulation with just a few pieces of information, such as the mean and standard deviation based on a sample of data or the probability of a likely range of values or of extreme values.

Mathematical formulas for a large number of continuous distributions are known and used in evaluating probabilities; however, the normal distribution with the familiar bell shape occurs widely in nature and in statistical applications, and is frequently used when the exact shape of the distribution is unknown.

Triangular and piecewise distributions can be used to reflect nonsymmetrical distributions and are included in the continuous distribution category (though they are not mathematically continuous) because their mathematical forms can be applied in the same way as continuous distribution mathematical representations.

## EXTRACTING INFORMATION FROM PROBABILITY DISTRIBUTIONS

Once determined, a probability distribution provides a comprehensive characterization of all possible outcomes and the probability of any single or any combination of outcomes. The next step is to extract information as required in the EBaR analysis.

Figure 7.9 illustrates the information content provided by a probability distribution. This example is related to a lighting efficiency investment where uncertainty is created by a lack of information on the number of hours the individual systems are operated over the year. This distribution was calculated with knowledge of building operating hours, an estimate of the portion of lighting turned off during the day, an estimate of lighting use by after-hours workers and janitorial staff, and an estimate of the fraction of lights inadvertently left on all night. The mean of the savings distribution is 50,000 kWh and its standard deviation is 10,000. The probability of the savings between 30,000 and 40,000 kWh is 13.6 percent. This probability can be calculated from the normal distribution equation (Equation 7.1) or it can be determined by referring to a table of the standard normal distribution values. Similarly the probability of any single savings figure or any range of savings can be calculated by referring to the figure.

It is possible to answer any question posed on the likelihood of lighting energy savings. What is the probability that the savings will be less than $20,000? (Answer: less than 1 percent.) What is the probability that savings will be greater than $60,000? (Answer: 15.9 percent.) What is the probability that the savings will be between $20,000 and $50,000? (Answer: 47.7 percent.)

Descriptions in this chapter make it appear that once probability distributions are developed, analysis results are provided almost mechanically.

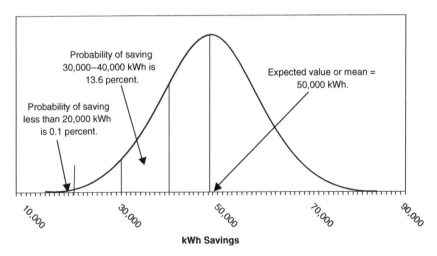

**FIGURE 7.9** Probability of Annual Lighting Electricity Savings

While that is accurate in some sense, distribution parameters and analysis results are always evaluated through rounds of sensitivity and other testing.

## APPLYING DISTRIBUTIONS WITH MONTE CARLO ANALYSIS

Monte Carlo analysis is a widely used numerical computational analysis tool that draws information from input probability distributions, applies the data in a process, and generates an outcome distribution. Monte Carlo analysis is an exceedingly powerful tool that is applied in virtually every field of science, business, and social science including physics, chemistry, transportation, medicine, sociology, psychology, economics, finance, computer science, engineering, and many more.

Figure 7.10 is a simplified schematic of the EBaR Monte Carlo process. Weather, performance and energy price are all subject to uncertainty and represented with probability distributions. This schematic reflects three input distributions; however, an actual EBaR analysis applies a distributional representation for each variable subject to uncertainty. A random number generator (RNG) is used to develop random draws from the individual

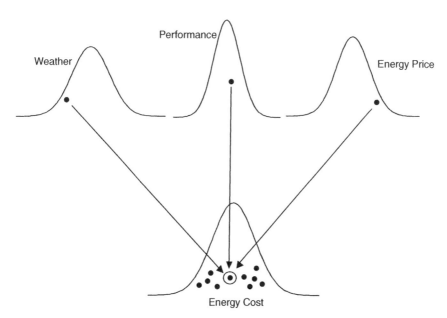

**FIGURE 7.10**   Simplified EBaR Monte Carlo Analysis Schematic

distributions, the inputs are processed to determine the energy cost associated with these values of the three variables and the results are stored in the output distribution of energy costs. The process continues until the output distribution is completely defined. A Monte Carlo run of the EBaR system with one million draws from the input distributions can be completed within a half minute on most computers.

Monte Carlo analysis is the analytical workhorse of EBaR, extracting information from diverse input probability distributions and providing a distribution of outputs and their probability of occurrence.

## energybudgetsatrisk.com

The procedures described above to develop input variables distributions and their application in Monte Carlo analysis reflect a conceptual description of the processes. These procedures are implemented in one of two ways:

1. Commercially available Monte Carlo software can be used with the Excel procedures described in the next chapter to conduct EBaR analysis.
2. In addition, EBaR software available at energybudgetsatrisk.com web site provides risk management software specifically customized for EBaR applications. EBaR software completes the distribution development process using any combination of the following inputs:
   - Historical data series.
   - Most likely values.
   - Extreme values.
   - Other user outcome-probability specifications.

EBaR software users may specify a distribution or have the software identify the appropriate normal, triangular, piecewise and other mathematically-based distribution. EBaR software also includes estimation processes described in the following chapter.

## SUMMARY

Energy risk management addresses risk by explicitly representing uncertainty in energy budgeting and investment analysis. Outcomes of uncertain processes, like energy use in a building are defined as probability distributions that reflect all possible outcomes and their associated probability of occurrence. Risk is defined as the probability of a negative outcome, and risk tolerance reflects the maximum acceptable probability of a negative outcome.

Probability distributions can be defined with observed data, or they can be specified mathematically using a limited number of parameters. Probability distribution parameters can be estimated using statistical approaches based on historical data and specifications of a range of most likely values or extreme values.

The symmetric bell-shaped or normal probability distribution occurs frequently in quantitative analysis and can be used to reflect probability distributions in EBaR analysis. Distributions like triangular and piecewise distributions can be used to reflect nonsymmetrical distributions.

All variables that are uncertain and help determine energy costs and efficiency investment returns are represented with probability distributions. These EBaR analysis inputs are applied with a widely used process called Monte Carlo analysis. Monte Carlo analysis applies repeated "draws" from each distribution to calculate a distribution of energy costs and investment returns.

The resulting distributions provide expected budgets and investment returns along with a full description of alternative outcomes and their probability of occurrence. These distributions form the basis of EBaR statistics and reported results.

## CHAPTER 8

# EBaR Budget Analysis Implementation—Developing Quantitative Relationships

**E**BaR analysis includes two distinct application areas: budget and investment analysis. Budget analysis includes an analysis of expected energy costs and risks. Investment analysis includes analysis of energy-efficiency investments, including investment returns and investment risks. Relationships developed in this chapter are applied in both budget and investment analysis.

EBaR budget analysis implementation is illustrated with an application to a case study facility. This chapter focuses on the first three steps in an EBaR application:

1. Budget variable identification.
2. Budget variable analysis.
3. Distribution parameter development.

As with the previous chapter, the primary objective of this chapter is to provide conceptual background to understand these processes and feel confident using the results of this or similar quantitative analysis. However, the processes are described in sufficient detail to provide a roadmap for readers to apply the analysis and develop distribution parameters using data for their facilities.

The quantitative applications described here are also provided as an automated process using software available at energybudgetsatrisk. com.

Readers whose interest is primarily developing an overview of the EBaR process may want to skim this chapter, focusing only on conceptual issues included in several of the sections that follow.

## EBaR ANALYSIS STEPS

EBaR budget analysis focuses on energy budgets and budget risk; efficiency investments are addressed with EBaR investment analysis. EBaR budget analysis determines the expected budget and budget variance, where the term *budget variance* reflects the expected maximum deviation of actual energy costs from the expected budget. EBaR investment analysis determines expected returns, both IRR and net savings, associated with an efficiency investment at different confidence levels. EBaR budget analysis is conducted before and after efficiency investments to assess investment impacts on budget risk.

The EBaR budget and investment analysis quantitative framework consists of six basic steps including:

1. Budget variable identification specifies variables likely to impact the energy budget and investment returns.
2. Variable analysis quantifies relationships used to describe variable distributions.
3. Distribution parameter development determines probability distributions for each variable.
4. Monte Carlo analysis extracts values for variables based on their distributions for use in budget and investment analysis.
5. Budget and investment analysis, evaluation, and assessment include calculations of distributions, EBaR statistics, sensitivity analysis, and other activities.
6. Documentation includes presentation of results at several levels ranging from a management overview report to technical documentation.

Each of these steps is illustrated with the case study of an Austin, Texas, office building. Before detailing the EBaR budget analysis process, several issues related to analysis complexity are addressed.

## ANALYSIS COMPLEXITY

This book provides an introduction to Energy Budgets at Risk concepts and applications. Examples are designed to be meaningful and to provide a template to guide applications at the reader's facilities.

### How Complicated Is EBaR Analysis?

There is generally, though not always, a trade-off between complexity of analysis, on the one hand, and reliability of results, on the other; the inadequacy of payback analysis in managing investment risks is a good example of an analysis approach that lacks the analytical ability to achieve its objective adequately. On the other hand, it is easy to mistake complexity in analysis with accuracy of results and to invest more in analysis refinements than justified by benefits derived from such refinements. For instance, complicated statistical time series analysis can be applied to develop future energy price estimates; however, given the importance of expected future energy market events described in Chapter 1, a most likely values distribution is often likely to provide a more accurate result than statistical techniques that cannot take into account changes in the structure of energy markets.

The standard applied in examples presented in this and the next several chapters, and recommended for applications at reader's facilities, is that initial analytical approaches should be reliable but no more advanced or complicated to apply than necessary.

Once initial results are developed and evaluated, additional analysis refinements can be considered. In most cases useful refinements will require no more demanding analysis than Excel-based regression estimation or variance analysis based on historical data series (also supported by an Excel tool). Examples of these applications are provided and explained in detail in the following chapters.

However, analysis extensions may not be necessary or desirable at many facilities because analysis refinements nearly always narrow the range of expected investment returns—that is, an investment that is desirable with less complex analysis will almost certainly be more desirable with more advanced analysis.

The analysis approaches provided in examples in this and the next several chapters provide a roadmap to apply basic EBaR analysis.

## Sensitivity Analysis

How does one decide when analysis refinements are useful? EBaR sensitivity analysis identifies critical quantitative parameters and relationships. Sensitivity analysis is the process of changing the value of an analysis input variable and assessing its impact on the analysis results. Sensitivity analysis can be conducted in a number of ways; however, the basis for most applications is a perturbation (increase and/or decrease) of a single variable or group of variables and an assessment of the impact on the results. Since the estimated spread of the input variable distribution reflects uncertainty in the distribution, perturbations based on increases and decreases in the standard deviations of the input variable distributions are also used.

Sensitivity analysis becomes a little more complicated when two or more variables in the EBaR analysis are related. For instance, in the case study example of this section, the Austin office building uses natural gas for space heating; however, natural gas is also used as a generating fuel by Austin Energy, the city's electric utility. Consequently, an attempt to quantify perturbation impacts of an increase or decrease in the price of natural gas should also reflect the associated increase or decrease in the price of electricity caused by the related increase or decrease in Austin Energy's generation fuel costs.

## Distribution Dynamics

The examples provided in previous sections and case study analyses in the remainder of the book use multiyear analyses that apply the same distributions for each year in the analysis. This specification is appropriate if the likely distribution of variable values is the same for all years in the analysis time period. For instance, uncertainty over operating hours of new fluorescent lamps is likely to be the same in each year. Some information may be gained over time; however, the focus here is on identifying changes in distributions through a planning horizon at the time the analysis is conducted.

This lack of temporal correlation is a reasonable characterization for a large number of distributions such as operating uncertainties, weather, and other variables whose trends are unpredictable at the time of the analysis. Other distributions like price distributions can reflect changes over time. Distributions that change over time are dynamic distributions that in most cases reflect a simple analysis extension. EBaR analysis is conducted for each month in the analysis period regardless of whether fixed or dynamic distributions are used, so, except for specifying the dynamic nature of distribution changes, the only difference is that in the dynamic case the distributions are updated for each month before being applied in the Monte Carlo analysis.

One advantage of using fixed distributions is that results are the same for each year so a single presentation of annual results is sufficient to describe the analysis. While dynamic distributions provide different results for each time period, analysis results are still presented as average annual decision variables with additional detail provided for each year in the analysis period.

For ease and clarity of presentation, most of the case study analysis presented in the remainder of this book uses fixed rather than dynamic distributions. The implied assumptions for the case study facility are that there are no temporal trends in weather, or other variable distributions including energy prices. That means that on average, Austin natural gas prices are expected to neither increase nor decrease over time from their current level, though, considerable uncertainty exists on the exact price level in any year of the ten-year analysis period used in the EBaR case study investment analysis. As of mid-2007, given alternative energy forecasts, this is a reasonable assumption.

An analysis of a dynamic distribution of natural gas prices is included in the next chapter as part of the EBaR investment analysis to illustrate its application.

## Balancing Methodology Requirements

The application of every quantitative analysis methodology utilizes certain assumptions, most of which are traditionally not specified or acknowledged. It is also true that most assumptions are never perfectly met and results are, to some extent, conditioned on the fact that violated assumptions have little impact on the results.

This book provides a practical guide to applying a limited number of statistical and methodological processes to offer the benefits of basic EBaR analysis to all facility and energy managers. Consequently, little space is devoted to academic nuances related to estimation issues. The suggested processes are chosen because they are easy to apply and provide reliable results, even when many of the classical assumptions associated with statistical analysis are imperfectly met. The suggested processes also reflect my personal judgment based on experience in estimating and applying these and similar methodologies in actual applications.

The intuitive interpretations of the procedures provided here can easily be supplemented by interested readers with web or textbook references.

## BUDGET VARIABLE IDENTIFICATION

Important energy budget variables depend on the facility and its operation. After a general characterization of budget variables, a summary of case study facility characteristics and case study budget variables are identified.

### Identifying Sources of Budget Variation

EBaR budget analysis considers impacts of all important variables that contribute to energy budget uncertainty.

#### Variables
A list of variables contributing to energy cost uncertainty includes:

- Weather variables (impacts on space heating, air conditioning, ventilation).
- Electric price.
- Natural gas price.

- Vacancy rates.
- Equipment characteristics.
- Operating schedules.
- Manufacturing process schedules.
- Other factors.

Important variables nearly always include the first three categories (weather and energy prices).

## Case Study Facility

The case study facility represents composite characteristics of several similar office buildings in Austin, Texas. The facility is an owner-occupied, five-story, 120,000 square foot office building, constructed in 1988. Primary building operating hours are 8:00 A.M. to 6:00 P.M. Monday through Friday. The facility uses natural gas for space heating and some water heating units and electricity for all other end uses. The HVAC system has a variable air volume ventilation system. HVAC system setbacks occur at 6:00 P.M. with normal settings restored at 7:30 A.M. Janitorial crews operate from approximately 6:00 to 9:00 P.M. each weekday. The building is open and is periodically used by staff during off hours.

The HVAC system in the building has not been recommissioned (that is, tuned up). The lighting system is typical of late 1980s design with an average connected load of 2.0 W/square feet. Standard high-efficiency ballasts are used with T12 lamps. Little attention has been paid to energy efficiency since the building was constructed. The annual electricity use is 16.3 kWh/square foot and natural gas use is 39.2 kBtu/square foot. These energy-use characteristics are reasonably close to the average central Texas office building in this size category (MAISY utility customer databases indicate that the the average is about 17.5 kWh/square foot and 29.6 kBtu/square foot; see www.maisy.com).

Energy bills are about $200,000 per year for electricity and $50,000 for natural gas, up by about 25 percent for electricity and 80 percent for natural gas since 2002.

The building owner is concerned about the continuing impact of high energy bills and wants to consider measures to reduce energy costs and to avoid the impacts of the volatile natural gas market.

The facility manager is responsible for energy use as well as other utilities management, waste services, security, building upkeep, and security. The facility has a contract with an HVAC company to do once-a-year maintenance. Other than HVAC maintenance, no energy management activities have been conducted since the building was first occupied.

### Analysis Variables

Variables contributing to energy cost uncertainty in the case study building include:

- Weather variables (impacts on space heating, air conditioning, ventilation).
- Electricity price.
- Natural gas price.

## BUDGET VARIABLE ANALYSIS

The second step in EBaR budget analysis is to analyze energy budget variables important in determining future budget variation. Readers can apply data from the case study facility as an exercise to become familiar with EBaR analysis and/or substitute information to immediately develop EBaR applications for their facilities.

Before embarking on variable analysis, the issue of systematic versus random influences is addressed.

### Separating Systematic from Random Influences

Energy use varies from month to month because of systematic influences, such as weather, and random influences that are not clearly discernable. An example of a random influence might be variations in customer traffic in a retail environment. Generally, systematic influences are far greater than random influences.

EBaR analysis separates systematic influences from random influences. Recognizing and quantifying systematic influences with historical data is necessary to develop empirical relationships that describe variations in energy use associated with variations in underlying causes. For instance, variations in cooling degree-days explain variations in air conditioning and ventilation electricity use.

Once systematic influences are quantified, the observed random variation is assigned to one or more end uses to proceed with budget analysis. For example, historical month-to-month changes in summer electricity use are unlikely to be fully explained by monthly cooling degree-days, in part, because cooling degree-days are an aggregate measure of air conditioning requirements. However, unless other factors are known to impact energy use in summer months, unexplained variations in summer electricity use are considered a random variation associated with air conditioning and ventilation use. Similarly, unexplained monthly kWh variation in winter months is assigned to ventilation electricity use.

The empirical approaches applied in this chapter to estimate systematic and random influences on energy use are appropriate for basic EBaR analysis.

## Facility Energy Use Detail

Annual and monthly energy use beginning in May, 2005 are shown in Table 8.1. Data for at least two years are useful; a minimum of one year's monthly data is required, though more limited utility billing data can be used with data from similar buildings to estimate energy use patterns.

**TABLE 8.1**   Case Study Facility Energy Use, 2005–2007

Facility square feet: 120,000
Average annual kWh: 1,961,072 kWh
Average annual natural gas use: 4,699 MMBtu (MM = 1,000,000)

| Year | Month | kWh | kW | kBtu (Ngas) | HDD | CDD |
|------|-------|-----|-----|-------------|-----|-----|
| 2005 | June | 239,275 | 781 | 3,572 | 0 | 541 |
| 2005 | July | 204,613 | 775 | 8,480 | 0 | 614 |
| 2005 | August | 241,084 | 824 | 10,215 | 0 | 621 |
| 2005 | Sept. | 220,100 | 766 | 9,300 | 0 | 583 |
| 2005 | Oct. | 158,675 | 582 | 229,951 | 57 | 205 |
| 2005 | Nov. | 116,321 | 416 | 405,801 | 171 | 116 |
| 2005 | Dec. | 118,032 | 522 | 1,023,737 | 459 | 5 |
| 2006 | Jan. | 129,265 | 417 | 983,876 | 282 | 2 |
| 2006 | Feb. | 115,719 | 442 | 973,320 | 342 | 14 |
| 2006 | March | 108,801 | 351 | 472,569 | 116 | 107 |
| 2006 | April | 148,987 | 572 | 42,822 | 3 | 289 |
| 2006 | May | 175,830 | 651 | 20,054 | 0 | 369 |
| 2006 | June | 207,847 | 694 | 1,889 | 0 | 497 |
| 2006 | July | 244,703 | 779 | 10,498 | 0 | 609 |
| 2006 | Aug. | 239,062 | 852 | 10,538 | 0 | 679 |
| 2006 | Sept. | 207,152 | 710 | 7,346 | 0 | 416 |
| 2006 | Oct. | 162,789 | 582 | 123,381 | 39 | 221 |
| 2006 | Nov. | 111,560 | 567 | 413,231 | 183 | 62 |
| 2006 | Dec. | 119,411 | 567 | 1,152,601 | 412 | 15 |
| 2007 | Jan. | 133,016 | 669 | 1,344,999 | 593 | 2 |
| 2007 | Feb. | 117,131 | 487 | 1,307,630 | 381 | 5 |
| 2007 | March | 111,503 | 364 | 389,847 | 149 | 84 |
| 2007 | April | 115,573 | 379 | 435,582 | 124 | 58 |
| 2007 | May | 175,695 | 600 | 16,234 | 0 | 286 |

The information in Table 8.1 provides valuable insights that can be used to determine both systematic and random variations in electricity and natural gas use. kWh reflects monthly electricity use, and kW is the maximum or peak 15-minute electricity use in the month. Systematic energy use variations result from variations in CDD (cooling degree-days) and HDD (heating degree-days) while random variations reflect impacts of influences that cannot be quantified.

Two approaches are applied here to estimate systematic relationships. Algebraic calculations are used to estimate summer and winter weather-sensitive energy use, yielding kWh/degree-day and kBtu/degree-day ratios. Excel-based linear regression analysis illustrates EBaR statistical analysis using the information in the tables and figures above. Both approaches described in this chapter typically provide reliable relationships between energy use and weather data, and are sufficient for all basic EBaR applications.

## Weather-Sensitive Energy Use

Electricity use (MWH), peak kW, and cooling degree-days (CDD) are graphed in Figure 8.1. One MWH (megawatt hour) equals 1,000 kWh (kilowatt hours). Peak kW (maximum kW in the month) is included because the case study facility, like most nonresidential electric utility customers, is billed each month based on total monthly electricity use (kWh) and peak kW. Natural gas use (MMBtu, million Btu) and heating degree-days (HDD) series are presented in Figure 8.2.

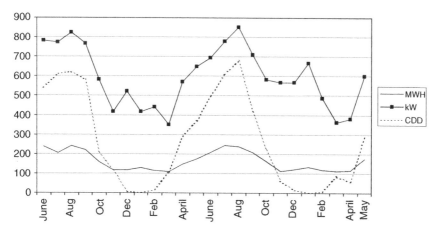

**FIGURE 8.1** Monthly kWh, kW, and CDD

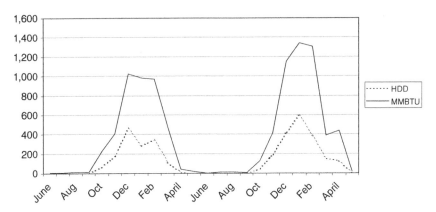

**FIGURE 8.2**   Monthly Natural Gas Use, and HDD

The data shown in the figures clearly indicate a relationship between cooling degree-days and air conditioning and heating degree-days and space heating. Cooling degree-days are calculated by subtracting 65 from the average of the maximum and minimum daily temperatures; any value less than zero is set to zero. Heating degree-days use the same concept by subtracting the average temperature from 65. Degree-days are summed across days to determine monthly and annual figures. The base value of 65 degrees is traditional and generally works reasonably well to explain variations in heating and air conditioning. Lower base values are sometimes found to be more effective in explaining weather-related energy use variations in nonresidential buildings and can be developed from NOAA weather data.

## Estimating Weather-Sensitive Relationships—Algebraic Method

Weather-sensitive relationships can be estimated using an algebraic analysis of the data, or elementary statistical analysis can be applied. If a statistical approach is preferred, the algebraic approach should still be used to verify the statistical results. A statistical approach is required if more advanced energy use weather data relationships are developed.

The algebraic method calculates kWh/CDD for summer months and kWh/CDD for winter months. The following steps are applied to calculate these ratios.

**Step 1. Identify Shoulder Month**   Identify a shoulder spring/fall month that has minimal weather-sensitive electricity use (electric heating, air conditioning, and ventilation). The case study building uses natural gas for space heating so variations in winter month kWh and kW in the figure and table are a result of an increased use of electricity for space heating ventilation, which includes fans and pumps to move heat through a facility. Winter months use somewhat more electricity for lighting and water heating; however, these impacts are typically small and can be ignored in this basic analysis. March of 2006 reflects the shoulder month with baseload electricity use of 108,801 kWh and 351 kW.

**Step 2. Calculate Air Conditioning/Ventilation kWh/CDD Ratio**  Identify months with CDD greater than 5 percent of the annual total. Using a threshold avoids months that may include heating/ventilation impacts and limits the impact of non–weather-related factors. Calculate the sum of kWh for each of these months and subtract the product of the shoulder-month use times the number of months. Divide the final kWh amount by the sum of CDD for these months. This ratio is an estimate of the kWh/CDD ratio.

Using the 13 months with CDD greater than 150, adding kWh for these months and subtracting 13 times 108,801 yields 1,211,396 for the numerator and 5,930 CDD for the denominator with a kWh/CDD ratio of 204.

**Step 3. Calculate Electric Space Heating/Ventilation kWh/CDD Ratio**  Identify months with HDD greater than 5 percent of the annual total. Calculate the sum of kWh for each of these months and subtract the product of the shoulder-month use times the number of months. Divide the kWh amount by the sum of HDD for these months. This ratio is an estimate of the kWh/HDD ratio.

Using the 11 months with CDD less than 150 and HDD greater than 75, adding kWh for these months and subtracting 11 times 108,801 yields 99,522 for the numerator and 3,212 HDD for the denominator with a kWh/HDD ratio of 31.

The kWh/HDD ratio reflects only ventilation, since the building is heated with natural gas. If a facility is electrically space heated the ratio will reflect both space heating and ventilation.

**Step 4. Calculate kW/CDD and kW/HDD**  An important part of electricity cost is the demand charge based on the maximum amount of electricity used in the month. kW/CDD and kW/HDD ratios are calculated using the same procedure applied in Steps 2 and 3. The same months are used for each ratio, and 351kW used in the shoulder month is multiplied by the number of months and subtracted from the total (rather than the 108,801 kWh used in the kWh ratios).

The kW/CDD ratio is 0.78, and the kW/HDD ratio is 0.41.

**Step 5. Calculate Natural Gas Btu/HDD**    Average natural gas used in months
with zero heating degree-days is 9,813 MBTU. This use reflects minor water heating uses and is considered the natural gas non–weather-sensitive
baseload. Adding natural gas use for the 12 months where HDD is greater
than 75 and subtracting the baseload natural gas use (12 times 9,813) give a
total of 8,908 MMBtu (1,000,000 Btu). Dividing by 3251, the sum of HDD
in those months, yields an average natural gas use of 2,740 MBtu/HDD.

**Estimating Monthly Energy Use**    The calculations in this section provide
a basis for estimating monthly electricity and natural gas use based on
heating and cooling degree-days. Relevant relationships developed above
include:

| | |
|---|---|
| Baseload (non-weather sensitive) electricity use | 108,801 kWh and 351 kW |
| Air conditioning/ventilation electricity use | 204 kWh/CDD |
| Ventilation electricity use (winter) | 31 kWh/HDD |
| Peak kW baseload | 351 kW |
| Air conditioning/ventilation peak kW | 0.78kW/CDD |
| Ventilation peak kW (winter) | 0.41kW/HDD |
| Baseload (non–weather-sensitive) natural gas use | 9,813 MBTU |
| Space heating natural gas use | 2,740 MBtu/HDD |

Equations for estimating monthly energy use are:

kWh = 108,801 + 204*CDD  (for 13 summer months identified above)
kWh = 108,801 + 31*HDD  (for 11 winter months identified above)
kW = 351 + 0.78*CDD  (for 13 summer months identified above)
kW = 351 + 0.41*HDD  (for 11 winter months identified above)
MBtu = 9813+2,740*HDD

Where the "*" symbol stands for multiplication.
    Actual and estimated values for kWh, kW are shown along with the
estimation error in Table 8.2. Actual and estimated kBtu values are shown
in Table 8.3.
    Results in Table 8.2 show average errors that are reasonably small for
monthly kWh and kW. Natural gas forecast errors are somewhat larger;
however, most of the large errors occur for months in which little space
heating occurred. These percentage errors are magnified because they are
calculated with a small base. For instance, actual natural gas use in June 2006
was 1,889; however, estimated use was the baseload, 9,813. The percentage
error is 419.5 percent; however, the absolute error of about 8,000 kBtu is
less than 1 percent of December's natural gas use.

**TABLE 8.2**   Estimated kWh, kW

| Year | Month | kWh | est kWh | % Error | kW | est kW | % Error |
|------|-------|-----|---------|---------|-----|--------|---------|
| 2005 | June | 239,275 | 219,165 | 8.4 | 781 | 773 | 1.1 |
| 2005 | July | 204,613 | 234,057 | −14.4 | 775 | 830 | −7.2 |
| 2005 | Aug. | 241,084 | 235,485 | 2.3 | 824 | 835 | −1.4 |
| 2005 | Sept. | 220,100 | 227,733 | −3.5 | 766 | 806 | −5.2 |
| 2005 | Oct. | 158,675 | 150,621 | 5.1 | 582 | 511 | 12.2 |
| 2005 | Nov. | 116,321 | 114,102 | 1.9 | 416 | 421 | −1.1 |
| 2005 | Dec. | 118,032 | 123,030 | −4.2 | 522 | 539 | −3.4 |
| 2006 | Jan. | 129,265 | 117,543 | 9.1 | 417 | 467 | −11.9 |
| 2006 | Feb. | 115,719 | 119,403 | −3.2 | 442 | 491 | −11.1 |
| 2006 | March | 108,801 | 112,397 | −3.3 | 351 | 399 | −13.6 |
| 2006 | April | 148,987 | 167,757 | −12.6 | 572 | 576 | −0.8 |
| 2006 | May | 175,830 | 184,077 | −4.7 | 651 | 639 | 1.8 |
| 2006 | June | 207,847 | 210,189 | −1.1 | 694 | 739 | −6.5 |
| 2006 | July | 244,703 | 233,037 | 4.8 | 779 | 826 | −6.0 |
| 2006 | Aug. | 239,062 | 247,317 | −3.5 | 852 | 881 | −3.3 |
| 2006 | Sept. | 207,152 | 193,665 | 6.5 | 710 | 675 | 4.9 |
| 2006 | Oct. | 162,789 | 153,885 | 5.5 | 582 | 523 | 10.0 |
| 2006 | Nov. | 111,560 | 114,474 | −2.6 | 567 | 426 | 24.9 |
| 2006 | Dec. | 119,411 | 121,573 | −1.8 | 567 | 520 | 8.3 |
| 2007 | Jan. | 133,016 | 127,184 | 4.4 | 669 | 594 | 11.1 |
| 2007 | Feb. | 117,131 | 120,612 | −3.0 | 487 | 507 | −4.2 |
| 2007 | March | 111,503 | 113,420 | −1.7 | 364 | 412 | −13.3 |
| 2007 | April | 115,573 | 112645 | 2.5 | 379 | 402 | −5.9 |
| 2007 | May | 175,695 | 167145 | 4.9 | 600 | 574 | 4.4 |

**Advantages and Limitations of the Algebraic Approach**   The algebraic approach to developing empirical relationships explaining changes in energy use as a result of changes in CDD and HDD should be conducted in every EBaR analysis to at least serve as a reference. As with any process, there are advantages and limitations.

Advantages
- Intuitive process
- Easy to apply

Limitations
- Algebraic-based reflect average kWh/CDD, kWh/HDD and Btu/HDD relationships. However, these relationships will be used in EBaR analysis to reflect monthly *changes* in electricity and natural gas use as a result

**TABLE 8.3**    Estimated Natural Gas Use (kBtu)

| Year | Month | kBtu (Ngas) | est kBtu | % Error |
|------|-------|-------------|----------|---------|
| 2005 | June  | 3,572       | 9,813    | −174.7  |
| 2005 | July  | 8,480       | 9,813    | −15.7   |
| 2005 | Aug.  | 10,215      | 9,813    | 3.9     |
| 2005 | Sept. | 9,300       | 9,813    | −5.5    |
| 2005 | Oct.  | 229,951     | 165,993  | 27.8    |
| 2005 | Nov.  | 405,801     | 478,353  | −17.9   |
| 2005 | Dec.  | 1,023,737   | 1,267,473 | −23.8  |
| 2006 | Jan.  | 983,876     | 782,493  | 20.5    |
| 2006 | Feb.  | 973,320     | 946,893  | 2.7     |
| 2006 | March | 472,569     | 327,653  | 30.7    |
| 2006 | April | 42,822      | 18,033   | 57.9    |
| 2006 | May   | 20,054      | 9,813    | 51.1    |
| 2006 | June  | 1,889       | 9,813    | −419.5  |
| 2006 | July  | 10,498      | 9,813    | 6.5     |
| 2006 | Aug.  | 10,538      | 9,813    | 6.9     |
| 2006 | Sept. | 7,346       | 9,813    | −33.6   |
| 2006 | Oct.  | 123,381     | 116,673  | 5.4     |
| 2006 | Nov.  | 413,231     | 511,233  | −23.7   |
| 2006 | Dec.  | 1,152,601   | 1,138,693 | 1.2    |
| 2007 | Jan.  | 1,344,999   | 1,634,633 | −21.5  |
| 2007 | Feb.  | 1,307,630   | 1,053,753 | 19.4   |
| 2007 | March | 389,847     | 418,073  | −7.2    |
| 2007 | April | 435,582     | 349,573  | 19.7    |
| 2007 | May   | 16,234      | 9,813    | 39.6    |

of *changes* in CDD and HDD. As long as changes in energy use are proportional to changes in CDD and HDD, relationships based on average are the same as those that represent marginal changes. However, if changes in CDD result in greater or smaller changes in kWh when CDD are large, the average and marginal relationships are no longer the same. This condition can be tested in the statistical approach described in the next section.

- Identifying shoulder months and estimating baseload, or the non–weather-sensitive portion of monthly energy use, can be difficult if shoulder months include significant heating and air conditioning loads.
- Algebraic development of these relationships is suitable only for relationships between energy use and a single variable. The statistical approach described in the next section can be used to relate monthly energy use to more than one weather or other variable.

## Weather-Sensitive Relationships—Statistical Method

Relationships between electricity and natural gas use and weather variables can also be developed with statistical methods. This section describes an Excel-based process to estimate the relationships developed in the preceding section with the algebraic method.

**Linear Regression Model** The estimation process applied in this chapter is ordinary least squares linear regression analysis (OLS). The estimation is initiated with the specification of a linear relationship between a dependent variable (Y) and one or more independent or explanatory variables (X). The relationship is represented as:

$$Y = b0 + b1 * X$$

Parameters or coefficients values b0 and b1 are estimated using data on the dependent and independent variables. The process used to estimate these coefficients is called linear because of the straight line or linear form of the estimated equation. The regression analysis estimates the parameters in this linear relationship by fitting a line through the points on the Y-X graph in a way that the square of the deviations from the estimated Y values to the actual Y values are minimized. Regression analysis, often called least squares regression because of this characteristic, has a variety of attractive statistical properties and is widely used in many application areas.

One characteristic of OLS that makes it attractive, compared to the algebraic approach described above, is its ability to reflect nonproportional relationships. Another way to state this property is that the b1 coefficient reflects the marginal impact of the X variable (the change in Y given a one-unit change in the value of X). This is an important characteristic in estimating weather-sensitive relationships using aggregate variables like CDD and HDD.

CDD and HDD are poor measures of heating, air conditioning, and ventilation energy use when these values are small. A 65 degree base degree reflects the difference between 65 degrees and the average of the high and low temperature for the day. As long as no air conditioning, ventilation, or heating is required when CDD or HDD are zero, there is no problem. However, the existence of internal loads in commercial buildings often requires air conditioning when the average outdoor temperature is less than 65 degrees and space heating is required only when the average temperature is greater than 65 degrees.

Sixty-five degree base CDD and HDD can still be used in statistical estimation; however, this situation requires avoiding months with few CDD and HDD in estimating the appropriate equation. It is also important to evaluate the pattern of residuals (difference between actual electricity use and electricity use estimated with the statistical equation). This latter issue is addressed below.

By omitting months with a small number of CDD and HDD, the OLS equations reflect the marginal impact of CDD on air conditioning and ventilation, and the marginal impact of HDD on ventilation and space heating. If the estimate of the intercept coefficient, b0, is 0.0, the b1 coefficient is the same as the average impact of degree-days on the energy use variables.

OLS models are estimated with Excel, which uses the Y and X variable designation in setting up the process. Steps required to estimate the models are provided in detail below.

**Step 1. Identify Shoulder Month**   This step is identical to Step 1 of the algebraic method. The objective is to identify a shoulder spring/fall month that has minimal weather-sensitive electricity use (electric heating, air conditioning, and ventilation). The case study building uses natural gas for space heating so variations in winter month MWh and kW in the figure and table are a result of an increased use of electricity for space heating ventilation, which includes fans and pumps to move heat through a facility. March of 2007 reflects the shoulder month with baseload electricity use of 108,801 kWh and 351 kW.

**Step 2. Estimate Air Conditioning/Ventilation kWh Relationship**   This step estimates the relationship between air conditioning and ventilation kWh and kW electricity use and cooling degree-days. As with the algebraic method, the 65-degree-based degree-days measures are used because they are already computed and accessible for virtually any U.S. location for individual years, 30-year normals, and standard deviations reflecting year-to-year variation. We assume that monthly kWh corresponds reasonably well to calendar months. If that is not the case, a billing month degree-day should be calculated for each day in the billing month and summed to get the monthly figure.

The estimation process is initiated with the specification of a linear relationship between air conditioning and ventilation (AC/Vent) and is represented as:

$$kWh = b0 + b1 * CDD$$

Where parameters or coefficients values b0 and b1 are estimated using kWh and CDD data in Table 8.1.

Months with CDDs greater than 5 percent of the annual total are used in the estimation process. Avoiding months with a small number of CDD avoids difficulties associated with selection of the CDD base (55 or 60 degree bases may be more appropriate for some nonresidential applications). Thirteen of the 24 months in Table 8.1 meet this requirement and are used in the following estimation.

The following steps provide weather-based relationships used in EBaR. The data in Table 8.1 are applied in this application.

Estimating a regression relationship between month kWh and CDD is referred to as regressing monthly kWh on monthly CDD. Excel is used to conduct the regression analysis.

The procedure for applying the analysis in Excel is as follows:

a. Enter data for the 13 months from Table 8.1 in a worksheet with each data item represented as a column as it is in the table. Add a column header (kWh and CDD) to each column. The data should look like Table 8.4.

b. Select the Excel Tools/Data Analysis/Regression option. The regression component is provided as an add-in module and may need to be loaded into Excel with the Tools/Add-Ins/Analysis ToolPak before the regression analysis can be conducted. A pop-up box is displayed on the screen

**TABLE 8.4**   Data Preparation for Regression Analysis

| Year | Month | CDD | kWh |
|------|-------|-----|-----|
| 2005 | June  | 541 | 239,275 |
| 2005 | July  | 614 | 204,613 |
| 2005 | Aug.  | 621 | 241,084 |
| 2005 | Sept. | 583 | 220,100 |
| 2005 | Oct.  | 205 | 158,675 |
| 2006 | April | 289 | 148,987 |
| 2006 | May   | 369 | 175,830 |
| 2006 | June  | 497 | 207,847 |
| 2006 | July  | 609 | 244,703 |
| 2006 | Sept. | 679 | 239,062 |
| 2006 | Oct.  | 416 | 207,152 |
| 2006 | Nov.  | 221 | 162,789 |
| 2007 | May   | 286 | 175,695 |

**TABLE 8.5** Air Conditioning/Ventilation kWh Coefficient Estimates[*]

|  | Coefficients | Standard Error | t Stat | P-value |
|---|---|---|---|---|
| Intercept | 116286.563 | 12096.13617 | 9.613529592 | 1.09456E-06 |
| CDD | 187.8725028 | 25.01580913 | 7.510150955 | 1.18495E-05 |

[*]Note: The "E-0x" notation signifies that the decimal point should be moved x digits to the left. 55.0 E-02 represents 0.55

to provide all analysis specifications. Select the Input Y-Range icon, click-and-drag over the kWh column including the header, and hit the Enter key. Select the Input X-Range icon, click-and-drag over the CDD column including the header, and hit the Enter key. Check the labels option. In the Output box of the pop-up window click on the New Worksheet radio button. In the Residuals box of the pop-up window check the Residuals and Residual Plot box. Click the OK button.

c. A new worksheet will open providing estimates of the parameters and a variety of statistics related to the estimation process.

The coefficient b1 reflects the contribution of air conditioning and ventilation to monthly electricity use and will be used to determine potential year-to-year variations in air conditioning electricity use that occurs because of weather fluctuations. The entry in the Coefficients column and CDD row is the estimate of the b1 parameter, 187.87.

The size of the parameters in this and the estimated equations that follow should be evaluated to insure reasonable values. The b0 parameter (the intercept) should generally be positive for electric equations (unless baseload electricity use is small) but can take on negative or positive values in the gas equation, depending on the slope of the line and the extent to which the relationship between kWh or natural gas is nonlinear for a small values of degree-days. The b1 (CDD) coefficient shows the increase in monthly electricity use for each degree-day increase. An increase of 100 monthly degree-days results, according to the estimated equation, is an increase of 18,787 kWh (see Table 8.5).

A linear relationship is specified in these relationships as an approximation to the true relationship and typically performs well. The difference between each actual kWh and the value calculated from the estimated relationship (the line in Figure 8.3) are called residuals. The predicted or estimated value is determined by multiplying a month's CDD times the CDD coefficient value (187.87) and adding 116,287. The actual and predicted kWh is shown in Figure 8.3.

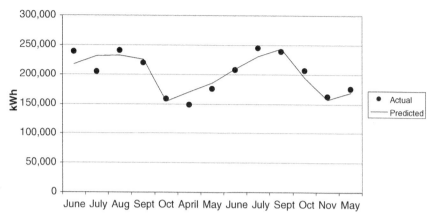

**FIGURE 8.3** Actual and Predicted kWh

If residuals generally reflect a random nature, in terms of being positive and negative (below and above the line) as one moves from lower to higher values of HDD or CDD, the linear representation is acceptable. However, grouped residual signs, for instance, 4 negative residuals, followed by 5 positive residuals and then 4 negative residuals, indicate a model specification problem. Statistical tests exist to evaluate this and other information gleaned from residuals; however, these issues do not need to be addressed in this basic analysis. The residual plot shown in Figure 8.4 is provided in the regression output worksheet. The negative and positive residuals are reasonably well distributed as one moves from lower to higher CDD values.

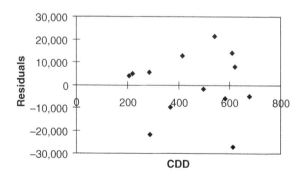

**FIGURE 8.4** CDD Residual Plot

If signs of residuals are grouped, a likely cause is a nonlinear relationship between kWh or natural gas and degree-days. Data should be inspected to insure against data errors, such as an estimated meter reading or erroneous CDD or HDD values. An unusually large residual for one or two observations is usually a tip-off on the presence of a data error.

If no data errors exist, a quadratic equation specification often resolves this problem. The resulting kWh equation specification is

$$kWh = b0 + b1 * CDD + b2 * CDD * CDD$$

Estimating a quadratic equation requires adding an additional column to the table of data reflecting the squared value of CDD.[1] The regression procedure is the same except that the CDD and CDD*CDD columns are selected as the X-range.

The simple functional forms used in the analysis in this section lend themselves to intuitive interpretation; estimated parameter values should always make sense.

Weather data for each month in the sample period can also be used to develop alternative weather representations. Average operating hours temperature and alternative degree-day bases (50, 55, 60) can also be applied. Degree-days and these other explanatory variables can also be transformed; for instance, the logarithm of degree-days, to reflect nonlinear relationships.

**Step 3. Estimate Winter Ventilation kWh Relationship**   Regress kWh on HDD for months with HDD greater than 5 percent of the annual. In the case study, these months are those that were not included in Step 2.

The relationship represented in this step is:

$$kWh = c0 + c1 * HDD$$

If this facility were electrically space heated, the regression results would reflect the impacts of heating degree-days on heating and ventilation energy use; however, with a facility heated by natural gas, the impacts of HDD on ventilation are represented in the estimated equation. Winter months tend to have fewer hours of natural daylight as well as cooler inlet water temperatures, so a small amount of variation in winter month kWh may be due to these influences. Including these refinements is not necessary for most applications.

**TABLE 8.6** Winter Ventilation Coefficient Estimates

|  | Coefficients | Standard Error | t Stat | P-value |
|---|---|---|---|---|
| Intercept | 108194.6114 | 3563.938789 | 30.35815647 | 2.23422E-10 |
| HDD | 33.06134873 | 10.84706718 | 3.047952795 | 0.013838662 |

The estimated equation results for this ventilation equation (Table 8.6) indicate an increase of 100 HDD results in an increased monthly ventilation electricity use of 3,306 kWh.

**Step 4. Estimate kW-CDD and kW-HDD Relationships** The impact of weather on peak demand is estimated with kW-CDD and kW-HDD regressions. The relationship for summer month peak demand is:

$$kW = d0 + d1 * CDD$$

Results are shown in Table 8.7.
The relationship for winter peak demand is:

$$kW = e0 + e1 * HDD$$

Results are shown in Table 8.8.

**Step 5. Estimate Natural Gas kBtu–HDD Relationships** Regress natural gas energy use on HDD to estimate the space heating-weather relationship. Use

**TABLE 8.7** Summer kW Coefficient Estimates

|  | Coefficients | Standard Error | t Stat | P-value |
|---|---|---|---|---|
| Intercept | 442.2167004 | 20.33237794 | 21.74938424 | 2.16989E-10 |
| CDD | 0.5766145062 | 0.0420490377 | 13.71290611 | 2.91903E-08 |

**TABLE 8.8** Winter kW Coefficient Estimates

|  | Coefficients | Standard Error | t Stat | P-value |
|---|---|---|---|---|
| Intercept | 291.361087 | 22.21693466 | 13.11436935 | 3.60156E-07 |
| HDD | 0.5725060456 | 0.0676186088 | 8.466693649 | 1.40327E-05 |

**TABLE 8.9**   Natural Gas kBtu Estimates

|              | Coefficients | Standard Error | t Stat      | P-value       |
| ------------ | ------------ | -------------- | ----------- | ------------- |
| Intercept    | 117514.6833  | 88681.40316    | 1.325133332 | 0.214605978   |
| X Variable 1 | 2342.786418  | 281.7286236    | 8.315755739 | 8.37562E-06   |

only those months where HDD are significant (more than several percent of the annual).

The relationship represented in this step is:

$$\text{Natural Gas kBtu} = f0 + f1 * HDD$$

Estimation results are shown in Table 8.9.

## Evaluating Estimated Relationships

Interpreting the estimated relationships developed in the previous steps includes two activities:

1. The interpretation of parameters.
2. The evaluation of statistical significance of parameters and relationships.

**Interpreting Parameters**   The interpretation of the two parameters in the linear relationships is straightforward. Parameters or coefficients with a 0 subscript (b0,c0,d0,e0,f0) represent the Y-axis intercept and coefficients with a 1 subscript (b1,c1,d1,e1,f1) represent the slope of the line. The slope shows the impacts of a 1 degree change in degree-days on either kWh or natural gas Btu's depending on the equation. The simple linear or quadratic equations lend themselves to intuitive interpretation; estimated parameter values should always be evaluated to insure that they make sense.

**Statistical Evaluation**   The extent to which the estimated equations explain the degree-day–related variation in monthly kWh and natural gas is indicated by statistics provided in the Excel regression output.

For linear regression equations with a constant term like those above, the p-values shown in the output table are a statistical measure of the likelihood that the slope parameters of the relationship (b1,c1,d1) are *not* zero. In statistical terms, the null hypothesis (the hypothesis being tested) is that there is no relationship between monthly energy use (kWh, kW or natural gas) and degree-days—that is, the slope parameters equal zero. This null hypothesis can be rejected with greater confidence as the p-value becomes smaller. Upper thresholds of 0.10 or 0.05 are traditional measures.

If the p-value is greater than 0.05 or 0.10, the null hypothesis of a slope parameter equal to zero cannot be rejected, and there is insufficient evidence to support the assumption that energy use varies as a function of degree-days. Stated another way, one cannot be confident that a relationship exists between degree-days and monthly energy use. When p-values are larger than the acceptable threshold, one of two actions is appropriate.

1. The slope parameter p-values may be low because there is not enough variation in monthly energy and degree-days in the estimation sample. In this case, extending the analysis to cover additional months is recommended. Extending the number of data points in the sample will generally improve the precision of the estimates. If the data are easily available, this extension will generally be advantageous in all applications (even those where p-values are acceptable with a single year's data). The only potential difficulty with this extension of the estimation time period is if some other event that impacts kWh or natural gas occurs in this period—for instance, variations in utilized floor space, changes in equipment or equipment operation and so on. In these cases, the other influences should be reflected as a separate variable in the estimated equation; for example, including the building vacancy rate.

2. The presence of a large p-value may also reflect the fact that (a) there is no statistically significant relationship between monthly energy use and degree-days, or (b) even though a relationship likely exists, existing data are not sufficient to estimate the parameters of the relationship. If a statistically significant relationship does not appear to exist, the algebraic ratios developed above can be applied in EBaR analysis to develop nonsystematic estimates of energy use described in a later section.

   If both statistical and ratio methods fail to provide a satisfactory relationship, no systematic relationship will be reflected in the EBaR analysis for this variable and historical data will be used to characterize observed random variations.

Regression analysis results include a graph of residuals (actual value–estimated values). An evaluation of these data is helpful in identifying (1) data outliers that may be a result of transcription error or other factors such as estimated meter readings and (2) model specification difficulties reflected by groupings of positive and negative residuals (discussed above).

**TABLE 8.10** Regression Results Summary

| Equation | Intercept | CDD/HDD |
|---|---|---|
| Summer kWh | 116,287 | 187.9 |
| Winter kWh | 108,195 | 33.06 |
| Summer kW | 442.2 | 0.577 |
| Winter kW | 291.4 | 0.573 |
| Natural Gas Btu | 117,515 | 2,343 |

**Estimating Monthly Energy Use** Monthly energy use is estimated with results of the estimated regression equations by adding the intercept term to the product of the CDD or HDD and the estimated slope term (b1,c1,d1,e1,f1). Summer refers to months with CDD greater than 5 percent of the annual total and winter refers to months with HDD greater than 5 percent of the HDD annual total. Regression results are summarized in Table 8.10.

Actual and estimated values for kWh, kW are shown along with the estimation error in Table 8.11. Actual and estimated natural gas values are shown in Table 8.12.

**Comparison with Algebraic Estimates** Statistically-based energy use estimates are always more accurate in estimating historical values of the energy use variables because of the ability of the linear model to reflect marginal relationships as compared to the average relationships represented with the algebraic method. These differences are illustrated in Figure 8.5 where eleven data points are estimated with the linear regression model and with the algebraic ratio method. The ratio method reflects a linear relationship with a Y-intercept of 0. The linear regression model estimates both the intercept and the slope permitting it to capture the change in Y associated with changes in X.

The benefit of the algebraic method relative to the statistical model is that it is easier to implement. What is the cost of using the algebraic method rather than the statistical method? The primary impact will nearly always be to overestimate the spread of weather-related distributions. Since statistical estimates can be counted on to improve the accuracy of distribution development which is described in a later section, an initial analysis can be conducted with ratio estimates. Any efficiency option that meets investment criteria with the ratio methods is almost guaranteed to meet investment criteria when statistical analysis results replace ratio applications. For options that are marginal under the ratio method, an extension to statistical analysis is appropriate.

**TABLE 8.11**   Estimated kWh, kW

| Year | Month | kWh | est kWh | % Error | kW | est kW | % Error |
|------|-------|-----|---------|---------|-----|--------|---------|
| 2005 | June  | 239,275 | 217,926 | 8.9 | 781 | 754 | 3.5 |
| 2005 | July  | 204,613 | 231,640 | −13.2 | 775 | 796 | −2.8 |
| 2005 | Aug.  | 241,084 | 232,955 | 3.4 | 824 | 800 | 2.8 |
| 2005 | Sept. | 220,100 | 225,816 | −2.6 | 766 | 778 | −1.6 |
| 2005 | Oct.  | 158,675 | 154,800 | 2.4 | 582 | 560 | 3.7 |
| 2005 | Nov.  | 116,321 | 113,848 | 2.1 | 416 | 389 | 6.5 |
| 2005 | Dec.  | 118,032 | 123,370 | −4.5 | 522 | 554 | −6.2 |
| 2006 | Jan.  | 129,265 | 117,518 | 9.1 | 417 | 453 | −8.6 |
| 2006 | Feb.  | 115,719 | 119,502 | −3.3 | 442 | 487 | −10.2 |
| 2006 | Mar.  | 108,801 | 112,030 | −3.0 | 351 | 358 | −1.9 |
| 2006 | April | 148,987 | 170,582 | −14.5 | 572 | 609 | −6.4 |
| 2006 | May   | 175,830 | 185,612 | −5.6 | 651 | 655 | −0.6 |
| 2006 | June  | 207,847 | 209,659 | −0.9 | 694 | 729 | −5.0 |
| 2006 | July  | 244,703 | 230,701 | 5.7 | 779 | 793 | −1.8 |
| 2006 | Aug.  | 239,062 | 243,852 | −2.0 | 852 | 834 | 2.2 |
| 2006 | Sept. | 207,152 | 194,442 | 6.1 | 710 | 682 | 4.0 |
| 2006 | Oct   | 162,789 | 157,806 | 3.1 | 582 | 570 | 2.1 |
| 2006 | Nov.  | 111,560 | 114,245 | −2.4 | 567 | 396 | 30.2 |
| 2006 | Dec.  | 119,411 | 121,816 | −2.0 | 567 | 527 | 7.0 |
| 2007 | Jan.  | 133,016 | 127,800 | 3.9 | 669 | 631 | 5.6 |
| 2007 | Feb.  | 117,131 | 120,791 | −3.1 | 487 | 509 | −4.6 |
| 2007 | March | 111,503 | 113,121 | −1.5 | 364 | 377 | −3.5 |
| 2007 | April | 115,573 | 112,294 | 2.8 | 379 | 362 | 4.5 |
| 2007 | May   | 175,695 | 170,018 | 3.2 | 600 | 607 | −1.2 |

Ratio estimates are also useful in evaluating the results of the statistical analysis. Outliers, or extreme data values can result in models that may not perform as well in estimating energy use with a different series of HDD or CDD. These outliers are generally identifiable in the graph of residuals; however, a series of outliers can sometimes be difficult to identify.

The average relationships developed with the algebraic method provide one way of assessing the "reasonableness" of the estimated coefficients. Table 8.13 shows estimated slope parameters and ratios for each of the weather-related relationships. Both of these values reflect the change in energy use for a 1 unit change in CDD or HDD. For instance, for summer kWh, a 1 degree change in CDD results in a change of 188 kWh using the estimated coefficient and a 204 kWh change using the ratio estimate. Values should be relatively similar between the estimates.

**TABLE 8.12** Estimated kBtu

| Year | Month | kBtu (Ngas) | est kBtu | % Error |
|------|-------|-------------|----------|---------|
| 2005 | June  | 3,572       | 4,089    | −14.5   |
| 2005 | July  | 8,480       | 4,089    | 51.8    |
| 2005 | Aug.  | 10,215      | 4,089    | 60.0    |
| 2005 | Sept. | 9,300       | 4,089    | 56.0    |
| 2005 | Oct.  | 229,951     | 251,054  | −9.2    |
| 2005 | Nov.  | 405,801     | 518,131  | −27.7   |
| 2005 | Dec.  | 1,023,737   | 1,192,854| −16.5   |
| 2006 | Jan.  | 983,876     | 778,180  | 20.9    |
| 2006 | Feb.  | 973,320     | 918,748  | 5.6     |
| 2006 | March | 472,569     | 389,278  | 17.6    |
| 2006 | April | 42,822      | 124,543  | −190.8  |
| 2006 | May   | 20,054      | 4,089    | 79.6    |
| 2006 | June  | 1,889       | 4,089    | −116.5  |
| 2006 | July  | 10,498      | 4,089    | 61.1    |
| 2006 | Aug.  | 10,538      | 4,089    | 61.2    |
| 2006 | Sept. | 7,346       | 4,089    | 44.3    |
| 2006 | Oct.  | 123,381     | 208,883  | −69.3   |
| 2006 | Nov.  | 413,231     | 546,245  | −32.2   |
| 2006 | Dec.  | 1,152,601   | 1,082,743| 6.1     |
| 2007 | Jan.  | 1,344,999   | 1,506,787| −12.0   |
| 2007 | Feb.  | 1,307,630   | 1,010,116| 22.8    |
| 2007 | March | 389,847     | 466,590  | −19.7   |
| 2007 | April | 435,582     | 408,020  | 6.3     |
| 2007 | May   | 16,234      | 4,089    | 74.8    |

How can one decide if the statistical estimates are preferred? P-values for the coefficient estimates of the Y-axis intercept $(b0,c0,d0,e0,f0)$ less than 0.10 indicate that the relationship is nonproportional, and that regression model is preferred. If p-values for the slope coefficients $(b1,c1,d1,d1,e1,f1)$ are greater than 0.10, ratio estimates should be used.

**TABLE 8.13** Estimated kWh, kW

| Equation | Estimated Coefficient | Calculated Ratio |
|----------|-----------------------|------------------|
| Summer kWh | 188.00 | 204 |
| Winter kWh | 33.00 | 31 |
| Summer kW | 0.58 | 0.78 |
| Winter kW | 0.57 | 0.41 |
| Natural Gas Btu | 2,343 | 2,324 |

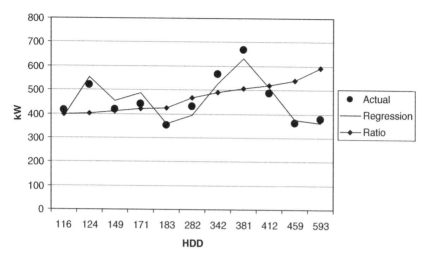

**FIGURE 8.5** Monthly kWh, kW, and CDD

**Advantages and Limitations of the Statistical Approach** Completing both the algebraic and statistical analysis is recommended with selection of the statistical approach if results indicate superior representation as described in the preceding section. However, as indicated earlier, the algebraic ratio method alone is sufficient to proceed with EBaR analysis.

A summary of statistical approach advantages and limitations include:

Advantages
- Ability to represent both proportional and nonproportional relationships between energy and degree-day.
- Indication of statistical significance in the output table of statistics.
- Indication of data problems and nonlinear relationships with estimation residuals.
- Easy estimation application using Excel.

Limitations
- More difficult to develop than the algebraic ratios.
- Requires evaluation of statistical results to determine acceptability relative to algebraic ratios.

## Systematic and Random Weather-Sensitive Energy Use

Weather-sensitive energy use relationships developed in the preceding sections are used to develop energy use distributions associated with variations in weather. Weather variations are developed from historical weather data.

Differences between actual energy use and estimated energy use shown in Tables 8.2 and 8.3 and Tables 8.11 and 8.12 are viewed as a random variation in energy use defined by the size of the difference and are carried forward in the distribution development.

The size of this random variation is shown in Tables 8.14 through 8.16 for the statistical application in the preceding section. Actual energy use is presented along with the systematic (related to weather plus the shoulder-month baseload) component and the difference between the two, which reflects the random variation component. Information for kWh, kW and natural gas are presented.

**TABLE 8.14**    Systematic and Random kWh Historical Components

| Year | Month | Actual kWh | Systematic Variation | Random Variation | RV as % of Actual |
|------|-------|-----------|---------------------|------------------|-------------------|
| 2005 | June  | 239,275 | 217,926 | 21,349  | 8.9   |
| 2005 | July  | 204,613 | 231,640 | −27,027 | −13.2 |
| 2005 | Aug.  | 241,084 | 232,955 | 8,129   | 3.4   |
| 2005 | Sept. | 220,100 | 225,816 | −5,717  | −2.6  |
| 2005 | Oct.  | 158,675 | 154,800 | 3,875   | 2.4   |
| 2005 | Nov.  | 116,321 | 113,848 | 2,473   | 2.1   |
| 2005 | Dec.  | 118,032 | 123,370 | −5,337  | −4.5  |
| 2006 | Jan.  | 129,265 | 117,518 | 11,747  | 9.1   |
| 2006 | Feb.  | 115,719 | 119,502 | −3,783  | −3.3  |
| 2006 | March | 108,801 | 112,030 | −3,229  | −3.0  |
| 2006 | April | 148,987 | 170,582 | −21,595 | −14.5 |
| 2006 | May   | 175,830 | 185,612 | −9,782  | −5.6  |
| 2006 | June  | 207,847 | 209,659 | −1,812  | −0.9  |
| 2006 | July  | 244,703 | 230,701 | 14,002  | 5.7   |
| 2006 | Aug.  | 239,062 | 243,852 | −4,790  | −2.0  |
| 2006 | Sept. | 207,152 | 194,442 | 12,710  | 6.1   |
| 2006 | Oct.  | 162,789 | 157,806 | 4,982   | 3.1   |
| 2006 | Nov.  | 111,560 | 114,245 | −2,684  | −2.4  |
| 2006 | Dec.  | 119,411 | 121,816 | −2,405  | −2.0  |
| 2007 | Jan.  | 133,016 | 127,800 | 5,216   | 3.9   |
| 2007 | Feb.  | 117,131 | 120,791 | −3,660  | −3.1  |
| 2007 | March | 111,503 | 113,121 | −1,618  | −1.5  |
| 2007 | April | 115,573 | 112,294 | 3,279   | 2.8   |
| 2007 | May   | 175,695 | 170,018 | 5,676   | 3.2   |

**TABLE 8.15**   Systematic and Random kW Historical Components

| Year | Month | Actual kW | Systematic Variation | Random Variation | RV as % of Actual |
|------|-------|-----------|---------------------|------------------|-------------------|
| 2005 | June  | 781 | 754 | 27  | 3.5 |
| 2005 | July  | 775 | 796 | −22 | −2.8 |
| 2005 | Aug.  | 824 | 800 | 23  | 2.8 |
| 2005 | Sept. | 766 | 778 | −12 | −1.6 |
| 2005 | Oct.  | 582 | 560 | 22  | 3.7 |
| 2005 | Nov.  | 416 | 389 | 27  | 6.5 |
| 2005 | Dec.  | 522 | 554 | −33 | −6.2 |
| 2006 | Jan.  | 417 | 453 | −36 | −8.6 |
| 2006 | Feb.  | 442 | 487 | −45 | −10.2 |
| 2006 | March | 351 | 358 | −7  | −1.9 |
| 2006 | April | 572 | 609 | −37 | −6.4 |
| 2006 | May   | 651 | 655 | −4  | −0.6 |
| 2006 | June  | 694 | 729 | −35 | −5.0 |
| 2006 | July  | 779 | 793 | −14 | −1.8 |
| 2006 | Aug.  | 852 | 834 | 19  | 2.2 |
| 2006 | Sept  | 710 | 682 | 28  | 4.0 |
| 2006 | Oct.  | 582 | 570 | 12  | 2.1 |
| 2006 | Nov.  | 567 | 396 | 171 | 30.2 |
| 2006 | Dec.  | 567 | 527 | 40  | 7.0 |
| 2007 | Jan.  | 669 | 631 | 38  | 5.6 |
| 2007 | Feb.  | 487 | 509 | −23 | −4.6 |
| 2007 | March | 364 | 377 | −13 | −3.5 |
| 2007 | April | 379 | 362 | 17  | 4.5 |
| 2007 | May   | 600 | 607 | −7  | −1.2 |

Tables 8.14, 8.15, and 8.16 provide a feeling for the relative size of random variations compared to the systematic component. For kWh and kW the average size of this variation is about 5 percent of the actual. Natural gas random variation averages 17 percent for months with more than 75 HDD.

Several approaches can be applied to incorporate the random source of variation in estimates of energy use including:

1. Maintain the differentials that exist in each historical month between forecast and actual data as a random component. With two years of data, the differentials from one or the other year can be chosen randomly.

**TABLE 8.16**  Systematic and Random kBtu Historical Components

| Year | Month | Actual kBtu | Systematic Variation | Random Variation | RV as % of Actual |
|------|-------|-------------|---------------------|------------------|-------------------|
| 2005 | June | 3,572 | 4,089 | −517 | −14.5 |
| 2005 | July | 8,480 | 4,089 | 4,391 | 51.8 |
| 2005 | Aug. | 10,215 | 4,089 | 6,126 | 60.0 |
| 2005 | Sept. | 9,300 | 4,089 | 5,211 | 56.0 |
| 2005 | Oct. | 229,951 | 251,054 | −21,103 | −9.2 |
| 2005 | Nov. | 405,801 | 518,131 | −112,330 | −27.7 |
| 2005 | Dec. | 1,023,737 | 1,192,854 | −169,116 | −16.5 |
| 2006 | Jan. | 983,876 | 778,180 | 205,696 | 20.9 |
| 2006 | Feb. | 973,320 | 918,748 | 54,573 | 5.6 |
| 2006 | March | 472,569 | 389,278 | 83,291 | 17.6 |
| 2006 | April | 42,822 | 124,543 | −81,721 | −190.8 |
| 2006 | May | 20,054 | 4,089 | 15,965 | 79.6 |
| 2006 | June | 1,889 | 4,089 | −2,200 | −116.5 |
| 2006 | July | 10,498 | 4,089 | 6,409 | 61.1 |
| 2006 | Aug. | 10,538 | 4,089 | 6,449 | 61.2 |
| 2006 | Sept. | 7,346 | 4,089 | 3,257 | 44.3 |
| 2006 | Oct. | 123,381 | 208,883 | −85,503 | −69.3 |
| 2006 | Nov. | 413,231 | 546,245 | −133,014 | −32.2 |
| 2006 | Dec. | 1,152,601 | 1,082,743 | 69,858 | 6.1 |
| 2007 | Jan. | 1,344,999 | 1,506,787 | −161,788 | −12.0 |
| 2007 | Feb. | 1,307,630 | 1,010,116 | 297,513 | 22.8 |
| 2007 | March | 389,847 | 466,590 | −76,742 | −19.7 |
| 2007 | April | 435,582 | 408,020 | 27,562 | 6.3 |
| 2007 | May | 16,234 | 4,089 | 12,145 | 74.8 |

2. Divide the 24 months of data into two summer and two winter periods based on CDD and HDD with approximately 6 months in each category. Use the mean and standard deviation for each group in developing a random component to be added to the forecast of the baseload plus systematic energy use.
3. Apply other statistical procedures to characterize the random activities including extensions of the estimated equations.

The third option is not appropriate for a basic application. The first option is preferred if month-specific residuals have the same sign and magnitude under similar CDD or HDD values (using three years of data in the estimation and analysis has considerable value in this component of the analysis). This relationship can exist if seasonal weather patterns exist but are not reflected in the CDD or HDD variables. When random components are of different signs for the same month in two or more different years, the second option is preferable, reflecting an influence that is random, even for the same month.

The second option is illustrated in this case study analysis. This application will generate random components to each month's energy forecast that reflect a size that is consistent with that shown in the tables above. The standard deviations and means for each of the periods is shown in Table 8.17. The average values of the actual variable in each segment are also included in the last column of the table for reference. These estimates were derived using the Excel STDEV function. These random variations are modeled using a normal distribution; consequently, the mean plus or minus the standard deviation includes 68 percent of all outcomes.

## Electricity and Natural Gas Price Analysis

Electricity and natural gas price variability are the other two variables that impact energy costs. While historical price series support the application of statistical analysis, the reality is that fuel oil, natural gas, and electricity prices are determined more by future demand and supply considerations that cannot be extrapolated from historical information.

Considering the limited usefulness of statistical estimates and models, a more qualitative approach is considered appropriate for developing quantitative estimates of future energy prices and their distributions. This topic is addressed in more detail in the following section on developing natural gas and electricity price distributions.

**TABLE 8.17**   Random Variation Specifications

| Energy Type | Period | HDD/CDD MAX | STD DEV | MEAN | Average Actuals |
|---|---|---|---|---|---|
| kWh | Summer1 | 150–416 | 12,592 | −689 | 171,521 |
| kWh | Summer2 | 417– | 15,837 | 590 | 228,098 |
| kWh | Winter1 | 75–183 | 3,020 | −356 | 112,752 |
| kWh | Winter2 | 184– | 6,733 | 297 | 122,096 |
| kW | Summer1 | 150–416 | 23.7 | 2.34 | 616 |
| kW | Summer2 | 417– | 24.7 | −2.01 | 782 |
| kW | Winter1 | 75–183 | 75.6 | 39.11 | 416 |
| kW | Winter2 | 184– | 38.3 | −9.72 | 517 |
| kBtu | Winter1 | 3–171 | 145,092 | 30,454 | 299,993 |
| kBtu | Winter2 | 172– | 306,184 | 3,389 | 1,028,485 |

## DISTRIBUTION DEVELOPMENT

Distribution development, the third step in the EBaR development process relies heavily on the preceding step, budget variable analyses. Estimated end-use (space heating, air conditioning, and so on are end uses) energy use equations developed above provide information required to develop distributions reflecting systematic variations in air conditioning, ventilation, and space heating energy uses and random variations revealed in historical data.

Energy price distributions are developed with the help of historical data analysis; however, the distributions are primarily determined with expectations on future energy prices.

Distribution development for each of the five distributions relevant to the case study facility is described here. Distributions include:

- AC/ventilation
- Winter ventilation
- Space heating
- Natural gas price
- Electricity price

It should be emphasized again that the detailed analysis descriptions are included here for the benefit of analysts who plan to implement these estimation components of EBaR analysis themselves. Others may want to skim these sections.

The quantitative applications described in this section are also provided as an automated process with software available at energybudgets atrisk.com.

### Summer kWh

Summer month kWh is determined by applying values of CDD to the equations that were estimated to reflect monthly variations in air conditioning and ventilation kWh. The estimated regression model plus the random variation is represented as:

$$\text{Summer kWh(dist)} = 116{,}287 + 187.87 * \text{CDD(mean, stdev)}$$

$$+\text{RV(mean, stdev)}$$

The kWh variable is indicated as a distribution, reflecting that its value depends on variables on the right hand side of the equation that also reflect a distribution of values. Two sources of variation in this relationship create a distribution of outcomes. The first is variation in CDD from month to month and year to year. The second is the random variation represented with the RV variable. A distribution of air conditioning and ventilation kWh is generated by applying a CDD and RV value many times to this equation and saving the results. The values of the CDD and RV variables are defined by historical data including 30 years for CDD and the 24 months of data on kWh in the estimation sample for RV as described in the previous section.

For example, Table 8.18 shows 30-year averages for Austin CDD and HDD and standard deviations provided by the National Climatic Data Center for this area of Texas.

Examining August, the 30-year average is 610 CDD with a standard deviation of 65 CDD. A set of observations consistent with this mean and standard deviation, following a normal distribution, can be developed using Excel's Tools/Data Analysis/Random Number Generation tool by specifying a normal distribution along with a mean and standard deviation. Ten thousand observations were specified to generate the histogram shown in

**TABLE 8.18**    CDD and HDD Random Variation Specifications

| Month | CDD | SDEVCDD | HDD | SDEVHDD |
|---|---|---|---|---|
| Jan. | 7 | 4 | 475 | 108 |
| Feb. | 18 | 7 | 319 | 89 |
| March | 59 | 24 | 163 | 56 |
| April | 147 | 42 | 44 | 33 |
| May | 323 | 77 | 2 | 7 |
| June | 495 | 64 | 0 | 0 |
| July | 605 | 68 | 0 | 0 |
| Aug. | 610 | 65 | 0 | 0 |
| Sept | 439 | 70 | 2 | 6 |
| Oct. | 207 | 32 | 32 | 34 |
| Nov. | 51 | 13 | 205 | 79 |
| Dec. | 13 | 2 | 406 | 99 |
| Annual | 2,974 | 241 | 1,648 | 218 |

*Source: Climatography of the United States* No. 85, Divisional Normals and Standard, Deviations of Temperature, Precipitation, and Heating and Cooling Degree-days 1971–2000 (and previous normals periods) National Climatic Data Center, Asheville, NC. Annuals from http://www.ncdc.noaa.gov/oa/climate/online/ccd/nrmcdd.html (AUSTIN)

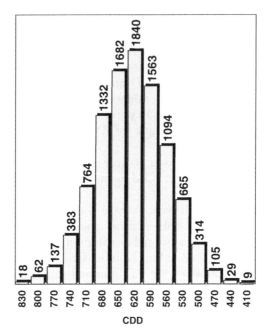

**FIGURE 8.6** August CDD Distribution

Figure 8.6. The numbers at the top of each bar show the number of observations for the category shown along the x-axis.

When the earlier equation is applied to these 10,000 CDDs (ignoring for the moment the RV term), the histogram of Summer AC/ventilation kWh which includes the shoulder-month baseload is generated (Figure 8.7). It is interesting to note that the weather histogram exhibits considerably more spread, relative to the value of the mean than does the kWh histogram. That is, the variation in CDD is much greater than the variation in the monthly kWh. This is a result of the fact that the baseload is not sensitive to CDD changes and it accounts for about 50 percent of monthly kWh use.[2]

All that is left in representing a distribution of August kWh use is to add the random variation represented by the RV term in the equation. Excel is used to generate 10,000 observations whose values follow a normal distribution with a mean of 590 kWh and a standard deviation of 15,837 kWh based on the RV specification in Table 8.17.

The distribution of August kW including RV is shown in Figure 8.8. Compared to the distribution without RV, the new distribution has spread out slightly and shifted to yield slightly larger values.

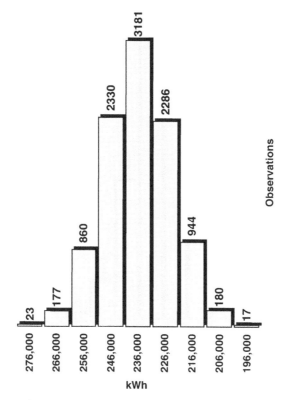

**FIGURE 8.7**   August kWh Distribution

## Other Energy Use Distributions

Other energy use distributions are developed with the same methodology applied in the previous section. Associated relationships are listed here.

$$\text{Winter kWh(dist)} = 108{,}195 + 33.06 * \text{HDD(mean, stdev)} + \text{RV(mean, stdev)}$$

$$\text{Summer kW(dist)} = 442.2 + 0.577 \, \text{CDD(mean, stdev)} + \text{RV(mean, stdev)}$$

$$\text{Winter kW(dist)} = 291.4 + 0.573 * \text{HDD(mean, stdev)} + \text{RV(mean, stdev)}$$

$$\text{Natural Gas kBtu(dist)} = 117{,}515 + 2{,}343 * \text{HDD(mean, stdev)} + \text{RV(mean, stdev)}$$

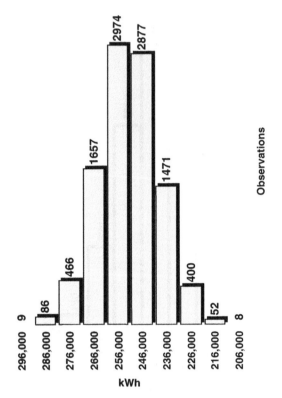

**FIGURE 8.8**  August kWh Distribution with
CDD and RV Impacts

Each of these equations is applied to a distribution of degree-days and random variations to generate a distribution of kWh, kW and natural gas uses for each month in the forecast horizon.

## Natural Gas Price

Historical natural gas prices are not available for the Austin area; consequently Texas natural gas prices are used for the case study EBaR analysis. Figure 8.9 shows Texas natural gas prices since 1990.

While the early 2007 consensus forecast calls for a decline in natural gas prices, events in mid-2007 oil markets and the most recent information on world economic growth would seem to lend more credence to the contrarian forecast that suggests little in the way of declines in international oil prices. While natural gas and oil are not perfect substitutes, high oil prices apply

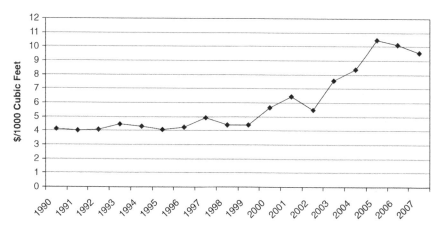

**FIGURE 8.9**  Texas Natural Gas Prices

upward pressure to natural gas prices. Since any estimate of world economic growth depends so heavily on nonquantifiable factors, and includes considerable uncertainty, any attempt to develop distributions based on statistical analysis is unwise.

It is possible, however, to develop boundaries on likely natural gas price outcomes based on information at hand. For instance, the natural gas price peak in 2005 that occurred because of hurricane Katrina damage can serve as a likely upper boundary. After a November 2005 price of $15.07/MMBtu, the price settled back to an average of $11.94 for the first two months of 2006. $12.00/MMBtu is selected as a reasonable upper boundary with this perspective. The current $9.57/MMBtu might serve as a reasonable expected price with an expected lower price matching the average of 2001–2004 prices of $7.00/MMBtu.

With lower, mean, and upper values of $7.00, $9.57 and $12.00 per MMBtu (MMBtu and 1000 cubic feet are interchangeable units) the symmetric normal distribution will work well to represent the distribution of natural gas prices. Several options are available when the expected distribution is nonsymmetrical, including the use of a triangular distribution, other distributions, and mixed distributions.

If the upper and lower limits reflect a probability less than 2.5 percent that the price will be above $12.00 and less than 2.5 percent that it will be below $7.00, the resulting distribution is shown in Figure 8.10.

This price distribution applies to all years in the planning horizon. Price distributions can also be specified to include trends in means, and upper and lower boundaries as illustrated in the next chapter.

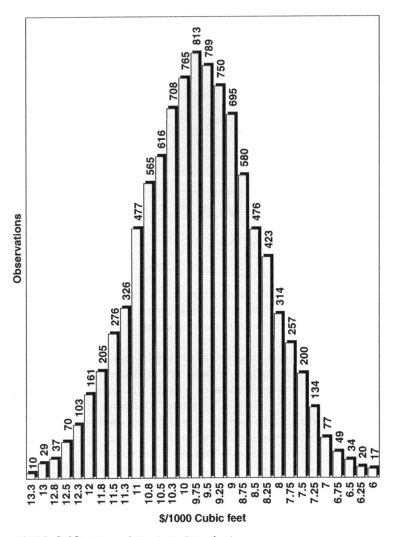

**FIGURE 8.10** Natural Gas Price Distribution

## Electricity Price

Figure 8.11 shows the Austin Energy average electricity energy price ($/kWh), excluding the demand charge ($/kW) for the case study facility and natural gas prices from Figure 8.9. About half of the electricity bill comes from the energy charge and half from the demand charge based on the monthly kW maximum use. The demand charge reflects primarily cost

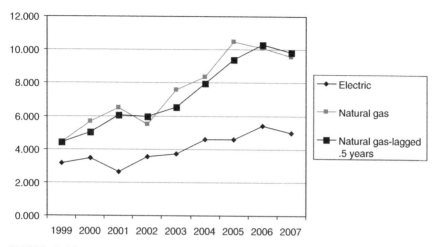

**FIGURE 8.11**   Electricity and Natural Gas Prices

recovery for generation facilities and remains relatively stable over most of the time period. The energy charge includes the cost of fuel used to generate electricity and reflects the most volatile component of electricity price series. Electricity price is represented in cents/kWh and gas prices is $/1000 cubic feet.

The figure shows that electricity prices in Texas, as in many other areas, have closely followed natural gas prices because natural gas reflects such a large fraction of electric generating fuel costs. A one/half-year lagged series (Gas-0.5 in the table below; the gas price shown for the year 2000 is an average of 1999 and 2000 gas prices) is also included in the figure. The city of Austin hedges its gas purchases and attempts to make relatively infrequent changes in the fuel adjustment component of the energy charge; consequently, it takes some time for the change in natural gas prices to impact electricity prices. That means that current electricity prices are more accurately represented as a function of lagged natural gas prices.

Given the causal relationship between natural gas and electric kWh prices, the distribution of electric prices is viewed as a function of natural gas prices. This relationship is implemented with the estimated regression equation of the two series shown in Figure 8.11. The estimation results are shown in Table 8.19.

The low p-values indicate a confident rejection of the null hypothesis that there is no relationship. The adjusted R-square statistic is 0.80, which indicates that 80 percent of the variation in the electric price series is explained by variation in the natural gas series faced by the customer. The

**TABLE 8.19**   kWh Prices and Natural Gas Price Relationship

|          | Coefficients | Standard Error | t Stat      | P-value     |
|----------|--------------|----------------|-------------|-------------|
| Intercept | 1.19593103  | 0.512009829    | 2.335757951 | 0.052169744 |
| Gas-0.5   | 0.38755796  | 0.067638018    | 5.72988347  | 0.00071302  |

average absolute error is 6.5 percent (errors are negative and positive and sum to zero as a characteristic of the regression process).

Natural gas prices are determined first by a draw from the natural gas price distribution. The gas price is supplied to the equation represented in Table 8.19, which determines the kWh price for electricity. A random variation associated with the relationship between electric and natural gas prices is also introduced that reflects the standard deviation of 0.387 for the residuals.

The peak demand price component ($/kW) does not vary with natural gas and is assumed to remain the same in the planning horizon.

## SUMMARY

This chapter illustrates the estimation of parameters used to define EBaR weather-related energy-use distributions as well as price distributions. The objective of the chapter is to provide a conceptual background on the estimation process; however, sufficient detail is included to serve as a roadmap for readers to apply the analysis and develop distribution parameters, using data for their facilities. Both an algebraic and statistical approach are described in the development of weather-related energy-use distributions. Analysis tools applied in the text are available in Excel, and their application is illustrated in detail. The quantitative applications described here are also provided as an automated process using software available at energybudgetsatrisk.com.

A variety of issues related to estimating distribution parameters is also discussed including analysis complexity. The chapter ends with a description of EBaR distribution development using parameters estimated in earlier sections.

# EBaR Budget Analysis (EBaR$_{budget}$)

**C**hapter 9 covers Steps 4 and 5 in the EBaR analysis framework for the energy budgets application including:

4. Monte Carlo analysis to extract values for variables based on their distributions.
5. Analysis evaluations and assessment.

## MONTE CARLO FRAMEWORK

EBaR Monte Carlo analysis is the process of extracting information from input variable distributions, calculating energy bills and generating a distribution of energy costs. Draws from the distribution are accomplished with a random number generator, and the energy cost calculation process is completed numerous times with the results of each calculation saved away. The Monte Carlo process can best be illustrated by describing individual steps undertaken by the software in the case study example.

Step 1. Draw one CDD value from each month's CDD distribution.

Step 2. Draw one HDD value from each month's HDD distribution.

Step 3. Draw random variation (RV) values for each month for each of the five equations estimated above (summer kWh, summer kW, winter kWh, winter kW, and winter natural gas equations).

Step 4. Apply CDD, HDD, and RV values to the appropriate equations to estimate monthly kWh, kW, and natural gas energy use.

Step 5. Draw natural gas price value from natural gas distribution.

Step 6. Apply the natural gas price to the electricity use equation in the previous section to estimate an electricity energy price ($/kWh).

Step 7. Apply electricity energy prices (\$/kWh), demand (\$/kW) charges and natural gas prices to monthly energy data to develop total energy cost.

Step 8. Save electricity cost, natural gas cost, and total energy cost.

Step 9. Repeat steps 1 through 8 until the distribution of electric, natural gas, and total costs undergo negligible changes with each succeeding group of 10,000 observations.

The end result of the process is a distribution of electric, natural gas, and total costs that reflect variations in weather and energy prices.

The number of distributions on the input side increases the number of observations required to achieve stability in the results. Given the four distributions applied above, the number of rounds required in the Monte Carlo process can become exceeding large, though a variety of techniques can be used to insure an efficient sampling of information from each of the distributions.

The steps described above apply empirical distributions developed in the previous chapter in a Monte Carlo process to translate information on electric and natural gas prices, summer and winter weather variables and random sources of energy use variation into a probability distribution of energy costs that provides the best estimate of next year's energy budget and budget contingencies.

It is important to remember that an EBaR application does not require users to conduct each of these steps themselves. Software available at energybudgetsatrisk.com automates the entire EBaR analysis.

## EVALUATION AND ASSESSMENT

Quantitative relationships developed in Chapter 8 form the basis for the case study results presented in this and following chapters. The Monte Carlo analysis framework summarized in the previous section is applied here.

### Point Estimates

Monte Carlo software can be applied with zero standard deviations for each of the distributions to get a single-point estimate of energy use and energy costs. All of the relationships developed in the previous chapter are applied with their mean values. Mean monthly CDD and HDD provide point estimates of monthly kWh, kW, and kBtu using the estimated equation for each variable and the mean values of the random variations for each equation. These monthly energy use estimates are applied to the mean estimate of

**TABLE 9.1**   Case Study Energy Use and Cost Characteristics

|  | Energy Use | Units | Annual Cost |
|---|---|---|---|
| Electricity | 1,939 | MWH | $207,752 |
| Natural gas | 5,559 | MMBtu | $53,201 |

natural gas price (9.57), and the mean gas price is applied to the electric price–natural gas price equation to determine the energy kWh charge. The resulting energy use represents the best point estimate of future energy one can derive without using distribution information. Annual energy use and cost estimates based on this information are presented in Table 9.1.

Monthly energy use and cost characteristics are shown in Table 9.2 and Figure 9.1. Electricity energy costs in Figure 9.2 are separated into energy (kWh) and demand (kW) costs. Demand charges are approximately equal to energy charges. The annual peak demand of 792 kW yields an annual load factor of 0.28 (average annual hourly electricity use divided by maximum kW in the year), which is lower than average for a 120,000 square foot office building, indicating a peaked electricity use profile. Natural gas use per square foot is also greater than average for office buildings. Both characteristics suggest inefficiencies in the HVAC system, which will be explored in the next chapter when efficiency investment options are considered.

**TABLE 9.2**   Case Study of Monthly Energy Use and Cost Characteristics

| Month | Electricity Use (kWh) | Peak kW | Electricity Cost ($) | Natural Gas Use (kBtu) | Natural Gas Cost ($) | Total Energy Cost() |
|---|---|---|---|---|---|---|
| Jan. | 124,196 | 603 | $14,665 | 1,253,830 | $11,999 | $26,664 |
| Feb. | 119,038 | 513 | $13,242 | 888,321 | $8,501 | $21,743 |
| March | 113,228 | 424 | $11,782 | 529,878 | $5,071 | $16,853 |
| April | 143,215 | 529 | $14,816 | 243,996 | $2,335 | $17,151 |
| May | 176,280 | 631 | $18,846 | 145,590 | $1,393 | $20,239 |
| June | 209,873 | 726 | $22,081 | 140,904 | $1,348 | $23,430 |
| July | 230,538 | 789 | $24,144 | 140,904 | $1,348 | $25,492 |
| Aug. | 231,478 | 792 | $24,237 | 140,904 | $1,348 | $25,586 |
| Sept. | 199,352 | 693 | $21,032 | 145,590 | $1,393 | $22,425 |
| Oct. | 154,487 | 564 | $16,671 | 215,880 | $2,066 | $18,737 |
| Nov. | 115,269 | 448 | $12,202 | 621,219 | $5,945 | $18,147 |
| Dec. | 121,914 | 563 | $14,036 | 1,092,160 | $10,452 | $24,488 |
| Annual | 1,938,868 | | $207,752 | 5,559,176 | $53,201 | $260,953 |

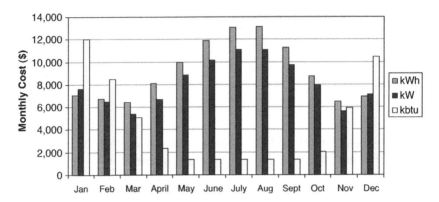

**FIGURE 9.1** Monthly Energy Costs

## Distribution Estimates

The Monte Carlo process is now applied with means and standard deviations (or lower and upper bound estimates in the case of natural gas prices), the systematic energy use (kWh, kW, kBtu) relationships and the relationship between natural gas and electricity prices. The Monte Carlo forecast reflects one million simulations with observations drawn from each of the distributions. The EBaR software uses a sample design that efficiently draws the sample observations from the distributions.

The distribution of natural gas costs, electric costs and total gas plus electric costs is shown in Figure 9.2. As indicated in the figure, the peaks of

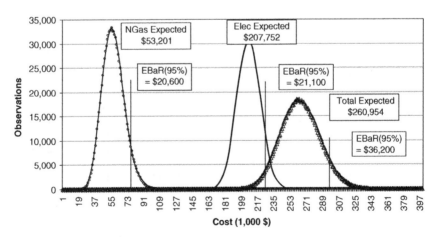

**FIGURE 9.2** Monthly Energy Cost Distributions

**TABLE 9.3**   Expected Energy Budgets and Variances

| | Budget and Variances | | | Budgets | | |
|---|---|---|---|---|---|---|
| | Electricity | Natural Gas | Total | Electricity | Natural Gas | Total |
| EBaR$_{budget,mean}$ | $207,752 | $53,201 | $260,953 | $207,752 | $53,201 | $260,953 |
| EBaR$_{budget,90}$ | $16,300 | $15,500 | $27,800 | $224,052 | $68,701 | $288,753 |
| EBaR$_{budget,95}$ | $21,100 | $20,600 | $36,200 | $228,852 | $73,801 | $297,153 |
| EBaR$_{budget,97.5}$ | $25,100 | $25,200 | $43,600 | $232,852 | $78,401 | $304,553 |

each distribution correspond to the point estimates and the expected values of electricity, natural gas and total utility costs. EbaR$_{budget,x}$ is the maximum budget variance likely to occur at a given confidence level, x. Thus, the expected electricity budget is $207,752 with an EbaR$_{budget,95}$ of $21,100 (maximum budget variance of $21,100 at a 95 percent confidence level). The interpretation of these results is straightforward; the energy manager can plan on a budget of $260,954 with confidence that the energy budget variance will be no greater than $36,200.

The distributions provide a great deal of additional information that is not detailed in the figure. For instance, the EBaR at a 97.5 level of confidence is $43,600. That is, the budget variance is nearly guaranteed to be no greater than $43,600. On the other hand, there is a 90 percent chance that the budget variance will not exceed $27,800. Of course, there is a 50 percent chance that energy costs will be less than the expected budget; in fact there is a 10 percent probability that energy costs will fall short of the expected budget by $28,000 or more. This and similar information is summarized in Table 9.3.

While the mean of electric and natural gas budgets equals the mean of the total budget, variances of the total budget are less, in absolute value, at each confidence level than the sum of the electricity and natural gas variances. The nature of the uncertainty in individual variables results in a smaller spread of the outcome distribution when all variables are considered at the same time.

## Sensitivity Analysis

Information on individual sources of budget variation are useful in evaluating these results. One way of evaluating contributions of the various inputs to the distribution of results is to examine each variable's individual contribution to variation in the analysis. Table 9.4 shows EbaR$_{budget,95}$ for the

**TABLE 9.4**  Baseline and Single Variable
Contributions to EBaR

| Application | EbaR$_{budget,95}$ |
|---|---|
| Baseline | $36,200 |
| Degree-days | $11,400 |
| Electricity price | $17,700 |
| Natural gas price | $18,800 |
| Model variables | $14,300 |

baseline analysis and contributions of individual variables. Figure 9.3 shows
the distributions associated with each of these analyses.

Budget uncertainty resulting from degree-days variation is the least at
$11,400 and natural gas is the greatest at $18,800. The contribution of
natural gas cost variation, however, is about four times more important
than one would expect based solely on its share of the total energy budget.

The nature of these distributions is such that variations in one distribution tend to somewhat offset variations in other distributions; consequently
the sum of the EbaR values is nearly twice the baseline EBaR of $36,200.

Relationships between kWh, kW and kBtu and degree days were estimated with the estimated systematic relationship and the random component. How important is the random component or model error in explaining
the variation shown in the EBaR budget results? This issue is addressed in

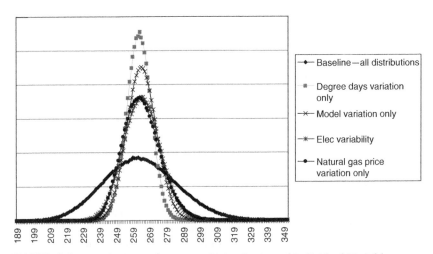

**FIGURE 9.3**  Baseline Distribution and Distribution of Individual Variables

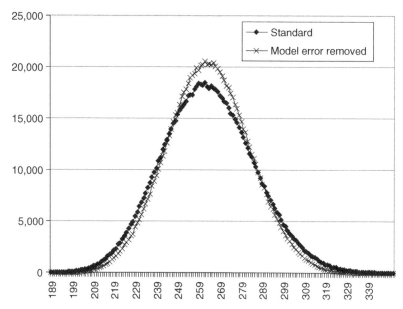

**FIGURE 9.4** Impact of Removing All Model Variation

Figure 9.4 where this source of variation is removed from the EbaR results. The figure indicates that this model error has minimal impact on the determination of expected budget variance. That is, the uncertainty reflected by errors in estimating relationships between degree-days and energy variables is relatively unimportant in the analysis.

## SUMMARY

EBaR budget analysis provides a baseline to plan current and future energy budgets, given existing equipment.

In the case study facility, an annual budget of $260,953 is the expected value. There is a 90 percent probability that the budget variance will be less than $27,800, a 95 percent probability of less than $36,200, and a worst-case outcome of $43,600 or more is likely to occur with a probability of 2.5 percent.

EbaR$_{budget}$ results are presented at different confidence levels to facilitate an assessment of the costs of bearing different levels of risk. If the EbaR$_{budget}$ value at the risk level used by the organization is greater than what can be absorbed, some action should be taken to hedge against this outcome.

A hedge is an investment designed to offset the risk associated with extreme budget variances. Hedging can take the form of a financial instrument. For instance, Wells Fargo recently announced a program to provide access to financial hedging instruments for its business customers. Another form of hedging is a physical hedge accomplished with an investment in energy efficiency technologies. In addition to reducing risk, or the size of the budget variance, investments in energy-efficiency technologies also reduce annual energy budgets by more than the cost of the investment. In this role, investments act to increase cash flows for the organization and add to the value of the facility as a capital asset.

Efficiency investment analysis is the topic of the next chapter.

## CHAPTER 10

# EBaR Efficiency Investment Analysis (EBaR$_{irr}$)

This chapter presents the heart of EBaR analysis including:

- Analysis of efficiency investment options
  - Internal rate of return
  - Net savings as a new revenue source
- Impacts of efficiency investments on
  - Energy budgets
  - Budget variances
  - Increased value of facility capital assets

The last section in this chapter addresses analysis of $CO_2$ and other emissions reductions achieved with energy efficiency investments.

## SOLVING THE EFFICIENCY INVESTMENT PROBLEM

Much of the material in the early part of this book addresses the difficulty organizations have in effectively evaluating investments in energy efficient technologies. Impressive market-tested energy efficient technologies are widely available; however, uncertainty associated with energy prices, weather, equipment performance, and a variety of other factors makes it difficult to evaluate these investments.

Traditional investment analysis taught in business schools recommends incorporating risk factors in discount rates used to assess the present value of future income streams. However, determining an appropriate discount rate is not a practical suggestion. Payback analysis and/or high internal rate of return thresholds are typically used to assess efficiency investments in practice. The conservative thresholds used in these analyses typically filter out all but sure-thing investments providing an imprecise approach to avoiding risk that also overlooks many profitable investments.

The Monte Carlo framework described in previous chapters applies an intuitive approach to evaluating the return on efficiency investments and risks associated with those investments. As illustrated in previous chapters, all important sources of variation in energy budgets can be quantified and brought together with Monte Carlo analysis to provide information on the likelihood of alternative outcomes including the traditional expected values or most likely point estimates.

As with the energy budgets analysis in the chapter, a sample of input variable values is drawn from each distribution, and energy costs are developed; however, in the investment application, energy savings associated with a specific technology investment is evaluated. This process generates a distribution of energy cost savings outcomes that present a comprehensive picture of an expected investment return as well as a distribution of returns. The distribution of outcomes permits investors to assess both the risk and rewards associated with the investments.

## CASE STUDY: EFFICIENCY INVESTMENT OPTIONS

Two efficiency options are considered for the case study facility. The first is a package of lighting technologies, and the second is an HVAC recommissioning effort.

Lighting efficiency options include replacing T12 lamp/ballast systems with super T8 lamp/electronic ballasts, delamping (removing some lighting fixtures), installation of occupancy and day lighting controls in selected areas, and replacement of selected incandescent lamps with compact fluorescent lamps. The lighting manufacturer's representatives conducted a lighting analysis and estimated savings of 483,000 kWh per year and 145 kW peak electricity use. Both of these figures include direct and indirect savings with the indirect savings coming from reduced air conditioning and ventilation loads as a result of less lighting waste heat. The total cost of the lighting retrofit program is $100,000 based on a fixed cost contract. Energy use savings are substantial reflecting approximately 20 percent of electricity use and 24 percent of average monthly kW savings. The impact on natural gas space heating is estimated to be negligible. The building energy manager's calculations of changes in connected loads applied to operating hours indicate savings within 15 percent of savings estimates provided by the contractor.

Analysis of the HVAC system showed an oversized and poorly designed system. The HVAC contractor has offered a recommissioning that will completely update the HVAC system in addition to a building energy management control system. The contractor estimates savings of 30 percent for AC electricity use (after lighting changes) and 65 percent for natural gas heating use. The fixed cost estimate for the recommissioning project is $125,000. The contractor estimates that achieved savings will be no less than 80 percent of the estimates, which is confirmed by independent analysis of the energy manager.

The lighting program has a payback of about 2.1 years, and the HVAC is expected to pay back in a little over three years. These investments would be viewed as marginal by many organizations and rejected out of hand by most because payback thresholds typically range from 1.5 to 2.0 years.

## REPRESENTING INVESTMENT ANALYSIS UNCERTAINTY

The same sources of uncertainty in budget analysis discussed in the last chapter are present in efficiency investment analysis; however, uncertainty concerning investment performance must be added to the analysis. Two results of the analysis are of primary interest: the impact of the investment on monthly energy costs and budget risk, and the financial returns associated with the investment.

The lighting investment is considered first. The efficiency measures being considered will significantly change HVAC needs, so tuning up the HVAC system must wait until after the lighting investment is completed unless the lighting program is rejected.

### Internal Rate of Return (IRR) Criterion

The internal rate of return measures the return on the energy efficiency investment over its lifetime. For instance, a one-time investment of $10,000 with a ten-year life (the lifetime of the case study fluorescent system) that returns $4,300 annually in savings has an IRR of 41.7 percent.

The IRR equation is:

$$\$10,000 = \$4,300/(1+\text{irr})^1 + \$4,300/(1+\text{irr})^2 + \cdots + \$4,300/(1+\text{irr})^{10}$$

Substituting 0.417 for the irr variable in the equation gives a sum on the right hand side that is equal to $10,000. As indicated by this equation, information on the initial investment cost and annual energy cost savings is used to solve the equation for an IRR value that makes the initial investment exactly equal to the discounted future cost savings over the investment lifetime. The IRR is perfect for representing returns in a Monte Carlo–based EBaR analysis. Each of the one million draws from the distributions reflects a single set of cost variables including electricity price, a natural gas price, and 12 monthly kWh, kW and kBtu energy uses. These data determine energy costs and savings associated with lighting and HVAC efficiency measures for this one observation. The output of the Monte Carlo analysis is one million observations on energy cost and savings, in the form of achieved IRR and net savings values (energy cost savings minus the amortized cost of the investment) associated with the efficiency investments. These observations form a distribution of IRRs and net savings that describe the expected return and the probabilities associated with the distribution of returns.

## Case Study IRR Results—Lighting

Monte Carlo analysis results are show in Figure 10.1 and Table 10.1. The most interesting characteristic of the IRR analysis is that the extreme values of expected IRR are so attractive. That is, using information only on the payback of 2.1 years for an expected IRR of 43.2 percent, this investment would appear to be too risky for most organizations to undertake. Risk in EBaR analysis is quantified as the probability of an IRR less than the required threshold. However, these results show that there is only a 2.5 chance of realizing an IRR of less than 33.9 percent and a 5 percent chance of a return less than 35.2 percent.

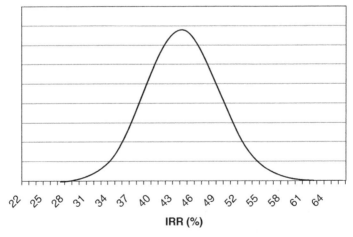

**FIGURE 10.1**  Distribution of Lighting Efficiency Measure IRRs

**TABLE 10.1**    EBaR Analysis of Lighting Energy Efficiency Measures

| IRR Measures | Values | Net Cash Flow |
|---|---|---|
| EBaR$_{irr,mean}$ | 43.2 | $26,800 |
| EBaR$_{irr,90}$ | 36.9 | $20,900 |
| EBaR$_{irr,95}$ | 35.2 | $19,400 |
| EBaR$_{irr,97.5}$ | 33.9 | $18,200 |

EBaR$_{irr,mean}$ and EBaR$_{irr,x}$ are used to characterize the expected IRR and the lowest IRR at the confidence level x. In this case EBaR$_{irr,mean}$ = 43.2 and EBaR$_{irr,95}$ = 35.2. Also included in the table and in Figure 10.2 are the expected net cash flows. Net refers to the fact that the annual financing costs have been deducted from the annual energy cost savings. This amount reflects the profit on this investment or the increased annual cash flow. Results in Table 10.1 reveal a minimum increased net cash flow of $18,200 and an expected net cash flow of $26,800. The net cash flow is especially important because it provides a new revenue incentive for making the investment.

The lighting efficiency measures (EEM) have also changed expected energy costs and EbaR budget values as shown in Table 10.2 and Figure 10.3. Expected energy costs are reduced by more than $44,000 and worst-case

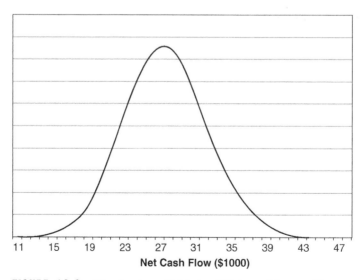

**FIGURE 10.2**    Distribution of Lighting Efficiency Measure Net Cash Flows

**TABLE 10.2**   Comparison of Expected Energy Costs and Variance with and without the lighting Energy Efficiency Measure (EEM)

|  | Lighting EEM | | | Baseline | | |
|---|---|---|---|---|---|---|
|  | Electricity | Natural Gas | Total | Electricity | Natural Gas | Total |
| EBaR$_{budget,mean}$ | $159,300 | $53,201 | $216,500 | $207,752 | $53,201 | $260,953 |
| EBaR$_{budget,90}$ | $13,600 | $15,500 | $25,200 | $16,300 | $15,500 | $27,800 |
| EBaR$_{budget,95}$ | $17,700 | $20,600 | $32,900 | $21,100 | $20,600 | $36,200 |
| EBaR$_{budget,97.5}$ | $21,200 | $25,200 | $39,600 | $25,100 | $25,200 | $43,600 |

energy budgets have been reduced even more, by $48,000. The distributions in Figure 10.3 show the significant shift to the left (lower costs) and a narrowing of the distributions reflecting a reduction in risk.

## Addressing the "What Ifs?"

While the results of the EBaR investment analysis look attractive for this investment option and the analysis has included major sources of uncertainty associated with returns on this investment—what if the energy manager's

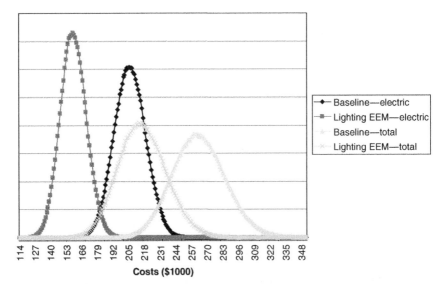

**FIGURE 10.3**   Energy Budget Distributions with and without Lighting EEM

expectation of savings is in error? The energy manager's original assessment may have relied on information provided by the manufacturer that may reflect a more positive statement of outcomes than warranted by experience. Or perhaps the analyst's views of future energy prices and their distributions may not correspond to those who are conducting the financial analysis at a higher management level.

These alternative views can be evaluated with scenario analysis that modifies input parameters to reflect alternative assumptions about future events.

An example is provided here to illustrate this process.

### Example

*What happens to the investment if the price of electricity declines because of a decline in natural gas prices of $2.00/1000 cubic feet from its current level of $9.57 per MMBtu? The impact of a natural gas price decline comes through the fuel adjustment component of the electric bill. This relationship was estimated in Chapter 8, so this scenario can be evaluated as shown in Table 10.3. Both IRR and net cash flows are reduced; however, the investment is highly profitable.*

### Case Study IRR Results—HVAC

It is important to evaluate each energy efficiency measure at the margin; that is, by comparing reductions in energy costs from a baseline that includes energy cost savings of all investments more profitable than the current investment. In some cases, energy efficiency program analysis must also consider the relationship between different energy efficiency measures. For instance, lighting energy efficiency measures change air conditioning and ventilation energy use so HVAC measures should be considered only after lighting measures are evaluated.

**TABLE 10.3**  Comparison of Expected Savings and Cost With $2 Reduction in Natural Gas Prices

|  | IRR | Net Cash Flow |
|---|---|---|
| EBaR$_{irr,mean}$ | 40.7 | $24,400 |
| EBaR$_{irr,90}$ | 34.6 | $18,800 |
| EBaR$_{irr,90}$ | 33.0 | $17,300 |
| EBaR$_{irr,90}$ | 31.6 | $16,100 |

**TABLE 10.4**  Evaluation of HVAC Efficiency Investment Analysis

|  | IRR | Net Cash Flow |
|---|---|---|
| $EBaR_{irr,mean}$ | 39.6 | $29,200 |
| $EBaR_{irr,90}$ | 28.3 | $16,400 |
| $EBaR_{irr,95}$ | 25.7 | $13,600 |
| $EBaR_{irr,97.4}$ | 23.5 | $11,300 |

In the case study application, HVAC efficiency measures are considered after the lighting measures have been incorporated. An important element of the EBaR analysis at this second stage is that uncertainty in results of the lighting program are incorporated in analysis of the HVAC program as well.

It is important to apply marginal efficiency investment analysis when several measures are being considered. If the results of two programs are combined, one of the programs may have a large enough IRR to more than make up for a program that does not meet IRR thresholds. In that case, investing in both programs is not economical. The organization's resources would be better spent investing only in those programs that pass marginal analysis.

Table 10.4 shows investment analysis results for the HVAC efficiency measures where IRR and net cash flow results are based on cost savings after lighting results have been accounted for. That is, savings from the lighting project are not included in analysis of the HVAC project. Both IRR and cash flow results recommend the HVAC investment.

Since the HVAC investment analysis results are acceptable and the lighting program was determined to be acceptable earlier, there is no real need to evaluate both the lighting and HVAC program together. However, if both measures are presented as a package for approval, the next step is to consider IRR and net cash flow for an investment package that includes both measures.

## CASE STUDY EFFICIENCY INVESTMENT ANALYSIS RESULTS

Table 10.5 shows energy efficiency investment IRRs, net cash flows, and energy cost distribution statistics for the combined lighting and HVAC package. Expected annual energy cost savings are $98,153 for an initial investment cost of $225,000. Analysis results indicate that $EBaR_{budget,95}$,

**TABLE 10.5**  Evaluation of HVAC and Efficiency Investment Analysis

|  | IRR | Net Cash Flow |
|---|---|---|
| EBaR$_{irr,mean}$ | 42.3 | $58,300 |
| EBaR$_{irr,90}$ | 35.5 | $44,000 |
| EBaR$_{irr,95}$ | 33.5 | $40,000 |
| EBaR$_{irr,97.5}$ | 32.4 | $37,800 |

|  | HVAC and Lighting Efficiency Measures Analysis | | | Baseline Analysis | | |
|---|---|---|---|---|---|---|
|  | Electricity | Natural Gas | Total | Electricity | Natural Gas | Total |
| EBaR$_{budget,mean}$ | $143,300 | $19,500 | $162,800 | $207,752 | $53,201 | $260,953 |
| EBaR$_{budget,90}$ | $12,200 | $5,100 | $15,500 | $16,300 | $15,500 | $27,800 |
| EBaR$_{budget,95}$ | $15,900 | $6,900 | $20,200 | $21,100 | $20,600 | $36,200 |
| EBaR$_{budget,97.5}$ | $19,000 | $8,500 | $24,200 | $25,100 | $25,200 | $43,600 |

the maximum expected budget variance, or budget risk, at a 95 percent confidence level is $16,000 less after the lighting and HVAC efficiency investments. The expected IRR is 42.3 percent with a net cash flow of $58,300; that is, an increase of $58,300 in operating income after financing costs are deducted from annual energy savings.

A worst-case outcome, with a 2.5 percent probability of occurrence, yields an IRR of 32.4 percent and a net cash flow of $37,800. Organizations that use payback to qualify project risk would likely have rejected the current project with its payback of 2.3 years; however, the Monte Carlo analysis shows that the investment has virtually no risk in achieving a minimum IRR of 32.4 percent.

With a capitalization rate of 8.0, the increase in the capital asset value of the office facility is $466,000 or $3.89 per square foot based on the increase in net income. After the investments have been paid off, the capital asset value of the facility will increase by $785,000, or $6.54 per square foot.

IRR and net cash flow investment analysis results are illustrated graphically in Figures 10.4 and 10.5. The improvement in both the expected budget and budget variance is clearly illustrated in Figure 10.6 with the new energy cost distribution shifted to the left by $98,153 and a variance that is almost half of the variance prior to the lighting and HVAC efficiency investments. The narrowing of the distribution is a graphical representation of the reduction in budget risk.

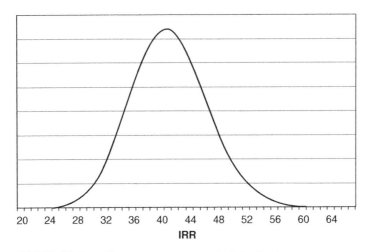

**FIGURE 10.4**   Efficiency Investment IRR Distribution

## ACHIEVING CO₂ AND OTHER GREEN GOALS

Private and public organizations are increasingly adopting sustainability goals to reduce direct and indirect emissions of $CO_2$ and other greenhouse gases. The single most important activity in meeting these goals for most organizations is the reduction of energy use in buildings. Facility emissions can be classified as direct and indirect. Nearly all direct emissions in

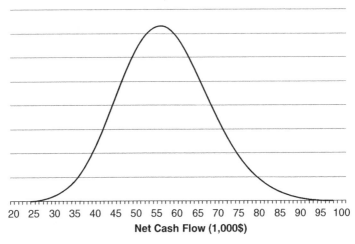

**FIGURE 10.5**   Efficiency Investment Net Cash Flow Distribution

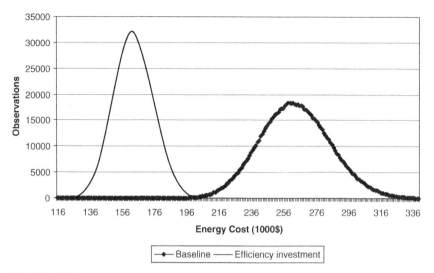

**FIGURE 10.6**   Energy Budget Distributions Before and After Lighting/HVAC
Investments

facilities come from fossil-fuel-fired space heating and water heating equipment. Indirect emissions are power plant emissions required to produce electricity used in the facility. As indicated in Chapter 1, 69 percent of electricity generated in the United States is generated by burning coal and natural gas. Any serious effort to reduce an organization's carbon footprint or to achieve other energy-related green goals begins with an assessment of current direct and indirect emissions. Environmental impacts of efficiency investments can then be evaluated relative to the baseline.

Table 10.6 and Figure 10.7 show baseline $CO_2$, NOx, particulate and $SO_2$ emissions along with emissions after the lighting and HVAC investments. As indicated, carbon emissions are reduced by 37.4 percent and reductions in other emissions range from 31 to 38 percent.

**TABLE 10.6**   Emissions Baseline and Impact of Efficiency Investment

|  | $CO_2$ (1,000 lbs) | NOx (lbs) | Particulates (lbs) | $SO_2$ (lbs) |
|---|---|---|---|---|
| Baseline | 3,293 | 3,796 | 631 | 2,526 |
| Efficiency Investment | 2,061 | 2,349 | 435 | 1,743 |
| Reduction | 1,232 | 1,447 | 196 | 784 |
| Reduction (%) | 37.4% | 38.1% | 31.0% | 31.0% |

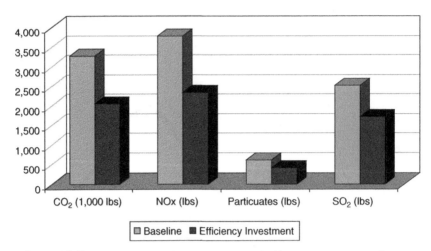

**FIGURE 10.7**   Emissions Baseline and Impact of Efficiency Investment (lbs/year)

EBaR analysis also provides estimates of emissions at alternative confidence levels. Figure 10.8 shows expected carbon emission reduction at various confidence levels. As indicated in the figure, a worst-case result provides $CO_2$ reductions of 808,721 pounds per year or a reduction of 24.6 percent of baseline use. This worst-case result would occur only with extremely

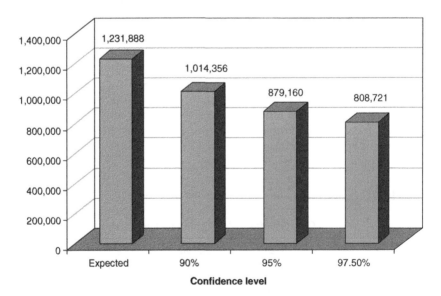

**FIGURE 10.8**   $CO_2$ Reductions at Alternative Confidence Levels (lbs/year)

warm winters, extremely cool summers, and extremely poor performance of the investment options as defined by the input distributions developed in Chapter 8.

The lighting and efficiency investment programs can be expected to provide a net cash flow of $58,300 per year, an internal rate of return of 42.3 percent, *and a reduction in the building's carbon footprint of 37.4 percent.*

## SUMMARY

This chapter applied Monte Carlo analysis to the empirical relationships developed in previous chapters to evaluate investments in two energy efficiency measures: a lighting package and an HVAC package. Lighting investment analysis was conducted first because changes in lighting waste heat affects HVAC options and cost savings. HVAC analysis considered the marginal energy cost improvements made after lighting effects were determined. Both packages, reflecting profitable investments, were then considered together as a single investment option.

The distribution of IRR and net cash flow (NCF) outcomes was determined with Monte Carlo analysis and investment risks were quantified and considered using IRR and net cash flow distributions. Investment risks associated with an alternative natural gas price forecast were also considered by applying scenario analysis.

The example illustrates the importance of considering net savings, the savings in energy costs beyond the cost of financing the equipment. In this example, efficiency investments reduce net operating costs by $58,300, which is equivalent to providing an annual increase in revenue of $58,300.

The last section of this chapter illustrates the use of EBaR analysis to support carbon reduction and other sustainability goals. The Austin office case study lighting investment is shown to reduce $CO_2$ emissions by 37.4 percent and other emissions from 31 to 38 percent.

## CHAPTER 11

# Energy Budgets at Risk in Competitive Markets

**S**everal states, most notably Texas and New York, have developed reasonably robust competitive electricity markets. A handful of states also have competitive natural gas markets. Business, institutional, and government energy customers in competitive energy states should consider energy pricing options as an additional dimension in EBaR analysis.

Energy customers in deregulated states have a wide choice of energy price options that can significantly impact energy costs and savings potentials that are associated with energy efficiency options. Poor energy pricing choices can provide the worst of all energy budget worlds: higher prices than would have occurred with regulated utilities and pricing terms that effectively limit net cash flow (NCF) benefits of energy efficiency options.

Competitive market EBaR applications are addressed in this chapter.

## COMPETITIVE ENERGY SUPPLIERS

Competitive energy suppliers buy energy on the market and resell that energy to individual customers. In the early days of competitive markets, relatively few pricing products were available to energy customers; they differed primarily in contract length and ranged from monthly to three or more years. Beginning around 2004 competitive electricity suppliers in deregulated states started advertising more complex pricing products including electric prices tied to the price of natural gas, options characteristics that allow customers to limit price swings, and products based on other hedging options. Electricity providers can now provide almost any electric pricing option imaginable, especially for larger customers.

As discussed in Chapter 3, the cost of providing service to an electricity customer depends on the hour of the day and the season when the electricity is produced. Competitive providers often provide quotes based on kWh use. However, these average price quotes are based on demand charges (\$ per monthly maximum kW use) payable to the local transmission and distribution (T&D) company, other system charges and charges for electricity (kWh). Consequently, retail providers must analyze data on customer energy use to determine price quotes.

Price quotes for smaller customers with electric meters that record only monthly kWh or monthly kWh and peak demand are easier for competitive suppliers to determine because most states use class load profiles to determine electricity supply requirements for these customers. Many of these customers can shop for electricity on supplier web sites.

Competitive retail electricity providers (REP) must estimate the cost of providing electricity to meet needs of both large and small customers and develop their own risk management strategies to supply electricity to the grid as required to meet customer electricity needs. REP strategy objectives are to maximize profit subject to specified risk tolerance. Most electricity pricing products offered to customers do not include factors like weather that determine actual 15-minute electricity uses of a customer; consequently, suppliers conduct weather analysis of historical customer energy use similar to that applied in EBaR analysis to quantify likely variations in energy use outcomes of their customers. This energy risk management is different from that applied to facilities because it deals only with the energy commodity. Competitive energy suppliers cannot make investments to trade efficiency for energy costs, as is the case in an energy-using physical facility. Energy commodity risk management is a well-developed field that uses a variety of financial derivatives to manage risk. Commodity energy risk management is practiced by both competitive energy providers and regulated utilities to manage risk and protect against adverse price movements.

## PRICING/EFFICIENCY MISCONCEPTIONS IN COMPETITIVE MARKETS

Chapter 3 included a list of issues to consider in dealing with competitive energy suppliers, especially issues that customers who previously dealt with regulated utilities might not consider in competitive market dealings. This section addresses several misconceptions about electricity purchase and efficiency choices based partly on attendee comments at Texas A&M University workshops.

### My Price Depends Only on kWh

REPs make money on the spread between power purchase (or purchase and delivery costs when electricity sales are bundled with T&D charges) and sales revenue. Since purchase and delivery depend on customer hourly load profiles, REPs estimate the cost of service with each customer's load profile. When providing price quotes to customers, REPs often deliver the quote based only on total electricity use ($/kWh), even though customer monthly kW use is important in determining the total cost. In considering price offerings and efficiency options, it is important to remember that facility load profiles determine energy price quotes, regardless of how the price is presented to the customer.

## I'll Find a Good Fixed Price and Then Deal with Efficiency Investments

One strategy that has an intuitive appeal is to first lock in a fixed price and then address energy efficiency issues after energy prices are set. This strategy should be avoided for a number of reasons; however, the most important one is that implementing energy efficiency options or contracting with a competitive supplier to recognize future improvements in energy use profiles can significantly reduce the quoted price of electricity.

Energy price choices and efficiency investment decisions are related because efficiency improvements change price offers and energy prices determine returns on efficiency investments. This relationship is illustrated in Figure 11.1. Starting with Step 1, an REP determines a competitive pricing offer based, in part, on customer efficiency characteristics. The customer selects terms of a pricing contract in Step 2 which, in part, determines electricity cost savings associated with individual efficiency investments in Step 3 and establishes new efficiency characteristics of the facility in Step 4.

If the process had started with the efficiency investment process (Step 4), a new efficiency profile would have been transmitted to the REP in Step 1 resulting in a more attractive set of pricing options in Step 2. Relating this process to the case study described in the previous chapter, lighting/HVAC efficiency investments reduced peak electricity demand (kW) by a greater percentage than electricity use (kWh). This greater relative reduction in the most expensive component of energy cost of service, peak kW, will generate a lower electricity price offering from an REP, even if the price quote is in $/kWh terms. In addition to losing out on a better price offer, REP customers may incur penalties if kWh usage falls below a certain level.

If contracting for electric prices occurs at the same time efficiency investment analysis occurs, the price contract should include provisions for lower prices if the facility meets specific kWh and kW targets.

## Locking in Prices Minimizes Risk

Fixed prices are a full hedge for the period of the contract; that is, prices will not increase regardless of the price of natural gas or other market factors.

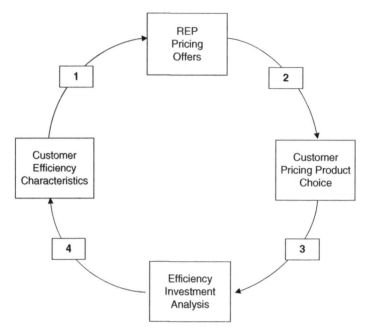

**FIGURE 11.1**   Pricing-Efficiency Choice Relationship

However, every hedge carries a cost. In this case the cost of the hedge is potential savings that could be achieved if the market price for electricity falls below the fixed price.

This cost can be quantified by examining the EBaR distributions for electricity price. For example, if an organization is buying electricity on a monthly basis, currently paying 12.0 cents/kWh and a competitive electricity supplier offers a price of 11.75 cents/kWh for the next 5 years, what are the costs and benefits of entering into the contract?

Locking in a price of 11.75 cents/kWh for the next 5 years would seem like a good choice, saving about $2,500 per year or $12,500 over the life of the contract for a facility that uses 1 million kWh annually. In addition, this fixed price offers protection in case natural gas prices increase, increasing the cost of electricity.

However, Figure 11.2 illustrates the costs associated with this choice based on the electricity price distribution used in the previous chapters. There is a 40 percent probability that the price of electricity will be less than the fixed price offer of 11.75 cents/kWh. Table 11.1 shows probabilities associated with other prices. There is a 31 percent chance that the price will be 11.5 cents or incurring a minimum annual cost of $5,000 associated

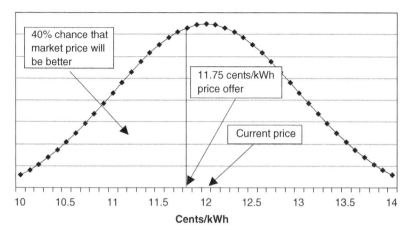

**FIGURE 11.2** EBaR Electricity Price Distribution

with taking the fixed price compared to continuing with monthly market pricing. Costs and probabilities associated with other market values are also included in Table 11.1.

While locking in electric and natural gas prices minimizes energy price risk, it carries a risk of forgone savings that cannot be captured if prices fall. One way of achieving the stability offered by a fixed price and limiting its cost is to negotiate a fixed price with the option of renegotiating if the market price falls below a specific threshold. On the other hand, an organization may want to use spot market pricing with an option to convert to a fixed price if the market price rises above a specific threshold. The value of these pricing options can be determined by applying EBaR analysis as described below.

**TABLE 11.1** Potential Costs of Locking in Electricity Price

| Market Price (cents/kWh) | Likelihood of Market Price or Lower | Annual Cost Savings at the Market Price ($) |
| --- | --- | --- |
| 11.75 | 40 | 2,500 |
| 11.5 | 31 | 5,000 |
| 11.25 | 23 | 7,500 |
| 11 | 16 | 10,000 |
| 10.75 | 11 | 12,500 |
| 10.5 | 5.5 | 15,000 |

## EBaR SIMULTANEOUS PRICING AND EFFICIENCY INVESTMENT CHOICE

Since energy price contracts impact efficiency investment returns and efficiency investments impact competitive price quotes, efficiency investment and purchasing decisions should be considered simultaneously. However, efficiency and purchasing decisions are almost always considered separately, usually by different departments within a single organization. There can be significant financial benefits to integrating these two decision processes. This section describes the use of the EBaR framework to integrate these decisions.

Prices for individual pricing options are referred to here as pricing products. Pricing products include fixed prices of various terms, heat rate products that tie electricity prices to natural gas prices and all other pricing specifications offered to customers. Prices for these products can change on a daily basis and are determined by REPs based in part on prices of futures and options contracts and prices of other financial derivatives they use to hedge their commodity price risk.

Provided with analysis of a facility's historical electricity use information, REPs provide price quotes, often in terms of $/kWh, though as mentioned above, this summary price is a final result of the REP's calculations that include costs associated with peak demand and other characteristics of customer hourly loads. Since this process requires calculations by REPs using up-to-date financial derivative prices, receiving pricing quotes is not currently a real-time process for medium and larger customers. For some smaller customers, standard or Web-based quotes that change less frequently are available from some REPs.

Organizations who have developed an EBaR analysis capability can easily evaluate various pricing products and the value of including options, like the option to renegotiate a fixed price and to cap a market price mentioned in the previous section.

This process is illustrated in Figure 11.3, which reflects the EBaR extension to Figure 11.1. Extra steps have been included in the retail energy provider-customer pricing process. The progression begins at Step 1 (the box indicates both Steps 1 and 5) with the REP providing a variety of pricing offers that differ in length of contract, options, and other characteristics of interest to the customers.

Potential efficiency investments are evaluated with each pricing product and the REP is asked to provide a second set of pricing products (step 5) based on the new efficiency characteristics (that is, new expected hourly electric loads). Significant changes in facility energy use patterns, like those of the case study application, can elicit significant reductions in price quotes ($/kWh), depending on the way efficiency programs impact on-peak

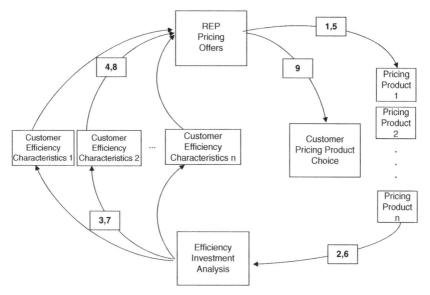

**FIGURE 11.3**   EBaR Pricing-Efficiency Choice Process

electricity use. Costs and benefits of undertaking each of the efficiency program options are evaluated with the new pricing products including costs of the business-as-usual case where no new efficiency investments are contemplated.

This process can continue for several rounds until the customer has identified the appropriate combination of a pricing product and energy efficiency investments. In order to secure a contract with the REP that takes advantage of the new efficiency investments, the customer will likely be required to meet energy and kW requirements upon which the future pricing contract is based.

EBaR analysis provides a quantitative framework for energy customers to simultaneously assess cost, benefits, and risks associated with alternative efficiency investments and competitive pricing offers. Without this tool, customers are left to subjective judgments regarding relative risks that, as discussed in previous chapters, generally lead to poor outcomes.

## SUMMARY

Competitive energy markets provide energy customers with a large number of energy pricing products not available in regulated markets. While market forces drive prices in both regulated and competitive markets, customers in regulated markets have few choices in selecting pricing products. Competitive markets permit (or perhaps *require* is a better word for most customers) energy customers to make a pricing choice. Options range from buying electricity and natural gas on the spot market to long-term fixed-price contracts.

In developing pricing offers, REPs estimate the cost of providing service to customers, which for electricity means the cost of supplying power on an hourly basis. Pricing offers are usually made on a kWh basis (for example 10 cents/kWh) without reference to monthly peak kW or hourly load profiles. However, a facility's hourly electricity characteristics still determine the quoted price.

This process means that, under most REP pricing contracts, when electric customers make efficiency investments that improve their cost of service characteristics, they continue to pay a price for electricity that reflects the more expensive cost of service characteristics used to calculate their initial price quotes. At the same time, customer energy cost savings are less than they would be if customers were allowed to get new price quotes that take into account their less costly load profile characteristics.

Customers in competitive markets can benefit from assessing competitive pricing offers and energy efficiency investments using the simultaneous EBaR process described in this chapter. This approach explicitly recognizes the fact that efficiency investments change price offers and price offers help define efficiency savings.

## CHAPTER 12

# EBaR Reports:
# Making the Case for Energy
# Efficiency Investments

EBaR transforms traditional energy efficiency and energy purchase decisions into a financial analysis framework compatible with best financial practices in today's business world. Organizations can evaluate financial risks and rewards of alternative energy-efficiency investments and achieve increased cash flows with decisions that are compatible with their budget flexibility and risk tolerance.

EBaR can also assist organizations in meeting sustainability goals. Energy efficiency is the primary opportunity to achieve reductions in carbon and other harmful emissions. EBaR provides a framework to assess carbon reduction impacts of energy efficiency investments and to evaluate risks and rewards of alternative sustainability strategies.

My experience working with corporate executives and energy managers over the last 30 years suggests that there is a critical analysis/communication gap in the energy-efficiency investment process. From the top down, CFOs and financial administrators see the details of efficient lighting, HVAC, and other systems as too technical and, with energy price volatility and other uncertainties, opt for a simple payback or internal rate of return hurdle rate screening process. Most energy efficiency capital budgeting proposals that come across their desks look good from an engineering analysis perspective; however, the inability to evaluate risk is a deal-breaker. Life cycle cost and net present value calculations simply contain too many uncertainties too feel comfortable with.

From the bottom up, energy managers struggle to put together energy efficiency projects they know will work and are generally frustrated that they are unable to convince the "financial people" that the investment will provide the kind of benefits they feel vindicate their engineering analysis.

## AN EBaR FACILITY ENERGY RISK
## MANAGEMENT STANDARD

JP Morgan's RiskMetrics service was instrumental in establishing VaR as a standard financial risk management tool in the 1990s. No similar resource has been available to show energy and financial managers how to develop and apply risk management techniques to minimize energy costs, subject to organizational risk tolerance. The objective of *Energy Budgets at Risk* is to provide such a guide.

EBaR analysis was developed to fill this analysis/communications gap. Financial administrators can view project risks and rewards within a familiar risk management framework, and energy managers can provide analysis in that same framework to make the case for investments they know will be profitable. At a recent luncheon address I delivered in Houston to the local Association of Energy Engineers chapter, one of the participants approached me after the talk and said "you've provided the missing link." I hope that EBaR does bridge the gap between financial decision-makers and all of the energy managers and energy engineers who can help their organizations benefit from the huge untapped energy efficiency potential that exists in most facilities.

Previous chapters have addressed the analysis part of the analysis/ communication gap mentioned above; this chapter focuses on the communications component. Specifically, this chapter provides::

1. A summary overview of EBaR analysis results.
2. A template for developing EBaR executive summary reports at readers' facilities.

Value is realized by EBaR analysis only when the results are applied in a decision-making process. Energy managers often report directly to the CFO or an equivalent chief financial or administrative position. Sometimes one or two layers of management exist between individuals responsible for energy risk management analysis and decision-makers.

Understanding the importance and applicability of EBaR results is self-evident to the individual who conducts the analysis; however, presenting the results of quantitative analysis to busy individuals at higher levels in the management chain is often a challenge.

To provide effective decision-making input, EBaR results must include a small number of easy-to-understand decision-variables characterizing energy budget and investment risk. It is important to present this information in a clear, concise way using standard tabular and graphics presentations as part of an EBaR report executive summary.

In addition to presenting information in an executive summary, it may be useful to include more detailed information. Decision makers who want to delve into detail themselves to consider scenario analysis and other supporting analysis issues, may value direct and immediate access to this material. On the other hand providing more information than necessary as part of a decision-supporting information package can create a diversion that easily obscures the primary results reflected in the decision variables. The appropriate amount of detail in the supporting analysis must be determined at individual organizations.

The remainder of this chapter presents a prototype EBaR Executive Summary Report that can be used as a basis for developing an EBaR report at any facility.

## EBaR BUDGET AND INVESTMENT ANALYSIS

### Executive Summary

#### AUSTIN OFFICE BUILDING, JANUARY 20, 2008

### Facility Description

Structure: Five-story, 120,000 square foot office building located at 210 West Madison, Austin, TX.

General energy efficiency characterization: No efficiency upgrades have been incorporated since construction in 1988. Lighting technologies are dated. Annual HVAC maintenance is conducted.

### Energy Costs

Expected current year and last year's actual energy costs are shown in Table 12.1. Expected costs reflect normal weather patterns and expected energy prices for the coming year. Expected monthly energy costs are shown in Figure 12.1 with electric costs detailed by monthly kWh and peak demand (kW) charges.

### Current Budget Risk

Current budget risk is the maximum expected budget variance based on current views of likely electricity and natural gas prices over the coming

**TABLE 12.1** Austin Office Building Expected and Previous Year's Energy Costs

|  | Energy Use | Units | Annual Cost | Last Year's Costs |
|---|---|---|---|---|
| Electricity | 1,939 | MWH | $207,752 | $206,472 |
| Natural gas | 5,559 | MMBtu | $53,201 | $49,896 |
|  |  | Totals | $260,953 | $256,368 |

year and normal summer and winter climatic variations. Budget variances are designated $EbaR_{budget,x}$, and represent the *largest* budget variance that can be expected to occur x percent of the time or with an x percent confidence level.

EBaR values for various confidence levels are shown in Table 12.2 and Figure 12.2. The $EbaR_{budget,90}$ variance amount of $27,800 is recommended as the energy budget contingency for the coming year.

### Recommended Efficiency Investment Option

Lighting efficiency and HVAC recommisioning investment options are recommended to reduce energy operating budgets and budget risk.

The project includes replacing existing fluorescent lamps and ballasts, lighting controls and replacing selected incandescent lamps with compact fluorescent lamps. The HVAC recommissioning will update the HVAC system and install a building energy management control system.

**Cost and Expected Energy Savings** The lighting manufacturer's estimate of savings is 483,000 kWh per year and 145 kW peak electricity use. The

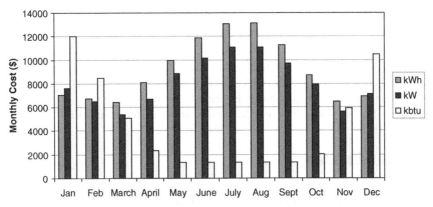

**FIGURE 12.1** Austin Office Building Expected Monthly Energy Costs

**TABLE 12.2**    Expected Energy Budgets and Variances (Annual $)*

| | Budget and Variances | | | Budgets | | |
|---|---|---|---|---|---|---|
| | Electricity | Natural Gas | Total | Electricity | Natural Gas | Total |
| EBaR$_{budget,mean}$ | $207,752 | $53,201 | $260,953 | $207,752 | $53,201 | $260,953 |
| EBaR$_{budget,90}$ | $16,300 | $15,500 | $27,800 | $224,052 | $68,701 | $288,753 |
| EBaR$_{budget,95}$ | $21,100 | $20,600 | $36,200 | $228,852 | $73,801 | $297,153 |
| EBaR$_{budget,97.5}$ | $25,100 | $25,200 | $43,600 | $232,852 | $78,401 | $304,553 |

*Note: Total budget variance at each EBaR confidence level is less than the sum of individual variances for electricity and natural gas reflecting some canceling of uncertainty when both energy sources are considered together.

total cost of the lighting retrofit program is $100,000 based on a fixed-cost contract.

The HVAC recommisioning and energy management control system is expected to achieve savings of 30 percent for air conditioning electricity use (after lighting changes) and 65 percent for natural gas heating use. The fixed-cost estimate for the recommissioning project is $125,000.

Total program cost is $225,000.

**Investment Analysis**    EBaR investment analysis was conducted using esti-mated variations in energy prices and weather. Variations of actual savings are assumed to be +/– 20 percent of estimates provided by manufacturer and vendor representatives. These performance assessments were developed

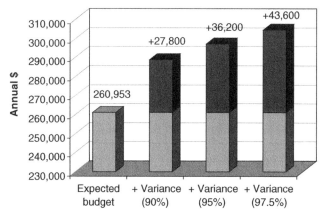

**FIGURE 12.2**    Expected Energy Budgets and Variances

**TABLE 12.3** Expected Investment
Analysis Summary

| | |
|---|---|
| Investment cost | $225,000 |
| Energy cost savings | $98,153 |
| Net cash flow | $58,300 |
| Internal rate of return | 42.3% |

by the in-house energy manager and accepted as reasonable variations by both manufacturers and vendors.

Expected annual energy cost savings are $98,153, reflecting a net cash flow of $58,300 assuming the investments are financed over a 10-year period at 12 percent interest. The expected internal rate of return (IRR) on the investment is 42.3 percent.

The $58,300 reflects energy cost savings after deducting the cost of the investment and is equivalent to $58,300 income derived from suggested efficiency investment.

Table 12.3 shows expected cost, savings, net cash flow, and IRR.

**Investment Risk**   Investment risk is defined by $EBaR_{IRR,x}$ (the lowest expected IRR at the x confidence level) and $EBaR_{netsave,x}$ (the lowest expected net savings, that is, annual energy cost savings minus annualized investment cost at the x confidence level).

Table 12.4 and Figures 12.3 and 12.4 show energy efficiency investment IRRs and net cash flows for three confidence levels. Net cash flow reflects the annual energy cost savings minus the annual cost of financing the investment.

**Impacts on Budget Risk**   Table 12.5 and Figure 12.5 show the impact of the efficiency investment on expected annual energy budgets and budget variances at the three confidence levels. Expected buget variances are reduced by about 45 percent.

**TABLE 12.4**   Efficiency Program Returns

| Confidence Level | Minimum IRR (%) | Minimum Net Cash Flow |
|---|---|---|
| Expected | 42.3 | $ 58,300 |
| 90% | 35.5 | $ 44,000 |
| 95% | 33.5 | $ 40,000 |
| 97.5% | 32.4 | $ 37,800 |

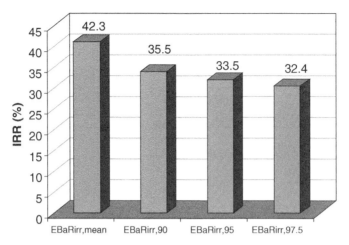

**FIGURE 12.3**  Efficiency Program IRRs

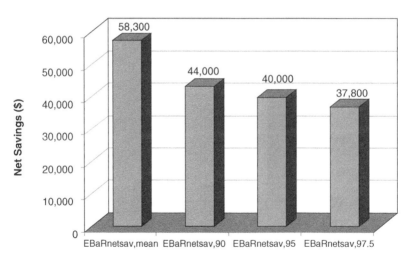

**FIGURE 12.4**  Efficiency Program Net Savings

**TABLE 12.5**   Evaluation of Efficiency Investment Impacts on Energy Budgets (annual $)

| Confidence Level | HVAC and Lighting Efficiency Measures Analysis | | | Baseline Analysis | | |
|---|---|---|---|---|---|---|
| | Electricity | Natural Gas | Total | Electricity | Natural Gas | Total |
| Expected Budgets | 143,300 | 19,500 | 162,800 | 207,752 | 53,201 | 260,953 |
| Maximum Budget Variances | | | | | | |
| 90% | 12,200 | 5,100 | 15,500 | 16,300 | 15,500 | 27,800 |
| 95% | 15,900 | 6,900 | 20,200 | 21,100 | 20,600 | 36,200 |
| 97.5% | 19,000 | 8,500 | 24,200 | 25,100 | 25,200 | 43,600 |

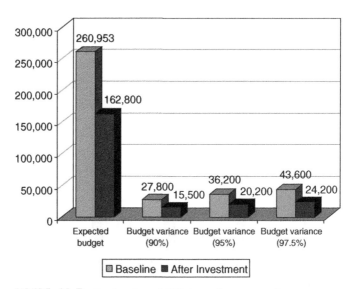

**FIGURE 12.5**   Evaluation of Efficiency Investment Impacts on Energy Budgets

**TABLE 12.6**   Annual Emissions Baseline and Impact of Efficiency Investment

|  | $CO_2$ (1000 lbs) | NOx (lbs) | Particulates (lbs) | $SO_2$ (lbs) |
|---|---|---|---|---|
| Baseline | 3,293 | 3,796 | 631 | 2,526 |
| Efficiency Investment | 2,061 | 2,349 | 435 | 1,743 |
| Reduction (lbs) | 1,232 | 1,447 | 196 | 784 |
| Reduction (%) | 37.4% | 38.1% | 31.0% | 31.0% |

**Contributions to $CO_2$ Reductions and Other Green Goals**   Table 12.6 and Figure 12.6 show annual baseline of $CO_2$, NOx, particulates and $SO_2$ emissions along with emissions after the lighting and HVAC investments. As indicated, carbon emissions are reduced by 37.4 percent and reductions in other emissions range from 31 to 38 percent.

**Opportunity Cost of Bypassing the Investment**   Bypassing this investment incurs costs in the form of foregone savings identified in Table 12.7 and Figure 12.7. Future net savings are discounted at 12 percent per annum.

**Loss in Facility Capital Value**   Bypassing the investment also reduces the market value of the facility, based on current capitalization rates used in the local real estate market. Table 12.8 and Figure 12.8 present these foregone capital value increases.

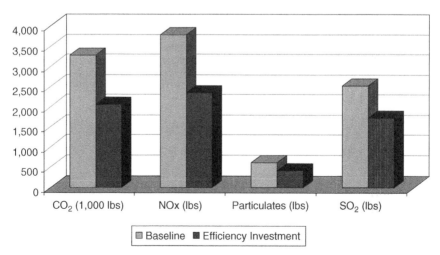

**FIGURE 12.6**   Annual Emissions Baseline and Impact of Efficiency Investment (lbs) Opportunity Cost of Bypassing the Investment

**TABLE 12.7**   EBaR Energy Efficiency Investment: Forgone Savings

| Confidence Level | Annual Savings | Total Discounted Savings | IRR | Description |
|---|---|---|---|---|
| Expected | $58,300 | $329,408 | 42.3 | Expected opportunity costs. |
| 90% | $44,000 | $248,610 | 35.5 | Probability is 90% that values will be larger than these. |
| 95% | $40,000 | $226,009 | 33.5 | Probability is 95% that values will be larger than these. |
| 97.5% | $37,800 | $213,578 | 32.4 | Probability is 97.5% that values will be larger than these. |

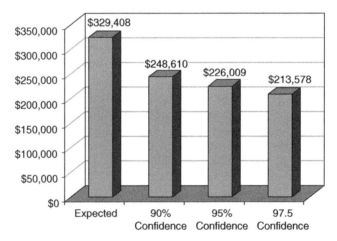

**FIGURE 12.7**   EBaR Energy Efficiency Investment: Foregone Savings

**TABLE 12.8**   EBaR Energy Efficiency Investment: Foregone Capital Value Increases

| Capitalization Factor | Expected | 90% probability | 97.5% probability |
|---|---|---|---|
| 5 | $291,500 | $220,000 | $189,000 |
| 8 | $466,400 | $352,000 | $302,400 |
| 10 | $583,000 | $440,000 | $378,000 |

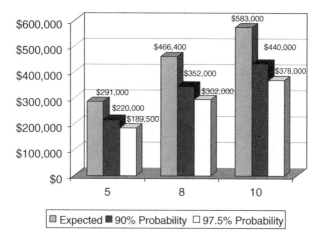

**FIGURE 12.8**    EBaR Energy Efficiency Investment: Foregone Capital Value Increases

## ADDITIONAL REPORT INFORMATION

Any of the graphical and tabular displays of information presented in Chapters 9 and 10 may also be included in EBaR reports as supporting documentation. Management attuned to risk management or quantitative management applications like Six-Sigma may be receptive and even prefer to see distribution representations of the data presented in the charts and graphs presented in the previous chapter.

Scenario analysis like that illustrated with alternative natural gas prices in Chapter 10 can also be presented to provide an indication of the sensitivity of EBaR analysis results to varying any of the input assumptions.

## ADDITIONAL INFORMATION ON EBaR APPLICATIONS, EXPERIENCE, AND REPORTING

energybudgetsatrisk.com is a companion web site for this book. Web contents include energy risk management software customized to support all aspects of EBaR analysis, additional discussion of EBaR-related issues and a section devoted to frequently asked questions about EBaR applications.

Questions concerning EBaR related topics may be addressed to the author via e-mail through the web site. Readers are invited to share their comments on EBaR and related energy management issues in a special Web section.

Information on EBaR workshops and training is also posted on energybudgetsatrisk.com.

# Benchmarking Your Facility's Energy Use with MAISY Data

This appendix provides a series of facility energy use tables designed to help you estimate potential energy savings at your facility. This evaluation does not take the place of more detailed analysis and evaluations of energy efficiency investments; however, it provides readers with a sense of the magnitude of energy and energy cost savings that may be available.

## TABLE USAGE

The tables in this Appendix have been developed with the widely-used MAISY® (Market Analysis and Information System) Commercial Energy Use Database (www.maisy.com). This database, developed and maintained by the author, has been expanded since its introduction in 1995 to include information on more than one million commercial, institutional, and government facilities. The database includes detailed information for each customer record including energy use by end use (space heating, air conditioning, and so on), equipment, building structure, operating characteristics and hourly loads for each of the 8,760 hours of the year.

The MAISY database has been used by equipment manufacturing companies to evaluate and design energy-using equipment (including Toyota, United Technologies, Ingersoll Rand, Aisin, and a variety of fuel cell, cool storage, and wind energy companies), retail electricity providers, and regulated utilities to better understand their customers' energy use patterns (including Reliant Energy, Texas Utilities, the Southern Company, Commonwealth Edison, Florida Power and Light, and several dozen more) and by energy service companies, national research laboratories, and other energy-related organizations.

Presenting information on facility energy use in appendix tables proved to be a serious challenge. Energy use varies across buildings as a result of operating hours, structure and equipment characteristics, and many other dimensions. However, tabular presentation of information permits only a few dimensions before the number of tables becomes unwieldy.

Analysis of facility energy use from the MAISY database indicated that, after considering variations in space heating and air conditioning by climate, the two best indicators of facility energy use per square foot of building area are building or business type and weekly operating hours. Consequently, 51 tables have been developed representing 20 building types and 3 operating hours categories (less than 50 hours, 50–85 hours, and more than 85 hours) for all building types except hospitals, nursing homes, hotels, and college dorms, where buildings operate at all hours and grocery stores where there were too few facilities that operated fewer than 50 hours per week.

For each building type/operating hours category, the tables report energy use for the 90th, 70th, 50th, 30th and 10th percentile of customers in each category. Comparing the difference in energy use between the median and the 30th percentile provides an indication of how much energy can be reduced for a typical facility within the category for a reasonable return on the efficiency investment. Operation at the 10th percentile reflects the most efficient buildings in the stock.

For instance, Table A.1 shows baseload electricity use characteristics for offices that operate between 50 and 85 hours per week. As with other appendix table entries, energy use is measured by dividing energy use by net square feet in the facility (net square feet excludes garage and other unconditioned space).

Baseload electricity use is electricity use for non–weather-sensitive uses, which excludes space heating, air conditioning and ventilation (HVAC). The interior lighting row indicates that the median facility in this category uses

**TABLE A.1** Baseload Electricity Use, Office Buildings, 50–85 Operating Hours per Week (kWh/square foot)

| End Use | 90% | 70% | Median | 30% | 10% | Facility Difference |
|---|---|---|---|---|---|---|
| Water heating | 2.71 | 1.42 | 0.92 | 0.48 | 0.21 | |
| Cooking | 1.15 | 0.71 | 0.61 | 0.40 | 0.11 | |
| Refrigeration | 0.77 | 0.37 | 0.22 | 0.12 | 0.05 | |
| Interior lighting | 9.48 | 6.07 | 4.28 | 2.36 | 1.19 | |
| Exterior lighting | 1.01 | 0.4 | 0.28 | 0.13 | 0.06 | |
| Equipment | 3.67 | 2.15 | 1.66 | 0.98 | 0.53 | |
| Miscellaneous | 3.93 | 2.12 | 1.65 | 0.87 | 0.39 | |
| *Total Baseload* | 22.72 | 13.24 | 9.62 | 5.34 | 2.54 | |

4.28 kWh/square foot, that the most efficient 30 percent use 2.36 kWh/square foot and the most efficient 10 percent use only 1.19 kWh/square foot.

Generally, reductions in energy use from the median to the 30 percent level can be achieved with paybacks of from two to four years, which means that much of this improvement is likely to win approval and provide net revenue increases under an EBaR analysis. Total baseload electricity use is 9.62 kWh/square feet at the median; and 5.34 kWh/square feet at the 30 percent level. The difference of 4.28 kWh/square foot in a 200,000 square foot facility paying $0.10/kWh reflects an energy cost savings of more than $85,600. Energy use figures on the left side of the median reflect significantly greater energy use in existing buildings and significantly greater efficiency investment potential.

Each table provides space heating, air conditioning, and ventilation uses detailed by several climate zones defined by heating and cooling degree-days. Space heating energy use is provided for electricity and natural gas.

Any attempt to develop general tables such as these may prove less useful when applied to unique situations. Users can, however, use the information on variation in energy use characteristics with modifications to evaluate potentials at their facilities.

## TABLE SPECIFICATIONS

The twenty building or business types in Table A.2 are presented alphabetically in the appendix. A single table is provided for hospitals, nursing homes, hotels, and college dormitories. For other building types, tables are presented for three operating hour categories: less than 50 hours, 50–85 hours, and more than 85 hours, except for grocery stores where establishments operating fewer than 50 hours were too few to include.

All energy use figures are presented as kWh/square foot and kBtu/square foot for natural gas and oil.

Climate zones are shown in Table A.3 for 65 degree base heating and cooling degree days values.

## CALCULATING YOUR POTENTIAL ENERGY SAVINGS

The following steps can be applied to develop a general idea of the energy cost savings available in your facility. An example application is shown in a later section in this Appendix.

**TABLE A.2** Building Types

Assembly (recreational, social, and so forth)
College dormitory
College office
College other
Dry warehouse
Educational
Federal government office
Federal government other
Grocery
Hospital
Hotel
Nursing home
Office
Refrigerated warehouse
Religious
Restaurant
Retail
Retail mall
State/local government office
State/ local government other

## Step 1. Developing Baseline Information

1.1. Gather electricity and natural gas bills for the previous 12 months.
1.2. Compute $/kWh and $/MMBtu for electricity and natural gas for the past year by dividing total electricity costs by the sum of monthly kWh and total natural gas cost by the sum of MMBtus or the equivalent unit of measurement, 1000 cubic feet.
1.3. Select the lowest monthly electricity use in the last year (this should coincide with a spring or fall month). Multiply this figure by 12 to get annual baseload electricity use and divide that figure by the net square

**TABLE A.3** Climate Zones

| Zone | Low | High | Zone | Low | High |
|------|-----|------|------|-----|------|
| HDD zone 1 | 0 | 2,000 | CDD zone 1 | 0 | 1,000 |
| HDD zone 2 | 2,000 | 4,000 | CDD zone 2 | 1,000 | 2,000 |
| HDD zone 3 | 4,000 | 6,000 | CDD zone 3 | 3,000 | |
| HDD zone 4 | 6,000 | | | | |

feet in your facility to get annual baseload kWh/square foot. Net square feet exclude unconditioned spaces like parking garages.

1.4. Subtract the minimum month's electricity use from each summer month and add the remainder for summer months to get air conditioning/ventilation electricity use. Divide by net square feet to determine air conditioning/ventilation kWh/square foot.

1.5. Subtract the minimum month's electricity use from each winter month and add the remainder for winter months to get either electric space heating/ventilation (in facilities with electric space heating) or winter ventilation electricity use (in facilities with natural gas space heating). Divide by net square feet to determine space heating/ventilation kWh/square foot or winter ventilation kWh/square foot (if there is no electric space heating in the facility, increases in winter electricity use reflect primarily increases in ventilation uses).

1.6. For natural gas, subtract the baseload month from winter months to get space heating energy use and divide by net square feet to get kBtu/square feet (multiply the MMBtu or 1000 cubic feet by 1000 before you divide to obtain kBtu/square feet rather than MMBtu/square feet).

1.7. Locate the table appropriate for your facility based on the building type and weekly operating hours.

## Step 2. Calculations

2.1. Compare your facility's annual baseload kWh/square foot figure to the Total Baseload row in the Baseload Electricity Use component of the table. If you fall very far from one of the five total baseload entries, calculate the kWh/square foot from the closest column by either interpolating or using the ratio of your annual baseload to the baseload in the table. For instance in Table A.1, if your baseload kWh/square foot is 8.0, multiply all of the entries in the column with the baseload total of 9.62 by 0.83 (8.0/9.62).

The difference between your baseload kWh/square foot and the 30 percent level is a good measure of what can be achieved with high yield investments. The difference using the 10 percent level reflects a more aggressive program.

2.2. Record the difference between your end-use (water heating, cooking, and so on) kWh/square foot and your target (30 percent or 10 percent or somewhere in between) in the space Facility Difference. Do not include entries for end uses not relevant to your facility.

2.3. If you have electric air conditioning, use the air conditioning/ventilation kWh/square calculated in Step 1.4. Identify the values in the CDD zone appropriate for your facility for the Air Conditioning and Summer Ventilation Electricity Use table. Calculate the difference between your current kWh/square foot for conditioning/ ventilation and your target and enter in the Facility Difference space.

2.4. If you have electric space heating, combine the "Space Heating Ventilation Electricity Use" and the "Electric Space Heating Electricity Use" table entries and identify the difference between the values for your facility and your target.

2.5. If you use natural gas for space heating:

    **a.** Use the Space Heating Ventilation Electricity Use table. Apply the ratio of your facility's Air Conditioning and Summer Ventilation Electricity Use identified in Step 2.3 to the Space Heating Ventilation Electricity Use table. In other words, if your air conditioning electricity use was 10 percent above the median, apply 1.1 to the median to get your Space Heating Ventilation Electricity value. Calculate the difference between your current kWh/square foot for space heating ventilation and your target.

    **b.** Use the natural gas heating kBtu/square foot calculated in step 1.6 above to identify an appropriate column and calculate the Facility Difference based on your target.

2.6. You should have identified each of the relevant end uses in your facility and identified its place in the distribution of energy use characteristics provided by the table. For each of these entries, you should also have calculated a Facility Difference that reflects the energy use savings in kWh/square foot or kBtu/square foot associated with meeting the 30th percentile or other target energy use.

## Step 3. Calculate Potential Cost Savings

3.1. Add all of the electric Facility Difference entries in your table to get a total kWh Facility difference. Multiply this total kWh/square foot savings by the net square feet in your facility by the average electricity price ($/kWh) calculated in Step 1.2. This is your potential electric cost savings.

3.2. Complete the same steps for natural gas to compute fossil fuel cost savings.

3.3. Apply Facility Differences for individual end uses to facility square feet and average energy prices to evaluate cost-saving potential by end use.

## Considering the Result

The energy use characteristics reflected at the 30th percentile level typically provide attractive returns on investments. Half or more of the cost savings can be realized as net savings, that is, savings after paying for the investments. These investment returns are comparable to a new source of revenue.

While the 10 percent level reflects a greater commitment to long-term efficiency investments, many of the investments represented in the range between 30 and 10 percent provide high returns and significant nets savings, especially when utility and other incentives are considered.

While this analysis is only general in nature, the distribution of energy use characteristics is based on real buildings and provides evidence that significant savings exist and can be achieved with considerable financial rewards to those willing to apply contemporary risk management principles to energy efficiency investments.

## EXAMPLE APPLICATION

The Austin office building used in previous chapters is applied in this section to illustrate the calculations and application of the table data described in Steps 1–3 above.

### Step 1. Developing Baseline Information

1.1. Gather electricity and natural gas bills for the previous 12 months.
 *Monthly energy use is shown in Table A.4. Table A.5 shows annual energy use, costs and prices for electricity and natural gas.*

**TABLE A.4**  Monthly Energy Use

| Year | Month | kWh | MMBtu (Natural Gas) |
|---|---|---|---|
| 2006 | June | 207,847 | 2 |
| 2006 | July | 244,703 | 10 |
| 2006 | Aug. | 239,062 | 11 |
| 2006 | Sept. | 207,152 | 7 |
| 2006 | Oct. | 162,789 | 123 |
| 2006 | Nov. | 111,560 | 413 |
| 2006 | Dec. | 119,411 | 1,153 |
| 2007 | Jan. | 133,016 | 1,345 |
| 2007 | Feb. | 117,131 | 1,308 |
| 2007 | March | 111,503 | 390 |
| 2007 | April | 115,573 | 436 |
| 2007 | May | 175,695 | 16 |

**TABLE A.5**　Annual Energy Use,
Costs and Prices for Electricity
and Natural Gas

| Electricity | |
| --- | --- |
| Use (kWh) | 1,945,442 |
| Cost | $208,657 |
| Price ($/kWh) | 0.107 |
| **Natural Gas** | |
| Use (MMBtu) | 5,214 |
| Cost | $49,897 |
| Price ($/MMBtu) | 9.57 |

1.2. Compute $/kWh and $/MMBtu for electricity and natural gas for the past year by dividing total electricity costs by the sum of monthly kWh and total natural gas cost by the sum of MMBtus or the equivalent unit of measurement, 1000 cubic feet.

$$\$208,657/1,945,442 = 0.107 \$/kWh$$
$$\$49,897/5,214 = 9.57 \$/MMBtu$$

1.3. Select the lowest monthly electricity use in the last year (this should coincide with a spring or fall month). Multiply this figure by 12 to get annual baseload electricity use and divide that figure by the net square feet in your facility to get annual baseload kWh/square foot. Net square feet exclude unconditioned spaces like parking garages.

$$111,503 * 12 = 1,338,036 \ kWh \ (annual \ baseload \ use)$$
$$1,338,036 \ kWh/120,000 \ square \ feet = 11.15 \ kWh/square \ feet$$
$$(baseload)$$

1.4. Subtract the minimum month's electricity use from summer months and add the remainder for summer months to get air conditioning/ventilation electricity use. Divide by net square feet to determine air conditioning/ventilation kWh/square foot.

$$Sum \ of \ May \ through \ October - 6 * 111,503 = 568,230$$
$$air \ conditioning/ventilation \ electricity \ use$$
$$568,230/120,000 \ square \ feet = 4.74 \ kWh/square \ feet$$
$$(air \ conditioning/ventilation \ electricity \ use)$$

1.5. Subtract the minimum month's electricity use from each winter month and add the remainder for winter months to get either electric space winter ventilation electricity use (in facilities with natural gas space heating). Divide by net square feet to determine space heating/ ventilation kWh/square foot or winter ventilation kWh/square foot (if there is no electric space heating in the facility, increases in winter electricity use reflect primarily increases in ventilation uses).

*Sum of November through April kWh − 6 ∗ 111,503 = 39,176*
*ventilation electricity use winter months*
*weather sensitive electricity use*

*39,176/120,000 square feet = 0.327 kWh/square feet (winter*
*ventilation electricity use)*

1.6. For natural gas, subtract the baseload month from winter months to get space heating energy use and divide by net square feet to get kBtu/square feet (multiply the MMBtu or 1000 cubic feet by 1000 before you divide to obtain kBtu/square feet rather than MMBtu/square feet).

*5,214 MMBtu − 12 ∗ 10 = 5,094 MMBtu*

*5,094 MMBtu ∗ 1,000 kBtu/MMBtu/120,000 square feet = 42.45*
*kBtu/square feet (space heating natural gas use)*

1.7. Locate the table appropriate for your facility based on the building type and weekly operating hours.

*The appropriate table is for offices operating from 50–85 hours/week. (See Table A.6).*

## Step 2. Calculations

2.1. Compare your facility's annual baseload kWh/square foot figure to the Total Baseload row in the Baseload Electricity Use component of the table. If you fall very far from one of the five total baseload entries, calculate the kWh/square foot from the closest column by using the ratio of your annual baseload to the baseload in the table. For instance in Table A.1, if your baseload kWh/square foot is 8.0, multiply all of the entries in the column with the baseload total of 9.62 by 0.83 (8.0/9.62).

The difference between your baseload kWh/square foot and the 30 percent level is a good measure of what can be achieved with high yield investments. The difference using the 10 percent level reflects a more aggressive program.

**TABLE A.6**  Appendix Table for Offices Operating between 50–85 Hours/Week*

| End Use | Baseload Electricity Use 90% | 70% | Median | 30% | 10% | Facility Difference |
|---|---|---|---|---|---|---|
| Water heating | 2.71 | 1.42 | 0.92 | 0.48 | 0.11 | |
| Cooking | 1.15 | 0.71 | 0.61 | 0.4 | 0.22 | |
| Refrigeration | 0.77 | 0.37 | 0.22 | 0.12 | 0.05 | |
| Interior lighting | 9.48 | 6.07 | 4.28 | 2.36 | 1.19 | |
| Exterior lighting | 1.01 | 0.4 | 0.28 | 0.13 | 0.06 | |
| Equipment | 3.67 | 2.15 | 1.66 | 0.98 | 0.53 | |
| Miscellaneous | 3.93 | 2.12 | 1.65 | 0.87 | 0.39 | |
| *Total Baseload* | 22.72 | 13.24 | 9.62 | 5.34 | 2.54 | |

| Climate Zone | Space Heating Ventilation Electricity Use 90% | 70% | Median | 30% | 10% | Facility Difference |
|---|---|---|---|---|---|---|
| HDD zone 1 | 0.56 | 0.28 | 0.21 | 0.08 | 0.04 | |
| HDD zone 2 | 0.58 | 0.32 | 0.19 | 0.15 | 0.09 | |
| HDD zone 3 | 1.89 | 1.08 | 0.62 | 0.41 | 0.23 | |
| HDD zone 4 | 1.96 | 1.47 | 1.02 | 0.87 | 0.27 | |

| Climate Zone | Air Conditioning and Summer Ventilation Electricity Use 90% | 70% | Median | 30% | 10% | Facility Difference |
|---|---|---|---|---|---|---|
| CDD zone 1 | 3.33 | 2.02 | 1.28 | 0.73 | 0.26 | |
| CDD zone 2 | 5.09 | 2.81 | 2.16 | 1.52 | 1.01 | |
| CDD zone 3 | 8.44 | 4.07 | 2.83 | 2.06 | 1.48 | |

| Climate Zone | Electric Space Heat 90% | 70% | Median | 30% | 10% | Facility Difference |
|---|---|---|---|---|---|---|
| HDD zone 1 | 1.63 | 0.64 | 0.40 | 0.28 | 0.14 | |
| HDD zone 2 | 3.04 | 1.58 | 1.09 | 0.70 | 0.35 | |
| HDD zone 3 | 4.92 | 2.12 | 1.63 | 1.10 | 0.98 | |
| HDD zone 4 | 7.85 | 5.66 | 3.51 | 2.02 | 0.87 | |

| Climate Zone | Natural Gas Space Heat 90% | 70% | Median | 30% | 10% | Facility Difference |
|---|---|---|---|---|---|---|
| HDD zone 1 | 28.9 | 14.98 | 8.98 | 5.84 | 3.59 | |
| HDD zone 2 | 59.55 | 26.08 | 18.37 | 13.54 | 11.14 | |
| HDD zone 3 | 56.04 | 29.26 | 20.93 | 14.49 | 8.53 | |
| HDD zone 4 | 79.47 | 37.42 | 30.44 | 19.79 | 7.00 | |

*All Electricity data are in kWh/square foot units and all natural gas data are in kBtu/square foot units. Source: MAISY® Commercial Energy Use Database, www.maisy.com

**TABLE A.7**    Baseload Electricity Savings

| End Use | Baseload Electricity Use | | | | | | Facility Difference |
|---|---|---|---|---|---|---|---|
| | 90% | 70% | Austin Office | Median | 30% | 10% | |
| Water heating | 2.71 | 1.42 | *1.07* | 0.92 | 0.48 | 0.21 | *0.59* |
| Cooking | 1.15 | 0.71 | *0.71* | 0.61 | 0.40 | 0.11 | *0.31* |
| Refrigeration | 0.77 | 0.37 | *0.25* | 0.22 | 0.12 | 0.05 | *0.13* |
| Interior lighting | 9.48 | 6.07 | *4.96* | 4.28 | 2.36 | 1.19 | *2.60* |
| Exterior lighting | 1.01 | 0.40 | *0.32* | 0.28 | 0.13 | 0.06 | *0.19* |
| Equipment | 3.67 | 2.15 | *1.92* | 1.66 | 0.98 | 0.53 | *0.94* |
| Miscellaneous | 3.93 | 2.12 | *1.91* | 1.65 | 0.87 | 0.39 | *1.04* |
| *Total Baseload* | 22.72 | 13.24 | *11.15* | 9.62 | 5.34 | 2.54 | *5.81* |

*The case study facility baseload electricity use/square foot is 11.15. The 70th percentile baseload is 13.24 and the median is 9.62. We will use the ratio 11.15/9.62 = 1.16 to create a new column in the table between the 70th percentile and the median. These calculations are shown in Table A.7.*

2.2. Record the difference between your end-use (water heating, cooking, and so on) kWh/square foot and your target (30 percent or 10 percent or somewhere in between) in the space Facility Difference. Do not include entries for end uses not relevant to your facility.

*We will use the 30th percentile as a reasonable goal and calculate the difference in our end-use estimates and the target (see Table A.7). Our entries in the table are identified in the Austin Office and Facility Difference column.*

*The results indicated that achieving a 30th percentile level of baseload electricity use can nearly cut our current baseload use by half. Most of these potential savings are associated with lighting.*

2.3. If you have electric air conditioning, use the air conditioning/ventilation kWh/square calculated in Step 1.4. Identify the values in the CDD zone appropriate for your facility for the Air Conditioning and Summer Ventilation Electricity Use table. Calculate the difference between your current kWh/square foot for conditioning/ ventilation and your target and enter in the Facility Difference space.

*Our air conditioning/ventilation electricity use is 4.74 kWh/square feet. The entry for our facility and the Facility Difference are indicated in Table A.8.*

**TABLE A.8** Air Conditioning Electricity Savings

| | Air Conditioning and Summer Ventilation Electricity Use | | | | | | |
|---|---|---|---|---|---|---|---|
| Climate Zone | 90% | Austin Office | 70% | Median | 30% | 10% | Facility Difference |
| CDD zone 3 | 8.44 | 4.74 | 4.07 | 2.83 | 2.06 | 1.48 | 2.68 |

2.4. If you have electric space heating, combine the Space Heating Ventilation Electricity Use and the Electric Space Heating Electricity Use table entries and identify the difference between the values for your facility and your target.

*We do not use electric space heating.*

2.5. If you use natural gas for space heating:
  a. Use the Space Heating Ventilation Electricity Use table (see Table A.9). Apply the ratio of your facility's Air Conditioning and Summer Ventilation Electricity Use identified in Step 2.3 to Table A.9. In other words, if your air conditioning electricity use was 10 percent above the median, apply 1.1 to the median to get your Space Heating Ventilation Electricity value. Calculate the difference between your current kWh/square foot for conditioning.
  b. Use the natural gas heating kBtu/square foot calculated in Step 1.6 to identify an appropriate column and calculate the Facility Difference based on your target.

  *Austin heating degree days are just slightly below 2,000; consequently we use HDD Zone 2 data.*

2.6. You should have identified each of the relevant end uses in your facility and identified its place in the distribution of energy use characteristics. For each of these entries, you should also have calculated a Facility

**TABLE A.9** Space Heating Ventilation Electricity Savings

| | Space Heating Ventilation Electricity Use | | | | | | |
|---|---|---|---|---|---|---|---|
| Climate Zone | 90% | Austin Office | 70% | Median | 30% | 10% | Facility Difference |
| HDD zone 2 | 0.58 | 0.32 | 0.32 | 0.19 | 0.15 | 0.09 | 0.17 |

**TABLE A.10**   Natural Gas Space Heating Savings

| | Natural Gas Space Heat | | | | | | |
|---|---|---|---|---|---|---|---|
| Climate Zone | 90% | Austin Office | 70% | Median | 30% | 10% | Facility Difference |
| HDD zone 2 | 59.55 | 42.45 | 26.08 | 18.37 | 13.54 | 11.14 | 28.91 |

Difference that reflects the energy use savings in kWh/square foot or kBtu/square foot associated with meeting the 30 percentile or other target energy use. (See Table A.10.)

## Step 3. Calculate Potential Cost Savings

3.1. Add all of the electric Facility Difference entries in your table to get a total kWh Facility difference. Multiply this total kWh/square foot savings by the net square feet in your facility by the average electricity price ($/kWh) calculated in Step 1.2. This is your potential electric cost savings.

3.2. Complete the same steps for natural gas to compute fossil fuel cost savings.

3.3. Apply Facility Differences for individual end uses to facility square feet and average energy prices to evaluate cost-saving potential by end use.

Remember to divide the product of kBtu/square foot for natural gas by 1,000 to convert to MMBtu required when applying the natural gas price. *Results of the analysis are shown in Tables A.11 and A.12.*

It is interesting to note that the lighting and HVAC efficiency investment program analyzed in Chapter 10 provided natural gas cost savings of

**TABLE A.11**   Potential Electric Energy and Cost Savings

| | kWh/square foot | kWh | Cost |
|---|---|---|---|
| Baseload | 5.81 | 697,200 | $74,600 |
| Air conditioning | 2.68 | 321,600 | $34,411 |
| Space heating ventilation | 0.17 | 20,400 | $2,183 |
| | Total | 1,038,548 | $111,194 |

**TABLE A.12**   Potential Natural Gas Energy and Cost Savings

|  | kBtu/Square Foot | MMBtu Savings | Cost Savings |
|---|---|---|---|
| Space heating | 28.91 | 3,469 | $33,200 |

$33,701 and electricity cost savings of $64,452, which is about 68 percent of the savings that can be achieved at the 30th percentile in energy use in the tables.

## SUMMARY

A variety of resources exist to analyze facility energy use in more detail and more accurately than what can be accomplished with 51 tables. (See Tables A.13 to A.63). Engineering heat load models represent physical characteristics of buildings and model heat gains and losses on an hour-by-hour basis including details of the HVAC system, solar radiation, and many other factors. I have used these models in many projects over the past 30 years and recommend their application as the ultimate in analyzing facility energy use characteristics.

The objective of this Appendix is not to dot i's and cross t's on facility energy use estimation; it is to provide readers with a sense of the magnitude of energy and energy cost savings likely to be available in their facilities. The fact that the results in the table reflect information from more than one million buildings is testament to the fact that significant efficiency potential exists in nearly all commercial, institutional, government, and industrial buildings.

Characteristics of an individual facility may, of course, make it atypical enough to fall outside the boundaries of the information presented in these tables. However, comparing medians and percentile energy use data in this Appendix should provide some sense of efficiency-related energy-saving potentials.

**TABLE A.13**    Assembly (Less than 50 hours/week)

| End Use | Baseload Electricity Use, kWh/square foot | | | | | Facility Difference |
|---|---|---|---|---|---|---|
| | 90% | 70% | Median | 30% | 10% | |
| Water heating | 0.94 | 0.47 | 0.20 | 0.14 | 0.07 | |
| Cooking | 1.84 | 0.45 | 0.24 | 0.18 | 0.12 | |
| Refrigeration | 1.10 | 0.47 | 0.18 | 0.09 | 0.02 | |
| Interior lighting | 3.12 | 1.90 | 1.22 | 0.49 | 0.26 | |
| Exterior lighting | 1.32 | 0.78 | 0.41 | 0.20 | 0.09 | |
| Equipment | 0.33 | 0.16 | 0.11 | 0.04 | 0.02 | |
| Miscellaneous | 0.41 | 0.21 | 0.14 | 0.04 | 0.03 | |
| *Total Baseload* | 9.06 | 4.44 | 2.50 | 1.18 | 0.61 | |

| Climate Zone | Space Heating Ventilation Electricity Use, kWh/square foot | | | | | Facility Difference |
|---|---|---|---|---|---|---|
| | 90% | 70% | Median | 30% | 10% | |
| HDD zone 1 | 0.36 | 0.10 | 0.06 | 0.02 | 0.01 | |
| HDD zone 2 | 0.29 | 0.20 | 0.15 | 0.11 | 0.02 | |
| HDD zone 3 | 1.31 | 0.55 | 0.34 | 0.14 | 0.05 | |
| HDD zone 4 | 1.07 | 0.64 | 0.44 | 0.19 | 0.12 | |

| Climate Zone | AC and Summer Ventilation Electricity Use, kWh/square foot | | | | | Facility Difference |
|---|---|---|---|---|---|---|
| | 90% | 70% | Median | 30% | 10% | |
| CDD zone 1 | 3.15 | 1.23 | 0.77 | 0.36 | 0.10 | |
| CDD zone 2 | 4.36 | 2.72 | 1.45 | 1.03 | 0.35 | |
| CDD zone 3 | 11.91 | 5.36 | 4.32 | 2.14 | 0.81 | |

| Climate Zone | Electric Space Heat, kWh/square foot | | | | | Facility Difference |
|---|---|---|---|---|---|---|
| | 90% | 70% | Median | 30% | 10% | |
| HDD zone 1 | 2.16 | 1.05 | 0.72 | 0.58 | 0.34 | |
| HDD zone 2 | 8.12 | 1.62 | 1.08 | 0.93 | 0.24 | |
| HDD zone 3 | 7.19 | 2.51 | 1.23 | 0.92 | 0.78 | |
| HDD zone 4 | 6.07 | 3.63 | 2.95 | 2.07 | 1.48 | |

| Climate Zone | Natural Gas Space Heat, kBtu/square foot | | | | | Facility Difference |
|---|---|---|---|---|---|---|
| | 90% | 70% | Median | 30% | 10% | |
| HDD zone 1 | 37.38 | 24.72 | 9.11 | 5.92 | 3.83 | |
| HDD zone 2 | 85.16 | 59.24 | 20.43 | 12.45 | 7.45 | |
| HDD zone 3 | 71.47 | 48.66 | 31.24 | 18.86 | 11.16 | |
| HDD zone 4 | 82.00 | 60.41 | 44.05 | 28.31 | 14.28 | |

**TABLE A.14** Assembly (50–85 hours/week)

| End Use | Baseload Electricity Use, kWh/square foot | | | | | Facility Difference |
| | 90% | 70% | Median | 30% | 10% | |
|---|---|---|---|---|---|---|
| Water heating | 1.07 | 0.75 | 0.60 | 0.41 | 0.25 | |
| Cooking | 1.67 | 1.46 | 1.20 | 0.81 | 0.32 | |
| Refrigeration | 2.30 | 0.88 | 0.58 | 0.08 | 0.03 | |
| Interior lighting | 6.56 | 4.35 | 3.16 | 1.62 | 0.62 | |
| Exterior lighting | 1.50 | 1.09 | 0.65 | 0.41 | 0.22 | |
| Equipment | 0.50 | 0.33 | 0.24 | 0.13 | 0.05 | |
| Miscellaneous | 0.58 | 0.42 | 0.27 | 0.14 | 0.06 | |
| *Total Baseload* | 14.18 | 9.28 | 6.70 | 3.60 | 1.55 | |

| Climate Zone | Space Heating Ventilation Electricity Use, kWh/square foot | | | | | Facility Difference |
| | 90% | 70% | Median | 30% | 10% | |
|---|---|---|---|---|---|---|
| HDD zone 1 | 0.63 | 0.34 | 0.08 | 0.04 | 0.01 | |
| HDD zone 2 | 0.32 | 0.25 | 0.12 | 0.06 | 0.03 | |
| HDD zone 3 | 1.53 | 0.87 | 0.63 | 0.34 | 0.19 | |
| HDD zone 4 | 1.75 | 0.92 | 0.71 | 0.47 | 0.22 | |

| Climate Zone | AC and Summer Ventilation Electricity Use, kWh/square foot | | | | | Facility Difference |
| | 90% | 70% | Median | 30% | 10% | |
|---|---|---|---|---|---|---|
| CDD zone 1 | 5.18 | 2.67 | 1.33 | 0.81 | 0.32 | |
| CDD zone 2 | 6.70 | 3.89 | 2.61 | 1.64 | 0.79 | |
| CDD zone 3 | 13.12 | 7.07 | 3.38 | 1.42 | 0.66 | |

| Climate Zone | Electric Space Heat, kWh/square foot | | | | | Facility Difference |
| | 90% | 70% | Median | 30% | 10% | |
|---|---|---|---|---|---|---|
| HDD zone 1 | 1.22 | 0.88 | 0.42 | 0.24 | 0.04 | |
| HDD zone 2 | 3.14 | 1.99 | 0.78 | 0.47 | 0.17 | |
| HDD zone 3 | 7.54 | 5.61 | 2.31 | 2.03 | 1.21 | |
| HDD zone 4 | 9.58 | 8.65 | 3.44 | 2.72 | 1.70 | |

| Climate Zone | Natural Gas Space Heat, kBtu/square foot | | | | | Facility Difference |
| | 90% | 70% | Median | 30% | 10% | |
|---|---|---|---|---|---|---|
| HDD zone 1 | 67.54 | 17.79 | 7.89 | 5.29 | 3.31 | |
| HDD zone 2 | 40.30 | 14.96 | 8.80 | 4.82 | 3.08 | |
| HDD zone 3 | 52.98 | 42.38 | 23.84 | 10.60 | 7.95 | |
| HDD zone 4 | 75.71 | 46.43 | 29.02 | 12.97 | 9.97 | |

**TABLE A.15**  Assembly (Greater than 85 hours/week)

| End Use | Baseload Electricity Use, kWh/square foot | | | | | Facility Difference |
|---|---|---|---|---|---|---|
| | 90% | 70% | Median | 30% | 10% | |
| Water heating | 0.63 | 0.37 | 0.36 | 0.26 | 0.08 | |
| Cooking | 1.90 | 0.84 | 0.71 | 0.21 | 0.10 | |
| Refrigeration | 4.67 | 1.31 | 0.35 | 0.24 | 0.09 | |
| Interior lighting | 8.49 | 5.85 | 2.65 | 1.67 | 1.26 | |
| Exterior lighting | 1.51 | 0.93 | 0.59 | 0.26 | 0.15 | |
| Equipment | 0.67 | 0.45 | 0.24 | 0.15 | 0.09 | |
| Miscellaneous | 0.77 | 0.55 | 0.27 | 0.16 | 0.10 | |
| *Total Baseload* | 18.64 | 10.30 | 5.17 | 3.25 | 1.87 | |

| Climate Zone | Space Heating Ventilation Electricity Use, kWh/square foot | | | | | Facility Difference |
|---|---|---|---|---|---|---|
| | 90% | 70% | Median | 30% | 10% | |
| HDD zone 1 | 0.44 | 0.20 | 0.17 | 0.12 | 0.05 | |
| HDD zone 2 | 0.55 | 0.23 | 0.15 | 0.08 | 0.03 | |
| HDD zone 3 | 1.48 | 1.01 | 0.57 | 0.23 | 0.12 | |
| HDD zone 4 | 1.57 | 0.98 | 0.72 | 0.69 | 0.27 | |

| Climate Zone | AC and Summer Ventilation Electricity Use, kWh/square foot | | | | | Facility Difference |
|---|---|---|---|---|---|---|
| | 90% | 70% | Median | 30% | 10% | |
| CDD zone 1 | 3.47 | 1.97 | 1.51 | 0.67 | 0.36 | |
| CDD zone 2 | 6.64 | 4.17 | 1.76 | 1.55 | 0.75 | |
| CDD zone 3 | 16.17 | 13.10 | 9.93 | 4.67 | 1.27 | |

| Climate Zone | Electric Space Heat, kWh/square foot | | | | | Facility Difference |
|---|---|---|---|---|---|---|
| | 90% | 70% | Median | 30% | 10% | |
| HDD zone 1 | 1.80 | 1.24 | 0.62 | 0.25 | 0.06 | |
| HDD zone 2 | 3.74 | 1.92 | 1.20 | 0.90 | 0.30 | |
| HDD zone 3 | 7.30 | 4.09 | 2.92 | 2.17 | 1.48 | |
| HDD zone 4 | 9.55 | 5.86 | 4.34 | 2.13 | 1.70 | |

| Climate Zone | Natural Gas Space Heat, kBtu/square foot | | | | | Facility Difference |
|---|---|---|---|---|---|---|
| | 90% | 70% | Median | 30% | 10% | |
| HDD zone 1 | 40.23 | 28.87 | 22.21 | 8.88 | 4.00 | |
| HDD zone 2 | 56.27 | 41.60 | 26.00 | 20.80 | 5.20 | |
| HDD zone 3 | 78.47 | 50.02 | 31.85 | 21.90 | 6.01 | |
| HDD zone 4 | 149.00 | 104.30 | 74.50 | 52.06 | 13.65 | |

**TABLE A.16**  College Dorm

| End Use | Baseload Electricity Use, kWh/square foot | | | | | Facility Difference |
|---|---|---|---|---|---|---|
| | 90% | 70% | Median | 30% | 10% | |
| Water heating | 5.40 | 3.78 | 2.70 | 2.00 | 1.08 | |
| Cooking | 1.50 | 1.08 | 0.76 | 0.30 | 0.07 | |
| Refrigeration | 0.77 | 0.21 | 0.02 | 0.01 | 0.01 | |
| Interior lighting | 8.74 | 5.79 | 4.40 | 3.12 | 1.55 | |
| Exterior lighting | 0.87 | 0.34 | 0.16 | 0.11 | 0.07 | |
| Equipment | 0.48 | 0.31 | 0.28 | 0.23 | 0.15 | |
| Miscellaneous | 1.65 | 1.09 | 0.72 | 0.50 | 0.28 | |
| *Total Baseload* | 20.31 | 13.30 | 9.04 | 6.58 | 3.31 | |

| Climate Zone | Space Heating Ventilation Electricity Use, kWh/square foot | | | | | Facility Difference |
|---|---|---|---|---|---|---|
| | 90% | 70% | Median | 30% | 10% | |
| HDD zone 1 | 0.36 | 0.23 | 0.15 | 0.04 | 0.02 | |
| HDD zone 2 | 1.16 | 0.72 | 0.38 | 0.19 | 0.06 | |
| HDD zone 3 | 1.88 | 1.40 | 0.59 | 0.24 | 0.09 | |
| HDD zone 4 | 2.38 | 1.44 | 1.12 | 0.74 | 0.11 | |

| Climate Zone | AC and Summer Ventilation Electricity Use, kWh/square foot | | | | | Facility Difference |
|---|---|---|---|---|---|---|
| | 90% | 70% | Median | 30% | 10% | |
| CDD zone 1 | 3.89 | 2.10 | 1.31 | 0.87 | 0.45 | |
| CDD zone 2 | 5.67 | 4.15 | 2.47 | 1.31 | 1.02 | |
| CDD zone 3 | 10.99 | 6.84 | 5.30 | 2.71 | 1.74 | |

| Climate Zone | Electric Space Heat, kWh/square foot | | | | | Facility Difference |
|---|---|---|---|---|---|---|
| | 90% | 70% | Median | 30% | 10% | |
| HDD zone 1 | 0.67 | 0.60 | 0.42 | 0.25 | 0.04 | |
| HDD zone 2 | 2.38 | 1.50 | 1.15 | 0.81 | 0.08 | |
| HDD zone 3 | 4.13 | 2.08 | 1.73 | 1.38 | 0.19 | |
| HDD zone 4 | 16.40 | 9.70 | 8.08 | 7.41 | 2.86 | |

| Climate Zone | Natural Gas Space Heat, kBtu/square foot | | | | | Facility Difference |
|---|---|---|---|---|---|---|
| | 90% | 70% | Median | 30% | 10% | |
| HDD zone 1 | 31.99 | 16.70 | 10.71 | 9.73 | 5.88 | |
| HDD zone 2 | 37.84 | 26.76 | 16.41 | 14.06 | 4.10 | |
| HDD zone 3 | 81.59 | 25.63 | 18.61 | 13.96 | 7.03 | |
| HDD zone 4 | 80.74 | 27.71 | 19.79 | 13.85 | 8.43 | |

**TABLE A.17**   College Office (Less than 50 hours/week)

| End Use | Baseload Electricity Use, kWh/square foot | | | | | Facility Difference |
|---|---|---|---|---|---|---|
| | 90% | 70% | Median | 30% | 10% | |
| Water heating | 1.86 | 1.39 | 0.38 | 0.25 | 0.06 | |
| Cooking | 0.22 | 0.14 | 0.10 | 0.03 | 0.02 | |
| Refrigeration | 0.72 | 0.60 | 0.13 | 0.09 | 0.04 | |
| Interior lighting | 7.26 | 5.85 | 5.08 | 2.62 | 1.60 | |
| Exterior lighting | 1.32 | 0.36 | 0.30 | 0.15 | 0.06 | |
| Equipment | 2.35 | 2.21 | 2.07 | 1.17 | 0.99 | |
| Miscellaneous | 2.67 | 2.35 | 2.08 | 1.11 | 0.66 | |
| *Total Baseload* | 16.40 | 12.90 | 10.14 | 5.42 | 3.43 | |

| Climate Zone | Space Heating Ventilation Electricity Use, kWh/square foot | | | | | Facility Difference |
|---|---|---|---|---|---|---|
| | 90% | 70% | Median | 30% | 10% | |
| HDD zone 1 | 0.20 | 0.14 | 0.10 | 0.05 | 0.02 | |
| HDD zone 2 | 0.64 | 0.46 | 0.34 | 0.20 | 0.14 | |
| HDD zone 3 | 1.00 | 0.78 | 0.53 | 0.36 | 0.19 | |
| HDD zone 4 | 1.23 | 1.08 | 0.94 | 0.60 | 0.53 | |

| Climate Zone | AC and Summer Ventilation Electricity Use, kWh/square foot | | | | | Facility Difference |
|---|---|---|---|---|---|---|
| | 90% | 70% | Median | 30% | 10% | |
| CDD zone 1 | 2.13 | 1.59 | 1.06 | 0.69 | 0.21 | |
| CDD zone 2 | 6.12 | 2.90 | 2.37 | 1.26 | 0.79 | |
| CDD zone 3 | 9.85 | 5.85 | 4.36 | 2.59 | 1.71 | |

| Climate Zone | Electric Space Heat, kWh/square foot | | | | | Facility Difference |
|---|---|---|---|---|---|---|
| | 90% | 70% | Median | 30% | 10% | |
| HDD zone 1 | 0.81 | 0.52 | 0.26 | 0.19 | 0.11 | |
| HDD zone 2 | 3.33 | 2.82 | 2.35 | 0.66 | 0.49 | |
| HDD zone 3 | 4.80 | 3.64 | 2.79 | 0.88 | 0.74 | |
| HDD zone 4 | 7.08 | 6.02 | 5.06 | 1.28 | 1.11 | |

| Climate Zone | Natural Gas Space Heat, kBtu/square foot | | | | | Facility Difference |
|---|---|---|---|---|---|---|
| | 90% | 70% | Median | 30% | 10% | |
| HDD zone 1 | 64.29 | 47.15 | 21.43 | 12.86 | 2.14 | |
| HDD zone 2 | 82.40 | 65.58 | 32.96 | 18.46 | 11.21 | |
| HDD zone 3 | 93.15 | 85.22 | 71.02 | 46.16 | 28.41 | |
| HDD zone 4 | 112.65 | 82.78 | 68.98 | 34.49 | 20.69 | |

**TABLE A.18**   College Office (50–85 hours/week)

| End Use | Baseload Electricity Use, kWh/square foot | | | | | Facility Difference |
| | 90% | 70% | Median | 30% | 10% | |
|---|---|---|---|---|---|---|
| Water heating | 4.01 | 2.60 | 1.10 | 0.76 | 0.33 | |
| Cooking | 0.19 | 0.16 | 0.15 | 0.09 | 0.06 | |
| Refrigeration | 0.35 | 0.13 | 0.09 | 0.04 | 0.02 | |
| Interior lighting | 10.42 | 7.77 | 4.34 | 3.04 | 1.90 | |
| Exterior lighting | 0.73 | 0.40 | 0.23 | 0.15 | 0.06 | |
| Equipment | 4.57 | 2.63 | 1.77 | 1.26 | 0.76 | |
| Miscellaneous | 4.98 | 2.76 | 1.65 | 1.24 | 0.71 | |
| *Total Baseload* | 26.15 | 16.45 | 9.33 | 6.88 | 3.94 | |

| Climate Zone | Space Heating Ventilation Electricity Use, kWh/square foot | | | | | Facility Difference |
| | 90% | 70% | Median | 30% | 10% | |
|---|---|---|---|---|---|---|
| HDD zone 1 | 0.81 | 0.45 | 0.20 | 0.16 | 0.04 | |
| HDD zone 2 | 1.28 | 0.82 | 0.62 | 0.48 | 0.17 | |
| HDD zone 3 | 1.70 | 1.16 | 0.89 | 0.54 | 0.26 | |
| HDD zone 4 | 2.88 | 2.05 | 1.09 | 0.83 | 0.55 | |

| Climate Zone | AC and Summer Ventilation Electricity Use, kWh/square foot | | | | | Facility Difference |
| | 90% | 70% | Median | 30% | 10% | |
|---|---|---|---|---|---|---|
| CDD zone 1 | 3.24 | 2.36 | 1.67 | 1.10 | 0.72 | |
| CDD zone 2 | 9.13 | 5.28 | 3.97 | 2.19 | 0.64 | |
| CDD zone 3 | 14.36 | 8.91 | 7.03 | 5.08 | 3.85 | |

| Climate Zone | Electric Space Heat, kWh/square foot | | | | | Facility Difference |
| | 90% | 70% | Median | 30% | 10% | |
|---|---|---|---|---|---|---|
| HDD zone 1 | 2.23 | 1.78 | 1.34 | 0.67 | 0.22 | |
| HDD zone 2 | 9.73 | 6.49 | 4.08 | 3.23 | 1.09 | |
| HDD zone 3 | 12.37 | 8.25 | 5.89 | 4.71 | 1.26 | |
| HDD zone 4 | 23.29 | 17.81 | 13.70 | 11.37 | 2.33 | |

| Climate Zone | Natural Gas Space Heat, kBtu/square foot | | | | | Facility Difference |
| | 90% | 70% | Median | 30% | 10% | |
|---|---|---|---|---|---|---|
| HDD zone 1 | 41.48 | 33.30 | 18.88 | 15.34 | 10.79 | |
| HDD zone 2 | 63.17 | 50.85 | 46.24 | 32.37 | 13.87 | |
| HDD zone 3 | 99.61 | 80.21 | 61.77 | 37.68 | 15.36 | |
| HDD zone 4 | 106.11 | 91.33 | 72.60 | 39.93 | 19.81 | |

**TABLE A.19**   College Office (Greater than 85 hours/week)

| End Use | Baseload Electricity Use, kWh/square foot | | | | | Facility Difference |
|---|---|---|---|---|---|---|
| | 90% | 70% | Median | 30% | 10% | |
| Water heating | 0.93 | 0.91 | 0.55 | 0.27 | 0.08 | |
| Cooking | 0.47 | 0.45 | 0.36 | 0.24 | 0.07 | |
| Refrigeration | 0.50 | 0.17 | 0.10 | 0.06 | 0.02 | |
| Interior lighting | 12.56 | 10.09 | 5.97 | 4.13 | 1.59 | |
| Exterior lighting | 0.32 | 0.22 | 0.11 | 0.08 | 0.04 | |
| Equipment | 4.60 | 3.09 | 2.22 | 1.59 | 0.68 | |
| Miscellaneous | 5.03 | 3.58 | 2.20 | 1.67 | 0.45 | |
| *Total Baseload* | 24.41 | 18.51 | 11.51 | 8.04 | 2.93 | |

| Climate Zone | Space Heating Ventilation Electricity Use, kWh/square foot | | | | | Facility Difference |
|---|---|---|---|---|---|---|
| | 90% | 70% | Median | 30% | 10% | |
| HDD zone 1 | 1.19 | 0.79 | 0.33 | 0.18 | 0.06 | |
| HDD zone 2 | 2.60 | 1.01 | 0.63 | 0.32 | 0.18 | |
| HDD zone 3 | 3.02 | 2.10 | 1.11 | 0.81 | 0.41 | |
| HDD zone 4 | 3.07 | 1.54 | 1.24 | 1.04 | 0.57 | |

| Climate Zone | AC and Summer Ventilation Electricity Use, kWh/square foot | | | | | Facility Difference |
|---|---|---|---|---|---|---|
| | 90% | 70% | Median | 30% | 10% | |
| CDD zone 1 | 4.92 | 2.08 | 1.01 | 0.64 | 0.27 | |
| CDD zone 2 | 8.58 | 5.12 | 2.94 | 1.96 | 1.36 | |
| CDD zone 3 | 19.45 | 9.96 | 6.07 | 3.95 | 2.07 | |

| Climate Zone | Electric Space Heat, kWh/square foot | | | | | Facility Difference |
|---|---|---|---|---|---|---|
| | 90% | 70% | Median | 30% | 10% | |
| HDD zone 1 | 2.84 | 1.66 | 1.28 | 0.51 | 0.28 | |
| HDD zone 2 | 4.49 | 2.35 | 2.14 | 1.18 | 0.64 | |
| HDD zone 3 | 5.20 | 2.78 | 2.26 | 1.68 | 1.23 | |
| HDD zone 4 | 10.90 | 6.17 | 5.14 | 3.69 | 1.54 | |

| Climate Zone | Natural Gas Space Heat, kBtu/square foot | | | | | Facility Difference |
|---|---|---|---|---|---|---|
| | 90% | 70% | Median | 30% | 10% | |
| HDD zone 1 | 53.68 | 25.77 | 8.59 | 6.01 | 3.44 | |
| HDD zone 2 | 77.36 | 38.31 | 9.60 | 6.24 | 4.32 | |
| HDD zone 3 | 119.61 | 42.03 | 16.81 | 10.09 | 6.97 | |
| HDD zone 4 | 110.28 | 36.76 | 18.38 | 12.87 | 8.14 | |

**TABLE A.20**   College Other (Less than 50 hours/week)

| End Use | Baseload Electricity Use, kWh/square foot | | | | | Facility Difference |
| --- | --- | --- | --- | --- | --- | --- |
| | 90% | 70% | Median | 30% | 10% | |
| Water heating | 7.36 | 5.59 | 3.96 | 1.66 | 0.77 | |
| Cooking | 3.91 | 3.07 | 2.79 | 1.53 | 0.84 | |
| Refrigeration | 5.98 | 0.87 | 0.13 | 0.04 | 0.01 | |
| Interior lighting | 12.19 | 7.51 | 2.99 | 2.18 | 0.82 | |
| Exterior lighting | 1.75 | 1.06 | 0.43 | 0.21 | 0.08 | |
| Equipment | 1.39 | 0.72 | 0.33 | 0.29 | 0.13 | |
| Miscellaneous | 4.90 | 2.54 | 1.09 | 0.83 | 0.23 | |
| *Total Baseload* | 37.48 | 21.36 | 11.72 | 6.74 | 2.88 | |

| Climate Zone | Space Heating Ventilation Electricity Use, kWh/square foot | | | | | Facility Difference |
| --- | --- | --- | --- | --- | --- | --- |
| | 90% | 70% | Median | 30% | 10% | |
| HDD zone 1 | 0.09 | 0.08 | 0.05 | 0.04 | 0.02 | |
| HDD zone 2 | 1.21 | 0.49 | 0.32 | 0.17 | 0.14 | |
| HDD zone 3 | 1.72 | 1.08 | 0.66 | 0.52 | 0.32 | |
| HDD zone 4 | 1.89 | 1.49 | 1.35 | 0.90 | 0.48 | |

| Climate Zone | AC and Summer Ventilation Electricity Use, kWh/square foot | | | | | Facility Difference |
| --- | --- | --- | --- | --- | --- | --- |
| | 90% | 70% | Median | 30% | 10% | |
| CDD zone 1 | 4.58 | 2.95 | 1.77 | 0.61 | 0.23 | |
| CDD zone 2 | 8.70 | 5.46 | 2.76 | 1.49 | 0.82 | |
| CDD zone 3 | 9.13 | 3.29 | 3.08 | 1.24 | 0.93 | |

| Climate Zone | Electric Space Heat, kWh/square foot | | | | | Facility Difference |
| --- | --- | --- | --- | --- | --- | --- |
| | 90% | 70% | Median | 30% | 10% | |
| HDD zone 1 | 2.09 | 1.70 | 1.50 | 1.19 | 0.38 | |
| HDD zone 2 | 6.92 | 5.95 | 4.77 | 3.34 | 1.43 | |
| HDD zone 3 | 10.63 | 8.72 | 7.59 | 6.07 | 1.90 | |
| HDD zone 4 | 14.62 | 11.10 | 10.99 | 9.57 | 2.20 | |

| Climate Zone | Natural Gas Space Heat, kBtu/square foot | | | | | Facility Difference |
| --- | --- | --- | --- | --- | --- | --- |
| | 90% | 70% | Median | 30% | 10% | |
| HDD zone 1 | 37.02 | 34.01 | 17.97 | 12.81 | 5.39 | |
| HDD zone 2 | 47.50 | 40.56 | 29.97 | 22.98 | 10.49 | |
| HDD zone 3 | 53.76 | 51.41 | 33.60 | 27.22 | 16.80 | |
| HDD zone 4 | 66.13 | 60.90 | 39.47 | 32.37 | 19.55 | |

**TABLE A.21**   College Other (50–85 hours/week)

| End Use | Baseload Electricity Use, kWh/square foot | | | | | Facility Difference |
|---|---|---|---|---|---|---|
| | 90% | 70% | Median | 30% | 10% | |
| Water heating | 9.30 | 3.70 | 3.07 | 0.61 | 0.31 | |
| Cooking | 3.67 | 2.62 | 2.05 | 1.55 | 0.41 | |
| Refrigeration | 2.41 | 1.33 | 0.64 | 0.10 | 0.05 | |
| Interior lighting | 11.69 | 7.24 | 3.34 | 2.24 | 0.39 | |
| Exterior lighting | 1.41 | 0.44 | 0.32 | 0.09 | 0.07 | |
| Equipment | 2.62 | 0.57 | 0.40 | 0.28 | 0.07 | |
| Miscellaneous | 8.58 | 2.00 | 1.28 | 0.83 | 0.16 | |
| *Total Baseload* | 39.68 | 17.90 | 11.10 | 5.70 | 1.46 | |

| Climate Zone | Space Heating Ventilation Electricity Use, kWh/square foot | | | | | Facility Difference |
|---|---|---|---|---|---|---|
| | 90% | 70% | Median | 30% | 10% | |
| HDD zone 1 | 0.75 | 0.46 | 0.30 | 0.06 | 0.03 | |
| HDD zone 2 | 2.13 | 0.87 | 0.40 | 0.31 | 0.09 | |
| HDD zone 3 | 2.61 | 1.28 | 1.13 | 1.05 | 0.55 | |
| HDD zone 4 | 2.25 | 1.36 | 1.24 | 0.83 | 0.67 | |

| Climate Zone | AC and Summer Ventilation Electricity Use, kWh/square foot | | | | | Facility Difference |
|---|---|---|---|---|---|---|
| | 90% | 70% | Median | 30% | 10% | |
| CDD zone 1 | 7.92 | 3.16 | 1.32 | 1.03 | 0.41 | |
| CDD zone 2 | 8.29 | 5.83 | 3.60 | 2.59 | 1.32 | |
| CDD zone 3 | 10.67 | 7.62 | 5.12 | 2.56 | 1.54 | |

| Climate Zone | Electric Space Heat, kWh/square foot | | | | | Facility Difference |
|---|---|---|---|---|---|---|
| | 90% | 70% | Median | 30% | 10% | |
| HDD zone 1 | 1.96 | 1.35 | 0.98 | 0.59 | 0.10 | |
| HDD zone 2 | 4.40 | 3.86 | 1.27 | 0.57 | 0.36 | |
| HDD zone 3 | 4.56 | 2.36 | 1.63 | 0.73 | 0.49 | |
| HDD zone 4 | 5.37 | 3.78 | 2.66 | 1.12 | 0.67 | |

| Climate Zone | Natural Gas Space Heat, kBtu/square foot | | | | | Facility Difference |
|---|---|---|---|---|---|---|
| | 90% | 70% | Median | 30% | 10% | |
| HDD zone 1 | 44.48 | 35.58 | 22.24 | 13.79 | 6.89 | |
| HDD zone 2 | 89.48 | 67.34 | 37.70 | 22.62 | 11.31 | |
| HDD zone 3 | 99.07 | 52.79 | 49.29 | 27.60 | 15.28 | |
| HDD zone 4 | 87.47 | 62.39 | 56.80 | 25.56 | 18.74 | |

**TABLE A.22**   College Other (Greater than 85 hours/week)

| End Use | Baseload Electricity Use, kWh/square foot | | | | | Facility Difference |
|---|---|---|---|---|---|---|
| | 90% | 70% | Median | 30% | 10% | |
| Water heating | 1.33 | 0.56 | 0.39 | 0.25 | 0.12 | |
| Cooking | 4.42 | 2.17 | 2.00 | 0.46 | 0.20 | |
| Refrigeration | 2.14 | 0.33 | 0.21 | 0.04 | 0.02 | |
| Interior lighting | 11.91 | 7.21 | 5.34 | 3.35 | 0.47 | |
| Exterior lighting | 1.20 | 0.69 | 0.24 | 0.13 | 0.08 | |
| Equipment | 1.82 | 1.04 | 0.62 | 0.38 | 0.08 | |
| Miscellaneous | 6.47 | 3.28 | 1.85 | 1.16 | 0.15 | |
| Total Baseload | 29.29 | 15.28 | 10.65 | 5.77 | 1.12 | |

| Climate Zone | Space Heating Ventilation Electricity Use, kWh/square foot | | | | | Facility Difference |
|---|---|---|---|---|---|---|
| | 90% | 70% | Median | 30% | 10% | |
| HDD zone 1 | 0.81 | 0.17 | 0.03 | 0.02 | 0.01 | |
| HDD zone 2 | 2.11 | 1.24 | 0.34 | 0.16 | 0.07 | |
| HDD zone 3 | 2.59 | 1.17 | 0.80 | 0.61 | 0.30 | |
| HDD zone 4 | 3.69 | 1.94 | 1.28 | 0.87 | 0.37 | |

| Climate Zone | AC and Summer Ventilation Electricity Use, kWh/square foot | | | | | Facility Difference |
|---|---|---|---|---|---|---|
| | 90% | 70% | Median | 30% | 10% | |
| CDD zone 1 | 4.65 | 2.56 | 1.52 | 0.94 | 0.17 | |
| CDD zone 2 | 6.01 | 3.59 | 2.10 | 0.48 | 0.31 | |
| CDD zone 3 | 17.97 | 7.80 | 1.38 | 0.80 | 0.53 | |

| Climate Zone | Electric Space Heat, kWh/square foot | | | | | Facility Difference |
|---|---|---|---|---|---|---|
| | 90% | 70% | Median | 30% | 10% | |
| HDD zone 1 | 0.17 | 0.14 | 0.10 | 0.05 | 0.02 | |
| HDD zone 2 | 2.76 | 2.25 | 1.90 | 0.97 | 0.47 | |
| HDD zone 3 | 4.87 | 4.16 | 3.14 | 1.04 | 0.71 | |
| HDD zone 4 | 6.67 | 5.83 | 5.58 | 2.34 | 0.79 | |

| Climate Zone | Natural Gas Space Heat, kBtu/square foot | | | | | Facility Difference |
|---|---|---|---|---|---|---|
| | 90% | 70% | Median | 30% | 10% | |
| HDD zone 1 | 37.33 | 20.30 | 15.61 | 12.89 | 2.97 | |
| HDD zone 2 | 35.77 | 21.97 | 18.98 | 10.25 | 4.75 | |
| HDD zone 3 | 78.48 | 39.09 | 30.30 | 17.57 | 6.67 | |
| HDD zone 4 | 92.23 | 51.77 | 41.26 | 17.74 | 11.14 | |

**TABLE A.23** Dry Warehouse (Less than 50 hours/week)

| End Use | Baseload Electricity Use, kWh/square foot | | | | | Facility Difference |
|---|---|---|---|---|---|---|
| | 90% | 70% | Median | 30% | 10% | |
| Water heating | 0.55 | 0.20 | 0.11 | 0.07 | 0.03 | |
| Cooking | 0.05 | 0.04 | 0.03 | 0.01 | 0.00 | |
| Refrigeration | 0.43 | 0.10 | 0.06 | 0.02 | 0.01 | |
| Interior lighting | 3.06 | 1.35 | 0.84 | 0.37 | 0.21 | |
| Exterior lighting | 1.28 | 0.67 | 0.32 | 0.17 | 0.05 | |
| Equipment | 0.28 | 0.13 | 0.07 | 0.03 | 0.02 | |
| Miscellaneous | 2.73 | 1.13 | 0.68 | 0.26 | 0.16 | |
| *Total Baseload* | 8.38 | 3.62 | 2.11 | 0.93 | 0.48 | |

| Climate Zone | Space Heating Ventilation Electricity Use, kWh/square foot | | | | | Facility Difference |
|---|---|---|---|---|---|---|
| | 90% | 70% | Median | 30% | 10% | |
| HDD zone 1 | 0.18 | 0.07 | 0.03 | 0.02 | 0.01 | |
| HDD zone 2 | 0.41 | 0.14 | 0.09 | 0.04 | 0.01 | |
| HDD zone 3 | 1.10 | 0.51 | 0.34 | 0.19 | 0.04 | |
| HDD zone 4 | 1.18 | 0.68 | 0.47 | 0.24 | 0.04 | |

| Climate Zone | AC and Summer Ventilation Electricity Use, kWh/square foot | | | | | Facility Difference |
|---|---|---|---|---|---|---|
| | 90% | 70% | Median | 30% | 10% | |
| CDD zone 1 | 1.64 | 0.66 | 0.32 | 0.18 | 0.05 | |
| CDD zone 2 | 2.58 | 1.48 | 0.84 | 0.45 | 0.17 | |
| CDD zone 3 | 5.03 | 2.94 | 1.80 | 1.33 | 0.45 | |

| Climate Zone | Electric Space Heat, kWh/square foot | | | | | Facility Difference |
|---|---|---|---|---|---|---|
| | 90% | 70% | Median | 30% | 10% | |
| HDD zone 1 | 1.46 | 0.37 | 0.25 | 0.14 | 0.07 | |
| HDD zone 2 | 1.10 | 0.67 | 0.57 | 0.41 | 0.23 | |
| HDD zone 3 | 3.70 | 1.08 | 0.85 | 0.69 | 0.23 | |
| HDD zone 4 | 4.20 | 2.94 | 1.13 | 0.39 | 0.22 | |

| Climate Zone | Natural Gas Space Heat, kBtu/square foot | | | | | Facility Difference |
|---|---|---|---|---|---|---|
| | 90% | 70% | Median | 30% | 10% | |
| HDD zone 1 | 20.95 | 14.67 | 8.38 | 6.83 | 4.84 | |
| HDD zone 2 | 31.64 | 21.15 | 16.40 | 10.43 | 8.65 | |
| HDD zone 3 | 56.94 | 39.90 | 31.11 | 21.69 | 10.49 | |
| HDD zone 4 | 78.54 | 49.88 | 29.81 | 20.53 | 9.41 | |

**TABLE A.24** Dry Warehouse (50–85 hours/week)

| End Use | Baseload Electricity Use, kWh/square foot | | | | | Facility Difference |
|---|---|---|---|---|---|---|
| | 90% | 70% | Median | 30% | 10% | |
| Water heating | 1.21 | 0.39 | 0.14 | 0.07 | 0.02 | |
| Cooking | 0.02 | 0.01 | 0.01 | 0.01 | 0.01 | |
| Refrigeration | 0.58 | 0.12 | 0.04 | 0.02 | 0.01 | |
| Interior lighting | 4.54 | 2.55 | 1.13 | 0.70 | 0.28 | |
| Exterior lighting | 1.34 | 0.85 | 0.40 | 0.18 | 0.08 | |
| Equipment | 0.35 | 0.19 | 0.09 | 0.05 | 0.03 | |
| Miscellaneous | 3.22 | 1.75 | 0.90 | 0.46 | 0.18 | |
| *Total Baseload* | 11.26 | 5.86 | 2.71 | 1.49 | 0.61 | |

| Climate Zone | Space Heating Ventilation Electricity Use, kWh/square foot | | | | | Facility Difference |
|---|---|---|---|---|---|---|
| | 90% | 70% | Median | 30% | 10% | |
| HDD zone 1 | 0.20 | 0.14 | 0.05 | 0.02 | 0.01 | |
| HDD zone 2 | 1.03 | 0.47 | 0.18 | 0.11 | 0.05 | |
| HDD zone 3 | 1.65 | 0.78 | 0.51 | 0.34 | 0.10 | |
| HDD zone 4 | 1.37 | 1.02 | 0.76 | 0.35 | 0.08 | |

| Climate Zone | AC and Summer Ventilation Electricity Use, kWh/square foot | | | | | Facility Difference |
|---|---|---|---|---|---|---|
| | 90% | 70% | Median | 30% | 10% | |
| CDD zone 1 | 3.09 | 1.09 | 0.52 | 0.22 | 0.04 | |
| CDD zone 2 | 6.43 | 2.41 | 1.20 | 0.75 | 0.34 | |
| CDD zone 3 | 6.59 | 3.27 | 1.59 | 0.90 | 0.34 | |

| Climate Zone | Electric Space Heat, kWh/square foot | | | | | Facility Difference |
|---|---|---|---|---|---|---|
| | 90% | 70% | Median | 30% | 10% | |
| HDD zone 1 | 2.03 | 0.28 | 0.19 | 0.16 | 0.04 | |
| HDD zone 2 | 2.31 | 0.66 | 0.22 | 0.08 | 0.02 | |
| HDD zone 3 | 2.70 | 0.86 | 0.45 | 0.32 | 0.27 | |
| HDD zone 4 | 10.12 | 6.55 | 0.44 | 0.40 | 0.19 | |

| Climate Zone | Natural Gas Space Heat, kBtu/square foot | | | | | Facility Difference |
|---|---|---|---|---|---|---|
| | 90% | 70% | Median | 30% | 10% | |
| HDD zone 1 | 15.62 | 13.16 | 10.88 | 6.53 | 4.26 | |
| HDD zone 2 | 42.32 | 34.14 | 20.69 | 12.78 | 5.46 | |
| HDD zone 3 | 78.33 | 41.85 | 22.88 | 11.51 | 7.80 | |
| HDD zone 4 | 83.75 | 42.29 | 26.33 | 18.07 | 13.17 | |

**TABLE A.25** Dry Warehouse (Greater than 85 hours/week)

| End Use | Baseload Electricity Use, kWh/square foot | | | | | Facility Difference |
|---|---|---|---|---|---|---|
| | 90% | 70% | Median | 30% | 10% | |
| Water heating | 1.09 | 0.53 | 0.29 | 0.23 | 0.10 | |
| Cooking | 0.09 | 0.05 | 0.02 | 0.02 | 0.01 | |
| Refrigeration | 3.83 | 0.20 | 0.08 | 0.03 | 0.01 | |
| Interior lighting | 9.06 | 2.87 | 0.61 | 0.41 | 0.17 | |
| Exterior lighting | 1.22 | 0.57 | 0.37 | 0.19 | 0.07 | |
| Equipment | 0.43 | 0.18 | 0.03 | 0.02 | 0.01 | |
| Miscellaneous | 4.69 | 1.49 | 0.21 | 0.16 | 0.05 | |
| *Total Baseload* | 20.41 | 5.89 | 1.61 | 1.06 | 0.42 | |

| Climate Zone | Space Heating Ventilation Electricity Use, kWh/square foot | | | | | Facility Difference |
|---|---|---|---|---|---|---|
| | 90% | 70% | Median | 30% | 10% | |
| HDD zone 1 | 0.15 | 0.08 | 0.07 | 0.05 | 0.01 | |
| HDD zone 2 | 0.52 | 0.21 | 0.20 | 0.13 | 0.07 | |
| HDD zone 3 | 0.86 | 0.43 | 0.38 | 0.23 | 0.05 | |
| HDD zone 4 | 1.45 | 0.68 | 0.54 | 0.16 | 0.13 | |

| Climate Zone | AC and Summer Ventilation Electricity Use, kWh/square foot | | | | | Facility Difference |
|---|---|---|---|---|---|---|
| | 90% | 70% | Median | 30% | 10% | |
| CDD zone 1 | 2.09 | 1.32 | 0.85 | 0.57 | 0.27 | |
| CDD zone 2 | 3.46 | 1.69 | 1.19 | 0.81 | 0.31 | |
| CDD zone 3 | 9.62 | 8.18 | 3.20 | 1.46 | 0.41 | |

| Climate Zone | Electric Space Heat, kWh/square foot | | | | | Facility Difference |
|---|---|---|---|---|---|---|
| | 90% | 70% | Median | 30% | 10% | |
| HDD zone 1 | 1.09 | 0.78 | 0.64 | 0.42 | 0.11 | |
| HDD zone 2 | 1.19 | 0.94 | 0.90 | 0.50 | 0.27 | |
| HDD zone 3 | 3.08 | 2.51 | 1.74 | 0.91 | 0.40 | |
| HDD zone 4 | 2.24 | 1.88 | 1.43 | 1.11 | 0.34 | |

| Climate Zone | Natural Gas Space Heat, kBtu/square foot | | | | | Facility Difference |
|---|---|---|---|---|---|---|
| | 90% | 70% | Median | 30% | 10% | |
| HDD zone 1 | 44.73 | 18.33 | 11.54 | 10.79 | 3.81 | |
| HDD zone 2 | 87.77 | 48.65 | 26.88 | 11.43 | 7.85 | |
| HDD zone 3 | 88.12 | 39.67 | 23.89 | 15.24 | 8.29 | |
| HDD zone 4 | 79.63 | 56.83 | 28.83 | 16.78 | 15.48 | |

**TABLE A.26** Educational (Less than 50 hours/week)

| End Use | Baseload Electricity Use, kWh/square foot | | | | | Facility Difference |
| | 90% | 70% | Median | 30% | 10% | |
| --- | --- | --- | --- | --- | --- | --- |
| Water heating | 1.32 | 0.79 | 0.54 | 0.42 | 0.16 | |
| Cooking | 1.24 | 0.73 | 0.47 | 0.38 | 0.16 | |
| Refrigeration | 0.87 | 0.43 | 0.26 | 0.15 | 0.04 | |
| Interior lighting | 5.45 | 3.25 | 2.54 | 1.75 | 0.91 | |
| Exterior lighting | 1.27 | 0.82 | 0.44 | 0.23 | 0.11 | |
| Equipment | 0.49 | 0.34 | 0.27 | 0.19 | 0.11 | |
| Miscellaneous | 0.53 | 0.34 | 0.24 | 0.17 | 0.09 | |
| *Total Baseload* | 11.17 | 6.70 | 4.76 | 3.29 | 1.58 | |

| Climate Zone | Space Heating Ventilation Electricity Use, kWh/square foot | | | | | Facility Difference |
| | 90% | 70% | Median | 30% | 10% | |
| --- | --- | --- | --- | --- | --- | --- |
| HDD zone 1 | 0.30 | 0.16 | 0.09 | 0.07 | 0.03 | |
| HDD zone 2 | 0.81 | 0.43 | 0.24 | 0.15 | 0.08 | |
| HDD zone 3 | 1.63 | 0.98 | 0.67 | 0.51 | 0.27 | |
| HDD zone 4 | 2.22 | 1.43 | 0.95 | 0.65 | 0.34 | |

| Climate Zone | AC and Summer Ventilation Electricity Use, kWh/square foot | | | | | Facility Difference |
| | 90% | 70% | Median | 30% | 10% | |
| --- | --- | --- | --- | --- | --- | --- |
| CDD zone 1 | 2.44 | 1.23 | 0.82 | 0.54 | 0.25 | |
| CDD zone 2 | 3.33 | 2.13 | 1.40 | 0.91 | 0.45 | |
| CDD zone 3 | 6.59 | 3.95 | 2.64 | 1.77 | 0.96 | |

| Climate Zone | Electric Space Heat, kWh/square foot | | | | | Facility Difference |
| | 90% | 70% | Median | 30% | 10% | |
| --- | --- | --- | --- | --- | --- | --- |
| HDD zone 1 | 2.25 | 0.89 | 0.46 | 0.26 | 0.10 | |
| HDD zone 2 | 5.45 | 3.46 | 1.23 | 0.94 | 0.67 | |
| HDD zone 3 | 8.25 | 4.91 | 3.27 | 1.90 | 1.45 | |
| HDD zone 4 | 7.87 | 7.09 | 5.28 | 2.49 | 1.94 | |

| Climate Zone | Natural Gas Space Heat, kBtu/square foot | | | | | Facility Difference |
| | 90% | 70% | Median | 30% | 10% | |
| --- | --- | --- | --- | --- | --- | --- |
| HDD zone 1 | 37.31 | 23.85 | 17.28 | 14.13 | 9.12 | |
| HDD zone 2 | 55.97 | 39.22 | 25.57 | 19.09 | 10.08 | |
| HDD zone 3 | 79.53 | 53.88 | 42.27 | 31.68 | 19.76 | |
| HDD zone 4 | 79.65 | 55.90 | 48.22 | 39.74 | 23.60 | |

**TABLE A.27**　Educational (50–85 hours/week)

| End Use | Baseload Electricity Use, kWh/square foot | | | | | Facility Difference |
|---|---|---|---|---|---|---|
| | 90% | 70% | Median | 30% | 10% | |
| Water heating | 1.61 | 0.87 | 0.55 | 0.26 | 0.14 | |
| Cooking | 2.28 | 1.38 | 0.93 | 0.49 | 0.26 | |
| Refrigeration | 1.96 | 0.56 | 0.28 | 0.16 | 0.05 | |
| Interior lighting | 8.54 | 4.56 | 3.39 | 1.90 | 1.20 | |
| Exterior lighting | 1.09 | 0.56 | 0.33 | 0.15 | 0.10 | |
| Equipment | 0.79 | 0.42 | 0.33 | 0.19 | 0.14 | |
| Miscellaneous | 0.82 | 0.43 | 0.31 | 0.17 | 0.10 | |
| *Total Baseload* | 17.09 | 8.78 | 6.12 | 3.32 | 1.99 | |

| Climate Zone | Space Heating Ventilation Electricity Use, kWh/square foot | | | | | Facility Difference |
|---|---|---|---|---|---|---|
| | 90% | 70% | Median | 30% | 10% | |
| HDD zone 1 | 0.39 | 0.18 | 0.12 | 0.06 | 0.03 | |
| HDD zone 2 | 0.80 | 0.42 | 0.27 | 0.17 | 0.03 | |
| HDD zone 3 | 1.55 | 0.87 | 0.67 | 0.38 | 0.17 | |
| HDD zone 4 | 1.91 | 1.12 | 0.78 | 0.49 | 0.26 | |

| Climate Zone | AC and Summer Ventilation Electricity Use, kWh/square foot | | | | | Facility Difference |
|---|---|---|---|---|---|---|
| | 90% | 70% | Median | 30% | 10% | |
| CDD zone 1 | 2.33 | 1.21 | 0.78 | 0.45 | 0.21 | |
| CDD zone 2 | 4.19 | 2.49 | 1.63 | 1.03 | 0.45 | |
| CDD zone 3 | 9.04 | 5.42 | 3.53 | 1.94 | 0.75 | |

| Climate Zone | Electric Space Heat, kWh/square foot | | | | | Facility Difference |
|---|---|---|---|---|---|---|
| | 90% | 70% | Median | 30% | 10% | |
| HDD zone 1 | 5.94 | 0.80 | 0.52 | 0.45 | 0.07 | |
| HDD zone 2 | 3.55 | 2.62 | 1.42 | 1.09 | 0.81 | |
| HDD zone 3 | 8.71 | 7.30 | 3.90 | 1.75 | 1.28 | |
| HDD zone 4 | 37.06 | 25.89 | 9.42 | 4.30 | 2.12 | |

| Climate Zone | Natural Gas Space Heat, kBtu/square foot | | | | | Facility Difference |
|---|---|---|---|---|---|---|
| | 90% | 70% | Median | 30% | 10% | |
| HDD zone 1 | 23.09 | 13.91 | 9.52 | 8.49 | 4.66 | |
| HDD zone 2 | 50.71 | 34.08 | 22.82 | 15.94 | 9.32 | |
| HDD zone 3 | 72.56 | 45.27 | 30.60 | 19.88 | 13.23 | |
| HDD zone 4 | 79.88 | 48.10 | 36.21 | 31.90 | 9.32 | |

**TABLE A.28** Educational (Greater than 85 hours/week)

| End Use | Baseload Electricity Use, kWh/square foot | | | | | Facility Difference |
|---|---|---|---|---|---|---|
| | 90% | 70% | Median | 30% | 10% | |
| Water heating | 1.01 | 0.83 | 0.62 | 0.27 | 0.14 | |
| Cooking | 1.49 | 0.95 | 0.89 | 0.45 | 0.19 | |
| Refrigeration | 1.86 | 0.66 | 0.53 | 0.29 | 0.04 | |
| Interior lighting | 10.21 | 6.31 | 3.56 | 2.67 | 1.40 | |
| Exterior lighting | 0.56 | 0.17 | 0.13 | 0.09 | 0.06 | |
| Equipment | 0.84 | 0.68 | 0.35 | 0.25 | 0.15 | |
| Miscellaneous | 0.86 | 0.66 | 0.33 | 0.28 | 0.11 | |
| *Total Baseload* | 16.82 | 10.26 | 6.41 | 4.30 | 2.09 | |

| Climate Zone | Space Heating Ventilation Electricity Use, kWh/square foot | | | | | Facility Difference |
|---|---|---|---|---|---|---|
| | 90% | 70% | Median | 30% | 10% | |
| HDD zone 1 | 0.40 | 0.27 | 0.22 | 0.13 | 0.04 | |
| HDD zone 2 | 0.68 | 0.37 | 0.26 | 0.19 | 0.06 | |
| HDD zone 3 | 1.52 | 0.92 | 0.80 | 0.61 | 0.46 | |
| HDD zone 4 | 1.30 | 1.01 | 0.50 | 0.45 | 0.32 | |

| Climate Zone | AC and Summer Ventilation Electricity Use, kWh/square foot | | | | | Facility Difference |
|---|---|---|---|---|---|---|
| | 90% | 70% | Median | 30% | 10% | |
| CDD zone 1 | 1.95 | 1.54 | 0.77 | 0.52 | 0.35 | |
| CDD zone 2 | 3.87 | 2.47 | 2.01 | 1.30 | 0.82 | |
| CDD zone 3 | 8.59 | 6.92 | 4.17 | 2.77 | 2.37 | |

| Climate Zone | Electric Space Heat, kWh/square foot | | | | | Facility Difference |
|---|---|---|---|---|---|---|
| | 90% | 70% | Median | 30% | 10% | |
| HDD zone 1 | 1.95 | 1.31 | 0.78 | 0.57 | 0.42 | |
| HDD zone 2 | 3.81 | 2.52 | 1.27 | 0.83 | 0.74 | |
| HDD zone 3 | 6.70 | 3.18 | 2.85 | 1.97 | 1.43 | |
| HDD zone 4 | 10.85 | 4.77 | 3.69 | 2.17 | 2.01 | |

| Climate Zone | Natural Gas Space Heat, kBtu/square foot | | | | | Facility Difference |
|---|---|---|---|---|---|---|
| | 90% | 70% | Median | 30% | 10% | |
| HDD zone 1 | 14.35 | 11.41 | 6.83 | 4.10 | 1.37 | |
| HDD zone 2 | 39.57 | 22.72 | 12.77 | 7.95 | 4.20 | |
| HDD zone 3 | 64.80 | 39.18 | 30.14 | 12.06 | 7.84 | |
| HDD zone 4 | 68.55 | 43.16 | 33.77 | 18.28 | 12.19 | |

**TABLE A.29**   Federal Office (Less than 50 hours/week)

| End Use | Baseload Electricity Use, kWh/square foot | | | | | Facility Difference |
| | 90% | 70% | Median | 30% | 10% | |
| --- | --- | --- | --- | --- | --- | --- |
| Water heating | 4.48 | 2.43 | 2.22 | 1.31 | 0.56 | |
| Cooking | 0.66 | 0.55 | 0.50 | 0.34 | 0.09 | |
| Refrigeration | 1.28 | 0.74 | 0.51 | 0.27 | 0.10 | |
| Interior lighting | 9.34 | 8.56 | 5.19 | 3.53 | 1.07 | |
| Exterior lighting | 1.62 | 0.99 | 0.74 | 0.46 | 0.12 | |
| Equipment | 4.48 | 4.14 | 2.24 | 1.12 | 0.54 | |
| Miscellaneous | 4.53 | 3.30 | 2.64 | 1.27 | 0.47 | |
| *Total Baseload* | 26.39 | 20.72 | 14.04 | 8.30 | 2.95 | |

| Climate Zone | Space Heating Ventilation Electricity Use, kWh/square foot | | | | | Facility Difference |
| | 90% | 70% | Median | 30% | 10% | |
| --- | --- | --- | --- | --- | --- | --- |
| HDD zone 1 | 0.56 | 0.35 | 0.14 | 0.06 | 0.04 | |
| HDD zone 2 | 0.65 | 0.31 | 0.25 | 0.19 | 0.12 | |
| HDD zone 3 | 1.91 | 0.57 | 0.46 | 0.21 | 0.14 | |
| HDD zone 4 | 0.86 | 0.70 | 0.59 | 0.19 | 0.17 | |

| Climate Zone | AC and Summer Ventilation Electricity Use, kWh/square foot | | | | | Facility Difference |
| | 90% | 70% | Median | 30% | 10% | |
| --- | --- | --- | --- | --- | --- | --- |
| CDD zone 1 | 2.74 | 1.59 | 1.26 | 0.71 | 0.34 | |
| CDD zone 2 | 5.89 | 4.85 | 2.84 | 2.02 | 1.13 | |
| CDD zone 3 | 11.81 | 6.24 | 3.83 | 3.01 | 2.16 | |

| Climate Zone | Electric Space Heat, kWh/square foot | | | | | Facility Difference |
| | 90% | 70% | Median | 30% | 10% | |
| --- | --- | --- | --- | --- | --- | --- |
| HDD zone 1 | 2.70 | 1.49 | 1.24 | 0.21 | 0.04 | |
| HDD zone 2 | 2.46 | 1.46 | 1.01 | 0.73 | 0.27 | |
| HDD zone 3 | 4.47 | 2.41 | 1.54 | 0.53 | 0.44 | |
| HDD zone 4 | 5.94 | 2.72 | 1.98 | 0.65 | 0.59 | |

| Climate Zone | Natural Gas Space Heat, kBtu/square foot | | | | | Facility Difference |
| | 90% | 70% | Median | 30% | 10% | |
| --- | --- | --- | --- | --- | --- | --- |
| HDD zone 1 | 44.49 | 23.50 | 12.84 | 9.83 | 7.80 | |
| HDD zone 2 | 64.02 | 33.12 | 28.08 | 20.16 | 12.20 | |
| HDD zone 3 | 76.28 | 42.75 | 38.14 | 25.17 | 17.00 | |
| HDD zone 4 | 88.16 | 73.73 | 40.07 | 27.25 | 18.43 | |

**TABLE A.30**   Federal Office (50–85 hours/week)

| End Use | Baseload Electricity Use, kWh/square foot | | | | | Facility Difference |
|---|---|---|---|---|---|---|
| | 90% | 70% | Median | 30% | 10% | |
| Water heating | 1.93 | 1.80 | 1.01 | 0.61 | 0.19 | |
| Cooking | 0.70 | 0.54 | 0.45 | 0.26 | 0.08 | |
| Refrigeration | 0.56 | 0.38 | 0.15 | 0.11 | 0.10 | |
| Interior lighting | 9.45 | 5.68 | 3.50 | 2.60 | 1.96 | |
| Exterior lighting | 1.25 | 0.73 | 0.34 | 0.17 | 0.09 | |
| Equipment | 6.59 | 2.50 | 1.19 | 1.03 | 0.92 | |
| Miscellaneous | 8.01 | 2.61 | 1.10 | 0.94 | 0.78 | |
| *Total Baseload* | 28.49 | 14.24 | 7.74 | 5.71 | 4.12 | |

| Climate Zone | Space Heating Ventilation Electricity Use, kWh/square foot | | | | | Facility Difference |
|---|---|---|---|---|---|---|
| | 90% | 70% | Median | 30% | 10% | |
| HDD zone 1 | 0.73 | 0.30 | 0.24 | 0.19 | 0.04 | |
| HDD zone 2 | 1.51 | 0.64 | 0.43 | 0.35 | 0.16 | |
| HDD zone 3 | 3.16 | 1.39 | 0.62 | 0.48 | 0.28 | |
| HDD zone 4 | 2.80 | 1.16 | 0.72 | 0.58 | 0.35 | |

| Climate Zone | AC and Summer Ventilation Electricity Use, kWh/square foot | | | | | Facility Difference |
|---|---|---|---|---|---|---|
| | 90% | 70% | Median | 30% | 10% | |
| CDD zone 1 | 4.74 | 2.68 | 1.52 | 1.24 | 0.33 | |
| CDD zone 2 | 6.59 | 3.69 | 2.54 | 1.92 | 0.56 | |
| CDD zone 3 | 12.91 | 7.85 | 5.38 | 3.55 | 0.99 | |

| Climate Zone | Electric Space Heat, kWh/square foot | | | | | Facility Difference |
|---|---|---|---|---|---|---|
| | 90% | 70% | Median | 30% | 10% | |
| HDD zone 1 | 0.22 | 0.15 | 0.09 | 0.04 | 0.03 | |
| HDD zone 2 | 5.08 | 4.15 | 2.86 | 1.14 | 0.63 | |
| HDD zone 3 | 6.82 | 6.52 | 4.40 | 1.65 | 0.52 | |
| HDD zone 4 | 8.27 | 7.28 | 5.02 | 2.26 | 1.59 | |

| Climate Zone | Natural Gas Space Heat, kBtu/square foot | | | | | Facility Difference |
|---|---|---|---|---|---|---|
| | 90% | 70% | Median | 30% | 10% | |
| HDD zone 1 | 40.16 | 21.84 | 14.09 | 10.15 | 3.52 | |
| HDD zone 2 | 59.82 | 49.06 | 31.65 | 19.94 | 8.56 | |
| HDD zone 3 | 71.35 | 59.12 | 40.77 | 25.69 | 18.33 | |
| HDD zone 4 | 83.06 | 77.55 | 50.04 | 30.02 | 22.12 | |

**TABLE A.31**    Federal Office (Greater than 85 hours/week)

| End Use | Baseload Electricity Use, kWh/square foot | | | | | Facility Difference |
|---|---|---|---|---|---|---|
| | 90% | 70% | Median | 30% | 10% | |
| Water heating | 2.35 | 2.31 | 0.60 | 0.33 | 0.15 | |
| Cooking | 2.32 | 1.29 | 0.53 | 0.34 | 0.12 | |
| Refrigeration | 0.60 | 0.59 | 0.17 | 0.09 | 0.06 | |
| Interior lighting | 9.78 | 6.16 | 3.26 | 2.61 | 1.96 | |
| Exterior lighting | 1.58 | 0.84 | 0.70 | 0.38 | 0.25 | |
| Equipment | 3.82 | 1.91 | 0.87 | 0.59 | 0.33 | |
| Miscellaneous | 4.59 | 2.16 | 0.80 | 0.50 | 0.18 | |
| *Total Baseload* | 25.04 | 15.27 | 6.93 | 4.85 | 3.04 | |

| Climate Zone | Space Heating Ventilation Electricity Use, kWh/square foot | | | | | Facility Difference |
|---|---|---|---|---|---|---|
| | 90% | 70% | Median | 30% | 10% | |
| HDD zone 1 | 1.50 | 1.24 | 0.12 | 0.07 | 0.01 | |
| HDD zone 2 | 2.30 | 1.54 | 1.03 | 0.38 | 0.19 | |
| HDD zone 3 | 2.83 | 2.65 | 1.36 | 0.64 | 0.37 | |
| HDD zone 4 | 3.10 | 2.23 | 2.07 | 1.39 | 0.60 | |

| Climate Zone | AC and Summer Ventilation Electricity Use, kWh/square foot | | | | | Facility Difference |
|---|---|---|---|---|---|---|
| | 90% | 70% | Median | 30% | 10% | |
| CDD zone 1 | 2.67 | 2.09 | 1.63 | 1.25 | 0.93 | |
| CDD zone 2 | 5.55 | 4.03 | 2.85 | 2.02 | 1.42 | |
| CDD zone 3 | 10.94 | 7.92 | 6.44 | 4.67 | 3.46 | |

| Climate Zone | Electric Space Heat, kWh/square foot | | | | | Facility Difference |
|---|---|---|---|---|---|---|
| | 90% | 70% | Median | 30% | 10% | |
| HDD zone 1 | 1.48 | 1.19 | 1.14 | 0.82 | 0.44 | |
| HDD zone 2 | 2.91 | 2.46 | 1.94 | 1.48 | 1.03 | |
| HDD zone 3 | 4.19 | 3.50 | 2.89 | 2.08 | 1.84 | |
| HDD zone 4 | 5.21 | 4.63 | 4.17 | 2.75 | 2.25 | |

| Climate Zone | Natural Gas Space Heat, kBtu/square foot | | | | | Facility Difference |
|---|---|---|---|---|---|---|
| | 90% | 70% | Median | 30% | 10% | |
| HDD zone 1 | 28.27 | 26.40 | 25.09 | 19.31 | 8.53 | |
| HDD zone 2 | 44.14 | 39.28 | 36.78 | 18.70 | 8.33 | |
| HDD zone 3 | 60.94 | 51.71 | 50.78 | 39.10 | 8.78 | |
| HDD zone 4 | 73.22 | 67.12 | 55.47 | 26.52 | 8.80 | |

**TABLE A.32**　Federal Other (Less than 50 hours/week)

| End Use | Baseload Electricity Use, kWh/square foot | | | | | Facility Difference |
|---|---|---|---|---|---|---|
| | 90% | 70% | Median | 30% | 10% | |
| Water heating | 2.40 | 1.62 | 0.40 | 0.18 | 0.13 | |
| Cooking | 2.37 | 1.51 | 0.83 | 0.27 | 0.14 | |
| Refrigeration | 2.69 | 1.34 | 0.75 | 0.36 | 0.08 | |
| Interior lighting | 9.33 | 6.64 | 1.86 | 1.61 | 0.27 | |
| Exterior lighting | 1.37 | 0.98 | 0.89 | 0.35 | 0.19 | |
| Equipment | 1.08 | 0.89 | 0.28 | 0.18 | 0.07 | |
| Miscellaneous | 3.34 | 2.73 | 0.65 | 0.29 | 0.06 | |
| *Total Baseload* | 22.58 | 15.71 | 5.66 | 3.24 | 0.94 | |

| Climate Zone | Space Heating Ventilation Electricity Use, kWh/square foot | | | | | Facility Difference |
|---|---|---|---|---|---|---|
| | 90% | 70% | Median | 30% | 10% | |
| HDD zone 1 | 0.38 | 0.31 | 0.25 | 0.15 | 0.05 | |
| HDD zone 2 | 0.94 | 0.75 | 0.39 | 0.20 | 0.08 | |
| HDD zone 3 | 1.62 | 1.02 | 0.53 | 0.21 | 0.11 | |
| HDD zone 4 | 3.95 | 1.72 | 1.31 | 0.86 | 0.08 | |

| Climate Zone | AC and Summer Ventilation Electricity Use, kWh/square foot | | | | | Facility Difference |
|---|---|---|---|---|---|---|
| | 90% | 70% | Median | 30% | 10% | |
| CDD zone 1 | 2.63 | 1.73 | 1.10 | 0.70 | 0.29 | |
| CDD zone 2 | 6.48 | 2.75 | 1.60 | 0.66 | 0.23 | |
| CDD zone 3 | 6.92 | 2.69 | 1.73 | 1.69 | 0.27 | |

| Climate Zone | Electric Space Heat, kWh/square foot | | | | | Facility Difference |
|---|---|---|---|---|---|---|
| | 90% | 70% | Median | 30% | 10% | |
| HDD zone 1 | 0.62 | 0.32 | 0.31 | 0.26 | 0.02 | |
| HDD zone 2 | 1.64 | 1.13 | 0.84 | 0.53 | 0.18 | |
| HDD zone 3 | 2.34 | 1.55 | 1.03 | 0.78 | 0.31 | |
| HDD zone 4 | 4.11 | 3.92 | 2.22 | 1.78 | 0.71 | |

| Climate Zone | Natural Gas Space Heat, kBtu/square foot | | | | | Facility Difference |
|---|---|---|---|---|---|---|
| | 90% | 70% | Median | 30% | 10% | |
| HDD zone 1 | 14.44 | 10.11 | 7.22 | 2.31 | 1.66 | |
| HDD zone 2 | 32.36 | 29.77 | 25.89 | 8.80 | 12.33 | |
| HDD zone 3 | 73.62 | 54.13 | 43.30 | 25.98 | 17.32 | |
| HDD zone 4 | 91.23 | 83.33 | 60.82 | 40.75 | 20.07 | |

**TABLE A.33**　Federal Other (50–85 hours/week)

| End Use | Baseload Electricity Use, kWh/square foot | | | | | Facility Difference |
|---|---|---|---|---|---|---|
| | 90% | 70% | Median | 30% | 10% | |
| Water heating | 2.93 | 1.54 | 0.77 | 0.44 | 0.09 | |
| Cooking | 0.68 | 0.54 | 0.45 | 0.12 | 0.08 | |
| Refrigeration | 0.41 | 0.33 | 0.27 | 0.15 | 0.08 | |
| Interior lighting | 8.78 | 6.59 | 5.23 | 1.51 | 1.47 | |
| Exterior lighting | 1.73 | 0.94 | 0.93 | 0.14 | 0.05 | |
| Equipment | 1.95 | 0.98 | 0.82 | 0.45 | 0.16 | |
| Miscellaneous | 6.70 | 3.04 | 2.57 | 0.93 | 0.36 | |
| *Total Baseload* | 23.18 | 13.96 | 13.28 | 3.73 | 2.29 | |

| Climate Zone | Space Heating Ventilation Electricity Use, kWh/square foot | | | | | Facility Difference |
|---|---|---|---|---|---|---|
| | 90% | 70% | Median | 30% | 10% | |
| HDD zone 1 | 0.80 | 0.26 | 0.20 | 0.09 | 0.03 | |
| HDD zone 2 | 1.50 | 0.60 | 0.48 | 0.31 | 0.12 | |
| HDD zone 3 | 1.85 | 1.02 | 0.84 | 0.57 | 0.32 | |
| HDD zone 4 | 4.18 | 1.87 | 1.44 | 0.59 | 0.45 | |

| Climate Zone | AC and Summer Ventilation Electricity Use, kWh/square foot | | | | | Facility Difference |
|---|---|---|---|---|---|---|
| | 90% | 70% | Median | 30% | 10% | |
| CDD zone 1 | 4.33 | 3.10 | 1.35 | 0.95 | 0.49 | |
| CDD zone 2 | 6.84 | 3.21 | 1.53 | 1.21 | 0.48 | |
| CDD zone 3 | 8.07 | 4.87 | 3.48 | 1.74 | 1.13 | |

| Climate Zone | Electric Space Heat, kWh/square foot | | | | | Facility Difference |
|---|---|---|---|---|---|---|
| | 90% | 70% | Median | 30% | 10% | |
| HDD zone 1 | 0.92 | 0.64 | 0.46 | 0.39 | 0.16 | |
| HDD zone 2 | 3.49 | 2.75 | 1.91 | 1.56 | 0.72 | |
| HDD zone 3 | 5.87 | 4.89 | 3.91 | 3.01 | 1.67 | |
| HDD zone 4 | 6.76 | 6.23 | 6.02 | 4.82 | 2.47 | |

| Climate Zone | Natural Gas Space Heat, kBtu/square foot | | | | | Facility Difference |
|---|---|---|---|---|---|---|
| | 90% | 70% | Median | 30% | 10% | |
| HDD zone 1 | 16.98 | 14.56 | 12.13 | 4.70 | 2.18 | |
| HDD zone 2 | 41.32 | 36.00 | 31.30 | 15.65 | 10.09 | |
| HDD zone 3 | 59.38 | 52.06 | 40.35 | 20.98 | 12.52 | |
| HDD zone 4 | 88.75 | 77.83 | 68.27 | 27.31 | 21.85 | |

**TABLE A.34** Federal Other (Greater than 85 hours/week)

| End Use | Baseload Electricity Use, kWh/square foot | | | | | Facility Difference |
| --- | --- | --- | --- | --- | --- | --- |
| | 90% | 70% | Median | 30% | 10% | |
| Water heating | 0.42 | 0.37 | 0.34 | 0.24 | 0.11 | |
| Cooking | 2.07 | 1.48 | 1.22 | 1.06 | 0.41 | |
| Refrigeration | 0.28 | 0.10 | 0.05 | 0.02 | 0.01 | |
| Interior lighting | 10.67 | 3.37 | 2.18 | 1.35 | 1.09 | |
| Exterior lighting | 0.60 | 0.56 | 0.50 | 0.39 | 0.28 | |
| Equipment | 0.51 | 0.16 | 0.15 | 0.13 | 0.11 | |
| Miscellaneous | 1.70 | 0.59 | 0.43 | 0.33 | 0.24 | |
| *Total Baseload* | 16.25 | 6.63 | 4.87 | 3.51 | 2.25 | |

| Climate Zone | Space Heating Ventilation Electricity Use, kWh/square foot | | | | | Facility Difference |
| --- | --- | --- | --- | --- | --- | --- |
| | 90% | 70% | Median | 30% | 10% | |
| HDD zone 1 | 0.44 | 0.14 | 0.11 | 0.02 | 0.01 | |
| HDD zone 2 | 0.74 | 0.44 | 0.40 | 0.04 | 0.03 | |
| HDD zone 3 | 3.17 | 1.37 | 1.32 | 0.79 | 0.46 | |
| HDD zone 4 | 3.43 | 1.61 | 1.46 | 0.88 | 0.51 | |

| Climate Zone | AC and Summer Ventilation Electricity Use, kWh/square foot | | | | | Facility Difference |
| --- | --- | --- | --- | --- | --- | --- |
| | 90% | 70% | Median | 30% | 10% | |
| CDD zone 1 | 4.83 | 1.38 | 1.14 | 0.54 | 0.32 | |
| CDD zone 2 | 4.33 | 1.73 | 1.44 | 1.07 | 0.56 | |
| CDD zone 3 | 5.14 | 3.81 | 2.72 | 0.77 | 0.65 | |

| Climate Zone | Electric Space Heat, kWh/square foot | | | | | Facility Difference |
| --- | --- | --- | --- | --- | --- | --- |
| | 90% | 70% | Median | 30% | 10% | |
| HDD zone 1 | 0.70 | 0.44 | 0.32 | 0.18 | 0.13 | |
| HDD zone 2 | 0.85 | 0.62 | 0.48 | 0.21 | 0.14 | |
| HDD zone 3 | 1.37 | 1.17 | 1.02 | 0.57 | 0.44 | |
| HDD zone 4 | 4.86 | 3.24 | 2.70 | 1.22 | 0.95 | |

| Climate Zone | Natural Gas Space Heat, kBtu/square foot | | | | | Facility Difference |
| --- | --- | --- | --- | --- | --- | --- |
| | 90% | 70% | Median | 30% | 10% | |
| HDD zone 1 | 49.50 | 19.80 | 9.00 | 6.75 | 4.50 | |
| HDD zone 2 | 73.74 | 27.65 | 12.29 | 9.83 | 7.18 | |
| HDD zone 3 | 77.68 | 66.58 | 36.99 | 24.04 | 12.21 | |
| HDD zone 4 | 99.32 | 70.28 | 46.85 | 28.11 | 16.40 | |

**TABLE A.35** Grocery (50–85 hours/week)

| End Use | Baseload Electricity Use, kWh/square foot | | | | | Facility Difference |
|---|---|---|---|---|---|---|
| | 90% | 70% | Median | 30% | 10% | |
| Water heating | 2.23 | 2.10 | 1.89 | 1.02 | 0.38 | |
| Cooking | 1.45 | 1.11 | 1.07 | 0.40 | 0.20 | |
| Refrigeration | 37.56 | 27.25 | 23.76 | 18.49 | 11.10 | |
| Interior lighting | 9.18 | 5.24 | 4.59 | 2.45 | 1.56 | |
| Exterior lighting | 1.51 | 1.00 | 0.83 | 0.66 | 0.28 | |
| Equipment | 0.75 | 0.53 | 0.47 | 0.26 | 0.15 | |
| Miscellaneous | 4.32 | 3.33 | 2.86 | 1.63 | 1.02 | |
| Total Baseload | 57.00 | 40.56 | 35.47 | 24.91 | 14.69 | |

| Climate Zone | Space Heating Ventilation Electricity Use, kWh/square foot | | | | | Facility Difference |
|---|---|---|---|---|---|---|
| | 90% | 70% | Median | 30% | 10% | |
| HDD zone 1 | 0.79 | 0.28 | 0.13 | 0.07 | 0.04 | |
| HDD zone 2 | 1.73 | 0.59 | 0.40 | 0.29 | 0.14 | |
| HDD zone 3 | 4.92 | 2.06 | 1.23 | 0.43 | 0.16 | |
| HDD zone 4 | 5.96 | 2.41 | 1.59 | 0.70 | 0.46 | |

| Climate Zone | AC and Summer Ventilation Electricity Use, kWh/square foot | | | | | Facility Difference |
|---|---|---|---|---|---|---|
| | 90% | 70% | Median | 30% | 10% | |
| CDD zone 1 | 8.87 | 6.43 | 3.68 | 2.63 | 1.36 | |
| CDD zone 2 | 16.00 | 8.99 | 5.88 | 3.52 | 1.55 | |
| CDD zone 3 | 20.18 | 14.43 | 11.62 | 8.00 | 5.38 | |

| Climate Zone | Electric Space Heat, kWh/square foot | | | | | Facility Difference |
|---|---|---|---|---|---|---|
| | 90% | 70% | Median | 30% | 10% | |
| HDD zone 1 | 1.19 | 0.80 | 0.69 | 0.33 | 0.11 | |
| HDD zone 2 | 3.92 | 2.94 | 2.46 | 2.11 | 1.53 | |
| HDD zone 3 | 7.11 | 5.31 | 4.60 | 3.92 | 3.50 | |
| HDD zone 4 | 15.10 | 8.23 | 6.73 | 5.62 | 5.18 | |

| Climate Zone | Natural Gas Space Heat, kBtu/square foot | | | | | Facility Difference |
|---|---|---|---|---|---|---|
| | 90% | 70% | Median | 30% | 10% | |
| HDD zone 1 | 49.67 | 38.58 | 13.36 | 8.82 | 7.09 | |
| HDD zone 2 | 73.59 | 41.04 | 15.45 | 13.29 | 8.83 | |
| HDD zone 3 | 63.22 | 48.66 | 16.58 | 13.29 | 9.47 | |
| HDD zone 4 | 77.36 | 45.38 | 20.42 | 15.52 | 10.21 | |

**TABLE A.36** Grocery (Greater than 85 hours/week)

| End Use | Baseload Electricity Use, kWh/square foot | | | | | Facility Difference |
|---|---|---|---|---|---|---|
| | 90% | 70% | Median | 30% | 10% | |
| Water heating | 5.27 | 3.58 | 2.68 | 1.50 | 0.88 | |
| Cooking | 1.94 | 1.53 | 1.13 | 0.91 | 0.66 | |
| Refrigeration | 50.88 | 37.47 | 31.39 | 27.71 | 18.37 | |
| Interior lighting | 17.85 | 12.57 | 10.20 | 7.59 | 3.30 | |
| Exterior lighting | 1.75 | 1.45 | 1.20 | 0.56 | 0.19 | |
| Equipment | 0.87 | 0.69 | 0.58 | 0.46 | 0.23 | |
| Miscellaneous | 5.72 | 4.15 | 3.66 | 2.88 | 1.51 | |
| *Total Baseload* | 86.36 | 61.44 | 50.84 | 41.61 | 25.14 | |

| Climate Zone | Space Heating Ventilation Electricity Use, kWh/square foot | | | | | Facility Difference |
|---|---|---|---|---|---|---|
| | 90% | 70% | Median | 30% | 10% | |
| HDD zone 1 | 0.64 | 0.31 | 0.18 | 0.07 | 0.03 | |
| HDD zone 2 | 2.22 | 0.76 | 0.46 | 0.30 | 0.15 | |
| HDD zone 3 | 2.93 | 1.68 | 0.86 | 0.53 | 0.31 | |
| HDD zone 4 | 3.60 | 1.61 | 1.22 | 1.01 | 0.54 | |

| Climate Zone | AC and Summer Ventilation Electricity Use, kWh/square foot | | | | | Facility Difference |
|---|---|---|---|---|---|---|
| | 90% | 70% | Median | 30% | 10% | |
| CDD zone 1 | 11.07 | 7.15 | 5.03 | 3.19 | 1.91 | |
| CDD zone 2 | 18.62 | 11.69 | 8.58 | 5.48 | 3.38 | |
| CDD zone 3 | 31.13 | 18.62 | 12.98 | 8.58 | 5.89 | |

| Climate Zone | Electric Space Heat, kWh/square foot | | | | | Facility Difference |
|---|---|---|---|---|---|---|
| | 90% | 70% | Median | 30% | 10% | |
| HDD zone 1 | 3.87 | 1.48 | 0.75 | 0.40 | 0.10 | |
| HDD zone 2 | 6.66 | 4.36 | 2.20 | 1.34 | 0.58 | |
| HDD zone 3 | 12.77 | 6.80 | 4.37 | 2.43 | 1.39 | |
| HDD zone 4 | 13.10 | 8.10 | 6.55 | 5.50 | 2.90 | |

| Climate Zone | Natural Gas Space Heat, kBtu/square foot | | | | | Facility Difference |
|---|---|---|---|---|---|---|
| | 90% | 70% | Median | 30% | 10% | |
| HDD zone 1 | 48.07 | 29.11 | 12.76 | 8.54 | 6.70 | |
| HDD zone 2 | 59.97 | 36.75 | 16.86 | 12.81 | 7.67 | |
| HDD zone 3 | 86.51 | 54.43 | 26.04 | 20.78 | 12.41 | |
| HDD zone 4 | 91.12 | 57.11 | 51.13 | 28.50 | 19.27 | |

**TABLE A.37**  Hospital

| End Use | Baseload Electricity Use, kWh/square foot | | | | | Facility Difference |
|---|---|---|---|---|---|---|
| | 90% | 70% | Median | 30% | 10% | |
| Water heating | 10.76 | 5.64 | 3.25 | 2.15 | 1.03 | |
| Cooking | 6.71 | 3.17 | 2.60 | 1.84 | 0.78 | |
| Refrigeration | 2.73 | 1.66 | 1.18 | 0.94 | 0.08 | |
| Interior lighting | 16.42 | 10.60 | 8.46 | 5.27 | 3.05 | |
| Exterior lighting | 0.41 | 0.23 | 0.09 | 0.06 | 0.03 | |
| Equipment | 2.45 | 1.80 | 1.41 | 0.86 | 0.49 | |
| Miscellaneous | 11.12 | 7.90 | 5.83 | 3.56 | 1.92 | |
| *Total Baseload* | 50.60 | 31.00 | 22.82 | 14.68 | 7.38 | |

| Climate Zone | Space Heating Ventilation Electricity Use, kWh/square foot | | | | | Facility Difference |
|---|---|---|---|---|---|---|
| | 90% | 70% | Median | 30% | 10% | |
| HDD zone 1 | 0.71 | 0.25 | 0.14 | 0.08 | 0.01 | |
| HDD zone 2 | 0.89 | 0.27 | 0.17 | 0.10 | 0.04 | |
| HDD zone 3 | 2.39 | 1.09 | 0.45 | 0.26 | 0.11 | |
| HDD zone 4 | 2.64 | 1.67 | 0.65 | 0.30 | 0.14 | |

| Climate Zone | AC and Summer Ventilation Electricity Use, kWh/square foot | | | | | Facility Difference |
|---|---|---|---|---|---|---|
| | 90% | 70% | Median | 30% | 10% | |
| CDD zone 1 | 7.08 | 4.65 | 3.21 | 2.13 | 1.20 | |
| CDD zone 2 | 11.23 | 6.98 | 4.74 | 2.91 | 1.75 | |
| CDD zone 3 | 19.91 | 11.85 | 7.87 | 4.21 | 2.24 | |

| Climate Zone | Electric Space Heat, kWh/square foot | | | | | Facility Difference |
|---|---|---|---|---|---|---|
| | 90% | 70% | Median | 30% | 10% | |
| HDD zone 1 | 2.26 | 2.21 | 1.19 | 0.45 | 0.22 | |
| HDD zone 2 | 5.34 | 3.89 | 2.48 | 0.74 | 0.27 | |
| HDD zone 3 | 8.52 | 6.70 | 5.47 | 2.13 | 0.62 | |
| HDD zone 4 | 11.53 | 9.65 | 6.10 | 5.37 | 0.78 | |

| Climate Zone | Natural Gas Space Heat, kBtu/square foot | | | | | Facility Difference |
|---|---|---|---|---|---|---|
| | 90% | 70% | Median | 30% | 10% | |
| HDD zone 1 | 32.62 | 20.25 | 13.57 | 6.80 | 4.25 | |
| HDD zone 2 | 89.56 | 34.14 | 27.38 | 17.50 | 9.77 | |
| HDD zone 3 | 86.76 | 56.92 | 38.44 | 24.59 | 13.00 | |
| HDD zone 4 | 82.16 | 65.39 | 46.22 | 27.43 | 16.64 | |

**TABLE A.38** Hotel

| End Use | Baseload Electricity Use, kWh/square foot | | | | | Facility Difference |
| | 90% | 70% | Median | 30% | 10% | |
|---|---|---|---|---|---|---|
| Water heating | 6.95 | 3.84 | 3.05 | 1.47 | 0.30 | |
| Cooking | 3.83 | 1.83 | 1.29 | 0.96 | 0.27 | |
| Refrigeration | 1.60 | 0.79 | 0.25 | 0.08 | 0.02 | |
| Interior lighting | 9.84 | 7.59 | 5.62 | 2.45 | 1.03 | |
| Exterior lighting | 1.46 | 0.83 | 0.48 | 0.27 | 0.13 | |
| Equipment | 0.64 | 0.42 | 0.27 | 0.16 | 0.09 | |
| Miscellaneous | 2.48 | 1.49 | 0.88 | 0.37 | 0.20 | |
| Total Baseload | 32.84 | 17.92 | 11.84 | 5.76 | 2.33 | |

| Climate Zone | Space Heating Ventilation Electricity Use, kWh/square foot | | | | | Facility Difference |
| | 90% | 70% | Median | 30% | 10% | |
|---|---|---|---|---|---|---|
| HDD zone 1 | 0.21 | 0.13 | 0.05 | 0.03 | 0.01 | |
| HDD zone 2 | 1.34 | 0.35 | 0.21 | 0.12 | 0.02 | |
| HDD zone 3 | 2.12 | 0.73 | 0.31 | 0.18 | 0.06 | |
| HDD zone 4 | 2.57 | 0.85 | 0.59 | 0.26 | 0.06 | |

| Climate Zone | AC and Summer Ventilation Electricity Use, kWh/square foot | | | | | Facility Difference |
| | 90% | 70% | Median | 30% | 10% | |
|---|---|---|---|---|---|---|
| CDD zone 1 | 8.31 | 3.15 | 1.76 | 0.74 | 0.22 | |
| CDD zone 2 | 12.91 | 6.94 | 4.47 | 3.01 | 1.44 | |
| CDD zone 3 | 13.13 | 7.49 | 4.31 | 2.90 | 1.94 | |

| Climate Zone | Electric Space Heat, kWh/square foot | | | | | Facility Difference |
| | 90% | 70% | Median | 30% | 10% | |
|---|---|---|---|---|---|---|
| HDD zone 1 | 2.88 | 0.98 | 0.77 | 0.55 | 0.14 | |
| HDD zone 2 | 6.70 | 3.60 | 2.33 | 1.46 | 0.73 | |
| HDD zone 3 | 12.18 | 5.61 | 4.64 | 3.63 | 1.31 | |
| HDD zone 4 | 15.07 | 7.81 | 5.85 | 3.19 | 0.88 | |

| Climate Zone | Natural Gas Space Heat, kBtu/square foot | | | | | Facility Difference |
| | 90% | 70% | Median | 30% | 10% | |
|---|---|---|---|---|---|---|
| HDD zone 1 | 25.50 | 18.84 | 12.43 | 9.09 | 3.98 | |
| HDD zone 2 | 42.16 | 28.40 | 22.19 | 18.24 | 5.69 | |
| HDD zone 3 | 65.09 | 38.73 | 34.26 | 23.44 | 9.59 | |
| HDD zone 4 | 77.88 | 54.33 | 38.80 | 20.27 | 15.41 | |

**TABLE A.39**   Nursing Home

| End Use | Baseload Electricity Use, kWh/square foot | | | | | Facility Difference |
|---|---|---|---|---|---|---|
| | 90% | 70% | Median | 30% | 10% | |
| Water heating | 3.95 | 2.43 | 1.62 | 0.57 | 0.34 | |
| Cooking | 3.53 | 2.29 | 1.41 | 0.85 | 0.56 | |
| Refrigeration | 1.72 | 1.26 | 0.89 | 0.52 | 0.22 | |
| Interior lighting | 10.66 | 7.80 | 6.66 | 4.93 | 2.41 | |
| Exterior lighting | 0.80 | 0.52 | 0.43 | 0.24 | 0.18 | |
| Equipment | 0.60 | 0.43 | 0.31 | 0.23 | 0.13 | |
| Miscellaneous | 2.20 | 1.58 | 1.12 | 0.80 | 0.43 | |
| *Total Baseload* | 23.45 | 16.31 | 12.44 | 8.13 | 4.27 | |

| Climate Zone | Space Heating Ventilation Electricity Use, kWh/square foot | | | | | Facility Difference |
|---|---|---|---|---|---|---|
| | 90% | 70% | Median | 30% | 10% | |
| HDD zone 1 | 0.46 | 0.14 | 0.06 | 0.03 | 0.01 | |
| HDD zone 2 | 1.04 | 0.48 | 0.28 | 0.13 | 0.05 | |
| HDD zone 3 | 2.39 | 1.24 | 0.58 | 0.30 | 0.17 | |
| HDD zone 4 | 2.80 | 1.88 | 0.94 | 0.52 | 0.26 | |

| Climate Zone | AC and Summer Ventilation Electricity Use, kWh/square foot | | | | | Facility Difference |
|---|---|---|---|---|---|---|
| | 90% | 70% | Median | 30% | 10% | |
| CDD zone 1 | 6.20 | 2.69 | 1.79 | 1.16 | 0.63 | |
| CDD zone 2 | 8.34 | 4.68 | 3.18 | 2.26 | 1.24 | |
| CDD zone 3 | 15.03 | 8.62 | 6.01 | 4.14 | 2.76 | |

| Climate Zone | Electric Space Heat, kWh/square foot | | | | | Facility Difference |
|---|---|---|---|---|---|---|
| | 90% | 70% | Median | 30% | 10% | |
| HDD zone 1 | 2.84 | 1.48 | 1.44 | 1.07 | 0.27 | |
| HDD zone 2 | 7.26 | 4.34 | 2.92 | 1.68 | 0.86 | |
| HDD zone 3 | 14.40 | 9.01 | 7.22 | 5.49 | 2.26 | |
| HDD zone 4 | 21.42 | 11.45 | 10.06 | 7.96 | 2.69 | |

| Climate Zone | Natural Gas Space Heat, kBtu/square foot | | | | | Facility Difference |
|---|---|---|---|---|---|---|
| | 90% | 70% | Median | 30% | 10% | |
| HDD zone 1 | 66.53 | 58.06 | 31.06 | 18.63 | 6.21 | |
| HDD zone 2 | 89.21 | 50.37 | 33.66 | 18.60 | 6.61 | |
| HDD zone 3 | 100.45 | 71.39 | 52.98 | 28.16 | 8.69 | |
| HDD zone 4 | 111.27 | 87.37 | 56.15 | 31.57 | 11.40 | |

**TABLE A.40**   Office (Less than 50 hours/week)

| End Use | Baseload Electricity Use, kWh/square foot | | | | | Facility Difference |
|---|---|---|---|---|---|---|
| | 90% | 70% | Median | 30% | 10% | |
| Water heating | 2.44 | 1.12 | 0.71 | 0.43 | 0.18 | |
| Cooking | 1.17 | 0.35 | 0.16 | 0.13 | 0.04 | |
| Refrigeration | 0.95 | 0.28 | 0.19 | 0.11 | 0.04 | |
| Interior lighting | 9.34 | 4.37 | 3.07 | 1.84 | 0.81 | |
| Exterior lighting | 1.20 | 0.69 | 0.44 | 0.29 | 0.09 | |
| Equipment | 3.75 | 1.78 | 1.22 | 0.84 | 0.44 | |
| Miscellaneous | 3.99 | 1.80 | 1.18 | 0.71 | 0.29 | |
| *Total Baseload* | 22.84 | 10.39 | 6.97 | 4.35 | 1.89 | |

| Climate Zone | Space Heating Ventilation Electricity Use, kWh/square foot | | | | | Facility Difference |
|---|---|---|---|---|---|---|
| | 90% | 70% | Median | 30% | 10% | |
| HDD zone 1 | 0.25 | 0.15 | 0.10 | 0.08 | 0.04 | |
| HDD zone 2 | 1.00 | 0.53 | 0.37 | 0.21 | 0.07 | |
| HDD zone 3 | 1.73 | 0.92 | 0.47 | 0.33 | 0.20 | |
| HDD zone 4 | 2.73 | 1.21 | 0.91 | 0.47 | 0.27 | |

| Climate Zone | AC and Summer Ventilation Electricity Use, kWh/square foot | | | | | Facility Difference |
|---|---|---|---|---|---|---|
| | 90% | 70% | Median | 30% | 10% | |
| CDD zone 1 | 3.48 | 1.87 | 0.98 | 0.48 | 0.23 | |
| CDD zone 2 | 5.41 | 3.48 | 2.14 | 1.43 | 0.70 | |
| CDD zone 3 | 8.97 | 5.80 | 3.89 | 2.91 | 1.93 | |

| Climate Zone | Electric Space Heat, kWh/square foot | | | | | Facility Difference |
|---|---|---|---|---|---|---|
| | 90% | 70% | Median | 30% | 10% | |
| HDD zone 1 | 1.35 | 0.82 | 0.54 | 0.45 | 0.17 | |
| HDD zone 2 | 2.94 | 1.85 | 1.24 | 0.77 | 0.25 | |
| HDD zone 3 | 2.99 | 2.76 | 1.71 | 0.87 | 0.47 | |
| HDD zone 4 | 7.15 | 4.70 | 1.76 | 1.64 | 0.65 | |

| Climate Zone | Natural Gas Space Heat, kBtu/square foot | | | | | Facility Difference |
|---|---|---|---|---|---|---|
| | 90% | 70% | Median | 30% | 10% | |
| HDD zone 1 | 26.67 | 17.56 | 14.28 | 8.57 | 4.28 | |
| HDD zone 2 | 33.93 | 30.40 | 21.21 | 13.96 | 5.70 | |
| HDD zone 3 | 61.77 | 38.19 | 28.37 | 18.90 | 13.36 | |
| HDD zone 4 | 81.43 | 65.01 | 46.18 | 31.92 | 15.30 | |

**TABLE A.41**   Office (50–85 hours/week)

| End Use | Baseload Electricity Use, kWh/square foot | | | | | Facility Difference |
|---|---|---|---|---|---|---|
| | 90% | 70% | Median | 30% | 10% | |
| Water heating | 2.71 | 1.42 | 0.92 | 0.48 | 0.21 | |
| Cooking | 1.15 | 0.71 | 0.61 | 0.40 | 0.11 | |
| Refrigeration | 0.77 | 0.37 | 0.22 | 0.12 | 0.05 | |
| Interior lighting | 9.48 | 6.07 | 4.28 | 2.36 | 1.19 | |
| Exterior lighting | 1.01 | 0.40 | 0.28 | 0.13 | 0.06 | |
| Equipment | 3.67 | 2.15 | 1.66 | 0.98 | 0.53 | |
| Miscellaneous | 3.93 | 2.12 | 1.65 | 0.87 | 0.39 | |
| *Total Baseload* | 22.72 | 13.24 | 9.62 | 5.34 | 2.54 | |

| Climate Zone | Space Heating Ventilation Electricity Use, kWh/square foot | | | | | Facility Difference |
|---|---|---|---|---|---|---|
| | 90% | 70% | Median | 30% | 10% | |
| HDD zone 1 | 0.56 | 0.28 | 0.21 | 0.08 | 0.04 | |
| HDD zone 2 | 0.58 | 0.32 | 0.19 | 0.15 | 0.09 | |
| HDD zone 3 | 1.89 | 1.08 | 0.62 | 0.41 | 0.23 | |
| HDD zone 4 | 1.96 | 1.47 | 1.02 | 0.87 | 0.27 | |

| Climate Zone | AC and Summer Ventilation Electricity Use, kWh/square foot | | | | | Facility Difference |
|---|---|---|---|---|---|---|
| | 90% | 70% | Median | 30% | 10% | |
| CDD zone 1 | 3.33 | 2.02 | 1.28 | 0.73 | 0.26 | |
| CDD zone 2 | 5.09 | 2.81 | 2.16 | 1.52 | 1.01 | |
| CDD zone 3 | 8.44 | 4.07 | 2.83 | 2.06 | 1.48 | |

| Climate Zone | Electric Space Heat, kWh/square foot | | | | | Facility Difference |
|---|---|---|---|---|---|---|
| | 90% | 70% | Median | 30% | 10% | |
| HDD zone 1 | 1.63 | 0.64 | 0.40 | 0.28 | 0.14 | |
| HDD zone 2 | 3.04 | 1.58 | 1.09 | 0.70 | 0.35 | |
| HDD zone 3 | 4.92 | 2.12 | 1.63 | 1.10 | 0.98 | |
| HDD zone 4 | 7.85 | 5.66 | 3.51 | 2.02 | 0.87 | |

| Climate Zone | Natural Gas Space Heat, kBtu/square foot | | | | | Facility Difference |
|---|---|---|---|---|---|---|
| | 90% | 70% | Median | 30% | 10% | |
| HDD zone 1 | 28.90 | 14.98 | 8.98 | 5.84 | 3.59 | |
| HDD zone 2 | 59.55 | 26.08 | 18.37 | 13.54 | 11.14 | |
| HDD zone 3 | 56.04 | 29.26 | 20.93 | 14.49 | 8.53 | |
| HDD zone 4 | 79.47 | 37.42 | 30.44 | 19.79 | 7.00 | |

**TABLE A.42**   Office (Greater than 85 hours/week)

| End Use | Baseload Electricity Use, kWh/square foot | | | | | Facility Difference |
|---|---|---|---|---|---|---|
| | 90% | 70% | Median | 30% | 10% | |
| Water heating | 2.76 | 2.44 | 1.14 | 0.47 | 0.20 | |
| Cooking | 0.75 | 0.44 | 0.43 | 0.17 | 0.14 | |
| Refrigeration | 1.22 | 0.92 | 0.51 | 0.20 | 0.08 | |
| Interior lighting | 12.58 | 8.17 | 5.03 | 1.39 | 1.02 | |
| Exterior lighting | 0.94 | 0.35 | 0.11 | 0.06 | 0.03 | |
| Equipment | 4.22 | 1.99 | 1.22 | 0.56 | 0.34 | |
| Miscellaneous | 4.25 | 2.12 | 1.09 | 0.36 | 0.15 | |
| *Total Baseload* | 26.72 | 16.43 | 9.53 | 3.21 | 1.96 | |

| Climate Zone | Space Heating Ventilation Electricity Use, kWh/square foot | | | | | Facility Difference |
|---|---|---|---|---|---|---|
| | 90% | 70% | Median | 30% | 10% | |
| HDD zone 1 | 1.12 | 0.31 | 0.22 | 0.08 | 0.06 | |
| HDD zone 2 | 1.93 | 1.09 | 0.71 | 0.34 | 0.15 | |
| HDD zone 3 | 1.35 | 0.78 | 0.51 | 0.26 | 0.10 | |
| HDD zone 4 | 2.11 | 0.93 | 0.53 | 0.24 | 0.15 | |

| Climate Zone | AC and Summer Ventilation Electricity Use, kWh/square foot | | | | | Facility Difference |
|---|---|---|---|---|---|---|
| | 90% | 70% | Median | 30% | 10% | |
| CDD zone 1 | 3.49 | 1.98 | 0.94 | 0.38 | 0.16 | |
| CDD zone 2 | 10.76 | 5.67 | 3.06 | 1.67 | 1.07 | |
| CDD zone 3 | 16.90 | 9.65 | 6.89 | 3.68 | 2.42 | |

| Climate Zone | Electric Space Heat, kWh/square foot | | | | | Facility Difference |
|---|---|---|---|---|---|---|
| | 90% | 70% | Median | 30% | 10% | |
| HDD zone 1 | 1.49 | 1.01 | 0.67 | 0.35 | 0.01 | |
| HDD zone 2 | 5.60 | 3.03 | 1.98 | 1.02 | 0.83 | |
| HDD zone 3 | 5.34 | 3.35 | 2.68 | 1.88 | 0.80 | |
| HDD zone 4 | 5.69 | 4.83 | 3.11 | 2.46 | 1.17 | |

| Climate Zone | Natural Gas Space Heat, kBtu/square foot | | | | | Facility Difference |
|---|---|---|---|---|---|---|
| | 90% | 70% | Median | 30% | 10% | |
| HDD zone 1 | 36.00 | 21.60 | 18.00 | 17.88 | 4.59 | |
| HDD zone 2 | 52.67 | 23.74 | 21.58 | 10.79 | 7.77 | |
| HDD zone 3 | 71.91 | 31.93 | 23.97 | 11.29 | 7.09 | |
| HDD zone 4 | 97.20 | 38.88 | 32.40 | 22.03 | 6.03 | |

**TABLE A.43**     Refrigerated Warehouse (Less than 50 hours/week)

| End Use | Baseload Electricity Use, kWh/square foot | | | | | Facility Difference |
|---|---|---|---|---|---|---|
| | 90% | 70% | Median | 30% | 10% | |
| Water heating | 0.95 | 0.94 | 0.93 | 0.63 | 0.40 | |
| Cooking | 0.00 | 0.00 | 0.00 | 0.00 | 0.00 | |
| Refrigeration | 13.93 | 13.70 | 9.20 | 6.44 | 2.76 | |
| Interior lighting | 4.60 | 3.88 | 3.23 | 0.95 | 0.65 | |
| Exterior lighting | 2.14 | 1.33 | 1.26 | 0.59 | 0.15 | |
| Equipment | 0.28 | 0.25 | 0.19 | 0.04 | 0.01 | |
| Miscellaneous | 2.05 | 1.86 | 1.63 | 0.38 | 0.07 | |
| *Total Baseload* | 24.51 | 21.96 | 16.44 | 9.03 | 4.04 | |

| Climate Zone | Space Heating Ventilation Electricity Use, kWh/square foot | | | | | Facility Difference |
|---|---|---|---|---|---|---|
| | 90% | 70% | Median | 30% | 10% | |
| HDD zone 1 | 1.27 | 0.15 | 0.05 | 0.03 | 0.02 | |
| HDD zone 2 | 2.01 | 0.51 | 0.35 | 0.18 | 0.05 | |
| HDD zone 3 | 3.24 | 1.03 | 0.91 | 0.59 | 0.15 | |
| HDD zone 4 | 3.11 | 1.29 | 0.98 | 0.46 | 0.25 | |

| Climate Zone | AC and Summer Ventilation Electricity Use, kWh/square foot | | | | | Facility Difference |
|---|---|---|---|---|---|---|
| | 90% | 70% | Median | 30% | 10% | |
| CDD zone 1 | 2.68 | 1.76 | 1.03 | 0.47 | 0.23 | |
| CDD zone 2 | 6.45 | 3.49 | 2.28 | 1.42 | 0.53 | |
| CDD zone 3 | 9.34 | 5.80 | 3.22 | 1.86 | 0.87 | |

| Climate Zone | Electric Space Heat, kWh/square foot | | | | | Facility Difference |
|---|---|---|---|---|---|---|
| | 90% | 70% | Median | 30% | 10% | |
| HDD zone 1 | 0.63 | 0.47 | 0.30 | 0.26 | 0.21 | |
| HDD zone 2 | 1.41 | 1.17 | 0.87 | 0.80 | 0.61 | |
| HDD zone 3 | 3.72 | 2.34 | 1.86 | 1.67 | 1.49 | |
| HDD zone 4 | 4.38 | 2.33 | 2.19 | 1.42 | 1.31 | |

| Climate Zone | Natural Gas Space Heat, kBtu/square foot | | | | | Facility Difference |
|---|---|---|---|---|---|---|
| | 90% | 70% | Median | 30% | 10% | |
| HDD zone 1 | 32.29 | 29.01 | 20.33 | 11.38 | 5.29 | |
| HDD zone 2 | 51.38 | 45.74 | 41.58 | 19.96 | 7.90 | |
| HDD zone 3 | 72.58 | 64.81 | 62.63 | 25.05 | 11.27 | |
| HDD zone 4 | 86.21 | 69.27 | 67.61 | 27.04 | 14.20 | |

**TABLE A.44** Refrigerated Warehouse (50–85 hours/week)

| End Use | Baseload Electricity Use, kWh/square foot | | | | | Facility Difference |
|---|---|---|---|---|---|---|
| | 90% | 70% | Median | 30% | 10% | |
| Water heating | 0.39 | 0.35 | 0.32 | 0.22 | 0.09 | |
| Cooking | 0.00 | 0.00 | 0.00 | 0.00 | 0.00 | |
| Refrigeration | 14.60 | 12.37 | 11.29 | 9.56 | 2.54 | |
| Interior lighting | 4.76 | 1.59 | 1.19 | 0.54 | 0.12 | |
| Exterior lighting | 1.12 | 0.83 | 0.55 | 0.13 | 0.06 | |
| Equipment | 0.31 | 0.11 | 0.09 | 0.03 | 0.01 | |
| Miscellaneous | 2.00 | 0.81 | 0.64 | 0.26 | 0.09 | |
| *Total Baseload* | 23.18 | 16.06 | 14.08 | 10.74 | 2.91 | |

| Climate Zone | Space Heating Ventilation Electricity Use, kWh/square foot | | | | | Facility Difference |
|---|---|---|---|---|---|---|
| | 90% | 70% | Median | 30% | 10% | |
| HDD zone 1 | 0.33 | 0.08 | 0.07 | 0.04 | 0.01 | |
| HDD zone 2 | 0.99 | 0.35 | 0.30 | 0.17 | 0.04 | |
| HDD zone 3 | 2.70 | 0.76 | 0.54 | 0.30 | 0.06 | |
| HDD zone 4 | 5.22 | 1.86 | 0.87 | 0.44 | 0.08 | |

| Climate Zone | AC and Summer Ventilation Electricity Use, kWh/square foot | | | | | Facility Difference |
|---|---|---|---|---|---|---|
| | 90% | 70% | Median | 30% | 10% | |
| CDD zone 1 | 5.61 | 1.11 | 0.75 | 0.52 | 0.24 | |
| CDD zone 2 | 7.14 | 1.65 | 1.13 | 0.85 | 0.59 | |
| CDD zone 3 | 8.68 | 3.16 | 2.08 | 1.46 | 1.03 | |

| Climate Zone | Electric Space Heat, kWh/square foot | | | | | Facility Difference |
|---|---|---|---|---|---|---|
| | 90% | 70% | Median | 30% | 10% | |
| HDD zone 1 | 0.42 | 0.26 | 0.16 | 0.10 | 0.06 | |
| HDD zone 2 | 1.67 | 1.02 | 0.84 | 0.50 | 0.32 | |
| HDD zone 3 | 2.89 | 2.37 | 1.67 | 0.86 | 0.60 | |
| HDD zone 4 | 3.63 | 2.78 | 2.30 | 1.76 | 0.78 | |

| Climate Zone | Natural Gas Space Heat, kBtu/square foot | | | | | Facility Difference |
|---|---|---|---|---|---|---|
| | 90% | 70% | Median | 30% | 10% | |
| HDD zone 1 | 17.43 | 11.44 | 8.72 | 7.31 | 5.45 | |
| HDD zone 2 | 18.59 | 12.66 | 8.45 | 5.92 | 3.38 | |
| HDD zone 3 | 62.95 | 18.91 | 14.12 | 10.46 | 8.47 | |
| HDD zone 4 | 71.60 | 20.31 | 18.48 | 14.78 | 7.76 | |

**TABLE A.45**    Refrigerated Warehouse (Greater than 85 hours/week)

| End Use | Baseload Electricity Use, kWh/square foot | | | | | Facility Difference |
| | 90% | 70% | Median | 30% | 10% | |
|---|---|---|---|---|---|---|
| Water heating | 0.34 | 0.30 | 0.06 | 0.03 | 0.01 | |
| Cooking | 0.00 | 0.00 | 0.00 | 0.00 | 0.00 | |
| Refrigeration | 23.30 | 17.67 | 5.26 | 4.21 | 3.16 | |
| Interior lighting | 6.82 | 2.87 | 2.04 | 1.25 | 0.50 | |
| Exterior lighting | 0.73 | 0.58 | 0.20 | 0.09 | 0.07 | |
| Equipment | 0.29 | 0.10 | 0.08 | 0.05 | 0.02 | |
| Miscellaneous | 2.10 | 0.66 | 0.59 | 0.35 | 0.14 | |
| *Total Baseload* | 33.58 | 22.18 | 8.23 | 5.98 | 3.90 | |

| Climate Zone | Space Heating Ventilation Electricity Use, kWh/square foot | | | | | Facility Difference |
| | 90% | 70% | Median | 30% | 10% | |
|---|---|---|---|---|---|---|
| HDD zone 1 | 0.39 | 0.06 | 0.03 | 0.02 | 0.01 | |
| HDD zone 2 | 0.62 | 0.36 | 0.23 | 0.10 | 0.04 | |
| HDD zone 3 | 1.02 | 0.85 | 0.69 | 0.28 | 0.08 | |
| HDD zone 4 | 1.44 | 1.10 | 0.94 | 0.64 | 0.11 | |

| Climate Zone | AC and Summer Ventilation Electricity Use, kWh/square foot | | | | | Facility Difference |
| | 90% | 70% | Median | 30% | 10% | |
|---|---|---|---|---|---|---|
| CDD zone 1 | 2.88 | 1.75 | 0.69 | 0.28 | 0.21 | |
| CDD zone 2 | 5.77 | 3.62 | 2.77 | 0.97 | 0.52 | |
| CDD zone 3 | 12.04 | 5.46 | 3.47 | 1.89 | 1.07 | |

| Climate Zone | Electric Space Heat, kWh/square foot | | | | | Facility Difference |
| | 90% | 70% | Median | 30% | 10% | |
|---|---|---|---|---|---|---|
| HDD zone 1 | 0.30 | 0.20 | 0.15 | 0.11 | 0.09 | |
| HDD zone 2 | 1.05 | 0.53 | 0.35 | 0.32 | 0.25 | |
| HDD zone 3 | 1.51 | 0.89 | 0.81 | 0.73 | 0.67 | |
| HDD zone 4 | 1.55 | 1.17 | 1.05 | 0.93 | 0.93 | |

| Climate Zone | Natural Gas Space Heat, kBtu/square foot | | | | | Facility Difference |
| | 90% | 70% | Median | 30% | 10% | |
|---|---|---|---|---|---|---|
| HDD zone 1 | 7.01 | 5.48 | 4.38 | 2.85 | 2.19 | |
| HDD zone 2 | 7.02 | 6.65 | 5.44 | 3.43 | 1.96 | |
| HDD zone 3 | 11.47 | 9.66 | 8.19 | 5.41 | 2.62 | |
| HDD zone 4 | 11.91 | 10.96 | 9.70 | 6.60 | 4.17 | |

**TABLE A.46** Religious (Less than 50 hours/week)

| End Use | Baseload Electricity Use, kWh/square foot | | | | | Facility Difference |
|---|---|---|---|---|---|---|
| | 90% | 70% | Median | 30% | 10% | |
| Water heating | 0.67 | 0.36 | 0.19 | 0.13 | 0.09 | |
| Cooking | 0.73 | 0.48 | 0.29 | 0.20 | 0.09 | |
| Refrigeration | 1.13 | 0.31 | 0.20 | 0.05 | 0.01 | |
| Interior lighting | 1.32 | 0.63 | 0.34 | 0.17 | 0.09 | |
| Exterior lighting | 1.13 | 0.64 | 0.39 | 0.25 | 0.11 | |
| Equipment | 0.29 | 0.18 | 0.13 | 0.08 | 0.05 | |
| Miscellaneous | 0.34 | 0.21 | 0.15 | 0.09 | 0.05 | |
| Total Baseload | 5.61 | 2.81 | 1.69 | 1.06 | 0.49 | |

| Climate Zone | Space Heating Ventilation Electricity Use, kWh/square foot | | | | | Facility Difference |
|---|---|---|---|---|---|---|
| | 90% | 70% | Median | 30% | 10% | |
| HDD zone 1 | 0.14 | 0.10 | 0.05 | 0.03 | 0.01 | |
| HDD zone 2 | 0.37 | 0.18 | 0.13 | 0.07 | 0.03 | |
| HDD zone 3 | 0.71 | 0.36 | 0.23 | 0.15 | 0.06 | |
| HDD zone 4 | 0.92 | 0.57 | 0.39 | 0.24 | 0.11 | |

| Climate Zone | AC and Summer Ventilation Electricity Use, kWh/square foot | | | | | Facility Difference |
|---|---|---|---|---|---|---|
| | 90% | 70% | Median | 30% | 10% | |
| CDD zone 1 | 1.10 | 0.57 | 0.39 | 0.25 | 0.11 | |
| CDD zone 2 | 2.35 | 1.30 | 0.84 | 0.55 | 0.22 | |
| CDD zone 3 | 3.43 | 2.03 | 1.32 | 0.94 | 0.66 | |

| Climate Zone | Electric Space Heat, kWh/square foot | | | | | Facility Difference |
|---|---|---|---|---|---|---|
| | 90% | 70% | Median | 30% | 10% | |
| HDD zone 1 | 0.56 | 0.32 | 0.22 | 0.12 | 0.04 | |
| HDD zone 2 | 1.75 | 1.03 | 0.50 | 0.42 | 0.32 | |
| HDD zone 3 | 2.22 | 1.57 | 0.86 | 0.68 | 0.51 | |
| HDD zone 4 | 3.66 | 2.49 | 1.64 | 1.37 | 0.87 | |

| Climate Zone | Natural Gas Space Heat, kBtu/square foot | | | | | Facility Difference |
|---|---|---|---|---|---|---|
| | 90% | 70% | Median | 30% | 10% | |
| HDD zone 1 | 36.79 | 12.80 | 6.50 | 5.12 | 4.94 | |
| HDD zone 2 | 40.14 | 24.42 | 17.28 | 9.32 | 6.59 | |
| HDD zone 3 | 71.52 | 48.31 | 34.79 | 21.35 | 14.01 | |
| HDD zone 4 | 78.72 | 50.49 | 39.76 | 26.78 | 13.12 | |

**TABLE A.47**   Religious (50–85 hours/week)

| End Use | Baseload Electricity Use, kWh/square foot | | | | | Facility Difference |
|---|---|---|---|---|---|---|
| | 90% | 70% | Median | 30% | 10% | |
| Water heating | 0.52 | 0.46 | 0.20 | 0.12 | 0.08 | |
| Cooking | 0.46 | 0.36 | 0.33 | 0.28 | 0.10 | |
| Refrigeration | 0.56 | 0.14 | 0.07 | 0.02 | 0.01 | |
| Interior lighting | 4.64 | 1.94 | 1.23 | 0.77 | 0.69 | |
| Exterior lighting | 0.66 | 0.33 | 0.15 | 0.14 | 0.06 | |
| Equipment | 0.25 | 0.10 | 0.08 | 0.06 | 0.04 | |
| Miscellaneous | 0.30 | 0.10 | 0.07 | 0.06 | 0.04 | |
| *Total Baseload* | 7.39 | 3.43 | 2.13 | 1.45 | 1.02 | |

| Climate Zone | Space Heating Ventilation Electricity Use, kWh/square foot | | | | | Facility Difference |
|---|---|---|---|---|---|---|
| | 90% | 70% | Median | 30% | 10% | |
| HDD zone 1 | 0.40 | 0.21 | 0.10 | 0.05 | 0.02 | |
| HDD zone 2 | 0.67 | 0.31 | 0.25 | 0.15 | 0.08 | |
| HDD zone 3 | 0.95 | 0.34 | 0.32 | 0.27 | 0.13 | |
| HDD zone 4 | 1.26 | 0.63 | 0.42 | 0.37 | 0.23 | |

| Climate Zone | AC and Summer Ventilation Electricity Use, kWh/square foot | | | | | Facility Difference |
|---|---|---|---|---|---|---|
| | 90% | 70% | Median | 30% | 10% | |
| CDD zone 1 | 0.86 | 0.63 | 0.41 | 0.31 | 0.17 | |
| CDD zone 2 | 3.27 | 2.20 | 1.10 | 0.81 | 0.44 | |
| CDD zone 3 | 4.77 | 2.54 | 1.60 | 1.11 | 0.77 | |

| Climate Zone | Electric Space Heat, kWh/square foot | | | | | Facility Difference |
|---|---|---|---|---|---|---|
| | 90% | 70% | Median | 30% | 10% | |
| HDD zone 1 | 0.26 | 0.16 | 0.09 | 0.07 | 0.04 | |
| HDD zone 2 | 0.99 | 0.91 | 0.54 | 0.36 | 0.34 | |
| HDD zone 3 | 2.09 | 1.65 | 1.11 | 0.62 | 0.66 | |
| HDD zone 4 | 2.23 | 0.99 | 0.78 | 0.46 | 0.32 | |

| Climate Zone | Natural Gas Space Heat, kBtu/square foot | | | | | Facility Difference |
|---|---|---|---|---|---|---|
| | 90% | 70% | Median | 30% | 10% | |
| HDD zone 1 | 26.74 | 10.89 | 7.51 | 4.96 | 4.94 | |
| HDD zone 2 | 56.72 | 28.28 | 17.24 | 12.07 | 6.38 | |
| HDD zone 3 | 53.60 | 28.15 | 19.53 | 12.65 | 9.37 | |
| HDD zone 4 | 62.69 | 41.97 | 40.42 | 39.71 | 13.36 | |

**TABLE A.48**   Religious (Greater than 85 hours/week)

| End Use | Baseload Electricity Use, kWh/square foot | | | | | Facility Difference |
|---|---|---|---|---|---|---|
| | 90% | 70% | Median | 30% | 10% | |
| Water heating | 0.31 | 0.07 | 0.04 | 0.01 | 0.01 | |
| Cooking | 0.12 | 0.10 | 0.08 | 0.06 | 0.04 | |
| Refrigeration | 0.38 | 0.20 | 0.15 | 0.09 | 0.01 | |
| Interior lighting | 2.80 | 2.24 | 1.72 | 1.37 | 0.60 | |
| Exterior lighting | 0.29 | 0.09 | 0.06 | 0.05 | 0.02 | |
| Equipment | 0.11 | 0.08 | 0.05 | 0.03 | 0.02 | |
| Miscellaneous | 0.11 | 0.10 | 0.05 | 0.02 | 0.01 | |
| *Total Baseload* | 4.12 | 2.87 | 2.01 | 1.63 | 0.71 | |

| Climate Zone | Space Heating Ventilation Electricity Use, kWh/square foot | | | | | Facility Difference |
|---|---|---|---|---|---|---|
| | 90% | 70% | Median | 30% | 10% | |
| HDD zone 1 | 0.51 | 0.39 | 0.30 | 0.21 | 0.03 | |
| HDD zone 2 | 0.59 | 0.37 | 0.31 | 0.25 | 0.19 | |
| HDD zone 3 | 0.61 | 0.44 | 0.34 | 0.27 | 0.10 | |
| HDD zone 4 | 1.13 | 1.07 | 0.29 | 0.13 | 0.11 | |

| Climate Zone | AC and Summer Ventilation Electricity Use, kWh/square foot | | | | | Facility Difference |
|---|---|---|---|---|---|---|
| | 90% | 70% | Median | 30% | 10% | |
| CDD zone 1 | 0.62 | 0.56 | 0.51 | 0.36 | 0.19 | |
| CDD zone 2 | 2.56 | 1.71 | 1.50 | 0.43 | 0.12 | |
| CDD zone 3 | 5.59 | 4.28 | 3.29 | 2.30 | 0.99 | |

| Climate Zone | Electric Space Heat, kWh/square foot | | | | | Facility Difference |
|---|---|---|---|---|---|---|
| | 90% | 70% | Median | 30% | 10% | |
| HDD zone 1 | 0.48 | 0.38 | 0.21 | 0.15 | 0.04 | |
| HDD zone 2 | 0.94 | 0.83 | 0.71 | 0.43 | 0.16 | |
| HDD zone 3 | 2.19 | 1.95 | 1.77 | 0.97 | 0.53 | |
| HDD zone 4 | 3.68 | 2.92 | 2.54 | 1.52 | 1.02 | |

| Climate Zone | Natural Gas Space Heat, kBtu/square foot | | | | | Facility Difference |
|---|---|---|---|---|---|---|
| | 90% | 70% | Median | 30% | 10% | |
| HDD zone 1 | 10.43 | 6.78 | 5.22 | 2.61 | 1.36 | |
| HDD zone 2 | 17.08 | 11.67 | 9.49 | 5.69 | 2.85 | |
| HDD zone 3 | 33.15 | 19.27 | 14.38 | 7.19 | 3.60 | |
| HDD zone 4 | 40.13 | 35.31 | 26.75 | 13.91 | 8.03 | |

**TABLE A.49**   Restaurant (Less than 50 hours/week)

| End Use | Baseload Electricity Use, kWh/square foot | | | | | Facility Difference |
|---|---|---|---|---|---|---|
| | 90% | 70% | Median | 30% | 10% | |
| Water heating | 14.14 | 10.25 | 7.07 | 5.02 | 0.77 | |
| Cooking | 11.09 | 8.73 | 7.90 | 4.60 | 2.89 | |
| Refrigeration | 9.46 | 5.43 | 2.42 | 1.76 | 0.33 | |
| Interior lighting | 12.05 | 5.29 | 4.20 | 2.22 | 0.74 | |
| Exterior lighting | 1.95 | 1.55 | 1.21 | 0.97 | 0.24 | |
| Equipment | 0.74 | 0.33 | 0.30 | 0.12 | 0.05 | |
| Miscellaneous | 2.45 | 1.02 | 0.92 | 0.35 | 0.14 | |
| *Total Baseload* | 51.88 | 32.60 | 24.02 | 15.04 | 5.16 | |

| Climate Zone | Space Heating Ventilation Electricity Use, kWh/square foot | | | | | Facility Difference |
|---|---|---|---|---|---|---|
| | 90% | 70% | Median | 30% | 10% | |
| HDD zone 1 | 0.28 | 0.13 | 0.10 | 0.03 | 0.01 | |
| HDD zone 2 | 1.14 | 0.45 | 0.35 | 0.25 | 0.14 | |
| HDD zone 3 | 1.73 | 1.06 | 0.80 | 0.61 | 0.40 | |
| HDD zone 4 | 2.08 | 1.33 | 0.92 | 0.67 | 0.27 | |

| Climate Zone | AC and Summer Ventilation Electricity Use, kWh/square foot | | | | | Facility Difference |
|---|---|---|---|---|---|---|
| | 90% | 70% | Median | 30% | 10% | |
| CDD zone 1 | 7.52 | 5.42 | 3.24 | 1.49 | 0.81 | |
| CDD zone 2 | 12.21 | 7.53 | 5.62 | 3.00 | 1.32 | |
| CDD zone 3 | 32.14 | 21.69 | 16.22 | 11.15 | 6.40 | |

| Climate Zone | Electric Space Heat, kWh/square foot | | | | | Facility Difference |
|---|---|---|---|---|---|---|
| | 90% | 70% | Median | 30% | 10% | |
| HDD zone 1 | 0.37 | 0.23 | 0.16 | 0.12 | 0.01 | |
| HDD zone 2 | 2.41 | 0.98 | 0.76 | 0.60 | 0.25 | |
| HDD zone 3 | 2.60 | 1.16 | 1.04 | 0.83 | 0.33 | |
| HDD zone 4 | 2.92 | 1.54 | 1.46 | 1.17 | 0.42 | |

| Climate Zone | Natural Gas Space Heat, kBtu/square foot | | | | | Facility Difference |
|---|---|---|---|---|---|---|
| | 90% | 70% | Median | 30% | 10% | |
| HDD zone 1 | 38.24 | 28.24 | 26.74 | 14.71 | 5.62 | |
| HDD zone 2 | 44.61 | 37.41 | 28.78 | 14.39 | 8.65 | |
| HDD zone 3 | 49.33 | 43.16 | 30.83 | 16.93 | 9.56 | |
| HDD zone 4 | 75.09 | 63.36 | 46.93 | 21.74 | 13.14 | |

**TABLE A.50**  Restaurant (50–85 hours/week)

| End Use | Baseload Electricity Use, kWh/square foot | | | | | Facility Difference |
| | 90% | 70% | Median | 30% | 10% | |
| --- | --- | --- | --- | --- | --- | --- |
| Water heating | 12.13 | 8.26 | 7.86 | 5.12 | 0.77 | |
| Cooking | 18.86 | 13.92 | 6.53 | 3.80 | 3.02 | |
| Refrigeration | 21.75 | 13.28 | 8.62 | 4.14 | 1.89 | |
| Interior lighting | 13.75 | 8.00 | 5.50 | 4.21 | 1.17 | |
| Exterior lighting | 1.94 | 1.37 | 1.23 | 0.53 | 0.21 | |
| Equipment | 0.81 | 0.37 | 0.26 | 0.20 | 0.06 | |
| Miscellaneous | 2.51 | 1.13 | 0.78 | 0.63 | 0.18 | |
| *Total Baseload* | 71.75 | 46.33 | 30.78 | 18.63 | 7.30 | |

| Climate Zone | Space Heating Ventilation Electricity Use, kWh/square foot | | | | | Facility Difference |
| | 90% | 70% | Median | 30% | 10% | |
| --- | --- | --- | --- | --- | --- | --- |
| HDD zone 1 | 0.27 | 0.13 | 0.08 | 0.05 | 0.02 | |
| HDD zone 2 | 0.89 | 0.38 | 0.26 | 0.20 | 0.12 | |
| HDD zone 3 | 1.27 | 0.81 | 0.51 | 0.37 | 0.25 | |
| HDD zone 4 | 1.71 | 1.20 | 0.88 | 0.58 | 0.29 | |

| Climate Zone | AC and Summer Ventilation Electricity Use, kWh/square foot | | | | | Facility Difference |
| | 90% | 70% | Median | 30% | 10% | |
| --- | --- | --- | --- | --- | --- | --- |
| CDD zone 1 | 13.50 | 6.77 | 4.71 | 3.21 | 1.78 | |
| CDD zone 2 | 20.65 | 12.04 | 7.80 | 5.57 | 3.47 | |
| CDD zone 3 | 39.51 | 23.89 | 16.27 | 12.00 | 5.40 | |

| Climate Zone | Electric Space Heat, kWh/square foot | | | | | Facility Difference |
| | 90% | 70% | Median | 30% | 10% | |
| --- | --- | --- | --- | --- | --- | --- |
| HDD zone 1 | 2.52 | 1.09 | 1.01 | 0.53 | 0.22 | |
| HDD zone 2 | 7.92 | 2.89 | 2.01 | 1.02 | 0.81 | |
| HDD zone 3 | 10.10 | 5.22 | 4.04 | 2.83 | 1.63 | |
| HDD zone 4 | 11.76 | 4.65 | 3.92 | 2.67 | 1.42 | |

| Climate Zone | Natural Gas Space Heat, kBtu/square foot | | | | | Facility Difference |
| | 90% | 70% | Median | 30% | 10% | |
| --- | --- | --- | --- | --- | --- | --- |
| HDD zone 1 | 61.41 | 33.96 | 23.74 | 16.94 | 7.12 | |
| HDD zone 2 | 78.43 | 56.37 | 39.16 | 28.20 | 9.40 | |
| HDD zone 3 | 98.64 | 58.76 | 46.34 | 33.83 | 11.82 | |
| HDD zone 4 | 91.97 | 59.43 | 49.17 | 30.09 | 12.78 | |

**TABLE A.51**   Restaurant (Greater than 85 hours/week)

| End Use | Baseload Electricity Use, kWh/square foot | | | | | Facility Difference |
|---|---|---|---|---|---|---|
| | 90% | 70% | Median | 30% | 10% | |
| Water heating | 22.30 | 14.22 | 10.04 | 5.85 | 2.08 | |
| Cooking | 67.42 | 28.92 | 16.59 | 8.10 | 2.20 | |
| Refrigeration | 20.54 | 13.07 | 8.89 | 5.23 | 0.93 | |
| Interior lighting | 15.58 | 10.89 | 7.79 | 5.02 | 1.20 | |
| Exterior lighting | 2.03 | 1.44 | 1.21 | 0.61 | 0.16 | |
| Equipment | 0.85 | 0.54 | 0.37 | 0.20 | 0.06 | |
| Miscellaneous | 2.61 | 1.65 | 1.09 | 0.61 | 0.18 | |
| *Total Baseload* | 131.33 | 70.73 | 45.98 | 25.62 | 6.81 | |

| Climate Zone | Space Heating Ventilation Electricity Use, kWh/square foot | | | | | Facility Difference |
|---|---|---|---|---|---|---|
| | 90% | 70% | Median | 30% | 10% | |
| HDD zone 1 | 0.94 | 0.22 | 0.13 | 0.06 | 0.02 | |
| HDD zone 2 | 1.61 | 0.57 | 0.33 | 0.21 | 0.10 | |
| HDD zone 3 | 2.09 | 1.05 | 0.71 | 0.48 | 0.24 | |
| HDD zone 4 | 2.17 | 1.26 | 1.00 | 0.70 | 0.33 | |

| Climate Zone | AC and Summer Ventilation Electricity Use, kWh/square foot | | | | | Facility Difference |
|---|---|---|---|---|---|---|
| | 90% | 70% | Median | 30% | 10% | |
| CDD zone 1 | 16.67 | 8.92 | 5.78 | 3.54 | 1.69 | |
| CDD zone 2 | 28.75 | 14.94 | 10.01 | 6.78 | 4.13 | |
| CDD zone 3 | 42.27 | 27.66 | 18.19 | 12.65 | 7.68 | |

| Climate Zone | Electric Space Heat, kWh/square foot | | | | | Facility Difference |
|---|---|---|---|---|---|---|
| | 90% | 70% | Median | 30% | 10% | |
| HDD zone 1 | 9.47 | 2.37 | 1.84 | 0.81 | 0.37 | |
| HDD zone 2 | 10.82 | 5.20 | 3.21 | 2.12 | 0.56 | |
| HDD zone 3 | 10.80 | 6.17 | 4.72 | 3.50 | 1.59 | |
| HDD zone 4 | 13.94 | 9.58 | 6.53 | 4.26 | 1.48 | |

| Climate Zone | Natural Gas Space Heat, kBtu/square foot | | | | | Facility Difference |
|---|---|---|---|---|---|---|
| | 90% | 70% | Median | 30% | 10% | |
| HDD zone 1 | 59.80 | 36.07 | 23.88 | 15.67 | 10.57 | |
| HDD zone 2 | 66.78 | 43.14 | 28.91 | 20.88 | 12.14 | |
| HDD zone 3 | 75.37 | 52.47 | 34.26 | 24.87 | 12.50 | |
| HDD zone 4 | 98.90 | 61.27 | 52.05 | 30.10 | 22.16 | |

**TABLE A.52**  Retail (Less than 50 hours/week)

| End Use | Baseload Electricity Use, kWh/square foot | | | | | Facility Difference |
|---|---|---|---|---|---|---|
| | 90% | 70% | Median | 30% | 10% | |
| Water heating | 2.02 | 1.23 | 0.78 | 0.31 | 0.20 | |
| Cooking | 0.24 | 0.21 | 0.20 | 0.14 | 0.09 | |
| Refrigeration | 1.48 | 0.28 | 0.09 | 0.04 | 0.02 | |
| Interior lighting | 4.65 | 2.08 | 1.13 | 0.74 | 0.36 | |
| Exterior lighting | 1.33 | 0.93 | 0.59 | 0.37 | 0.16 | |
| Equipment | 0.66 | 0.39 | 0.23 | 0.16 | 0.10 | |
| Miscellaneous | 1.17 | 0.66 | 0.35 | 0.21 | 0.11 | |
| *Total Baseload* | 11.55 | 5.78 | 3.37 | 1.97 | 1.04 | |

| Climate Zone | Space Heating Ventilation Electricity Use, kWh/square foot | | | | | Facility Difference |
|---|---|---|---|---|---|---|
| | 90% | 70% | Median | 30% | 10% | |
| HDD zone 1 | 0.50 | 0.22 | 0.11 | 0.05 | 0.04 | |
| HDD zone 2 | 0.65 | 0.31 | 0.20 | 0.16 | 0.08 | |
| HDD zone 3 | 1.58 | 1.06 | 0.43 | 0.22 | 0.11 | |
| HDD zone 4 | 2.09 | 1.34 | 0.50 | 0.34 | 0.14 | |

| Climate Zone | AC and Summer Ventilation Electricity Use, kWh/square foot | | | | | Facility Difference |
|---|---|---|---|---|---|---|
| | 90% | 70% | Median | 30% | 10% | |
| CDD zone 1 | 3.32 | 1.26 | 0.62 | 0.37 | 0.17 | |
| CDD zone 2 | 4.80 | 2.01 | 1.28 | 0.63 | 0.25 | |
| CDD zone 3 | 8.29 | 4.29 | 3.61 | 1.82 | 0.72 | |

| Climate Zone | Electric Space Heat, kWh/square foot | | | | | Facility Difference |
|---|---|---|---|---|---|---|
| | 90% | 70% | Median | 30% | 10% | |
| HDD zone 1 | 1.08 | 0.52 | 0.46 | 0.17 | 0.11 | |
| HDD zone 2 | 2.20 | 1.56 | 1.36 | 0.82 | 0.44 | |
| HDD zone 3 | 4.69 | 2.53 | 1.47 | 0.98 | 0.51 | |
| HDD zone 4 | 6.19 | 3.32 | 2.21 | 1.65 | 0.83 | |

| Climate Zone | Natural Gas Space Heat, kBtu/square foot | | | | | Facility Difference |
|---|---|---|---|---|---|---|
| | 90% | 70% | Median | 30% | 10% | |
| HDD zone 1 | 17.95 | 7.85 | 5.61 | 5.11 | 4.56 | |
| HDD zone 2 | 53.52 | 30.76 | 20.51 | 11.48 | 10.54 | |
| HDD zone 3 | 74.38 | 40.78 | 26.95 | 18.33 | 13.85 | |
| HDD zone 4 | 86.26 | 52.31 | 40.60 | 28.83 | 16.24 | |

**TABLE A.53**   Retail (50–85 hours/week)

| End Use | Baseload Electricity Use, kWh/square foot | | | | | Facility Difference |
| | 90% | 70% | Median | 30% | 10% | |
| --- | --- | --- | --- | --- | --- | --- |
| Water heating | 3.32 | 1.51 | 0.84 | 0.62 | 0.25 | |
| Cooking | 2.36 | 1.30 | 1.29 | 0.38 | 0.32 | |
| Refrigeration | 1.60 | 0.34 | 0.17 | 0.09 | 0.04 | |
| Interior lighting | 9.78 | 5.11 | 3.26 | 1.65 | 0.76 | |
| Exterior lighting | 1.38 | 0.93 | 0.53 | 0.29 | 0.14 | |
| Equipment | 1.30 | 0.61 | 0.40 | 0.26 | 0.11 | |
| Miscellaneous | 2.31 | 1.02 | 0.63 | 0.36 | 0.16 | |
| *Total Baseload* | 22.05 | 10.82 | 7.12 | 3.65 | 1.78 | |

| Climate Zone | Space Heating Ventilation Electricity Use, kWh/square foot | | | | | Facility Difference |
| | 90% | 70% | Median | 30% | 10% | |
| --- | --- | --- | --- | --- | --- | --- |
| HDD zone 1 | 0.39 | 0.17 | 0.08 | 0.05 | 0.02 | |
| HDD zone 2 | 1.36 | 0.53 | 0.32 | 0.19 | 0.09 | |
| HDD zone 3 | 1.57 | 1.05 | 0.67 | 0.44 | 0.17 | |
| HDD zone 4 | 2.84 | 1.55 | 0.93 | 0.53 | 0.25 | |

| Climate Zone | AC and Summer Ventilation Electricity Use, kWh/square foot | | | | | Facility Difference |
| | 90% | 70% | Median | 30% | 10% | |
| --- | --- | --- | --- | --- | --- | --- |
| CDD zone 1 | 3.68 | 1.64 | 0.77 | 0.45 | 0.16 | |
| CDD zone 2 | 7.63 | 2.63 | 1.64 | 0.96 | 0.49 | |
| CDD zone 3 | 10.33 | 5.09 | 3.43 | 1.46 | 0.86 | |

| Climate Zone | Electric Space Heat, kWh/square foot | | | | | Facility Difference |
| | 90% | 70% | Median | 30% | 10% | |
| --- | --- | --- | --- | --- | --- | --- |
| HDD zone 1 | 1.12 | 0.38 | 0.32 | 0.28 | 0.11 | |
| HDD zone 2 | 2.52 | 1.25 | 0.66 | 0.52 | 0.40 | |
| HDD zone 3 | 6.68 | 3.10 | 2.16 | 1.80 | 0.87 | |
| HDD zone 4 | 5.25 | 4.22 | 2.59 | 1.93 | 0.62 | |

| Climate Zone | Natural Gas Space Heat, kBtu/square foot | | | | | Facility Difference |
| | 90% | 70% | Median | 30% | 10% | |
| --- | --- | --- | --- | --- | --- | --- |
| HDD zone 1 | 31.66 | 22.28 | 12.51 | 7.83 | 3.75 | |
| HDD zone 2 | 69.42 | 39.27 | 27.95 | 12.69 | 5.76 | |
| HDD zone 3 | 74.26 | 47.71 | 37.26 | 23.79 | 11.18 | |
| HDD zone 4 | 79.18 | 56.46 | 44.66 | 23.40 | 12.22 | |

**TABLE A.54**   Retail (Greater than 85 hours/week)

| End Use | Baseload Electricity Use, kWh/square foot | | | | | Facility Difference |
|---|---|---|---|---|---|---|
|  | 90% | 70% | Median | 30% | 10% |  |
| Water heating | 5.30 | 2.98 | 1.84 | 1.08 | 0.74 |  |
| Cooking | 2.74 | 1.89 | 1.29 | 0.86 | 0.43 |  |
| Refrigeration | 5.54 | 3.02 | 2.52 | 0.33 | 0.06 |  |
| Interior lighting | 15.55 | 11.06 | 9.37 | 6.32 | 3.37 |  |
| Exterior lighting | 1.29 | 1.16 | 0.83 | 0.54 | 0.19 |  |
| Equipment | 1.29 | 0.86 | 0.49 | 0.38 | 0.18 |  |
| Miscellaneous | 2.19 | 1.44 | 0.81 | 0.64 | 0.30 |  |
| *Total Baseload* | 33.91 | 22.41 | 17.15 | 10.15 | 5.27 |  |

| Climate Zone | Space Heating Ventilation Electricity Use, kWh/square foot | | | | | Facility Difference |
|---|---|---|---|---|---|---|
|  | 90% | 70% | Median | 30% | 10% |  |
| HDD zone 1 | 0.53 | 0.35 | 0.12 | 0.08 | 0.05 |  |
| HDD zone 2 | 0.73 | 0.57 | 0.44 | 0.34 | 0.16 |  |
| HDD zone 3 | 2.89 | 2.04 | 1.60 | 0.71 | 0.17 |  |
| HDD zone 4 | 6.22 | 3.11 | 2.41 | 1.23 | 0.23 |  |

| Climate Zone | AC and Summer Ventilation Electricity Use, kWh/square foot | | | | | Facility Difference |
|---|---|---|---|---|---|---|
|  | 90% | 70% | Median | 30% | 10% |  |
| CDD zone 1 | 8.77 | 4.57 | 2.79 | 1.32 | 0.46 |  |
| CDD zone 2 | 6.88 | 4.59 | 3.59 | 2.03 | 1.38 |  |
| CDD zone 3 | 21.57 | 18.18 | 10.64 | 8.00 | 3.92 |  |

| Climate Zone | Electric Space Heat, kWh/square foot | | | | | Facility Difference |
|---|---|---|---|---|---|---|
|  | 90% | 70% | Median | 30% | 10% |  |
| HDD zone 1 | 1.49 | 0.66 | 0.25 | 0.18 | 0.08 |  |
| HDD zone 2 | 3.84 | 3.38 | 2.74 | 1.13 | 0.76 |  |
| HDD zone 3 | 4.28 | 3.76 | 3.42 | 2.25 | 1.25 |  |
| HDD zone 4 | 7.33 | 6.52 | 5.43 | 3.26 | 2.00 |  |

| Climate Zone | Natural Gas Space Heat, kBtu/square foot | | | | | Facility Difference |
|---|---|---|---|---|---|---|
|  | 90% | 70% | Median | 30% | 10% |  |
| HDD zone 1 | 85.20 | 36.46 | 15.69 | 11.16 | 7.34 |  |
| HDD zone 2 | 46.62 | 17.57 | 16.23 | 9.90 | 8.07 |  |
| HDD zone 3 | 65.81 | 65.24 | 41.13 | 19.25 | 5.59 |  |
| HDD zone 4 | 81.72 | 68.58 | 45.72 | 31.09 | 13.72 |  |

**TABLE A.55**     Retail—Mall (Less than 50 hours/week)

| End Use | Baseload Electricity Use, kWh/square foot | | | | | Facility Difference |
|---|---|---|---|---|---|---|
| | 90% | 70% | Median | 30% | 10% | |
| Water heating | 7.23 | 1.77 | 1.02 | 0.46 | 0.17 | |
| Cooking | 2.95 | 1.78 | 1.34 | 0.61 | 0.03 | |
| Refrigeration | 0.55 | 0.22 | 0.11 | 0.06 | 0.01 | |
| Interior lighting | 8.12 | 3.95 | 2.41 | 1.49 | 0.62 | |
| Exterior lighting | 1.78 | 0.81 | 0.54 | 0.35 | 0.14 | |
| Equipment | 1.10 | 0.60 | 0.36 | 0.23 | 0.10 | |
| Miscellaneous | 2.06 | 0.96 | 0.53 | 0.35 | 0.13 | |
| *Total Baseload* | 23.79 | 10.09 | 6.31 | 3.55 | 1.20 | |

| Climate Zone | Space Heating Ventilation Electricity Use, kWh/square foot | | | | | Facility Difference |
|---|---|---|---|---|---|---|
| | 90% | 70% | Median | 30% | 10% | |
| HDD zone 1 | 0.17 | 0.13 | 0.10 | 0.06 | 0.03 | |
| HDD zone 2 | 0.91 | 0.48 | 0.19 | 0.12 | 0.10 | |
| HDD zone 3 | 1.65 | 1.00 | 0.66 | 0.43 | 0.20 | |
| HDD zone 4 | 2.02 | 1.52 | 1.01 | 0.76 | 0.33 | |

| Climate Zone | AC and Summer Ventilation Electricity Use, kWh/square foot | | | | | Facility Difference |
|---|---|---|---|---|---|---|
| | 90% | 70% | Median | 30% | 10% | |
| CDD zone 1 | 2.96 | 1.11 | 0.74 | 0.52 | 0.23 | |
| CDD zone 2 | 5.96 | 3.07 | 1.49 | 1.04 | 0.45 | |
| CDD zone 3 | 8.35 | 4.41 | 3.39 | 2.31 | 0.84 | |

| Climate Zone | Electric Space Heat, kWh/square foot | | | | | Facility Difference |
|---|---|---|---|---|---|---|
| | 90% | 70% | Median | 30% | 10% | |
| HDD zone 1 | 2.40 | 1.36 | 0.80 | 0.48 | 0.24 | |
| HDD zone 2 | 3.68 | 1.67 | 0.96 | 0.57 | 0.40 | |
| HDD zone 3 | 2.36 | 2.04 | 1.07 | 0.75 | 0.54 | |
| HDD zone 4 | 3.27 | 3.10 | 1.67 | 1.44 | 1.14 | |

| Climate Zone | Natural Gas Space Heat, kBtu/square foot | | | | | Facility Difference |
|---|---|---|---|---|---|---|
| | 90% | 70% | Median | 30% | 10% | |
| HDD zone 1 | 14.25 | 11.95 | 9.96 | 6.67 | 3.69 | |
| HDD zone 2 | 38.12 | 29.26 | 20.90 | 16.27 | 9.03 | |
| HDD zone 3 | 63.86 | 42.17 | 31.93 | 20.75 | 6.86 | |
| HDD zone 4 | 80.47 | 39.00 | 30.95 | 21.67 | 12.38 | |

**TABLE A.56**    Retail—Mall (50–85 hours/week)

| End Use | Baseload Electricity Use, kWh/square foot | | | | | Facility Difference |
|---|---|---|---|---|---|---|
| | 90% | 70% | Median | 30% | 10% | |
| Water heating | 2.25 | 1.68 | 1.41 | 0.56 | 0.30 | |
| Cooking | 1.31 | 1.16 | 0.71 | 0.31 | 0.16 | |
| Refrigeration | 2.00 | 1.16 | 0.50 | 0.17 | 0.10 | |
| Interior lighting | 8.59 | 5.70 | 4.38 | 2.51 | 0.84 | |
| Exterior lighting | 1.20 | 0.79 | 0.48 | 0.25 | 0.07 | |
| Equipment | 1.07 | 0.69 | 0.47 | 0.27 | 0.14 | |
| Miscellaneous | 1.72 | 1.12 | 0.64 | 0.43 | 0.15 | |
| *Total Baseload* | 18.14 | 12.30 | 8.59 | 4.50 | 1.76 | |

| Climate Zone | Space Heating Ventilation Electricity Use, kWh/square foot | | | | | Facility Difference |
|---|---|---|---|---|---|---|
| | 90% | 70% | Median | 30% | 10% | |
| HDD zone 1 | 1.05 | 0.81 | 0.70 | 0.35 | 0.02 | |
| HDD zone 2 | 0.72 | 0.36 | 0.24 | 0.17 | 0.09 | |
| HDD zone 3 | 2.48 | 0.84 | 0.53 | 0.19 | 0.16 | |
| HDD zone 4 | 3.04 | 1.24 | 0.95 | 0.48 | 0.28 | |

| Climate Zone | AC and Summer Ventilation Electricity Use, kWh/square foot | | | | | Facility Difference |
|---|---|---|---|---|---|---|
| | 90% | 70% | Median | 30% | 10% | |
| CDD zone 1 | 3.39 | 1.82 | 0.88 | 0.46 | 0.21 | |
| CDD zone 2 | 5.55 | 3.12 | 2.52 | 1.38 | 0.46 | |
| CDD zone 3 | 9.01 | 7.70 | 3.37 | 2.80 | 0.79 | |

| Climate Zone | Electric Space Heat, kWh/square foot | | | | | Facility Difference |
|---|---|---|---|---|---|---|
| | 90% | 70% | Median | 30% | 10% | |
| HDD zone 1 | 1.01 | 0.77 | 0.71 | 0.32 | 0.21 | |
| HDD zone 2 | 1.35 | 1.20 | 1.04 | 0.67 | 0.33 | |
| HDD zone 3 | 1.81 | 1.47 | 1.21 | 0.62 | 0.46 | |
| HDD zone 4 | 3.94 | 3.08 | 0.94 | 0.66 | 0.25 | |

| Climate Zone | Natural Gas Space Heat, kBtu/square foot | | | | | Facility Difference |
|---|---|---|---|---|---|---|
| | 90% | 70% | Median | 30% | 10% | |
| HDD zone 1 | 16.65 | 12.09 | 6.13 | 4.11 | 2.82 | |
| HDD zone 2 | 29.08 | 22.86 | 16.57 | 11.60 | 6.18 | |
| HDD zone 3 | 57.06 | 25.63 | 17.80 | 10.53 | 5.08 | |
| HDD zone 4 | 76.82 | 27.38 | 18.29 | 10.39 | 9.21 | |

**TABLE A.57**  Retail—Mall (Greater than 85 hours/week)

| End Use | Baseload Electricity Use, kWh/square foot | | | | | Facility Difference |
|---|---|---|---|---|---|---|
| | 90% | 70% | Median | 30% | 10% | |
| Water heating | 2.03 | 1.27 | 1.04 | 0.45 | 0.19 | |
| Cooking | 2.39 | 1.51 | 1.07 | 0.40 | 0.13 | |
| Refrigeration | 1.93 | 1.36 | 1.07 | 0.48 | 0.26 | |
| Interior lighting | 13.53 | 6.98 | 3.76 | 3.01 | 0.93 | |
| Exterior lighting | 1.36 | 0.52 | 0.29 | 0.14 | 0.08 | |
| Equipment | 1.46 | 0.79 | 0.46 | 0.27 | 0.14 | |
| Miscellaneous | 2.27 | 1.21 | 0.62 | 0.50 | 0.13 | |
| *Total Baseload* | 24.97 | 13.64 | 8.31 | 5.24 | 1.86 | |

| Climate Zone | Space Heating Ventilation Electricity Use, kWh/square foot | | | | | Facility Difference |
|---|---|---|---|---|---|---|
| | 90% | 70% | Median | 30% | 10% | |
| HDD zone 1 | 0.26 | 0.18 | 0.08 | 0.03 | 0.02 | |
| HDD zone 2 | 0.94 | 0.19 | 0.12 | 0.07 | 0.04 | |
| HDD zone 3 | 1.54 | 0.88 | 0.39 | 0.30 | 0.20 | |
| HDD zone 4 | 1.91 | 0.50 | 0.40 | 0.32 | 0.28 | |

| Climate Zone | AC and Summer Ventilation Electricity Use, kWh/square foot | | | | | Facility Difference |
|---|---|---|---|---|---|---|
| | 90% | 70% | Median | 30% | 10% | |
| CDD zone 1 | 2.41 | 1.80 | 1.44 | 1.08 | 0.21 | |
| CDD zone 2 | 6.91 | 3.73 | 3.60 | 2.34 | 0.94 | |
| CDD zone 3 | 16.73 | 12.12 | 9.44 | 5.12 | 2.08 | |

| Climate Zone | Electric Space Heat, kWh/square foot | | | | | Facility Difference |
|---|---|---|---|---|---|---|
| | 90% | 70% | Median | 30% | 10% | |
| HDD zone 1 | 1.04 | 0.78 | 0.40 | 0.32 | 0.05 | |
| HDD zone 2 | 1.97 | 0.74 | 0.71 | 0.50 | 0.14 | |
| HDD zone 3 | 3.05 | 1.93 | 1.30 | 0.95 | 0.60 | |
| HDD zone 4 | 4.64 | 3.99 | 3.52 | 2.18 | 1.31 | |

| Climate Zone | Natural Gas Space Heat, kBtu/square foot | | | | | Facility Difference |
|---|---|---|---|---|---|---|
| | 90% | 70% | Median | 30% | 10% | |
| HDD zone 1 | 27.91 | 23.61 | 20.97 | 11.47 | 6.92 | |
| HDD zone 2 | 45.83 | 25.37 | 20.46 | 11.25 | 7.98 | |
| HDD zone 3 | 72.00 | 47.95 | 22.50 | 14.03 | 9.00 | |
| HDD zone 4 | 96.82 | 46.51 | 29.25 | 19.60 | 12.29 | |

**TABLE A.58**    State-Local Office (Less than 50 hours/week)

| End Use | Baseload Electricity Use, kWh/square foot | | | | | Facility Difference |
|---|---|---|---|---|---|---|
| | 90% | 70% | Median | 30% | 10% | |
| Water heating | 3.73 | 1.47 | 0.50 | 0.32 | 0.07 | |
| Cooking | 1.23 | 0.57 | 0.40 | 0.21 | 0.10 | |
| Refrigeration | 0.94 | 0.25 | 0.14 | 0.08 | 0.02 | |
| Interior lighting | 7.77 | 2.63 | 1.30 | 0.39 | 0.22 | |
| Exterior lighting | 1.39 | 0.61 | 0.44 | 0.18 | 0.07 | |
| Equipment | 4.07 | 1.52 | 0.92 | 0.73 | 0.31 | |
| Miscellaneous | 4.92 | 1.70 | 0.78 | 0.64 | 0.22 | |
| Total Baseload | 24.05 | 8.75 | 4.48 | 2.55 | 1.09 | |

| Climate Zone | Space Heating Ventilation Electricity Use, kWh/square foot | | | | | Facility Difference |
|---|---|---|---|---|---|---|
| | 90% | 70% | Median | 30% | 10% | |
| HDD zone 1 | 0.70 | 0.27 | 0.20 | 0.08 | 0.04 | |
| HDD zone 2 | 1.30 | 0.61 | 0.34 | 0.14 | 0.07 | |
| HDD zone 3 | 1.56 | 1.03 | 0.59 | 0.37 | 0.24 | |
| HDD zone 4 | 2.45 | 1.11 | 1.10 | 0.83 | 0.43 | |

| Climate Zone | AC and Summer Ventilation Electricity Use, kWh/square foot | | | | | Facility Difference |
|---|---|---|---|---|---|---|
| | 90% | 70% | Median | 30% | 10% | |
| CDD zone 1 | 3.86 | 1.73 | 1.26 | 0.64 | 0.18 | |
| CDD zone 2 | 6.53 | 2.24 | 1.57 | 1.09 | 0.32 | |
| CDD zone 3 | 16.12 | 9.84 | 4.54 | 3.35 | 2.29 | |

| Climate Zone | Electric Space Heat, kWh/square foot | | | | | Facility Difference |
|---|---|---|---|---|---|---|
| | 90% | 70% | Median | 30% | 10% | |
| HDD zone 1 | 1.25 | 0.64 | 0.38 | 0.21 | 0.05 | |
| HDD zone 2 | 2.69 | 1.40 | 0.62 | 0.49 | 0.24 | |
| HDD zone 3 | 4.57 | 2.65 | 2.33 | 1.96 | 0.82 | |
| HDD zone 4 | 7.11 | 3.53 | 2.97 | 2.83 | 1.31 | |

| Climate Zone | Natural Gas Space Heat, kBtu/square foot | | | | | Facility Difference |
|---|---|---|---|---|---|---|
| | 90% | 70% | Median | 30% | 10% | |
| HDD zone 1 | 36.67 | 25.61 | 18.43 | 10.13 | 4.79 | |
| HDD zone 2 | 50.19 | 32.78 | 25.49 | 15.27 | 13.90 | |
| HDD zone 3 | 76.85 | 58.33 | 39.41 | 29.49 | 15.76 | |
| HDD zone 4 | 91.55 | 63.68 | 48.16 | 24.06 | 18.30 | |

**TABLE A.59**   State-Local Office (50–85 hours/week)

| End Use | Baseload Electricity Use, kWh/square foot | | | | | Facility Difference |
|---|---|---|---|---|---|---|
| | 90% | 70% | Median | 30% | 10% | |
| Water heating | 2.17 | 1.79 | 1.33 | 0.82 | 0.52 | |
| Cooking | 0.49 | 0.45 | 0.42 | 0.16 | 0.11 | |
| Refrigeration | 1.00 | 0.56 | 0.48 | 0.12 | 0.04 | |
| Interior lighting | 9.01 | 8.31 | 2.95 | 1.55 | 0.54 | |
| Exterior lighting | 1.25 | 0.97 | 0.43 | 0.28 | 0.17 | |
| Equipment | 3.48 | 3.04 | 1.54 | 0.89 | 0.39 | |
| Miscellaneous | 4.09 | 3.23 | 1.50 | 0.80 | 0.14 | |
| *Total Baseload* | 21.49 | 18.35 | 8.65 | 4.62 | 1.91 | |

| Climate Zone | Space Heating Ventilation Electricity Use, kWh/square foot | | | | | Facility Difference |
|---|---|---|---|---|---|---|
| | 90% | 70% | Median | 30% | 10% | |
| HDD zone 1 | 0.34 | 0.22 | 0.19 | 0.07 | 0.04 | |
| HDD zone 2 | 0.73 | 0.64 | 0.41 | 0.30 | 0.23 | |
| HDD zone 3 | 1.44 | 0.75 | 0.57 | 0.44 | 0.25 | |
| HDD zone 4 | 3.96 | 2.08 | 0.92 | 0.80 | 0.43 | |

| Climate Zone | AC and Summer Ventilation Electricity Use, kWh/square foot | | | | | Facility Difference |
|---|---|---|---|---|---|---|
| | 90% | 70% | Median | 30% | 10% | |
| CDD zone 1 | 9.59 | 8.00 | 1.88 | 0.83 | 0.34 | |
| CDD zone 2 | 9.41 | 7.50 | 4.03 | 2.21 | 1.08 | |
| CDD zone 3 | 8.92 | 7.09 | 5.54 | 2.20 | 1.38 | |

| Climate Zone | Electric Space Heat, kWh/square foot | | | | | Facility Difference |
|---|---|---|---|---|---|---|
| | 90% | 70% | Median | 30% | 10% | |
| HDD zone 1 | 1.53 | 0.93 | 0.68 | 0.45 | 0.23 | |
| HDD zone 2 | 2.98 | 0.96 | 0.82 | 0.57 | 0.53 | |
| HDD zone 3 | 4.63 | 4.22 | 3.75 | 2.81 | 0.75 | |
| HDD zone 4 | 4.81 | 4.37 | 3.79 | 3.03 | 1.29 | |

| Climate Zone | Natural Gas Space Heat, kBtu/square foot | | | | | Facility Difference |
|---|---|---|---|---|---|---|
| | 90% | 70% | Median | 30% | 10% | |
| HDD zone 1 | 35.02 | 25.39 | 17.51 | 11.73 | 2.45 | |
| HDD zone 2 | 53.30 | 45.21 | 36.76 | 23.82 | 7.32 | |
| HDD zone 3 | 71.38 | 47.06 | 35.12 | 22.13 | 9.13 | |
| HDD zone 4 | 96.58 | 86.92 | 74.81 | 50.12 | 17.95 | |

**TABLE A.60**  State-Local Office (Greater than 85 hours/week)

| End Use | Baseload Electricity Use, kWh/square foot | | | | | Facility Difference |
|---|---|---|---|---|---|---|
| | 90% | 70% | Median | 30% | 10% | |
| Water heating | 1.58 | 1.28 | 1.11 | 0.48 | 0.19 | |
| Cooking | 0.65 | 0.47 | 0.27 | 0.21 | 0.10 | |
| Refrigeration | 0.57 | 0.43 | 0.19 | 0.12 | 0.05 | |
| Interior lighting | 12.00 | 7.34 | 4.41 | 2.53 | 1.32 | |
| Exterior lighting | 0.57 | 0.32 | 0.24 | 0.12 | 0.04 | |
| Equipment | 3.39 | 1.72 | 1.03 | 0.79 | 0.58 | |
| Miscellaneous | 3.21 | 1.53 | 0.92 | 0.48 | 0.29 | |
| *Total Baseload* | 21.97 | 13.09 | 8.17 | 4.73 | 2.57 | |

| Climate Zone | Space Heating Ventilation Electricity Use, kWh/square foot | | | | | Facility Difference |
|---|---|---|---|---|---|---|
| | 90% | 70% | Median | 30% | 10% | |
| HDD zone 1 | 0.51 | 0.24 | 0.10 | 0.07 | 0.02 | |
| HDD zone 2 | 1.25 | 0.96 | 0.43 | 0.33 | 0.20 | |
| HDD zone 3 | 1.48 | 0.91 | 0.69 | 0.55 | 0.31 | |
| HDD zone 4 | 2.42 | 1.15 | 0.77 | 0.59 | 0.53 | |

| Climate Zone | AC and Summer Ventilation Electricity Use, kWh/square foot | | | | | Facility Difference |
|---|---|---|---|---|---|---|
| | 90% | 70% | Median | 30% | 10% | |
| CDD zone 1 | 3.29 | 1.65 | 0.88 | 0.68 | 0.20 | |
| CDD zone 2 | 7.40 | 3.17 | 1.86 | 1.26 | 0.64 | |
| CDD zone 3 | 15.78 | 6.54 | 5.07 | 3.12 | 1.72 | |

| Climate Zone | Electric Space Heat, kWh/square foot | | | | | Facility Difference |
|---|---|---|---|---|---|---|
| | 90% | 70% | Median | 30% | 10% | |
| HDD zone 1 | 1.55 | 1.24 | 0.76 | 0.48 | 0.25 | |
| HDD zone 2 | 2.49 | 1.72 | 1.14 | 0.65 | 0.39 | |
| HDD zone 3 | 9.86 | 4.52 | 3.64 | 2.84 | 2.43 | |
| HDD zone 4 | 12.69 | 8.68 | 6.07 | 4.07 | 3.89 | |

| Climate Zone | Natural Gas Space Heat, kBtu/square foot | | | | | Facility Difference |
|---|---|---|---|---|---|---|
| | 90% | 70% | Median | 30% | 10% | |
| HDD zone 1 | 68.24 | 37.73 | 18.18 | 12.20 | 8.04 | |
| HDD zone 2 | 92.73 | 56.66 | 23.60 | 16.05 | 6.14 | |
| HDD zone 3 | 61.44 | 47.00 | 28.59 | 12.29 | 10.29 | |
| HDD zone 4 | 86.16 | 70.16 | 37.85 | 24.60 | 16.27 | |

**TABLE A.61**   State-Local Other (Less than 50 hours/week)

| End Use˙ | Baseload Electricity Use, kWh/square foot | | | | | Facility Difference |
|---|---|---|---|---|---|---|
| | 90% | 70% | Median | 30% | 10% | |
| Water heating | 3.57 | 2.36 | 1.19 | 0.28 | 0.22 | |
| Cooking | 2.20 | 1.08 | 0.96 | 0.27 | 0.13 | |
| Refrigeration | 1.33 | 0.15 | 0.07 | 0.03 | 0.01 | |
| Interior lighting | 4.42 | 2.66 | 1.61 | 0.52 | 0.34 | |
| Exterior lighting | 1.40 | 0.92 | 0.45 | 0.20 | 0.07 | |
| Equipment | 0.54 | 0.26 | 0.17 | 0.12 | 0.07 | |
| Miscellaneous | 1.81 | 0.69 | 0.47 | 0.19 | 0.09 | |
| *Total Baseload* | 15.27 | 8.12 | 4.92 | 1.47 | 0.93 | |

| Climate Zone | Space Heating Ventilation Electricity Use, kWh/square foot | | | | | Facility Difference |
|---|---|---|---|---|---|---|
| | 90% | 70% | Median | 30% | 10% | |
| HDD zone 1 | 0.83 | 0.16 | 0.10 | 0.04 | 0.02 | |
| HDD zone 2 | 1.12 | 0.44 | 0.30 | 0.13 | 0.07 | |
| HDD zone 3 | 1.26 | 0.79 | 0.48 | 0.30 | 0.17 | |
| HDD zone 4 | 1.70 | 0.88 | 0.51 | 0.29 | 0.20 | |

| Climate Zone | AC and Summer Ventilation Electricity Use, kWh/square foot | | | | | Facility Difference |
|---|---|---|---|---|---|---|
| | 90% | 70% | Median | 30% | 10% | |
| CDD zone 1 | 2.71 | 1.32 | 0.52 | 0.19 | 0.08 | |
| CDD zone 2 | 6.95 | 2.88 | 1.46 | 0.52 | 0.16 | |
| CDD zone 3 | 10.96 | 4.03 | 2.26 | 1.19 | 0.54 | |

| Climate Zone | Electric Space Heat, kWh/square foot | | | | | Facility Difference |
|---|---|---|---|---|---|---|
| | 90% | 70% | Median | 30% | 10% | |
| HDD zone 1 | 1.92 | 1.21 | 0.57 | 0.23 | 0.15 | |
| HDD zone 2 | 1.34 | 1.16 | 0.45 | 0.34 | 0.28 | |
| HDD zone 3 | 1.77 | 1.40 | 0.56 | 0.31 | 0.28 | |
| HDD zone 4 | 5.06 | 1.93 | 0.77 | 0.74 | 0.35 | |

| Climate Zone | Natural Gas Space Heat, kBtu/square foot | | | | | Facility Difference |
|---|---|---|---|---|---|---|
| | 90% | 70% | Median | 30% | 10% | |
| HDD zone 1 | 57.31 | 41.57 | 12.75 | 10.50 | 7.55 | |
| HDD zone 2 | 63.91 | 54.86 | 32.75 | 23.13 | 14.17 | |
| HDD zone 3 | 97.49 | 87.29 | 36.38 | 25.83 | 14.15 | |
| HDD zone 4 | 108.13 | 73.22 | 36.65 | 26.75 | 14.66 | |

**TABLE A.62**   State-Local Other (50–85 hours/week)

| End Use | Baseload Electricity Use, kWh/square foot | | | | | Facility Difference |
|---|---|---|---|---|---|---|
| | 90% | 70% | Median | 30% | 10% | |
| Water heating | 6.18 | 2.93 | 2.42 | 0.77 | 0.42 | |
| Cooking | 2.18 | 0.71 | 0.52 | 0.19 | 0.09 | |
| Refrigeration | 2.64 | 0.70 | 0.44 | 0.17 | 0.05 | |
| Interior lighting | 10.36 | 4.41 | 2.40 | 2.07 | 0.89 | |
| Exterior lighting | 1.30 | 0.58 | 0.37 | 0.22 | 0.06 | |
| Equipment | 0.91 | 0.49 | 0.29 | 0.15 | 0.12 | |
| Miscellaneous | 3.21 | 1.43 | 0.72 | 0.38 | 0.16 | |
| *Total Baseload* | 31.69 | 12.04 | 7.16 | 5.00 | 1.88 | |

| Climate Zone | Space Heating Ventilation Electricity Use, kWh/square foot | | | | | Facility Difference |
|---|---|---|---|---|---|---|
| | 90% | 70% | Median | 30% | 10% | |
| HDD zone 1 | 0.95 | 0.83 | 0.22 | 0.11 | 0.05 | |
| HDD zone 2 | 1.20 | 0.83 | 0.39 | 0.21 | 0.10 | |
| HDD zone 3 | 1.81 | 0.86 | 0.51 | 0.44 | 0.27 | |
| HDD zone 4 | 1.35 | 0.92 | 0.69 | 0.58 | 0.27 | |

| Climate Zone | AC and Summer Ventilation Electricity Use, kWh/square foot | | | | | Facility Difference |
|---|---|---|---|---|---|---|
| | 90% | 70% | Median | 30% | 10% | |
| CDD zone 1 | 7.12 | 1.60 | 0.89 | 0.68 | 0.27 | |
| CDD zone 2 | 9.59 | 3.36 | 2.36 | 1.04 | 0.34 | |
| CDD zone 3 | 11.78 | 9.36 | 5.28 | 3.09 | 1.30 | |

| Climate Zone | Electric Space Heat, kWh/square foot | | | | | Facility Difference |
|---|---|---|---|---|---|---|
| | 90% | 70% | Median | 30% | 10% | |
| HDD zone 1 | 0.68 | 0.66 | 0.39 | 0.26 | 0.03 | |
| HDD zone 2 | 1.88 | 1.63 | 1.10 | 0.76 | 0.13 | |
| HDD zone 3 | 6.46 | 2.44 | 2.07 | 1.52 | 0.58 | |
| HDD zone 4 | 7.01 | 2.65 | 2.19 | 1.85 | 1.62 | |

| Climate Zone | Natural Gas Space Heat, kBtu/square foot | | | | | Facility Difference |
|---|---|---|---|---|---|---|
| | 90% | 70% | Median | 30% | 10% | |
| HDD zone 1 | 40.18 | 23.25 | 16.86 | 13.19 | 5.57 | |
| HDD zone 2 | 54.00 | 33.28 | 24.47 | 17.52 | 7.30 | |
| HDD zone 3 | 59.80 | 55.96 | 41.15 | 33.04 | 12.35 | |
| HDD zone 4 | 93.69 | 60.09 | 40.60 | 30.34 | 19.23 | |

**TABLE A.63**    State-Local Other (Greater than 85 hours/week)

| End Use | Baseload Electricity Use, kWh/square foot | | | | | Facility Difference |
| | 90% | 70% | Median | 30% | 10% | |
|---|---|---|---|---|---|---|
| Water heating | 5.27 | 2.82 | 1.36 | 2.03 | 0.84 | |
| Cooking | 5.14 | 1.65 | 1.63 | 0.65 | 0.18 | |
| Refrigeration | 1.43 | 0.78 | 0.52 | 0.22 | 0.03 | |
| Interior lighting | 14.91 | 8.03 | 3.99 | 3.39 | 0.56 | |
| Exterior lighting | 1.03 | 0.45 | 0.31 | 0.23 | 0.09 | |
| Equipment | 0.93 | 0.53 | 0.22 | 0.19 | 0.08 | |
| Miscellaneous | 3.18 | 1.69 | 0.71 | 0.61 | 0.12 | |
| *Total Baseload* | 31.89 | 15.95 | 8.74 | 7.32 | 1.90 | |

| Climate Zone | Space Heating Ventilation Electricity Use, kWh/square foot | | | | | Facility Difference |
| | 90% | 70% | Median | 30% | 10% | |
|---|---|---|---|---|---|---|
| HDD zone 1 | 0.58 | 0.22 | 0.03 | 0.02 | 0.01 | |
| HDD zone 2 | 1.63 | 0.74 | 0.50 | 0.15 | 0.06 | |
| HDD zone 3 | 1.90 | 0.95 | 0.66 | 0.32 | 0.20 | |
| HDD zone 4 | 2.71 | 0.94 | 0.65 | 0.23 | 0.08 | |

| Climate Zone | AC and Summer Ventilation Electricity Use, kWh/square foot | | | | | Facility Difference |
| | 90% | 70% | Median | 30% | 10% | |
|---|---|---|---|---|---|---|
| CDD zone 1 | 7.02 | 5.05 | 2.81 | 1.08 | 0.29 | |
| CDD zone 2 | 11.24 | 6.29 | 2.97 | 2.06 | 0.89 | |
| CDD zone 3 | 13.36 | 5.93 | 4.15 | 2.31 | 1.57 | |

| Climate Zone | Electric Space Heat, kWh/square foot | | | | | Facility Difference |
| | 90% | 70% | Median | 30% | 10% | |
|---|---|---|---|---|---|---|
| HDD zone 1 | 1.06 | 0.84 | 0.70 | 0.33 | 0.08 | |
| HDD zone 2 | 2.34 | 2.00 | 1.67 | 1.08 | 0.42 | |
| HDD zone 3 | 8.50 | 6.04 | 4.83 | 3.71 | 1.59 | |
| HDD zone 4 | 9.81 | 6.57 | 4.98 | 3.92 | 1.84 | |

| Climate Zone | Natural Gas Space Heat, kBtu/square foot | | | | | Facility Difference |
| | 90% | 70% | Median | 30% | 10% | |
|---|---|---|---|---|---|---|
| HDD zone 1 | 15.26 | 11.69 | 6.49 | 4.22 | 1.95 | |
| HDD zone 2 | 37.00 | 13.92 | 12.88 | 8.37 | 4.12 | |
| HDD zone 3 | 51.72 | 45.67 | 26.36 | 10.54 | 8.70 | |
| HDD zone 4 | 108.86 | 84.21 | 38.10 | 19.11 | 14.72 | |

# Notes

## Preface

1. More precise estimates of energy-efficiency savings can be developed with a detailed assessment of each facility's building, equipment and operating characteristics. These assessments can range from brief walk-through audits to more detailed analysis conducted with computer models of facility energy use calibrated to actual energy use derived from utility bills or utility meter data.

## Chapter 1

1. Adjusting prices for inflation using traditional price indexes can provide a distorted picture of increases in energy costs for an individual organization depending on how accurately the price index used in the adjustment reflects increases in other costs for that organization, especially since price indexes include the cost of energy. However, "deflating" nominal prices with a general price index provides a reasonable general estimate of changes in energy prices relative to all costs.

   Some price indexes, such as the core producer price index exclude food and energy prices; however, true measures of energy price increases relative to other costs for business, institutions and governments vary significantly across individual organizations. The GDP chain-type price index is used here to be consistent with the Energy Information Administration's inflation-adjusted series.

2. The other top cost concern is health care. The Business Roundtable is an association of U.S. CEOs representing more than ten million employees and $4.5 trillion in annual revenues. Press release: "Business Roundtable Releases Fourth Quarter 2006 CEO Economic Outlook Survey," http://www.businessroundtable.org/. (December 12, 2006).

3. Glyn A. Holton, Contingency Analysis, Boston, Working Paper: "History of Value-at-Risk: 1922–1998," http://129.3.20.41/eps/mhet/papers/0207/0207001.pdf (July 25, 2002).

4. One of the conclusions of this study was that government information programs appear to have little impact on encouraging investment in energy efficiency. See S. T. Anderson and R. Newell, "Information Programs for Technology Adoption: The Case of Energy-Efficiency Audits." Resources for the Future Discussion Paper 02-58 (2002). http://www.rff.org/Documents/RFF-DP-02-58.pdf.

5. A statistical analysis of this relationship for the period 1989 to 2005 is provided in Jose A. Villar and Frederick L. Joutz, "The Relationship Between Crude Oil and Natural Gas Prices." Energy Information Administration, Office of Oil and Gas (October 2006). http://tonto.eia.doe.gov/FTPROOT/features/reloilgaspri.pdf.

6. Energy Information Administration, http://www.eia.doe.gov/emeu/cabs/China/Background.html).

7. Energy Information Administration, *International Energy Outlook 2007* (May 2007). OECD countries include Australia, Austria, Belgium, Canada, Czech Republic, Denmark, Finland, France, Germany, Greece, Hungary, Iceland, Ireland, Italy, Japan, Korea, Luxembourg, Mexico, Netherlands, New Zealand, Norway, Poland, Portugal, Slovak Republic, Spain, Sweden, Switzerland, Turkey, United Kingdom, and the United States.

8. Baker Hughes North American Rotary Rig Count, http://www.bhi.bhi-net.com/investor/rig/rig_na.htm.

9. Reuters, "OPEC research head: fair oil price $60–$65" (July, 22 2007).

10. Energy Information Administration, "The National Energy Modeling System: An Overview 2003" DOE/EIA-0581 (Washington, DC, March 2003).

11. See, for example, Jerry Jackson and Robert Lann, "Development and Application of the Northwest Power Planning Council Commercial Energy Demand Models." Jackson Associates Research Report (November 1982); Jerry Jackson and Peter DeGenering, "Development and Application of a Commercial Sector Energy Use Model for New York State." Charles River Associates, CRA Report #438 (April 1980), prepared for the New York State Energy Office; and Jerry Jackson, Steve Cohn, Jane Cope, and William S. Johnson, "The Commercial Demand for Energy: A Disaggregated Approach." Oak Ridge National Laboratory, ORNL/CON-14 (April 1978).

12. Energy Information Administration, *Annual Energy Outlook 2007, with Projections to 2030*. U.S. Department of Energy, Washington, DC 20585, www.eia.doe.gov/oiaf/aeo/ (February 2007).

13. International Energy Agency, *Medium-Term Oil Market Report*. (Paris: July, 2007).

14. S.T. Anderson and R. and Newell, "Information Programs for Technology Adoption: The Case of Energy-Efficiency Audits." Resources for the Future Discussion Paper 02-58 (2002), http://www.rff.org/Documents/RFF-DP-02-58.pdf.

## Chapter 2

1. Albert Thumann and Ruth Marie, "The Market Survey of the Energy Industry 2007," Association of Energy Engineers (released to members, May 30, 2007).
2. Nicole Hopper, Charles Goldman, Donald Gilligan, and Terry E. Singer, "A Survey of the U.S. ESCO Industry: Market Growth and Development from 2000 to 2006," Ernest Orlando Lawrence Berkeley National Laboratory, May 2007, http://eetd.lbl.gov/ea/EMS/EMS_pubs.html.
3. Energy Systems Laboratory, Texas A&M University, http://esl.eslwin.tamu.edu/continuous-commissioning-.html.
4. Albert Thumann and Ruth Marie, "The Market Survey of the Energy Industry 2007," Association of Energy Engineers (released to members, May 30, 2007).

## Chapter 3

1. For a description of retail market activity in the various states see Alliance for Retail Choice, "ARC's Baseline Assessment of Choice in the United States: An Assessment of Restructured Markets," http://www.allianceforretailchoice.com/ProjectCenter/ (May 2007).
2. A summary of these issues is available in "Energy Efficiency Policy Toolkit," Cheryl Harrington, Cathie Murray and Liz Baldwin, The Regulatory Assistance Project, http://www.raponline.org/Pubs/Efficiency_Policy_Toolkit_1_04_07.pdf, January 2007.

## Chapter 4

1. This quote is from Paul G. Keat and Philip K.Y. Young, *Managerial Economics: Economic Tools for Today's Decision Makers,* 5th ed. (Upper Saddle River, NJ: Pearson Prentice Hall, 2006). Chapter 12 of this reference provides a good overview of capital budgeting and the traditional treatment of risk.
2. M. Ross, "Capital Budgeting Practices of Twelve Large Manufacturers," *Financial Management* 15 (Winter 1986): 15–22.
3. R. Pike, "A Longitudinol Survey on Capital Budgeting Practices," *Journal of Business Finance and Accounting*, 24, No. 1 (January, 1996): 79–92.

4. F. Lefley, "Capital Investment Appraisal of Advanced Manufacturing Technology." *International Journal of Production Research*, 32, No. 12 (1994): 2751–2776.

## Chapter 5

1. Numerous risk typologies exist, Crouhy et al. identify eight major categories including market, credit, liquidity, operational, legal and regulatory, business, strategic and reputation. Michel Crouhy, Dan Galai, and Robert Mark, *The Essentials of Risk Management* (New York: McGraw-Hill, 2006).
2. Much of the information in this section was developed from Glyn A. Holton, "History of Value-at-Risk: 1922–1998." Working Paper, July 25, 2002; and Peter L. Bernstein, *Against the Gods, The Remarkable Story of Risk*. (New York: John Wiley & Sons, 1996).
3. Markowitz, Harry M. "Portfolio Selection". *Journal of Finance* 7, no. 1 (1952): 77–91.
4. Peter L. Bernstein, *Against the Gods, The Remarkable Story of Risk*. (New York: John Wiley & Sons, 1996).
5. Quarterly Derivatives Fact Sheet, Comptroller of the Currency, http://www.occ.treas.gov/ftp/deriv/dq107.pdf.
6. Research on individual decision making and risk behavior has led to development of a field within finance called behavioral finance (also claimed by economists as behavioral economics). Daniel Kahneman received the 2002 Nobel prize in economics for his work in recognizing behavioral aspects of decision making under uncertainty.

## Chapter 7

1. See David R. Anderson, Dennis J. Sweeney, and Thomas A. Williams, *Statistics for Business and Economics* (Mason, Ohio: Southwestern, 2005) for a good applied statistics textbook.

## Chapter 8

1. The two variables, CDD and CDD*CDD, are typically highly correlated, making it difficult for the OLS process to separate influences of the two. This problem can be avoided by using "centered" data; that is, calculate and subtract the mean of the CDD series from each CDD value to form a new series, say CDDc. Square the CDDc variables to create the second variable. Use these two new variables in place of CDD and CDD*CDD in the regression analysis.

2. Austin monthly CDD and HDD distributions are specified as independent distributions. With this specification, a warmer than usual August does not imply a warmer than usual September. A statistical analysis of historical weather data can be applied to evaluate the evidence of a joint distributions that can reflect month-to-month and season-to-season relationships; however, that analysis is beyond the scope of a basic application.

# Index

Printed and bound by CPI Group (UK) Ltd, Croydon, CR0 4YY

16/04/2025

14658457-0001